Soviet Foreign Policy Since World War II

Soviet Foreign Policy Since World War II: Imperial and Global

Third Edition

ALVIN Z. RUBINSTEIN
University of Pennsylvania

Scott, Foresman/Little, Brown Series in Political Science
SCOTT, FORESMAN AND COMPANY
Glenview, Illinois Boston London

Library of Congress Cataloging in Publication Data

Rubinstein, Alvin Z.
Soviet foreign policy since World War II : imperial and global / Alvin Z. Rubinstein. — 3rd ed.
p. cm.
Includes bibliographies and index.
ISBN 0-673-39893-5
1. Soviet Union—Foreign relations—1945- I. Title.
DK276.R76 1989 88-19923
327.47—dc 19 CIP

2 3 4 5 6 7 8 9 10 — KPF — 94 93 92 91 90 89

Printed in the United States of America

Acknowledgments

Maps on pp. 33, 71, and 199 reprinted by permission from Alvin Z. Rubinstein. *The Foreign Policy of the Soviet Union,* 3rd ed. (Random House, 1972).

Chapter 14 is based on "Prospects" in Alvin Z. Rubinstein, *Moscow's Third World Strategy.* Copyright © 1989 by Princeton University Press. Excerpts reprinted with permission of Princeton University Press.

This book is dedicated to
Ruda Frankie

Preface to the Third Edition

Mikhail S. Gorbachev's rise to the position of secretary general of the Communist Party of the Soviet Union is part of a larger generational transfer of power underway in the USSR. His agenda at home requires a major overhaul of the Soviet system. Thus far, there has been liberalization in the cultural field, easing of pressure on dissidents, and extensive legislation designed to stimulate the stagnating economy and attract foreign investment. The intelligentsia is benefiting visibly from Gorbachev's policy of *glasnost* (openness), but the working class and peasantry have little to show from *perestroika* (restructuring); and ultimately it is on their greater productivity and innovation that the success of his domestic program depends.

In the realm of foreign policy, Gorbachev's call for "new thinking" has yet to manifest itself operationally. However, there are hints of flexibility and impending changes on arms control, the Middle East, Afghanistan, and China, among other issues, and these may well presage new opportunities and new challenges for the Western world. An October 1987 report by the Institute for East-West Security Studies noted that "the new Soviet leadership seems to recognize that serious economic and technological deficiencies jeopardize the USSR's international position, and that reversing these trends requires not only major economic modernization, but also many new foreign policy approaches." As we enter a period of uncertainty in Soviet foreign policy and in Soviet-American relations, it is essential that we keep the lessons of the past clearly in mind.

In this new edition I seek to better fulfill the objectives that were set forth in the first edition. The basic structure of the book is retained, but Chapters 1 and 14 are new; the former provides background on the czarist period, the assumptions that underlie my analysis of Soviet foreign policy, and the role of ideology as a determinant of policy; the latter offers some tentative comparisons of the Khrushchev and Gorbachev eras and speculates on the probable lines of Soviet policy to the year 2000. The intervening chapters have been revised in order to clarify the unfamiliar and to update the material, particularly as it relates to developments under Gorbachev.

I acknowledge with appreciation the helpful suggestions made by Norma C. Noonan, Karl W. Ryavec, Wallace Spaulding, Peter Vigor, and Frank W. Wayman. John S. Covell, my editor in this enterprise, provided timely encouragement; he and Yvonne Mottershead guided the manuscript into the editorial process. Susan Hunsberger and the staff of Editing, Design & Production, Inc. were a pleasure to work with in the final production stage.

Preface to the First Edition

Soviet foreign policy has weathered crises and catastrophes, persisted, and flourished. Lenin, Stalin, and Khrushchev are long since dead, their roles in developing the Soviet system and Soviet foreign policy only dimly known by a Western generation now coming to political maturity. As a new group of leaders prepares to assume power in the Soviet Union, Brezhnev himself is on the threshold of becoming more a historical than a political figure. Because of the power of the Soviet Union, what the future obligarchs do in the world arena will have far-reaching consequences for the stability and security of Western civilization.

This book is intended to provide a concise, comprehensive account of the evolution, aims, and impact of Soviet foreign policy, primarily in the period since 1945; to bring coherence to complexity; to identify continuity and change; and to establish a foundation for in-depth exploration of the rich specialized literature that has been published over the past generation. For those who follow the vicissitudes of Soviet policy, the past is part of the present and contributes to speculations about the future. Hopefully, this volume will give the neophyte this needed perspective. The approach is eclectic, historical, policy-oriented, and analytical. It focuses on the USSR's actual behavior and on the external consequences of its policies, and not on the possible motivations and decisional inputs that produced the behavior. It pleads no theory, no fashionable model. A work of synthesis, this study draws freely on the storehouse of knowledge created by scholars, whose major works are cited in the bibliographies at the end of each chapter, and to whom I am indebted.

Inevitably, interpretative evaluations have been made, where it is not feasible to examine in detail the domestic determinants of policy and all the possible options available to Soviet leaders at any crucial period. No doubt policy differences and conflicting perceptions of unfolding situations exist; yet, once a policy is adopted, it acquires a life of its own and is the proper unit for examination. I have tried to sift fact from conjecture and to keep the analysis or "guesstimates" as dispassionate as possible. Throughout, I have attempted to draw attention to the concrete and specific issues that faced Soviet leaders at different times, to enable the reader to formulate an evaluation of the situation and gain an understanding of international politics. The term "Communist" not "socialist" is used to describe the Soviet Union and the Soviet-dominated regimes or bloc in Eastern Europe, because the ruling political organization is the "Communist party," the leaders call themselves "Communists," and the ideology of Marxism-Leninism is differentiated from other varieties of socialism. Also, Moscow prefers the term "socialist" in its relations with non-Communist countries and individuals, because the term has universal appeal and far fewer sinister connotations.

Grateful acknowledgment is made to the following publishers for their permission to use parts of my work which appeared in their publications: Random House, Inc.; Westview Press; *The World Today,* a monthly journal issued under the auspices of the Royal Institute of International Affairs; *Optima,* a review published by the Anglo-American Corporation of De Beers and Charter Consolidated Groups of Companies; and *Orbis,* a quarterly journal of the Foreign Policy Research Institute. I wish also to thank the Center for Advanced Studies at the University of Virginia for handling the typing of the final manuscript.

Contents

PART III. INSTRUMENTS OF SOVIET DIPLOMACY 253

Week of 26th

I

Historical Foundations: From Czarism to Bolshevism and the Eras of Lenin and Stalin

1
Sources of Soviet Policy

The foreign policy of the Soviet Union, like that of any great power, is a combination of discrete determinants. These include geopolitical considerations, historical memory, external threats, bureaucratic intriguing, exigencies of political power, economic capabilities, ideology, skill of the ruling elite, and so forth. At any given time, policy develops as the product of a complex process in which these determinants, although always changing, are in some fashion always present. Throughout Russia's modern history, from the late fifteenth century on, its physical attributes—geography, climate, population, and resources—have played important roles. They have influenced the unique characteristics of the country's political, social, military, and economic developments; its belief system and culture; its reaction to external challenge; and the key figures in its history.

Historical Legacy

The history of Russia is dramatic and complex. Between the sixth and ninth centuries, various tribes or groups of East Slavs settled the vast East European plain. In time, they developed into Russian, Ukrainian, and Belorussian or White Russian subdivisions, of which the former was the largest and most influential. The harsh climate and poor soil led to reliance on the numerous rivers for trade. Especially important was the contact between Kiev, which is situated on the Dnieper River, and the Byzantine Empire, which dominated the southern and western littorals of the Black Sea. It was from Byzantium, whose center was Constantinople, that the Eastern Orthodox branch of Christianity was introduced into Rus' (the Russian nation) through Kiev in 988. At the time, Kiev was the leading Russian center, though there were also principalities in Novgorod, Pskov, Suzdal, Chernigov, and Smolensk, among others.

Besides climate and geography, religion (in the form of Eastern Orthodoxy) was an early determinant of foreign policy. It contributed later to Russia's religious and cultural isolation from the rest of Europe; proved to be a source of tension with Russia's neighbors, especially as the Ukrainians and Belorussians came under the influence of Roman Catholicism during periods of Lithuanian and Polish domination; and shaped subsequent political culture and institutions, with evident effects on Czarist and Soviet society.

But before these events happened, a shared language, religion, and ethos had enabled the Russians to survive and eventually surmount three centuries of Mongol domination. In the mid-thirteenth century, the expanding Mongols subjugated all of Russia. From 1240 to 1380 they were unquestioned masters, exacting tribute, yet permitting cultural and religious autonomy to the many vassal princes.

In 1380, the prince of Moscow defeated a Mongol army at Kulikovo Pole (field) on the Don River. Though short-lived, the victory greatly enhanced the prestige of the principality of Moscow, which had emerged as a separate entity in the middle of the twelfth century, and which had by then become the seat of the Russian Orthodox Church. In 1480, Moscow's Prince Ivan III (1462–1505) cast off the Mongol yoke once and for all and absorbed rival Russian principalities such as Yaroslavl, Rostov, Novgorod, and Tver, more than doubling the size of the Muscovite domain. In a sense, he was the creator of a unified Russian state.

The Mongol period had been traumatic for Russia, arresting economic and social development, severing close ties to Byzantium, and accentuating the hierarchical and autocratic rule associated with Russia's Byzantine heritage. The end of Mongol overlordship and the ascendancy of Moscow as the center of Russian power ushered in several centuries of continual war between Russia and its western neighbors—Lithuania, Poland, and Sweden. These wars were fought as much for religious reasons as for real estate and for stable frontiers.

The clerically inspired animosities between the Byzantine church and the Papacy in Rome dated from the schism in 1054. The sack of Constantinople in 1204 by Frankish and Venetian crusaders intensified the Orthodox clergy's incitement of anti-Catholic feelings among the Rus', whose attachment to the Church had deepened during the harsh period of Mongol rule. A national Church suited the political aims of the Muscovite princes, who used it to expand their authority. In 1472, Ivan III assumed the title of czar and acquired an aura of Byzantine legitimacy by means of his marriage to a niece of the last Byzantine emperor to rule in Constantinople before it was overrun by the Ottoman Turks in 1453. From the time of his reign on, czars nurtured the view of Moscow as the "Third Rome" (Rome, Constantinople, Moscow)— "a fourth there cannot be."

For the next several hundred years, the struggle to determine the western borders of Russia in the vast area from the Baltic Sea to the Black Sea was invested with a religious as well as a strategic-political dimension: religious in that the Russian Orthodox czars of Moscow were pitted against the Roman Catholic rulers of Lithuania and Lithuania-Poland; strategic-political in that each sought to expand and consolidate control over peoples and societies in transition and across lands with no natural defensible frontiers. The indeterminacy of societies and borders promoted conflict.

There was no accommodation; none was desired. Czar Ivan IV (*Grozny,* the Terrible) (1530–1584) invaded Livonia (essentially today's Estonia and Latvia) in 1558 but his invasion failed dismally, and in the process of a 25-year war with Lithuania, Poland, and Sweden, he lost the fortified port of Ivangorod on the Gulf of Finland, which had been acquired by Ivan III. However, defeated in the West, Ivan spread to the East, conquering the Muslim khanates Kazan (in 1552) and Astrakhan (in 1556). It was he who extended Russia's control over the entire length of the Volga River and turned it into a multinational empire. This eastward expansion succeeded throughout the otherwise trying seventeenth century, when Russia experienced serious internal problems and repeated wars in the West. The conquest of Siberia advanced Russia's border to the Pacific, and in 1689 Moscow imposed on a weak China the Treaty of Nerchinsk, which moved the border to the Argun River and the Stanovoi Mountain range, where it remained until 1858 when the seizure of additional Chinese territory up to the Amur and Ussuri rivers established the current boundary between the Soviet Union and China.

Moscow's ambivalence toward the West became manifest in the mid-sixteenth century, when Ivan IV used a German adventurer, Hans Schlitte, to recruit Western technicians and specialists for service in Russia. The government feared outside intriguing but needed the knowledge foreigners could provide. As long as their numbers were relatively small, the solution was to restrict them to one area of Moscow. In Poland, Austria, and Sweden, Russia's interest in new technology, coupled with its expansionist policy, gave rise, according to Russian historian S. F. Platonov, to the "problem of the 'Russian peril' and the necessity of conducting a policy of isolation and repression vis-a-vis Moscow."[1] Surmounting the political upheavals and foreign interventions of the early seventeenth century, a new dynasty was established, the Romanov (1613–1917). This was a time of peasant rebellions, economic stringency, schisms in the Church, and recurring wars. The wars with Poland were long and difficult; particularly important was the uprising of the Zaporozhiye Cossacks against the Poles, which, in 1654, led to the incorporation of the Ukraine into the Russian empire.

Russia's imperial age and emergence as a European power began in earnest during the reign of Peter the Great (1682–1725). So, too, did its interest in the West. Peter borrowed ideas, technology, and personnel from the West on a scale unmatched in Russian history, and he introduced far-reaching military, administrative, and economic reforms. Epitomizing his determination to modernize Russia was his moving of the capital to St. Petersburg (Leningrad), a new city that he built on the Gulf of Finland in a style befitting the center of an empire. The capital remained there until necessity forced the Bolsheviks to relocate it back to Moscow in early 1918.

Peter's foreign policy focused on securing Russia's northern flank. He fought Sweden for over 20 years (1700–1721), defeating Charles XII, the most brilliant military commander of the early eighteenth century. The Treaty of Nystadt (1721) gave Russia control of the Gulf of Finland—its maritime route to the West—and the Baltic provinces of Estonia and Latvia. Henceforth Russia, not Sweden, was the foremost power in northern Europe.

Peter's successors added to this legacy, especially Catherine the Great (1762–1796), who expanded Russia's southern and western borders by defeating Ottoman Turkey and Poland, respectively. Catherine's humiliating defeat of Turkey and the consequent Treaty of Kuchuk Kainardji in 1774 advanced Russian territory to the Black Sea and led to the absorption of the Crimea, whose Muslim Tartars had previously relied on Turkish protection. Even more impressive was her role in effecting the successive partitions of Poland, which in 1795 ceased to be an independent state, until it was recognized again as such by the Provisional Government that succeeded the toppled czarist regime in February 1917. Poland's internal weakness had left it incapable of resisting the rapacious appetites of its increasingly powerful neighbors, Russia, Prussia, and Austria.

By the beginning of the nineteenth century, Russia was one of the great powers of Europe, its empire "an accomplished and firmly established fact. Even at that time it was by far the largest state in Europe. It had spread all over the east-European plain from the Baltic and the Arctic Ocean in the north to the Black Sea and the Caspian in the south; in Asia it possessed the whole of Siberia. Further expansion during the nineteenth century made the territory of the Empire equal to one-sixth of the surface of the globe."[2] After the defeat of Napoleon in 1815, Russia's foreign policy in Europe followed a course that was shaped more by imperial ambitions than by security. Friendship with Prussia and Austria—which had been since 1795 Russia's powerful neighbors in the West—would have assured stability and security. However, expansion at the expense of the weak Ottoman empire caused friction with Austria in the Balkans and with Britain in the Middle East. Still, Germany (as the expanded Prussian state was called after 1870) under Chancellor Otto von Bismarck kept the peace between the Hapsburgs and the Romanovs. But with his dismissal in 1890 the high-strung young Kaiser Wilhelm II decided to support Austria against Russia, thus turning Russia to an alliance with France, its longtime adversary.

Just as Russia's aims in the Balkans had nothing to do with security, so, too, its pressure on the Ottoman Turks for concessions on the Straits (the Dardanelles and the Bosporus) was dictated by impulses—historical, economic, and religious—that had little to do with security. Russia's defeat of the Turks in 1833 had turned the Black Sea into a Russian lake; under the Treaty of Unkiar Skelessi, access was forbidden to Turkish warships, and a weak Turkey, which Czar Nicholas had in 1844 dubbed the "sick man" of Europe, was no threat.

Imperial rivalry made much of the nineteenth century a period of Anglo-Russian "Cold War" and superseded Russia's traditional friendship with England, which had dated back to the 1550s. It extended along the rimland of Russia's southern border, from Ottoman Turkey to Iran, Afghanistan, and China. By 1907, however, fear of Germany led both powers to accommodation and a common alliance with France.

In the Far East, Russian imperialism took advantage of a weak China to extract additional real estate in the Amur-Ussuri region and de facto control of the provinces of Sinkiang and Mongolia. In northern Manchuria and Korea, the spread of Russian commercial interests precipitated a war with Japan, which was also bent on expansion into these areas. Russia's stunning defeat in the 1904–1905 war gave Japan a free hand, and for most of the period prior to 1914, social unrest in St. Petersburg and the revolution of 1905 kept the czar occupied with internal reforms.

In August 1914, Russia entered World War I on the side of France and Britain, optimistic about the prospects for substantial territorial gains at the expense of Turkey. Within a year, however, it had for all practical purposes been eliminated from the war. Its fate was sealed by Britain's failure to capture the Dardenelles, to knock Turkey out of the war, and to open a reliable supply route to help provision the poorly equipped Russian army. Faced with growing shortages, economic dislocation, and communications breakdowns, the corrupt and inefficient czarist regime proved incapable of stemming disaffection among the masses. Antiwar sentiment permeated the army. The regime's last safety net collapsed in February 1917. Food riots in the capital brought out the usually efficient crowd-busting Cossacks; this time, in contrast to 1905, the regime's protectors joined the protesters. The czar abdicated, and a provisional government was established. One autocracy ended, and another was soon to begin.

The Provisional Government, headed by Alexander Kerensky, groped for a way of mitigating the domestic crisis while keeping Russia in the war. Meanwhile, as part of its policy of cautious liberalization, it permitted the return of political exiles, among whom was Vladimir Ilyich Ulyanov, better known to history as V. I. Lenin. His Bolshevik party, one of several hitherto illegal revolutionary groups, had opposed Russia's participation in the "imperialist" war. From the moment he arrived on April 16, 1917, in Petrograd (as St. Petersburg had been renamed in 1914 to make it sound more Russian), he called for opposition to the government and to continuation in the war. His "April Theses" laid out the party's revolutionary line. Lenin hammered away at the need for "Bread, Land, and Peace," a slogan that distinguished the Bolsheviks from all other political groups. Conditions deteriorated; much-needed reforms were deferred, and participation in the war eroded the rapidly waning popular support for the government, which was further sapped by an attempted military coup in September.

Lenin's political genius was never more apparent than in his insistence on a sudden grab for power. On November 6–7 (October 24–25 of the old calendar), the Bolshevik forces seized key points such as the Fortress of Peter and Paul, located just opposite the former czar's Winter Palace on an island in the Neva River, and found themselves in control as the government's support melted away. In 1902, in *What Is to Be Done?* Lenin had written, "Give us an organization of revolutionaries, and we will overturn the whole of Russia!" On November 7, 1917, he did just that.

Lenin modernized the czarist system of rule. He centralized power in the Communist party; reaffirmed the preeminence of the state over society by renovating the inherited system of hierarchical and bureaucratic governmental institutions; foreclosed the emergence of a strong judiciary or any countervailing economic, social, or cultural institutions that might limit the power of the party (the new autocracy); and made extensive use of the secret police as an instrument for repression and control. (The evolution of the secret police from Ivan the Terrible's *Oprichnina* to Mikhail Gorbachev's KGB—Committee for State Security—has been characterized by its ever increasing efficiency and more pervasive penetration of society.)

Looking back, we see that the autocracy underwent changes in response to the outlook of a particular czar or the impact of secularization and industrialization. The Russia of Nicholas II (the last Romanov) differed from that of Nicholas I, just as Gorbachev's Soviet Union differs from Stalin's. However, the persistence of certain essentials—the concentration of power in the hands of a few, the assumption that "revolution" and reform should come from above, and the hostility to any political pluralism or institutional restraints on the rulers—suggests that there is a continuity of outlook in czarist and Communist institutions and methods of rule.

Autocracy does not require unanimity among those advising the ruler. There were always competing conceptions of how the country should move and develop. Ivan the Terrible, Catherine the Great, and Alexander I, among others, had to make momentous choices—though far fewer in foreign policy than in the domestic realm. For example, in the mid-to-late nineteenth century, a "debate" developed between two groups—the Slavophiles and the Westernizers—intent on influencing the course of autocratic rule. The Slavophiles' remarkably coherent ideology "centered on their belief in the superior nature and supreme historical mission of Orthodoxy and of Russia."[3] At its best, their vision was of a Camelot-like integration in which the Slavs would live in harmony in simple institutions; at its worst, their belief was expressed in the quasi-racist, messianic, and narrow nationalistic views of writers like Nicholas Danilevsky, whose famous work, *Russia and Europe,* was published in 1869. However, such views had little effect on the actual policy pursued by the czars, either in the Balkans, where Pan-Slavism was manipulated for imperial purposes, or in Central Asia, where Russification and Orthodoxy were not imposed. The Westernizers argued that Russia was part of Europe, albeit at a less advanced economic and political stage of development; and they pressed for liberalization and a constitutional system modeled on the British experience. But their outlook, too, had little impact on the czar in the 1890s, when he was assessing the relative advantages of aligning with Paris or Berlin.

Key foreign policy issues were decided on the basis of regional and international configurations of power and the ambitions and skill of the individual czar, and not according to any preconceived "ideological" blueprints. Periodically, simplistic attempts are made to equate the messianic Slavophilic view of Russia's uniqueness, sense of mission, and commitment to the Orthodox faith to the "internationalism" of Marxism-Leninism, whose doctrines include the vanguard leadership role of the Communist Party of the Soviet Union (CPSU), the incessant struggle against capitalism, and the inevitability of communism as the carrier of future civilization. However, no czarist government ever accepted Danilevsky's doctrine as official policy, and no Soviet ruler ever used the messianic aspects of ideology to guide fundamental decisions in world affairs.

Whenever the security of Russia was at stake and "contradictions" between ideological postulates and national interests existed, decisions were made on the basis of the latter.

A number of generalizations relevant to understanding Soviet foreign policy may be adduced from the czarist experience, without contravening analyses that maintain that czarist foreign policy was the consequence of individual mood as well as material calculations; was seldom formulated with a broad conception of what is today called "the national interest"; and was "never materially affected" by the pressures of domestic politics.[4]

First, much of Russia's expansion at the expense of other nations and peoples can be attributed to the quest for strategic frontiers. The association of territorial depth with security was a conception of defense that came naturally to successive czars whose realm had no formidable mountain ranges, deserts, or sea barriers to deter its enemies. From Moscow west to the North Sea, east to the Ural Mountains, and south to the Black Sea and the Caucasus the terrain is flat or gentle, a tempting course for invaders and restless nomadic peoples. Once freed from the Mongol yoke, Russia's main threats came from the west. After defeating Sweden and acquiring the eastern shore of the Baltic in 1721, its subsequent expansion was always against weak and anachronistic regimes. Although often attacked, after the eighteenth century, Russia was far more often the aggressor than the aggrieved.

Second, Russia's political elite never questioned the wisdom of expansion. Ambition reinforced the quest for security and the attachment to empire, whose increasingly multinational character, in turn, deepened the perceived need for strong, centralized, autocratic rule. There was no need to cloak expansionism in universalistic or pious cant.

Third, Russia's empire endured because it consisted of one geographic entity that was permeated with and settled by Russians who upheld czarist rule and because there was no power strong enough to conquer it (though, on occasion, some defeated it in limited wars fought for limited objectives).

Fourth, strategic considerations were invariably preeminent. Economic motivations were seldom important. Even when present, as in the conquest of the Central Asian khanates of Khiva and Bokhara in the 1860s and 1870s, such motivations were imbued with military objectives as well.

Finally, foreign policy decisions were the domain of the few and the powerful. They were made, wisely or not, unencumbered by public opinion or moral considerations; the purpose was to preserve and strengthen the imperial system. Czarist regimes moved in the international arena according to variants of traditional balance-of-power politics. The record shows that czarist as well as Soviet rulers were usually willing to negotiate, especially with whoever was the greatest threat, provided there was advantage to be gained. Their approach has been unsentimental, historically rooted, and quintessentially pragmatic, irrespective of the personality or ideology of the adversary.

Perspectives

Confronted by the multiplicity of determinants, Western analysts offer diverse interpretations of present-day Soviet foreign policy. Some claim that "communism is czarism in overalls," meaning that Soviet foreign policy is essentially a continuation of traditional czarist objectives and attitudes, which fused a concern for security with a covetous drive for real estate, resources, and international influence. Given the logic of geographic determinism, the quest for strategically secure borders led to the expansion westward toward Central Europe and an urge to the sea—the historic Russian drive for ports on the Baltic, the Mediterranean, the Yellow Sea, and the Persian Gulf.

Others believe that adherence to Marxism-Leninism impels the USSR to seek "Pax Sovietica," with Moscow as the center of authority of a network of Communist countries and parties having close links to tactical allies in the Third World. Despite the ecumenical pretensions of the ideology, they see in its doctrines an unremitting hostility toward the non-Communist world and a dangerous insularity and resistance to long-term accommodation. The ideology, they say, induces in the Kremlin a state of anxiety over security and gives rise to policies that are in turn deemed threatening by the objects of these policies, the opponents of Soviet hegemony, whose efforts to counter Soviet ambitions result in tensions that create the very conflictual situation originally forecast by the ideology. To an already strong and historically conditioned Russian paranoia, Marxism-Leninism brings a conception of the world that predisposes Soviet leaders to view the non-Communist world in the worst possible light—and to proceed accordingly. When, during his visit to Britain, Khrushchev was told that his harsh anti-British sentiments were defeating his own purpose, he remarked: "I know this is true, but I cannot stop myself. We Russians have lived surrounded by dangers in a state of siege for a generation. So we are apt to be afraid, and to say and do the wrong things."[5]

There are those who think Soviet policy is motivated by a relentless opportunism. Whether this is a response to perceived threats or the prospects for gain arising from the changing international system, the result is an active search for advantage, a policy of continual pressure on adversaries, a disposition toward exploitation and aggravation of regional conflicts. According to this view, the Soviet Union is unable or unwilling to cooperate for long with other governments, or to build lasting friendships based on mutual respect and mutual self-interest. Others see in the USSR's behavior in the world arena a stubborn insistence on recognition from the United States of coequal status in the management of the evolving international system, a determination to be accorded the prestige and role in world affairs consonant with its power and resources. Still others argue that the USSR is an authoritarian system, whose rulers require an external threat and an assertive foreign policy in order to direct outward the frustrations of the population and justify the continued monopoly of power by the Communist party.

Western analysts have studied such themes as Soviet perceptions of the military balance and the ups and downs of Soviet-American relations; the Kremlin's view of the "correlation of forces," interdependence, the energy crisis, intra-NATO tensions, and the causes of regional conflict and instability; and Soviet conceptions of the relative strengths of the détentist and antidétentist forces in American political life. Though based on careful examinations of Soviet writings, these analyses cannot tell us how key decisions are made in the Kremlin, who stands with whom on what issue, and what particular determinants or priorities prompt the adoption of policy option A rather than B, C, or D. The wellspring of Kremlin policy remains as much a riddle as ever.

Perhaps Winston Churchill gave us a clue for understanding Soviet foreign policy when he said, in a broadcast on October 1, 1939, apropos the Soviet Union's collusion with Nazi Germany to dismember Poland: "I cannot forecast to you the action of Russia. It is a riddle wrapped in a mystery inside of an enigma; but perhaps there is a key. That key is Russian national interest."[6] Those wishing to convey the image of an ideologically driven, relentlessly expansionist, difficult-to-comprehend Soviet leadership frequently omit the last twelve words. Admittedly, the term *national interest* is imprecise and infinitely malleable, and it can be used to justify any neutrality, any alliance, or any war. Yet it conveys responses to concrete situations in which the leadership acts in light of the constraints placed upon it by domestic and international pressures and considerations, and not in ways that reflect what the leadership would really like to do. The term *national interest* places foreign policy behavior in a specific context and requires that we make detailed examination of the actual nature of the threat or challenge, the range of options, the dilemmas, and the probable reasons for the choice that emerges. It does not provide answers to all questions, but shows the force of continuity of concerns and aims. Above all, it sheds light on the limitations, be they military, political or economic, that must be considered in evaluating Soviet policy.

Attempts to interpret Soviet behavior become more important as Soviet power grows. Though beset with pitfalls and subject to widespread disagreement, interpretations and analyses must be made: in great measure, an effective U.S. foreign policy depends upon an accurate appraisal of the strengths and weaknesses, the ambitions and fears, the options and dilemmas, and the domestic and international inhibitions of the Soviet leadership. Speculations about probable Soviet *behavior* rely on very different data and methods from those determining the Soviet Union's *capability.* In this process, it is important that we identify the assumptions on which our assessments are based. John Reshetar's pertinent comments help illumine the scope of the task:

> If, for example, it is assumed that fear plays a determining role in Soviet policy, then the possibility of actions committed out of desperation is correspondingly increased and looms larger in any estimate of what the Kremlin might do in a given situation. If it is assumed that the Soviet leadership always means what it says in its policy pronouncements and does not bluff, then such statements must be taken at face value. If it is assumed that what is said is not always meant to be taken literally . . . then it is necessary to distinguish between what might be an actual ultimatum and what might be a calculated attempt to dissuade without entailing sanctions. If it is assumed that the principal Soviet technique is military rather than economic or propaganda-oriented, then the tendency will be to overlook the degree of flexibility which the Soviet leadership can be said to permit itself, even though it is limited and possibly only tactical in nature.[7]

Underlying Assumptions

In any analysis of Soviet policy, whether it interprets past actions or speculates about future ones, the assumptions of the analyst are crucial. These, however, are rarely specified; instead they lie hidden in a line of analysis or advocacy—and the boundary between the two is not always clear to the reader. Making them explicit may clarify not only the assessment, but also the salience of the data, the suitability of the methods, and the rigor of the logic. This becomes particularly important when we realize that assumptions in the analysis of Soviet foreign policy are based on few reliable data from an arcane Soviet decision-making process, are not easily tested, are dependent in great measure on one's interpretation of the past, are influenced by a priori beliefs and preferences, and thus are peculiarly resistant to revision. We know that facts do not speak for themselves; they are construed by well-intentioned analysts who seek, reasonably, to rely on evidence that conforms to and buttresses their own predilections. Assumptions are omnipresent in political analysis: obscured in the interstices of formulations and arguments, they inexorably determine the choice of alternative explanations for policy outcomes.

Soviet foreign policy over the years and in different regions provides us with a solid record of what the Kremlin leaders have done. But it does not supply the reasons for any specific Soviet action. What one chooses from among several alternative explanations leads to one's assessment of Soviet concerns, aims, accomplishments, and motivations. And one's choice, without full information (which is impossible to obtain anyway), is influenced by one's basic assumptions about Soviet policy.

Mindful of Paul Winterton's observation that "there are no experts on the Soviet Union, only varying degrees of ignorance," I shall here briefly identify some of the principal assumptions that guide my approach to synthesizing Soviet behavior and that are meant to disclose what the Russians are up to.

First, there are no isolationists in the Kremlin. The urge to acquire influence and play a global role is not peculiar to the Soviet Union; it is a trademark of any powerful, ambitious imperial system. The Soviet Union has paid dearly for its newly acquired status as a superpower: three generations have sacrificed and suffered to modernize Russia, to expand its borders in search of strategically secure frontiers, to ensure that decisions affecting its national security will never again be arrived at without its full participation. Having driven itself to the center of the world stage, Moscow is not likely to retire to the wings soon or gracefully. In its determination, willingness to bear the cost of an imperial policy is implicit.

Second, Soviet initiatives will be undertaken in response to concrete threats to security and opportunities for gain. Contrary to the generally accepted view, Soviet diplomacy is flexible, adaptive, open to deals, and alert to "contradictions" in the non-Communist world. As befits the style of a calculating, tough-minded, sober elite, Soviet leaders will continue to respond pragmatically to events and opportunities, weighing the risks and rewards, the difficulties and dilemmas, careful to avoid war with the United States but increasingly resolved not to forgo cheaply the advantages they have obtained. They have a strong sense of continuity and a clear perception of their priorities. Soviet resources are limited and the Soviet economy has its troubles, but the Kremlin has the wherewithal and the will to make such commitments as are required to preserve its imperial system in Eastern Europe and the Far East, and to follow its ventures in the Third World, in support of its policy and current status in these areas.

Third, Soviet state-to-state relations are determined primarily by strategic and political calculations; ideological and economic considerations are secondary. Moscow's assessments are built around calculations of what will strengthen the Soviet Union and complicate the diplomacy of its main adversary, the United States, and not what will foster communism and the prospects of local Communist parties. Whatever legitimizing function ideology plays within the Soviet hierarchy, and whatever its importance as a medium for communication and conflict within the world Communist movement, ideology is not primary in Soviet foreign-policy formulation; it is more a potent stimulus to Western imagination than a determinant of Soviet policy.

Fourth, though differences over this issue or that issue (for example, whether to invade Czechoslovakia in August 1968 or Afghanistan in December 1979) may well have existed, and may indeed from time to time occasion some oligarchic tension over foreign policy, nonetheless an essential consensus is shared by the top Soviet leadership; no wide dichotomy separates "hawks" and "doves." Soviet leaders believe that military power is necessary and useful for preserving their system and promoting their foreign policy. As such, military considerations are prominent in Soviet thinking, but they do not result in any indiscriminate reliance on force to achieve political aims. The military instrument is intended to protect the USSR; but outside of the core Soviet security community it is used as an adjunct of diplomacy, not its master. Soviet leaders have read Clausewitz; they accept war as a permanent factor in international relations, but regard it as "nothing but the continuation of policy with other means." War and the use of force are viewed as means to achieve political goals.

Fifth, given the historical experience of czarist and Soviet Russia, I assume, looking to the 1990s, that the Soviet Union is a territorially satisfied power and will not resort to a major war with the United States or any of its allies in order to acquire additional real estate; and that as long as its own security community is not threatened, it will not seek to alter the superpower relationship by nuclear strike or conventional war in Europe or the Far East. The territorial expansion of the USSR into the Baltic region and Eastern Europe at the end of the Second World War was a consequence of a war that the Soviets did not start and, viewed from a long-term strategic perspective, may be considered as being in line with the strategic borders that had defined the czarist empire at the height of its power. The situation in Afghanistan, while showing that Moscow was not averse to projecting military power for strategic advantage in circumstances that seemed propitious and that posed no danger of confrontation with the United States, is not a model of probable Soviet behavior in situations in which the vital interests of principal adversaries are at stake.

Sixth, domestic difficulties and dilemmas are unlikely to change significantly the foreign policy interests, priorities, and preferences of the oligarchy. The Soviet domestic power base is secure, the institutions and loci of power are firmly in place, and the ruling elite consists of prudent authoritarians, not restless risk-takers bent on world conquest. Although the Soviet system faces major difficulties—the consequences of pervasive police controls, excessive centralization, and overbureaucratization of the economy—it is not on the verge of an internal crisis that threatens the rule of the Communist party or the integrity of the Soviet Union. By most objective criteria, the USSR is well-endowed with raw materials, especially energy and scarce minerals. It does, however, face a crisis in efficiency and requires a way of increasing productivity, making better use of available resources, and fostering innovation. These changes are necessary for the USSR to move into the next century in a strong position for sustaining growth and keeping abreast of the industrial-technological development of key rivals. Its ability to offer the Soviet people a better quality of life is tied to the leadership's willingness to make major changes in the way the system operates.

Seweryn Bialer, among others, has written on the difficulties of reforming the Soviet system:

> The basic truth about effective reforms is that they cannot be made on the installment plan. An incentive structure will remain ineffective unless the price system reflects real costs and supply and demand pressures. A more realistic price system will have very limited impact on the effectiveness of production if the centralized economic administration remains intact.[8]

The structural changes that Western analysts believe are necessary entail overcoming the resistance of vested political and bureaucratic interests, permeating the system with new attitudes of accountability and a new work ethic, and resolving the fundamental dilemmas of who will wield political power and what kind they will wield. An example may be illustrative of the problem.

The Soviet Union is composed of 15 union republics divided along ethnic lines and has a population of more than 280 million, only slightly more than half of whom are Russians and a quarter of whom are completely non-Slavic in language, nationality, culture, or tradition. There is a severe labor shortage, especially in the Russian SFSR. A surplus of labor exists in Muslim Central Asia, but these individuals are unwilling to relocate to the Slavic heartland. Should Moscow invest heavily in the non-Russian regions and risk providing these peoples with a strong socioeconomic base, which could be used to demand more political power; or does it "make do"? The non-Russians are increasing faster than the Slavs. Demographic projections estimate that by the early 21st century the Russians will have become a minority in the country. How will this affect the composition of the Red Army, the national consciousness of hitherto quiescent groups, and, above all, the psychological outlook of the centralized, absolutist, Great Russian leadership that rules in the Kremlin?

Since coming to power in March 1985, CPSU leader Mikhail S. Gorbachev has moved forcefully to energize and transform the system and society; *glasnost* (openness), *perestroika* (restructuring, of which democratization is supposed to be an essential part), and *uskoreniye* (acceleration) have become bywords of his agenda. However, he has yet to grapple with dilemmas affecting the future of the party and the modalities of how it rules.

A seventh assumption underlying my approach is that a strong pragmatic strain runs through Soviet foreign policy. Whatever their ideological predisposition, the men in the Kremlin are committed to careful analysis of the world scene—as they perceive it—and will act after sober calculation. This does not, of course, preclude mistakes, since several courses of action may seem "rational." Indeed, the USSR's foreign policy behavior over the past seven decades conforms far more closely to the model of the rational actor operating in the international system to optimize its security and ambitions than does that of its supposedly less ideologically influenced antagonists, for example, the United States, Great Britain, and France.

Soviet leaders are intent on the preservation and strengthening of their imperial system at home and in Eastern Europe and believe that their political patrimony can best be safeguarded by a strong military establishment. The respect for power is rooted in historical memory. Defense of the motherland and of the socialist commonwealth mandate sustained efforts in the military sphere. Moreover, given the traditional Russian propensity toward building redundancy into force levels and the conviction that the more power one has, the greater the prospect of one's affecting the course of events and attaining key objectives, military considerations are likely to loom large in Soviet thinking, despite progress in arms control.

Eighth, the Sino-Soviet rift will not easily or soon be bridged, which means that Russian leaders must deal with powerful adversaries on both flanks, as they did in the decades when Japan was the preeminent power in the Far East. Though normalization of sorts is proceeding slowly, the relationship will be characterized by residual suspicion and intrinsic rivalry in the foreseeable future. Given their obsession with security, Soviet planners must assume the worst, and this is likely to foreclose a significant reduction of forces along the Chinese border, thereby perpetuating the mistrust that hinders reconciliation.

Finally, there is the putative role of ideology in shaping Soviet foreign policy, a contentious subject that goes to the very heart of one's assumptions about the motivations and aims underlying the USSR's behavior. In other words, does the Soviet regime conduct its external relations in light of the canons of Marxist-Leninist doctrine, or is it guided by practical steps that will advance the national ambitions of the Russian component of the Soviet leadership?

My assumption is that, by now, the relevant postulates of Marxism-Leninism have been thoroughly Russified and converted into a tool of Soviet foreign policy. They have been integrated into the elite's value system, so that the ultimate goals postulated by the ideology are generally subordinate to the needs of the moment and the preservation of the state and its imperium. Just as a belief in Christianity has rarely affected the foreign policy decisions made by Christian rulers, so, too, a belief in Marxism-Leninism has rarely led Soviet leaders to act in a manner contrary to their perceptions of what is necessary and good for the "national interest" of the Soviet Union. The question for the Kremlin is not whether to advance "the cause of communism" at some expense to itself, but whether, in any given case, it would benefit more from flying the banner of world proletarian solidarity in the expectation that a parade of spiritual virtue will yield proximate material gain, or from concentrating instead on garnering immediate substantive dividends. Either way, the goal is advantage for the Soviet Union, and only the method varies.

Ever since the Treaty of Brest-Litovsk in March 1918, it has been evident that in Soviet foreign policy, security and survival have taken precedence over the spread of communism and revolution. Soviet leaders seldom have had difficulty reconciling the dualism between their perceived national interests and internationalist ambitions and between safeguarding the Soviet state and taking risks abroad on behalf of revolutionary movements. Part of the confusion in the West over the role that ideology plays in the determination of Soviet policy on any given issue stems from the attribution of maximalist belligerence to the Kremlin's aims. Such a view is based on reading selectively in the Communist scriptures and ignoring those passages that convey elements of ambivalence and permit practitioners to proceed with flexibility in the pursuit of allegedly unswerving ideological imperatives. For example, one popularly cited selection is the classic formulation of the irreconcilability between capitalism and communism, which Lenin made in March 1919:

> We are living not merely in a state but in a system of states, and the existence of the Soviet Republic side by side with imperialist states for a long time is unthinkable. One or the other must triumph in the end. And before this end supervenes, a series of frightful collisions between the Soviet Republic and the bourgeois states will be inevitable.[9]

But in December, he also declared that "the Russian Socialist Federal Soviet Republic wishes to live in peace with all peoples and to direct all of its strength on internal construction." And in a more Machiavellian vein, on December 21, 1920, he noted:

> Our policy is to use the differences of the imperialist powers in order to make agreement difficult, or to make such agreement temporarily impossible. . . . Our main interests in negotiating concessions are political.[10]

These largely contradictory statements described what was important for Lenin to convey at those different periods. Each of them can be used to support whatever a priori set of assumptions one holds about Soviet policy, but none completely describes the totality of Soviet aims and attitudes. Reality is far more complex than that.

True, ideology has occasionally led the Kremlin into serious miscalculations, such as Stalin's ordering the German Communists to support the Nazi party in the early 1930s, thereby inadvertently helping to destroy the strong social democratic movement and bring Hitler to power; or the USSR's expectation that Eastern Europe would follow the path of Soviet social and economic development. The latter error was acknowledged in June 1983 by party leader Yuri Andropov; in the wake of the Polish crisis, which proved the Polish Communist Party to be inept and to have no popular support, and which led the military to take over, Andropov remarked:

> There are major differences among the individual Socialist countries in the economy, in the culture, and in the ways and methods of solving the tasks of Socialist development. This is natural, even if in the past it seemed to us that it would be more uniform. . . . The time comes when the dues have to be paid for mistakes in politics.[11]

Ideology may intensify the Kremlin's suspicions of the outside ("capitalist") world and make agreements more difficult to reach, but it is no bar to pragmatism. Readiness to veer, yield, or retreat temporarily in the face of resistance by an adversary in order to effect a future advance is elevated to the status of a permanent operational principle for all communists in Lenin's *One Step Forward, Two Steps Backward,* published in 1904. This title, repeated as a tactical injunction only once in the book, is perhaps the most regularly misquoted phrase from Lenin's writings. Logic seems to suggest transposing the number of steps if progress is to be made toward an objective. Everything, however, depends on the relative size of the steps. Lenin knew that minor tactical retreats or concessions could confound an opponent and result in a major stride forward; this applies not only to the struggle for control of the party organization but also to foreign policy. Nor does ideology preclude making those deals that are deemed advantageous. In May 1942, Foreign Minister V. M. Molotov told President Franklin D. Roosevelt, who had asked him of his impressions of Hitler, that it was, after all, possible to come to an understanding with almost anyone, and that he himself had never met two more disagreeable people than Hitler and Nazi Foreign Minister Joachim von Ribbentrop.[12]

Moreover, this generation of Soviet leaders does not feel that before deciding on a course of action it must look to see what Lenin or Stalin or Khrushchev wrote; these men are fully capable of thinking for themselves. They may use appropriate quotations to lend ideological sanction to a particular decision, but that practice is rationalization after the fact and not a determinant of policy itself.

Throughout this study I have assumed that with each successive generation, ideology, though retaining some relevance, counts for less and less in the mix of determinants shaping day-to-day responses on this or that foreign-policy issue. Whatever ideology's continuing role as an instrument of control, be it a mode of esoteric communication among its adherents or a source of self-legitimation, in the formulation of foreign policy its utility is minimal; certainly, it is not central in determining the policy option selected on key questions. There is nothing enigmatic about the Soviet Union's changing relationships with the various major international actors. The Soviet elite may be influenced by Marxist beliefs in the centrality of economic factors in the shaping of conflicts among groups, in the inevitability of "socialism," in the role of revolution, and so on, but, as Barrington Moore has noted, its foreign policy behavior is more readily understandable as adaptation to the changing balance of power in the international system:

> Quite justifiably, international relations has been compared to a quadrille, in which the dancers change their partners at a definite signal. But no two dancers execute the steps in precisely the same fashion. Some, who are new to the steps, may try to stop the dance altogether, or call for a new tune. For this they may be sent to the corner (behind a *cordon sanitaire*), to emerge later as seeking and sought-after partners . . .
>
> The several phases of Soviet foreign policy in Europe and Asia represent in their essentials a single, continuous pattern. In this pattern the . . . Soviet Union has reacted to the shifting distribution of power in international politics. Sooner or later . . . the Soviets have danced the power political quadrille, throwing the weight of their force against any grouping of powers that showed signs of threatening their security. They have always aligned themselves against their "natural" antagonists in the balance of power at a given time. The choice of antagonist or allies had been determined not primarily by ideological factors, but by the structure of the balance-of-power system itself.[13]

Still, assessments of the role of ideology remain a matter of controversy because we have no way of knowing what determinants finally tip the scale in any given Kremlin decision; because we know little about factional rivalries in the Soviet leadership on foreign policy issues; and because Soviet leaders conduct diplomacy on two levels—state-to-state relations through the USSR's Ministry of Foreign Affairs and party-to-party relations with the world communist movement through the International Department of the CPSU's Central Committee. The world communist movement heightens suspicions of the USSR, which Moscow would like to allay, but Soviet leaders are unwilling or unable to disband this instrumental source of internal legitimacy and external support.

In general, Western analyses of Soviet policy and intentions suffer from numerous fallacies, enumerated as follows by Raymond L. Garthoff, a senior fellow at the Brookings Institution, former Foreign Service officer, and longtime specialist on Soviet affairs: (1) when in doubt, assume the worst; (2) never estimate intentions, only capabilities; (3) assume that Soviet leaders always (or never) have the same perceptions and aims as their Western counterparts; (4) assume that the Soviets never (or always) mean what they say; (5) consider Soviet capabilities to be larger than are needed—or than they believe are needed—for deterrence; (6) assert a Soviet intention to seek military superiority; and (7) believe that the "facts" speak for themselves, ignoring selection and definition of data.[14] These cautionary reminders merit attention. Too often, Soviet strengths are emphasized and Soviet weaknesses are neglected. Moreover, neither strengths nor weaknesses should be evaluated solely in military terms. In addition, it is common for analysts to dwell on the opportunities that may arise for Moscow and ignore the constraints that limit how far it can push its advantage without incurring risks that may outweigh the possible benefits.

If it is important to avoid preconceived conceptual traps, it is equally essential to learn from the Soviet record. A few propositions may be gleaned from the Kremlin's behavior in foreign affairs.

First, the Soviet leadership believes in the utility of force as a means of preserving or promoting strategic interests. The Kremlin is not embarrassed by its power or unduly worried about international public opinion. It is, of course, willing to utilize diplomacy and negotiation to achieve its goals, but Moscow has demonstrated—in Eastern Europe in 1953, 1956, and 1968, and increasingly in the Third World—an equal readiness to use the powerful force that it has built up. Its military intervention in Afghanistan in December 1979, when for the first time it used force in a Third World country in order to effect a change of leadership and secure the Soviet position within the country, is compelling evidence of this readiness.

Second, the Kremlin leadership is wedded to the preservation of its imperial system; it has little interest in interdependence or involvement with the outside world beyond what it sees as necessary for strengthening its own society. Moscow may not be isolationist, but neither is it internationalist in the Western sense of the word.

Third, Soviet leaders respect power and correlate power with diplomatic moves; they disdain weakness and equivocation. They are not captivated by appeals to friendship and humanitarian ideals. What motivates Moscow is a restless search for strategic advantages—an imperial ambition that is the other side of the obsessiveness with security. To the extent that Soviet leaders perceive a weak, vacillating, and muscle-bound United States that is stymied by domestic bickering, unsure of its priorities, and unwilling or unable to project military power in defense of clients or allies, they will exploit existing opportunities. Moscow will be influenced not by what Washington wants, but by its own capabilities.

Finally, the Soviets have an outlook that generates the all-pervasive political and strategic rivalry with the United States. The distinguished Russian historian Vasily O. Kliuchevsky has been quoted as saying, "Russia cannot be a country like the West, anymore than a tenor can be a bass." As long as the reality that Soviet leaders perceive offers corroborative evidence for the continuation of ideological-political struggle with all its implications, they will be encouraged to use their relationship with the West to secure an increasing imbalance of forces in their favor in the military and political spheres so as to advance the "profound revolutionary changes" that they believe to be characteristic of the present epoch. There is no writ for an end to imperial rivalry or an agreement to live and let live, much less for friendly cooperation to address regional and global problems.

Notes

1. S. F. Platonov, as translated and edited by Joseph L. Wieczynski, *Moscow and the West* (Hattiesburg, Miss.: Academic International, 1972), 5.
2. Michael Karpovich, *Imperial Russia, 1801–1917* (New York: Henry Holt, 1932), 4.
3. Nicholas V. Riasanovsky, *A History of Russia,* 3rd ed. (New York: Oxford, 1977), 401.
4. For example, see Richard E. Pipes, "Domestic Politics and Foreign Affairs," in Ivo J. Lederer (ed.), *Russian Foreign Policy* (New Haven: Yale University Press, 1962), 148.
5. Lord Taylor, "Deep Analysis of the Russian Mind," *New York Times Magazine,* January 7, 1962.

6. Winston S. Churchill, *The Gathering Storm* (New York: Houghton Mifflin, 1948), 449.

7. John S. Reshetar, Jr., *Problems of Analyzing and Predicting Soviet Behavior* (New York: Random House, 1955), 44–45.

8. Seweryn Bialer, *The Soviet Paradox: External Expansion, Internal Decline* (New York: Knopf, 1986), 128.

9. V. I. Lenin, *Selected Works,* Vol. 8 (New York: International Publishers, 1943), 33.

10. V. I. Lenin, *Sochinenia,* Vol. XXVI (Moscow: Institute of Marx-Engels-Lenin, 1930), 6–10.

11. Quoted in Roman Solchanyk, "Making Soviet Ideology Relevant," Radio Liberty Research, RL 1/84, December 29, 1983, 2.

12. Robert E. Sherwood, *Roosevelt and Hopkins: An Intimate History,* (New York: Harper & Bros., 1948), 565.

13. Barrington Moore, Jr., *Soviet Politics—The Dilemma of Power,* (Cambridge: Harvard University Press, 1950), 351–2; 382–3.

14. Raymond L. Garthoff, "On Estimating and Imputing Intentions," *International Security,* Vol. 2, No. 3 (Winter 1978), 22–32.

Selected Bibliography

BECKER, SEYMOUR. *Russia's Protectorates in Central Asia: Bukhara and Khiva, 1865-1924.* Cambridge: Harvard University Press, 1968.

BOBRICK, BENSON. *Fearful Majesty: The Life and Reign of Ivan the Terrible.* New York: Putnam, 1987.

CURTISS, JOHN SHELTON. *Russia's Crimean War.* Durham: Duke University Press, 1979.

DUNLOP, JOHN B. *The Faces of Contemporary Russian Nationalism.* Princeton: Princeton University Press, 1983.

GEYER, DIETRICH. *Russian Imperialism: The Interaction of Domestic and Foreign Policy 1860-1914.* New Haven: Yale University Press, 1987.

KENNAN, GEORGE F. *The Fateful Alliance: France, Russia, and the Coming of the First World War.* New York: Pantheon, 1984.

LEDERER, IVO J. (ED.). *Russian Foreign Policy.* New Haven: Yale University Press, 1962.

MADARIAGA, ISABEL DE. *Russia in the Age of Catherine the Great.* New Haven: Yale University Press, 1981.

MALOZEMOFF, ANDREW. *Russian Far Eastern Policy 1881-1904.* Berkeley: University of California Press, 1958.

MITCHELL, R. JUDSON. *Ideology of a Superpower: Contemporary Soviet Doctrine on International Relations.* Stanford: Hoover Press, 1982.

PIPES, RICHARD. *Russia Under the Old Regime.* New York: Scribner's, 1974.

RAEFF, MARC. *Understanding Imperial Russia: State and Society in the Old Regime.* New York: Columbia University Press, 1984.

SETON-WATSON, HUGH. *The Russian Empire 1801–1917.* Oxford: Clarendon Press, 1967.

VENTURI, FRANCO. *Roots of Revolution.* New York: Knopf, 1960.

VIGOR, P. H. *The Soviet View of War, Peace, and Neutrality.* London: Routledge & Kegan Paul, 1975.

YANOV, ALEXANDER. *The Origins of Autocracy: Ivan the Terrible in Russian History.* Berkeley: University of California Press, 1981.

2
The Beleaguered Soviet State, 1917–1939

When the Bolsheviks seized power in Russia on November 7, 1917, they faced challenges for which their experiences as underground revolutionaries and exiled members of an obscure political movement had not prepared them. During their early days they were absorbed with consolidating the regime and had no real understanding of the nature of foreign policy. Leon Trotsky, in his autobiography, comments on the prevailing naiveté: the expectation was, he states, that upon assuming the position of commissar of foreign affairs, "I will issue a few revolutionary proclamations to the peoples of the world and then shut up shop."

Burdened with the czarist legacy of a dispirited, disorganized army, a population weary of war, and an internal order on the brink of collapse, the Bolsheviks considered that their first task in foreign policy was to take Russia out of the "imperialist" First World War. "Peace, bread, and land" had been a compelling slogan in their mobilization of popular support. The promise of peace represented a major political commitment—one that they neither dared nor desired to break. Furthermore, since they viewed World War I as an imperialist war started by rival capitalists seeking to redivide the world, they rejected traditional norms of international law and diplomacy as alien to a proletarian state. Accordingly, on November 8, the Bolsheviks issued the Decree of Peace, proposing "to all warring peoples and their Governments to begin immediately negotiations for a just and democratic peace," which they defined as "an immediate peace without annexations and without indemnities." They proclaimed the abolition of secret diplomacy and the firm intention "to carry on all negotiations absolutely openly before all the people" and to publish in full the secret treaties of the preceding czarist government.

An appeal directed as much to the peoples and governments of

Western Europe as to the people of Russia, the decree was the first use by the Bolsheviks of what was later to be known as "demonstrative diplomacy," which George F. Kennan described as "diplomacy designed not to promote freely accepted and mutually profitable agreement as between governments, but rather to embarrass other governments and stir up opposition among their own peoples."[1]

The first step toward taking Russia out of the imperialist war was the preliminary armistice agreement signed with the Central Powers at Brest-Litovsk on December 15, 1917. At the time, some of the Bolsheviks balked at the Germans' insistence upon detaching those parts of the Russian empire then under German control, notably parts of Lithuania, Poland, and the Ukraine. They procrastinated in expectation of the coming revolution in Germany. Remember: these revolutionaries, who had emerged so suddenly from obscurity, lacked any experience in foreign affairs and shared an outlook that believed that world revolution was imminent, that the success of the revolution in Russia depended upon the spread of the revolution to highly industrialized Germany, and that all capitalist states were committed to the destruction of the newborn socialist state.

The Bolsheviks' unorthodox delaying tactics at the Brest-Litovsk negotiations irritated the Germans, who were eager for a speedy conclusion of peace. Only then could they transfer the bulk of their formidable army from the Eastern front to the West and hope to knock out the Allies before significant American reinforcements arrived. The impatient German military commander, Major-General Max von Hoffmann, presented Trotsky with alternatives: sign a peace treaty on German terms or face an immediate resumption of the German offensive.

Trotsky, the chief Russian negotiator and the commissar for foreign affairs, returned to Petrograd (later renamed Leningrad) on January 19, 1918, to consult with party leaders. He found that the recently elected and convened Constituent Assembly had been dissolved and that the Bolsheviks had assumed absolute power. Russia's brief flirtation with democracy, epitomized by the free elections held at the end of November 1917, had ended.

Lenin's First Foreign Policy Crisis

Now began the first momentous debate on foreign policy. The Bolsheviks had to face up to the realities of an international system of which they were inextricably a part. They had hitherto assumed that after appropriate agitation and propaganda, the German troops would revolt against their imperialist masters, thereby sparking a revolution that would spread to the rest of Europe. As committed (and still doctrinaire) Marxists, they believed that the loyalty of the proletariat of all countries was to class, not country. Despite this, and despite Lenin's espousal in the years before he came to power of the principle of national self-determination, their own nationalistic sentiments impelled them to oppose a peace with Germany that would require the dismantling of the Russian empire and the granting of independence to non-Russian peoples. At heart, most Bolsheviks remained attached to their czarist patrimony. The onrushing German advance confronted them with serious dilemmas and stark options.

Ever the realist and tactician, Lenin argued that a revolutionary outlook was not incompatible with realpolitik. He insisted that the preservation of the revolution (that is, the Bolshevik retention of political power) must outweigh all other considerations; that for the immediate future at least, the interests of world revolution and the international proletariat must be subordinated to the task of consolidating the new Soviet state; and indeed, that the best way to ensure the eventual success of world revolution was first to safeguard and strengthen the socialist state in Russia. This had to take precedence over all else, including the waging of a revolutionary war that, in any event, the Russian army was absolutely in no condition to undertake. Therefore, Lenin called for an immediate end to hostilities in his brilliant exposition "Theses on the Question of the Immediate Conclusion of a Separate and Annexationist Peace" (January 20, 1918).

Long-held and deeply felt beliefs were, however, difficult to shed. Those in the Central Committee who opposed Lenin's harsh decision hoped to prolong the negotiations and give time for the revolution to spread. They adopted Trotsky's formula of "no war, no peace," but agreed that should the Germans resume their advance, a peace treaty would be signed. Lenin felt that delay would be costly, but reluctantly concurred, adding facetiously that "for the sake of good peace with Trotsky, Latvia and Estonia are worth losing."

On January 30, 1918, Trotsky returned to Brest-Litovsk. He found the Germans in a far less patient mood and in the process of recognizing as spokesman for the Ukraine a splinter anti-Bolshevik group, with whom they signed a separate peace treaty on February 9, thereby obtaining badly needed grain and raw materials.

On February 18, the Central Powers launched a general offensive and advanced rapidly against virtually nonexistent Russian resistance. In Petrograd the Central Committee hurriedly convened and, after some heated discussion, voted to sue for peace, as the Germans rolled onward. (In March the Bolsheviks moved the capital to Moscow and renamed themselves the Communist party.) Lacking any alternative, the Bolsheviks quit the war. On March 15, 1918, Soviet leaders ratified the "Carthaginian" peace with the Central Powers and agreed to the loss of a third of Russia's population, cultivated land, and industry.

The Brest-Litovsk crisis served as a crucible from which emerged the outlines of a foreign policy. First, Soviet leaders recognized that military weakness left them prey to foreign attack and increased the likelihood of their deposition. Second, the absence of expected revolutions in Germany and Western Europe meant that they could not depend on world revolution to strengthen the socialist revolution in Russia; therefore, though continuing to anticipate world revolution as the only ultimate security, they undertook the creation of a Red Army to provide for their short-term safety. Finally, the policies both of the Central Powers and of the Entente buttressed their conviction (held to this day) that the capitalist world, irrespective of its internal rivalries, was basically hostile and would undermine the Communist regime if it could. Only world revolution could guarantee the success of the socialist revolution in Russia; yet the success of socialism in the new Soviet state was deemed a prerequisite for the advancement of world revolution. Thus Soviet leaders identified their own political survival with the good of the international proletariat. This dualism—the furthering of revolution abroad and the quest for national security—has remained a salient feature of Soviet foreign policy.

War Communism

The assumption concerning capitalist hostility was ominously confirmed by the Allied intervention, which started with the landing of Japanese troops at Vladivostok on April 5, 1918. Before it ended, British, French, American, and Japanese troops would be involved, a bitter all-out civil war would run its course, and communism would be entrenched in Russia. Confused and contradictory motives prompted the halfhearted, inept intervention in Russia's internal turmoil: the Japanese sought to carve out a sphere of influence from Russia's Far Eastern territories; the Americans wanted to check Japanese ambitions; the British landed at Murmansk to prevent the Germans from capturing stores of arms. The Western powers sought to use Czech and Slovak troops, who had originally been part of the Austro-Hungarian armies that were taken prisoner and then, when the Bolsheviks left the war, were freed and transported across Siberia for shipment to the Western front. These troops became pawns in Western efforts to weaken the Bolsheviks and encourage anti-Bolshevik forces. Allied strategists hoped in unspecified fashion to recreate an eastern front against the Germans.

Whatever military rationale the intervention originally had was no longer valid when World War I ended on November 11, 1918, but growing British and French commitments to anti-Bolshevik forces, American inertia, and Japanese persistence precluded any immediate disengagement. Fear of bolshevism's spread to the rest of Europe, French resentment over the Bolshevik repudiation of the prewar czarist debts and the influence of émigré and pro-White (anti-Bolshevik) groups in Western capitals all hardened the hostility of the interventionists, who sought, in Winston S. Churchill's words, "to strangle the infant bolshevism in its cradle."

On November 13, 1918, the Soviet government abrogated the Brest-Litovsk treaty, declaring its provisions null and void. During the autumn and winter, a Red Army was conscripted, trained, and toughened for battle. Under Trotsky's driving leadership, it proved superior to the smorgasbord of armies and leaders that constituted the opposition, the White Guard counterrevolutionaries. A centralized military command, a compact geographical base and internal lines of communication, effective appeals to patriotism against foreign armies, and the inability of the Whites to coordinate their military activities or agree on a common political program worked to the Bolsheviks' benefit. In addition, the Bolshevik promise of national self-determination, including the right of secession, induced nationalists in Armenia, Georgia, and Central Asia to resist attempts by the White armies to reimpose Russian domination. However, once the civil war was won, the Communist proceeded to reincorporate the non-Russian nationalities in the Caucasus and Central Asia into the Soviet state and suppress all separatist movements.

The year 1919 was crucial. At Versailles, a treaty was summarily handed to the Germans, and with it were sown the seeds of the next war in a Europe that did not realize the extent to which it had been weakened. In Germany, revolution met defeat at the hands of the military, and the fledgling Weimar Republic started its tragic, short life. In America, Wilson's dream of a League of Nations was defeated in the Senate and soon gave way to a "return to normalcy"—a phrase symbolizing America's abdication of international responsibility for two decades. The "Balkanized" area of central and southeastern Europe (the consequence of the collapse of the Austro-Hungarian empire) had not yet been linked with France in the unstable network of military alliances that was to give the French an illusion of security; in Paris fear of bolshevism dominated French policy, and émigré Russians pushed for all-out war against the Bolsheviks. And in Russia, after the excesses and suffering of "war communism," as the period is called in the Soviet Union, bolshevism emerged victorious. The Allies, forced to compromise by the unwillingness of their armies to fight in Russia in a struggle they did not understand, reluctantly abandoned their interventionist adventures.

In his military weakness Lenin relied heavily on the power of ideas and propaganda to defeat his enemies. Indeed, he was the first revolutionary in the twentieth century to sense the political potency of the mass media. In March 1919, at an ebb in Soviet fortunes, he established the Communist International (Comintern), nominally to further world revolution but actually to serve the interests of the Soviet state. Specifically, through a network of foreign Communist parties, the Comintern agitated against the Allied intervention and anti-Soviet activity by capitalist governments. The weapons it used to defend the weak Soviet state were revolutionary propaganda, labor strife, protest movements, and subversion. Soviet leaders probed the antagonisms within the capitalist world, not only between the great and lesser powers but also within the individual countries themselves; and they capitalized on the conciliatory, frequently sympathetic attitudes of bourgeois intellectuals toward the Soviet Union. In Lenin's words, "Our policy is to use the differences of the imperialist powers in order to make agreement [between them] difficult or to make such agreement temporarily impossible."[2] This was done with increasing skill through the pen and the podium.

A confident Lenin delivered the key address to the seventh All-Russian Congress on December 5, 1919.[3] The danger from the Allied intervention had been successfully countered and the civil war had passed its most acute phase. The principal White armies had been defeated, namely, those under Admiral Aleksandr V. Kolchak, who in November 1918 had seized control of the anti-Bolshevik coalition "government," the so-called All-Russian Provisional Government based in Omsk; and those led by General Anton Denikin, commander of the White forces in southern Russia. Moreover, the pressures for peace in war-weary Western Europe and for an end to the Allied intervention had increased, and nowhere more than among the small nations bordering on European Russia—in 1920, Finland, Latvia, and Estonia concluded formal peace treaties with the Bolshevik regime, which recognized their independence and secession from the Russian Empire, of which they had been a part for more than a century. Implicit in Lenin's analysis of the main stages of the capitalist intervention and civil war were two assumptions: first, that the capitalist world, though hostile, was divided and that these divisions could be exploited to consolidate the revolution and promote Soviet security—a major adaptation to classical balance of power theory; and second, that unconventional diplomacy (as represented by propaganda, peace movements, and front organizations) could be a valuable weapon, especially for a militarily weak Soviet Russia that had very limited options.

At the second congress of the Comintern in August 1920, a high degree of centralization and discipline was introduced. The Comintern adapted its structure and operating procedures to that of the Communist Party of the Soviet Union (CPSU). The twenty-one conditions for membership made certain that the Comintern would, in fact, be "a single

Communist party having branches in different countries." Moscow laid down the fundamentals of policy on all significant questions and disseminated them through the worldwide system of pro-Soviet Communist parties, whose subservience to the Soviet Union became total in the Stalin period. Unconventional diplomacy, epitomized by the Comintern, was adopted as a characteristic feature of Soviet foreign policy; it included the establishment and manipulation of political front organizations in order to weaken the anti-Soviet policies of capitalist governments, the support for revolutionary movements abroad, the use of mass media and propaganda, the recruitment of disaffected foreigners to serve the Soviet state, the use of cultural and commercial organizations for espionage, the fomenting of social and political unrest, and the concomitant promotion of normal government-to-government relations at one level and subversion at another. Developed as an arm of Soviet diplomacy in a period of military weakness, these techniques have been perfected, richly financed, and often skillfully utilized through the decades of growing Soviet power.

The Comintern congress had ended on August 7 amidst great expectations of a revolutionary surge into Central Europe: by late July the Red Army under General Mikhail Tukhachevsky was at the outskirts of Warsaw, having driven the Poles, who had taken Kiev on May 6, into headlong retreat. By August 15, however, the Poles launched a powerful counter offensive aided by the French, and the overextended Red Army retreated in haste. Contrary to hopes in the Kremlin, the Polish proletariat did not revolt, but fought as Poles against the historic and hated enemy, Russia. With this defeat, the lingering Soviet belief in an imminent world revolution ended. An armistice negotiated on October 12, 1920, led to a treaty of peace signed on March 18, 1921, at Riga, which governed Soviet-Polish relations until the partition of Poland in September 1939 by the Soviet Union and Nazi Germany.

By 1921 the new Soviet regime had withstood the twin threats of foreign intervention and civil war. With the end of "war communism," it turned to the tasks of internal recovery, consolidation of power, and "coexisting" in a hostile world. One period of Soviet foreign policy came to a successful conclusion. A second was about to begin.

Adaptation and Accommodation

The parish Soviet state also utilized conventional diplomacy to coexist with the capitalist states. While insisting upon the need for military preparedness in the expectation of a future military intervention, Lenin pioneered coexistence with the capitalists "to utilize the differences between them in order to make it difficult for them to unite" against the

Soviet Union. He needed time to consolidate Communist rule. The economy was in shambles, unrest was growing in the countryside, food shortages and industrial bottlenecks were endemic, and a revolt at Kronstadt in March 1921 by naval cadres (who had been stalwarts of the revolution) all militated for a breathing spell. Moreover, by 1921 the revolutionary mood in Europe had subsided and capitalism had entered a period of stabilization. The Allied powers, too, needed to tend to domestic matters and lifted the blockade of Russia, after reaching agreements on the repatriation of prisoners of war and on trade.

To promote Russia's economic recovery, Lenin instituted the New Economic Policy (NEP). This gave the peasants monetary incentives to produce, allowed a revival of free enterprise for small firms, and relaxed governmental controls on the economy; it also welcomed foreign capital and encouraged trade with capitalist countries to meet the urgent Soviet need for industrial machinery and credits. Lenin sought to strengthen the Soviet state and safeguard it from a feared coalition of capitalist powers bent on its overthrow.

Diplomatic recognition and "normalization" of relations were key objectives, not only to ensure legitimacy at home and abroad, but also to discourage intriguing against the new Soviet regime, for example, supporting exile groups dedicated to the restoration of a non-Communist regime. The end of isolation was accomplished first in Europe, then in Asia.

The Anglo-Soviet trade agreement of March 16, 1921, was an important step toward the Soviets' gaining acceptance internationally, as was Moscow's acceptance of the country's new frontiers (see map), which involved the loss of Finland, Estonia, Latvia, Lithuania, eastern Poland, Bessarabia (Romania), and Kars and Ardahan (to Turkey). But the momentous development was the agreement with Germany in April 1922, ending the isolation of the two outcasts of Europe. Russia and Germany had been invited to the Genoa economic conference called by British Prime Minister David Lloyd George in an effort to stimulate Europe's economic recovery. On Easter Sunday, April 16, 1922, the Soviet and German foreign ministers—Georgii V. Chicherin (1918–1929) and Walther Rathenau—met at Rapallo, near Genoa, and signed an agreement. The rapprochment was the first significant diplomatic triumph achieved by the Soviets through traditional norms of bourgeois diplomacy and power politics. It immeasurably enhanced the bargaining position of each country. For Britain and France, though they were not then aware of this, it signified the end of political preeminence on the continent of Europe.

Diplomatically, the Treaty of Rapallo brought the Soviet regime *de jure* recognition from Germany—the first major country to grant it. Eco-

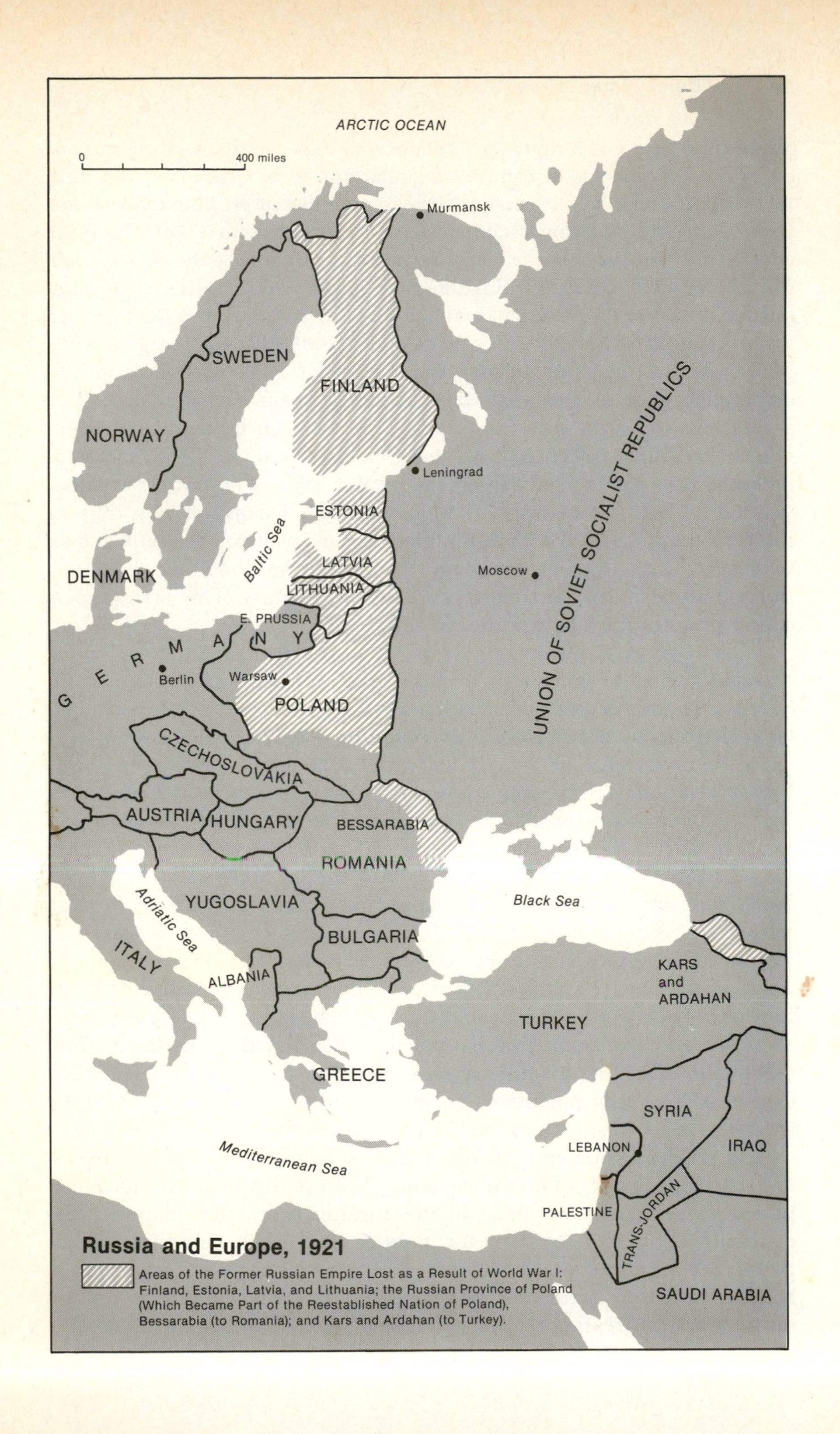

Russia and Europe, 1921

Areas of the Former Russian Empire Lost as a Result of World War I: Finland, Estonia, Latvia, and Lithuania; the Russian Province of Poland (Which Became Part of the Reestablished Nation of Poland), Bessarabia (to Romania); and Kars and Ardahan (to Turkey).

nomically, there was a mutual cancellation of existing financial claims, and expansion of trade with commercial relations to be "based on the most favored nation principle," and a German promise of economic assistance. Psychologically, Moscow established close contact with a key European country and believed that it had forestalled formation of the feared coalition of capitalist countries. Rapallo gave new impetus to the clandestine military collaboration that had already begun to develop a year earlier, when Lenin had decided to seek German assistance for the reorganization of the Red Army after signing the Treaty of Riga with Poland.[4] To accomplish this; he had used the Comintern agent Karl Radek to hold secret talks in Berlin with the Chief of the German General Staff, Hans von Seeckt. Military cooperation began in the spring of 1921, under the umbrella of a commercial agreement in May 1921. The Soviets obtained valuable assistance for construction of an advanced arms industry, training for their troops, and experience in modern warfare from the tank and air maneuvers that the German army, in circumvention of the Versailles treaty, was permitted to conduct on Russian territory. This arrangement continued until the rise of Hitler in 1933.

The essentials of Soviet foreign policy during the interwar period emerged clearly in Lenin's time: the primacy of the preservation of the Soviet state over revolutionary aspirations; the courtship of Germany; the normalization of relations with all capitalist countries and promotion of "peaceful coexistence" as a norm for Soviet behavior; the establishment of correct relations and nonaggression pacts with the bordering Baltic and East European countries that had previously been wholly or partially subdivisions of the czarist empire; the quest for close ties with China to counter Japanese expansion against the USSR and its client state, Mongolia; and finally, the use of the Comintern and other nongovernmental organizations to manipulate public opinion in support of Soviet policies and foment trouble in capitalist and colonial countries. National, not international, priorities predominated. Not until 1939 and the radical shift in the European balance of power would the USSR have the military capability to pursue an expansionist foreign policy, either directly or through political threats backed up by military means; or would it have the luxury of a choice from among potentially advantageous options and not be forced merely to react to situations over which it had little control.

In the succession struggle that followed Lenin's death on January 21, 1924, and brought Stalin absolute power, differences over foreign policy played a decidedly minor role. In the ensuing years, foreign policy was primarily a function of domestic politics. Intent on consolidating his power, Stalin courted the new elites—who were weary of war and eager to benefit from their status and position—by disclaiming interest in world revolution and stressing the construction of "socialism in one country."

Diplomatic recognition did not bring the expected surge in trade and investment credits. The Western countries were wary of Moscow's revolutionary doctrine, its official commitment to conflict between socioeconomic systems, and its unwillingness to settle prerevolutionary czarist debts; and they were suspicious of the Comintern and its network of communist parties.

The two major foreign-policy setbacks that Moscow experienced in the 1924-to-1930 period were in its relations with Britain and China and were the result of developments in the internal affairs of these countries. In Britain, the Labour party—which had established full diplomatic relations with the Soviet Union in January 1924—fell in elections in late October, on the heels of a "Red scare" that was triggered by publication of a letter allegedly signed by Grigorii Zinoviev, the head of the Comintern, but since proven to be a forgery concocted by a group of anti-Soviet émigrés. The Zinoviev letter called on the British Communist party to intensify its revolutionary activity and infiltration of British army units. The Conservative government severed diplomatic relations, and not until 1930 did British-Soviet relations again move onto a normal track.

In China, too, Moscow's position was abruptly shaken as a consequence of domestic turnabouts that were not directly attributable to Soviet policy, though in both the British and Chinese cases, the Comintern's espousal of world revolution and undoubted intrigues created a climate of suspicion that undercut Moscow's efforts to promote better relations on a government-to-government level. The result was cynical disbelief in Moscow's policy of peace, which included signing the 1928 Kellogg-Briand Pact, which outlawed war as an instrument of national policy; supporting the League of Nations' efforts to promote disarmament; and concluding treaties of nonaggression with Poland, Romania, and Estonia. These measures were inadequate to overcome the widespread antipathy that was felt everywhere in official circles in Europe. As a consequence, the great powers ignored Russia's traditional interests in Eastern Europe, and all major steps affecting the area in the interwar period were taken without Soviet participation. Stalin was to reverse this exclusionist policy in 1939, with far-reaching results for all of Europe.

In the 1920s no immediate threat to Soviet security was posed by any neighboring state in Europe, but the Soviet Union did have reason to fear a powerful and expansionist Japan. Japanese intervention in the Russian civil war and their attempt to detach the Maritime Province (containing the vital port of Vladivostok) had failed, largely because of Western pressure. Japan was induced to withdraw its troops at the Washington naval disarmament conference (November 12, 1921, to February 6, 1922). In a twist of irony—for which history is often noted—the Soviet Union, though not invited despite its protest that as a Far Eastern power it should have a voice in matters affecting regional security, was the principal beneficiary. Thanks to the Japanese withdrawal, in November 1922 Moscow greatly improved its military position vis-à-vis the Japanese by reincorporating Vladivostok and the puppet Far Eastern Republic, which it had created in eastern Siberia in April 1920 to serve as a buffer separating the weak Soviet State from the expansionist Japanese.

To the south, China loomed large in Soviet thinking. The ripening revolutionary situation, a desire to see Japan exhaust herself in expansion against China, and harassment from anti-Soviet forces operating in adjacent Manchuria, Outer Mongolia, and Xinjiang (Sinkiang)—areas nominally part of China but long vulnerable to Russian influence—heightened Soviet interest. In the early years when its military weakness was most evident, the Soviet state had disclaimed any desire for special privileges in China. For example, the Karakhan Declaration of 1919 renounced all former czarist spheres of influence in Manchuria and the Chinese Eastern Railroad (CER), the trunk line across northern Manchuria that connected with the Trans-Siberian line to Vladivostok and extended down to Port Arthur at the tip of the Liaotung Peninsula. But as the USSR's military position improved, such idealistic manifestos were superseded by a quest for the very same kind of concrete privileges enjoyed by the preceding czarist regime.

From the first, Moscow wanted diplomatic recognition from the internationally recognized but weak government in Beijing (Peking); every revolutionary regime seeks legitimacy as much to cripple counterrevolutionary elements as to entrench its own power. But the Beijing regime was pro-Japanese and until 1924 refused to deal with the Soviet Union. Elsewhere in China, the absence of a strong central government magnified the regional power of local warlords, who were generally hostile to Moscow and therefore poor prospects for Soviet infiltration. Particularly worrying was the anti-Soviet activity in Manchuria, which was ruled by Marshal Chang Tso-lin, who followed a pro-Japanese policy until 1928.

Frustrated in these directions, Moscow in 1921 made contact through the Comintern with Dr. Sun Yat-sen, the founder of the revolutionary Kuomintang (KMT) party, who had established a political base in Canton, in the south of China. It was through the Comintern that Moscow supported Sun's aim of overthrowing the very same government in Beijing from which the Soviet government was seeking diplomatic recognition. In this way conventional Soviet diplomacy and unconventional Comintern activity pursued common goals by different routes.

By supporting the KMT, Moscow aligned itself with an emerging revolutionary movement and hoped to weaken the Japanese position in China. For the first time it began cooperating with a bourgeois nationalist leadership, in accordance with a policy laid down by Lenin at the 1920

Comintern congress. Under this approach, when "imperialism" (in this instance, Japan) was the main threat, cooperation with a progressive stratum (defined by its readiness to work with the Soviet Union and local Communists) of capitalism was justifiable. Under the agreement entered into in January 1923 by Sun Yat-sen and Comintern representative A. A. Joffe (who was supposedly acting on behalf of the nongovernmental Communist International and not the Soviet government), both signatories acknowledged that China was not suitable for communism and that its "most pressing problems are the completion of national unification and the attainment of full independence." Joffe assured Dr. Sun "that Russia is willing and ready to enter into negotiations with China on the basis of Russia's abandonment of all treaties, and of the rights and privileges (conceded by China) under duress, secured by the Czarist Government from China," including treaties concerning the Chinese Eastern Railway [the key to control of Manchuria: when Russia had expanded in the Far East in the late nineteenth century, it had constructed the CER, thus entrenching its influence in Manchuria at the expense of a weak China and a jealous but as yet militarily inferior Japan]. Joffe declared "that it is not, and never has been, the intention or objective of the present Russian Government to carry out imperialistic policies in Outer Mongolia, or to work for Outer Mongolia's independence from China."[5] However, only one year later Moscow showed that its aim was to retain control, if possible, over both.

Nonetheless, the Sun-Joffe agreement brought immediate help to the Kuomintang, which remained the centerpiece of Soviet policy in China until 1927. Comintern advisers flocked to aid the Kuomintang: General Vasily K. Blucher helped found the Whampoa Military Academy outside Canton, and Michael Borodin, the most important of all the Comintern agents in China, reorganized the KMT along the lines of the CPSU. (Both men were executed by Stalin during the purges of 1937–1938.) The agreement was also instrumental in persuading the Chinese Communist party (CCP), which was created with Comintern support in 1921, to subordinate immediate prospects for power by joining the KMT in 1923, albeit under conditions that permitted the CCP to retain its identity as a party within a party.

In May 1924, three months after London had granted the USSR diplomatic recognition, Beijing followed suit. The weak Chinese government, desperate for any help it could get, made far-reaching concessions to the Soviet Union. Not only did Moscow keep ownership of the Chinese Eastern Railroad and retain its special position in Manchuria, but it also secured Beijing's recognition of autonomy for Outer Mongolia, whose actual status since 1921 had been that of Soviet satellite. The consolidation of control over Mongolia (and Xinjiang province) and reaffirmation of privileges in Manchuria were further examples of Moscow's familiar amalgam of security considerations and imperialist ambitions.

Three years later Soviet policy and prospects in China suffered a series of sharp setbacks. Sun Yat-sen died in March 1925 and was succeeded by Chiang Kai-shek, who felt strong enough by March 1926, because of Comintern assistance in training his troops, to launch his northern expedition to unify China under the KMT. Within a year, sweeping all before him, Chiang turned on the Communists and improved relations with the Western powers, seeing in them a more lucrative source of assistance against Japan and for China's economic development. Stalin finally broke off relations with Chiang in late 1927, but Soviet policy was not without some lasting benefit: though Chiang was ideologically hostile to Moscow, he was a nationalist whose anti-Japanese position came to be a basis for Sino-Soviet cooperation after Japan invaded Manchuria in September 1931.

Strained relations with Great Britain and the disappointments in China and elsewhere in Asia (that is, in Indonesia, India, Japan, and French Indochina) made the Soviets more insecure than ever. Internally they intensified the drive to develop "socialism in one country," introducing five-year plans for accelerated industrial growth. International events continued to be interpreted within the Marxist/Leninist mode of analysis, but Moscow's behavior generally accorded with more traditional norms of balance-of-power considerations and alignments against the main enemies of the moment; its policy was primarily reactive. Regardless of what Moscow may have wanted, it was constrained by a weak military position, absorption with its succession crisis, and an international environment that offered no opportunities for expansion or political maneuvering.

At the diplomatic level, in 1928 Stalin followed a cautious foreign policy, but at the same time he set the Comintern on an ultrarevolutionary tack. At its sixth congress in September, the Comintern enunciated guiding principles for foreign Communist parties; specifically, it held that (1) the Soviet Union was the citadel of world revolution — "She is the international driving force of proletarian revolution that impels the proletariat of all countries to seize power . . . she is the prototype of the fraternity of nationalities in all lands . . . that the world proletariat must establish when it has captured political power"; (2) the preservation of the Soviet Union must be the primary concern of the international proletariat — "In the event of the imperialist states declaring war upon and attacking the USSR, the international proletariat must retaliate by organizing bold and determined mass action and struggle for the overthrow of the imperialist governments"; and (3) all Communist parties owed exclusive allegiance to Moscow.[6] These principles were to be at the heart of the cleavages that beset the Communist world in the period after World War II when national communism and Eurocommunism became prominent political phenomena.

In the 1930s, Moscow faced serious threats to its security in Europe and the Far East. It maneuvered as best it could in an international system in which the significant decisions were made in Berlin, London, Paris, and Tokyo. Not until the spring of 1939 did Moscow become an important actor.

Like Lenin, Stalin preferred alignment with Germany, rather than Britain or France. Rapallo was insurance against the gnawing fear of a capitalist coalition's mounting another intervention; it provided much-needed economic and military assistance, and it forestalled isolation. The renewal of the Berlin treaty in 1931 signified continuation of the special Soviet-German relationship. Stalin saw no reason to heed the warnings of his exiled arch-opponent, Trotsky, about the rising danger from fascism (he had Trotsky murdered in Mexico in 1940). In keeping with the hard line that he had imposed on the Comintern in 1928, Stalin identified the Social Democrats, not the Nazis, as the main enemy of international communism, and actually contributed to Hitler's rise to power in early 1933 and to the consequent destruction of the German Communist party. Despite Hitler's public diatribes against the Communist menace, Stalin hoped that Germany and the USSR could do business. Machiavelli, not Marx, inspired Stalin's foreign policy.

The Quest for Security

A militarily weak and politically stigmatized Soviet Union sought security in various ways. To ensure that the nations on her western border would not serve as a staging ground for an interventionist-minded capitalist coalition, the USSR moved to neutralize the nations of Eastern Europe by negotiating treaties of nonaggression and friendship. Aided by the fears that Poland's pretensions to great power status engendered among the Baltic countries, Moscow succeeded in negotiating a friendship treaty with Lithuania in 1926 and a trade pact with Latvia in 1927. But not until after the Kellog-Briand pact of 1928 were the Soviets able to induce Poland, Romania, Latvia, and Estonia to agree to treaties of nonaggression. In Moscow, on February 9, 1929, these nations signed the East Pact (often called the Litvinov Protocol). At the time Soviet diplomats considered it a signal achievement: it served to foreclose any possible anti-Soviet coalition of powers involving the USSR's immediate neighbors. But the pact proved to be more form than substance.

Prior to 1939, the countries of Eastern Europe were united in their mistrust and fear of bolshevism. Only Czechoslovakia, which had no border with the USSR, did not regard Soviet policy, ideology, and objectives as threatening. However, the Versailles system of economic and political fragmentation in eastern Europe did little to encourage cooperative approaches to mutual problems; and, since the USSR posed no immediate military danger, the nations of the area took no important measures to improve relations with the neighboring colossus. Instead, ideological antipathy toward communism led them to look to France and its system of alliances for security. Trade between the USSR and Eastern Europe remained insignificant; political ties were weak and proved incapable of being strengthened when both were confronted by a resurgent and aggressive Germany. Russia's traditional interests in Eastern Europe were ignored in the councils of Europe, and all major steps affecting the area in the interwar period were taken without Soviet participation.

The Soviet Union continued to pursue friendly relations with Germany, initially viewing the Nazi movement with "total misapprehension." As Max Beloff noted, "Communist theory made no allowance for a movement which was at once revolutionary and non-proletarian."[7] Nazism, with its virulent anti-Communist appeal, was considered merely another manifestation of bourgeois ideology aimed at attracting the support of middle class constituents shaken by the disruptive social and economic consequences of the worldwide depression; and Hitler, the tool of German big business. None of this, Moscow reasoned, should preclude continued good government-to-government relations in the spirit of Rapallo. But Hitler's policy, especially the termination of military cooperation at the end of 1933, foreshadowed trouble in Soviet-German relations.

Stalin waited in silence and with growing anxiety, refraining for almost a year from any comment about events in Germany and thus adding to the confusion of an already sorely bewildered Comintern, which was still echoing an essentially anti-Western line. At the seventeenth congress of the CPSU in January 1934, Stalin at last spoke about the developments in Germany, as well as the overall international situation. Throughout his speech, he proffered the olive branch to Germany and made unmistakable his desire for continued relations in the tradition of Bismarck and Rapallo:

> Some German politicians say that the USSR has now taken an orientation towards France and Poland; that from being an opponent of the Versailles Treaty it has become a supporter of it, and that this change is to be explained by the establishment of the fascist regime in Germany. That is not true. Of course, we are far from being enthusiastic about the fascist regime in Germany. But it is not a question of fascism here, if only for the reason that fascism in Italy, for example, has not prevented the USSR from establishing the best relations with that country. Nor is it a question of any

alleged change in our attitude towards the Versailles Treaty. It is not for us, who have experienced the shame of the Brest Peace, to sing the praises of the Versailles Treaty. We merely do not agree to the world being flung into the abyss of a new war on account of that treaty. The same must be said of the alleged new orientation taken by the USSR. We never had any orientation towards Germany, nor have we any orientation towards Poland and France. Our orientation in the past and our orientation at the present time is towards the USSR, and towards the USSR alone. And if the interests of the USSR demand rapprochement with one country or another which is not interested in disturbing peace, we adopt this course without hesitation.

No, that is not the point. The point is that Germany's policy has changed. The point is that even before the present German politicians came to power, and particularly after they came to power, a contest began in Germany between two political lines: between the old policy, which was reflected in the treaties between the USSR and Germany, and the "new" policy, which in the main, recalls the policy of the former German Kaiser, who at one time occupied the Ukraine and marched against Leningrad, after converting the Baltic countries into a *place d'armes* for this march; and this "new" policy is obviously gaining the upper hand over the old policy.[8]

By late 1933, concern over its relationship with Germany stimulated interest in closer ties with the West, especially with France, whom Moscow courted even while it continued friendly relations with Germany. At all costs, Stalin worked to prevent a Franco-German understanding that would neutralize France and give Germany the green light to expand to the east.

Faced with growing Nazi hostility and rejection of Rapallo (that is, of a special relationship), Moscow accepted the French-sponsored invitation and on September 18, 1934, joined the League of Nations, where it became the leading exponent of collective security. The address of Soviet Foreign Minister Maxim Litvinov (1929–1939) before the League on the occasion of the USSR's becoming a member set the pattern for subsequent Soviet disquisitions on the potential positive role of the organization. Litvinov acknowledged an early Soviet fear that the nations of the League "might give collective expression to their hostility toward the Soviet Union and combine their anti-Soviet activities," but called now for cooperation of all peace-minded states, in the face of growing threats to their security.[9] Repeatedly during the next few years the USSR called upon the League of Nations to resist aggression in Ethiopia, Spain, China, Austria, and Czechoslovakia—to no avail.

Moscow's bilateral relationship with France foundered on a deep mutual suspicion of each other's motives and an ideological antipathy that blinded each to the common danger they faced. The two countries signed a treaty of mutual assistance on May 2, 1935, and the USSR signed a similar treaty with Czechoslovakia two weeks later. The purpose was to create an interlocking alliance system; the actual result was to give Stalin flexibility in responding to the German threat. Stalin effectively prevented any Franco-German agreement and avoided isolation in Europe. Under the Soviet-Czechoslovak treaty, the Soviet Union was committed to aiding Czechoslovakia, but only if France first took action in fulfillment of its treaty obligations. France's failure to live up to its commitment to Prague in September 1938 led to the dismemberment of Czechoslovakia, and it freed the USSR from any obligation to act on Czechoslovakia's behalf. However, that time of testing was still in the future.

In 1935, to stiffen the resolve of the Western countries to resist Hitler, Stalin ordered the Comintern to press for a popular front and to cooperate with all bourgeois parties, regardless of past differences, in the creation of this anti-Fascist front. But throughout 1935, 1936, 1937, and 1938, the Western powers gave way before Nazi Germany's relentless pressure, fearful of precipitating a showdown for which they were ill-prepared, hoping, ostrichlike, that each concession would be the last, and uneasy over stumbling into a situation that would entail really meaningful cooperation with a Soviet Union they detested and mistrusted. In this sense, ideologically derived perceptions shaped the behavior of Western leaders to a greater extent than they did Soviet policy.

For his part, Stalin continued in secret to put out feelers to Berlin for a new Rapallo-type agreement. He secretly admired Hitler and "appreciated" warnings in early 1937 from the German secret service suggesting that his former chief of staff, Marshal Mikhail Tukhachevsky, was part of a plot to seize power. Stalin was especially appreciative since the allegations against Tukhachevsky had been planted abroad by the NKVD (that is, the KGB) on his orders, "in the hope — perhaps even the knowledge — that they would return to Moscow in a form which could be used to frame" Tukhachevsky and other revolutionary heroes whom Stalin was determined to destroy in order to consolidate his absolute power.[10] A speculation that has less to commend it is that Stalin's purpose was to get rid of all possible opposition to a deal with Hitler, and Tukhachevsky's fear of Nazi Germany and interest in recultivating close links with France were not shared by Stalin. What was paramount for Stalin in 1935 and 1936 was carrying through his revolution from above: he wanted to eliminate all the old Bolsheviks who might oppose the new totalitarian socioeconomic order he was intent on creating. In this he owed more to Peter the Great than to Marx or even Lenin. The purges of the 1930s were intended to leave Stalin undisputed master of the Soviet Union. However, the external threats, which were manipulated as symbols, soon became realities Stalin could not ignore.

On March 7, 1936, Hitler marched into the Rhineland in violation of the 1925 Locarno Treaty. France, beset with one of its perennial cabinet crises, did nothing. Hitler had won his great gamble: from captured German government documents we know that the German army had orders to withdraw at once if the French gave any indication of opposition. How different the subsequent history of Europe might have been had France acted! Hitler's move not only set Germany irrevocably on the path to conquest and war, but strengthened his power in Germany. The last potential restraint — the German General Staff — was cowed into silence and submission by his stunning success. In the Kremlin, the French paralysis was viewed with concern, for it highlighted the lack of determination of the West to resist German remilitarization and expansion. Moscow may also have begun to reassess the value of the alliance with France.

Events in Spain soon revealed further vacillation and feebleness on the part of the French and British governments, which feared to intervene lest they push Nazi Germany and Fascist Italy into permanent alliance and be required to increase defense expenditures at a time when this would have been unpopular with their electorates. The newly formed French Popular Front Government of Léon Blum was scarcely two months old when, on July 19, 1936, General Francisco Franco turned the army against the Spanish republic. The Spanish Civil War of 1936–1939 accelerated the disintegration of the Popular Front, provided the first European battleground for World War II, and split West European political circles. It confronted Soviet leaders with a serious dilemma. A victory of the fascist Franco might push Paris into more intimate ties with Moscow. On the other hand, a Loyalist victory achieved with open communist support, though it would undoubtedly raise Soviet prestige, might paradoxically frighten France and lead her to view Hitler less belligerently. A different line of argument is suggested by General W. G. Krivitsky, then Chief of Soviet Military Intelligence in Western Europe, who contended that Stalin wanted to establish a Soviet-controlled regime in Spain in order to "command the respect of France and England, win from them the offer of a real alliance, and either accept it or — with that as a bargaining point — arrive at his underlying steady aim and purpose, a compact with Germany."[11] According to David Cattell, the rationale for this thesis is that Stalin, preoccupied at home with the Great Purge that decimated military and party cadres, "weak militarily, intensely adverse to and distrustful of the capitalist powers, had only the one alternative of negotiating a pact with Hitler. Stalin's problem was to show Hitler that Russia had something to offer and was a power of enough consequence to negotiate with Hitler as an equal."[12] But the evidence for this position is circumstantial and strained, whereas there are specific Soviet actions and statements suggesting that Stalin was still essentially committed to the rapprochement with France and support for collective action through the League of Nations.

The Spanish Civil War was one of the major tragedies of the twentieth century. Like any civil war, it involved great bitterness and bloodshed. The Spanish Communists took advantage of the situation to increase their influence in Loyalist circles. When it was evident that the republican cause would be defeated, pro-Moscow Communists initiated a purge of Communist and socialist elements critical of Stalin that was comparable to the one then going on in the Soviet Union, the net effect of which was to intensify French and British suspicion of the Soviets.

By 1938 Nazi Germany was a power to be reckoned with. After a lightning annexation of Austria on March 12, 1938, Hitler turned on Czechoslovakia. His ostensible objective was integration of the predominantly German-speaking Sudetenland region with Germany. Litvinov's repeated calls for "collective actions" to check "the further development of aggression," which now reflected Stalin's growing perception of danger, were ignored. Hitler's threat of war prompted a hurried British-French intercession that led to an agreement with Germany for the dismemberment of Czechoslovakia. The Munich Agreement of September 15 was signed without the participation of the victim or the USSR. The British and French dismissed Soviet expressions of a readiness to act in concert with them as meaningless: the fact that the Red Army had been weakened by purges, the absence of a common border between the USSR and Czechoslovakia, and the unwillingness of either Poland or Romania to grant permission to Soviet troops to pass through its country convinced Paris and London that Moscow was not a credible partner. The fact of the matter was that Britain and France were not ready for war and suspected that Moscow hoped to see them embroiled in a conflict that it would avoid. Suspicion of Moscow ran too deep in the West for political cooperation.

Stalin watched Hitler's success, the West's surrender, and the Soviet Union's growing isolation. Whatever hope he might have had for collective action to stymie Nazi aggression disappeared at Munich. In early March 1939, a few days before Hitler occupied all of Czechoslovakia (contrary to his solemn declaration at Munich that he had no further territorial demands), Stalin delivered a major address to the CPSU's Eighteenth Party congress. He derided France and Britain for their pusillanimity and Germany and Japan for their aggressive acts, and conveyed his belief that war was inevitable; that the nonaggressive states "draw back and retreat, making concession after concession to the aggressors;" and that a new situation was being created that the USSR could not ignore. He did not elaborate on his plans for the future, other than to say that the Soviet Union must be cautious and not allow itself "to be drawn into conflicts by warmongers who are accustomed to have others pull the chestnuts out of the fire for them." The general tenor of his speech was anti-Nazi, but the price for Soviet agreement with either coalition was left open for negotiation. For the first time in its young history, the Soviet leadership was in a strong bargaining position: it could come to terms with Hitler or join with a Britain and France now thoroughly alarmed by Germany's expansionist appetite. Stalin was waiting for the best offer.

Unimpressed by the British government's belated diplomatic activity (essentially a unilateral guarantee to Poland in March 1939), knowing Poland's anti-Soviet attitude and unwillingness to allow any Soviet troops on Polish soil even against the Nazi threat, eager to keep the USSR out of the new "imperialist" war that he sensed was imminent, and very much occupied with containing the Japanese in the Far East, Stalin let Hitler know that he was prepared for a deal. His clearest signal was the replacement on May 3, 1939, of Foreign Minister Litvinov, a Jew, by Vyacheslav M. Molotov (1939–1949, 1953–1956), one of Stalin's closest aides. This move signified the abandonment of efforts to work with the Western powers and the League of Nations—a policy Hitler associated with Litvinov—and the start of active talks with Germany.

The infamous Soviet agreement with Nazi Germany was signed on August 23, 1939. The ten-year nonaggression treaty obligated each party to neutrality in the event that the other became involved in a war with a third power. Actually, it was the green light Hitler needed to make sure that Germany could go to war without worrying about conflict on two fronts. Stalin knew of Hitler's plan to invade Poland, and the last article of the treaty stated that it was to "enter into force as soon as it is signed," an unusual diplomatic provision. Moreover, in a secret protocol (which is never mentioned in Soviet writings on the period), Stalin and Hitler agreed to a division of the spoils: Stalin's booty for signing the pact was eastern Poland, "bounded approximately by the line of the rivers Narew, Vistula, and San," Estonia, Latvia, Finland, and Bessarabia; the rest of Poland and all of Lithuania were allotted to Germany. Stalin's delight at the turn of events may be inferred from the toast he made with the German foreign minister: "I know how much the German people loves its Führer. I should therefore like to drink his health."

One eminent scholar has described the importance of the Nazi-Soviet pact for Stalin as follows:

> August 1939 represented the fruition of Stalin's whole complex conception of the means of Soviet survival in a hostile world and emergence into a commanding international position. It embraced the presumption of the inevitability of a great new war: the idea that, through divisive diplomacy in the Lenin tradition, Russia could both help to precipitate the conflict and preserve neutrality during its earlier stages, allowing the combatants to exhaust themselves whilst she grew stronger and stronger; and the notion

> that at some point Russia would be able to take over territories to which she had historical claim and contiguous countries whose ensuing Soviet-guided revolutions would advance the world-revolutionary cause while creating the "socialist encirclement" that would give Russia's revolution the still missing guaranteed security.[13]

Stalin looked to the coming war in Western Europe with equanimity. As he viewed the situation, the Soviet Union could sit out the European war, wait for a further weakening of the capitalist world, and prepare for the inevitable revolutionary situation that would offer new opportunities for the spread of Soviet power and the proletarian revolution.

The Nazi-Soviet pact also contributed to Soviet security in the Far East. For Soviet leaders, more than for their czarist counterparts, there has always been a discernible relationship between security in Europe and security in Asia. Fear of attack from both directions had been a Soviet nightmare ever since the Allied intervention of 1918–1920. The threat from Japan in the 1930s, coming as it did at a time when relations with Germany were deteriorating, heightened Moscow's fear of involvement in a two-front war and greatly influenced Stalin's decisions in 1939, a consideration generally given too little attention in Western writings.

After Japan's invasion and occupation of Manchuria in 1931, the main Soviet problem in Asia was determining whether Japan would strike south into China and eventually toward the raw materials of Southeast Asia, or north against Siberia. The ineffectiveness of the League of Nations and the unwillingness of the great powers to do more than protest Japanese aggression exacerbated Moscow's sense of isolation and danger. The threat from Japan brought the Soviet Union and China together again, and relations with Beijing were restored on December 12, 1932, to the detriment of Moscow's ties with the Chinese Communist party, then being relentlessly attacked by the KMT.

Moscow's diplomacy was to encourage Chiang Kai-shek to resist Japan and simultaneously to appease Japan and encourage it to expand at China's expense. In this, the Soviet Union practiced the same kind of above-the-counter and below-the-counter diplomacy in the Far East that it did in Europe. On numerous occasions Litvinov proposed a nonaggression pact to Japan; he was repeatedly rebuffed. Japan was interested, however, in purchasing the northern trunk lines of the Manchurian railroad, which were still controlled by the Soviet Union. Negotiations began in Tokyo in June 1933 and continued intermittently for almost two years until, in March 1935, Moscow finally agreed—over bitter Chinese protests—to sell its interest in the railroad and grant fishing concessions in Soviet Far Eastern waters. This appeasement was due in part to concern over secret Japanese-German military talks and to a desire to remove all possible pretexts for a Japanese attack, which the USSR was not then in condition to repel.

The Japanese, satisfied in Manchuria, restlessly probed Soviet determination and defenses farther to the east. In an attempt to discourage Japanese expansion into the Chinese provinces of Jehol and Chabar in Inner Mongolia, Moscow revealed that a mutual defense treaty with the Mongolian People's Republic (MPR) had been signed in March 1936, despite Beijing's claim that the MPR was juridically part of China. Since 1924, Moscow's control over the MPR had been such that it could have annexed the area, but it chose to encourage Mongol separatism from China and use the MPR as a buffer state. By contrast, further to the east, in Xinjiang, where Soviet influence was also preeminent, the USSR did not detach Chinese territory but chose to deal with compliant warlords, possibly because it feared that an independent Turkic-speaking Muslim people's republic in Central Asia might act as a catalyst for separatism in the USSR's own Turkic-speaking subdivisions—the Kazakh, Uzbek, and Kirghz SSRs.

As for the Chinese, their protests against these extensions of Soviet influence gave way to their urgent need for Soviet help following the full-scale Japanese invasion of July 1937. Concerned over the implications of the anti-Comintern pact among Germany, Italy, and Japan, Moscow had pushed for a popular front in China during the previous year. In December 1936, Chiang Kai-shek was dramatically kidnapped. His captors insisted that he stop the enervating punitive expeditions against the Communists and devote himself to leading the struggle against Japan. Reluctantly, he consented. The cooperation (for the most part half-hearted) between the KMT and the CCP strengthened the resistance to Japan and thus helped promote Soviet security; and Moscow provided China with important, though limited, quantities of military supplies, particularly during the period before Hitler's invasion of the Soviet Union.

From 1931 on, Moscow had striven to counter the Japanese threat. Its army east of the Urals was expanded from 100,000 in 1931 to about 600,000 in 1939; thousands of tanks and hundreds of planes were deployed. Between 1934 and 1936 there were many small but sharp military clashes along the Manchurian-Mongolian-Soviet border. Japanese probes, often in great strength, were repulsed: in July–August 1938, in the Lake Khasan (Changkufeng) area of the Manchurian-Korean-Soviet border; in 1939, along the Amur River; and in the spring and summer of 1939, in the Khalkingol (Nomonhan) steppe region along the Halka River that generally delineated the Manchurian-Mongolian border.

The latter was a full-fledged war that sharpened Stalin's interest in a nonaggression pact with Nazi Germany that would insulate Moscow from involvement in a European war. Buttressed by intelligence information on

Japanese military intentions from Richard Sorge, the USSR's master spy in Tokyo, the Soviets' superior generalship and weaponry bloodied the Japanese Kwangtung Army and deflected the war party in Tokyo from pushing a major war against the Soviet Union. (Purges in the forces in the Far East were nowhere near as extensive as those that wracked the Red Army's combat effectiveness in Europe. In 1941, when Western experts assessed the USSR's ability to resist the Nazi onslaught, they used as their standard the poor performance of the Red Army in the 1939–1940 Winter War against Finland—in which more than one million troops were required to overcome a Finnish army one-fifth that size—and ignored the impressive Soviet showing against Japan in the 1938–1939 battles). After the signing of the Nazi-Soviet pact, which apparently caught the Japanese by surprise, an uneasy quiet settled along the entire border, and the USSR concentrated on affairs in Europe. Soviet victories on the battlefield set the stage for the Soviet-Japanese neutrality pact of April 1941.

Stalin's diplomacy and military power in the Far East showed a sure sense of balance-of-power realities. Ideology and revolutionary agitation took a back seat to the pursuit of tactical objectives whose aim was to dissuade Japan from striking the Soviet Union and induce it to move south for satisfaction of its imperialist ambitions.

On August 31, 1939, Molotov defended the decision to conclude a pact with Nazi Germany in a major speech to the Soviet parliament. Criticizing Britain and France for the "howling contradictions" in their professed interest in cooperating with the Soviet Union, he emphasized the willingness of Germany to reach concrete and immediate agreements that were in the national interest of the Soviet Union, irrespective of the differences in the internal systems of the countries: "The art of politics in the sphere of foreign relations does not consist in increasing the number of enemies for one's country. . . . It is our duty to think of the interests of the Soviet people, the interests of the Union of the Soviet Socialist Republics." He stressed the importance of good relations with Germany and never alluded to the secret protocol:

> Is it really difficult for these [British and French] gentlemen to understand the purpose of the Soviet-German Nonaggression Pact, on the strength of which the USSR is not obligated to involve itself in war either on the side of Great Britain against Germany or on the side of Germany against Great Britain? Is it really difficult to understand that the USSR is pursuing and will continue to pursue its own independent policy, based on the interests of the peoples of the USSR and only their interests? If these gentlemen have such an uncontrollable desire to fight, let them do their own fighting without the Soviet Union. We will see what fighting stuff they are made of . . . .[14]

The next day German troops invaded Poland. As the curtain rose on World War II, the Soviet Union was on the sidelines.

Stalin had become master of the Soviet Union, surmounting the enormous resistance from the peasantry to his revolution from above in the 1930s, the debilitation and reconstitution of key institutions of Soviet society, the political isolation that foreign powers had sought to impose on a distrusted Soviet Union, and the vulnerability resulting from military weakness during most of the interwar period. None of his past foreign-policy blunders seemed to have been costly: not the exaggerated fear that Britain and France were plotting another intervention to topple the Soviet regime; not the misjudgment of nazism's inherent dynamism and expansionist threat to the Soviet Union; not the detrimental effects that the Comintern, as an instrument of Kremlin diplomacy, had on cooperation with the Western powers. On the eve of World War II, it appeared that Stalin's duplicity in handling the Western powers publicly and Germany privately had been practiced with great skill. The pact with Hitler had yielded fruits—a return of former czarist lands that added strategic depth to the USSR's western defenses, and a neutrality that seemed to guarantee the nation against involvement in a two-front war or in the European war that was to change the political complexion of the continent forever.

No Soviet official has ever criticized Stalin for his deal with Hitler. For example, on November 2, 1987 in a celebratory speech commemorating the 70th anniversary of the Bolshevik revolution, Gorbachev said the West resorted "to all sorts of lies to put the blame for World War II on the Soviet Union, alleging that the way to war was opened up by the Ribbentrop-Molotov nonaggression pact"

> They say that the decision that the Soviet Union made by signing the nonaggression pact with Germany was not the best one. Maybe so, if one is guided not by harsh reality but by speculative abstractions divorced from the context of the time. And in those conditions the question stood in about the same way as it did during the Brest [-Litovsk] peace treaty. Would our country be independent or not, would there be socialism in the world or not? . . .
>
> It is known from documents that the date for Germany's invasion of Poland, no later than 1 September, had been set as early as 3 April 1939, that is long before the Soviet-German pact. London, Paris, and Washington knew everything, down to the smallest details of the preparations for the Polish campaign, just as they knew that the only obstacle capable of stopping the Hitlerites could be the conclusion, no later than August 1939, of an Anglo-Franco-Soviet military alliance. Those plans were also known to the leadership of our country, and for this reason it tried to convince Britain and France of the need for collective measures. It also appealed to the Polish Government of the time for cooperation in order to end aggression.

> But the Western powers had other calculations: to lure the USSR with a promise of an alliance, and thereby to hamper the conclusion of the non-aggression pact which had been offered to us, to deprive us of the possibility of better preparing ourselves for the inevitable attack by Hitlerite Germany against the USSR.[15]

However, neither Gorbachev nor any other Soviet source ever mentioned the secret protocol that carved Eastern Europe into Soviet and German spheres of influence. One authoritative Soviet book, attempting to explain the territorial realignments that occurred, noted that the Soviet government regarded it as a "duty to prevent the fascist enslavement of the Ukrainian and Byelorussian populations that had been living with the Polish border since 1920":

> On September 17 in view of the fact that the Polish army had disintegrated under the blows of the German war machine the Red Army entered Western Byelorussia and Western Ukraine. The long-cherished dream of the Western Ukrainians and Byelorussians for reunification with the Soviet Ukraine and Byelorussia became a reality. In Moscow on September 28, 1939, a treaty was signed between the USSR and Germany establishing the Western border of the Soviet state approximately along the so-called "Curzon" line, which in 1919 Britain, France, the United States and other countries had proposed as the border between Soviet Russia and Poland based on ethnographical principles.[16]

There was no mention that these lines of division had been fixed *before*, not *after*, the Nazi invasion of Poland.

Notes

1. George F. Kennan, *Russia Leaves the War* (Princeton: Princeton University Press, 1956), 75–76.
2. V. I. Lenin, *Sochinenia,* Vol. XXVI, 2nd ed. (Moscow: State Publishing House, 1930), 8–14, excerpts. From a report presented by Lenin to the Eighth Congress of Soviets of the RSFSR on December 21, 1920.
3. V. I. Lenin, *Sochinenia,* Vol. XXX, 4th ed. (Moscow: Institute of Marx-Engels-Lenin, 1950), 185–97.
4. John W. Wheeler-Bennett, *The Nemesis of Power: The German Army in Politics 1918–1945* (New York: St. Martin's Press, 1954), 127–28.
5. Conrad Brandt, Benjamin Schwartz, and John K. Fairbank (eds.), *A Documentary History of Chinese Communism* (Cambridge: Harvard University Press, 1952), 70–71.

6. The Comintern's 1928 Program, as quoted in the U.S. Congress House Committee on Foreign Affairs, *The Strategy and Tactics of World Communism,* 80th Cong., 2nd Sess. (1948), H. Doc. 619, 121–40, excerpts.
7. Max Beloff, *The Foreign Policy of Soviet Russia 1929-1941,* Vol. 1 (New York: Oxford University Press, 1947), 61.
8. J. Stalin, *Problems of Leninism* (Moscow: Foreign Languages Publishing House, 1953), 592–93.
9. League of Nations, *Official Journal: Special Supplement to No. 125* (Geneva, September 1934), 67–69, excerpts.
10. Malcolm MacKintosh, *Juggernaut: A History of the Soviet Forces* (New York: Macmillan, 1967), 92.
11. W. G. Krivitsky, *I Was Stalin's Agent* (London: Hamish Hamilton, 1939), 99. Krivitsky, who defected in 1938, was murdered, presumably by the KGB, in a Washington hotel in February 1941.
12. David T. Cattell, *Soviet Diplomacy and the Spanish Civil War* (Berkeley: University of California Press, 1957), 36.
13. Robert C. Tucker, "The Emergence of Stalin's Foreign Policy," *Slavic Review,* Vol. 36, No. 4 (December 1977), 588–89.
14. U.S. House of Representatives, Committee on Foreign Affairs, 80th Cong., 2nd Sess., House Document No. 619, *The Strategy and Tactics of World Communism,* 160–65, excerpts.
15. Foreign Broadcast Information Service/Soviet Union (hereafter referred to as FBIS/SOV), November 3, 1987, 46.
16. A. A. Gromyko and B. N. Ponomarev (eds.), *Soviet Foreign Policy 1917-1945,* Vol. 1 (Moscow: Progress Publishers, 1981), 384.

Selected Bibliography

ALEXANDROV, VICTOR. *The Tukhachevsky Affair.* Englewood Cliffs, N.J.: Prentice-Hall, 1964.

BELOFF, MAX. *The Foreign Policy of Soviet Russia, 1929-1936.* Vol. 1. New York: Oxford University Press, 1947.

BRANDT, CONRAD. *Stalin's Failure in China 1924-1927.* Cambridge: Harvard University Press, 1958.

CARR, EDWARD HALLETT. *The Bolshevik Revolution, 1917-1923.* 4 vols. New York: Macmillan, 1950, 1952, 1953, 1954.

———. *German-Soviet Relations Between the World Wars, 1919-1939.* Baltimore: Johns Hopkins Press, 1951.

DALLIN, DAVID J. *The Rise of Russia in Asia.* New Haven: Yale University Press, 1949.

DEAKIN, F. W., and G. R. STORRY. *The Case of Richard Sorge.* New York: Harper & Row, 1966.

DEUTSCHER, ISAAC. *Stalin: A Political Biography.* New York: Oxford University Press, 1949.

———. *The Prophet Armed: Trotsky, 1879–1921.* New York: Oxford University Press, 1954.

DYCK, HARVEY L. *Weimar Germany and Soviet Russia 1926–1933: A Study in Diplomatic Instability.* New York: Columbia University Press, 1966.

EUDIN, XENIA, and HAROLD H. FISHER (EDS.). *Soviet Russia and the West, 1920–1927.* Stanford: Stanford University Press, 1957.

———, and ROBERT C. NORTH (EDS.). *Soviet Russia and the East, 1920–1927.* Stanford: Stanford University Press, 1957.

———, and ROBERT M. SLUSSER (EDS.). *Soviet Foreign Policy 1928–1934.* 2 vols. University Park: Pennsylvania State University Press, 1967.

FISCHER, LOUIS. *The Soviets in World Affairs.* 2 vols. New York: Vintage, 1960.

FREUND, GERALD. *Unholy Alliance: Russian-German Relations from the Treaty of Brest-Litovsk to the Treaty of Berlin.* New York: Harcourt Brace Jovanovich, 1957.

HASLAM, JONATHAN. *The Soviet Union and the Struggle for Collective Security in Europe, 1933–1939.* New York: St. Martin's Press, 1984.

HILGER, GUSTAV, and ALFRED G. MEYER. *The Incompatible Allies.* New York: Macmillan, 1953.

HOCHMAN, JIRI. *The Soviet Union and the Failure of Collective Security, 1934–1938.* Ithaca: Cornell University Press, 1984.

KENNAN, GEORGE F. *Russia Leaves the War.* Princeton: Princeton University Press, 1956.

———. *The Decision to Intervene.* Princeton: Princeton University Press, 1958.

———. *Russia and the West Under Lenin and Stalin.* Boston: Little, Brown, 1960.

LENSEN, GEORGE A. *Japanese Recognition of the USSR: Soviet-Japanese Relations, 1921–1930.* Tallahassee, Fla.: Diplomatic Press, 1970.

———. *The Damned Inheritance: The Soviet Union and the Manchurian Crisis, 1924–1935.* Tallahassee, Fla.: Diplomatic Press, 1974.

MCKENZIE, KERMIT E. *Comintern and World Revolution, 1928–1943.* New York: Columbia University Press, 1964.

MCSHERRY, JAMES E. *Stalin, Hitler, and Europe: The Origins of World War II, 1933–1939.* New York: World Publishing Co., 1968.

NORTH, ROBERT C. *Moscow and Chinese Communists.* Stanford: Stanford University Press, 1953.

ROSENBAUM, KURT. *Community of Fate: German-Soviet Diplomatic Relations, 1922–1933.* 2nd ed. Syracuse: Syracuse University Press, 1965.

ULAM, ADAM B. *Expansion and Coexistence: Soviet Foreign Policy, 1917-1973.* 2nd ed. New York: Praeger, 1974.

ULLMAN, RICHARD H. *Anglo-Soviet Relations 1917-1921.* 2 vols. Princeton: Princeton University Press, 1961, 1968.

WEINBERG, GERHARD L. *Germany and the Soviet Union, 1939-1941.* Leyden: Brill, 1954.

WHEELER-BENNETT, JOHN W. *The Forgotten Peace: Brest-Litovsk, March 1918.* New York: Morrow, 1939.

WHITE, STEPHEN. *The Origins of Détente: The Genoa Conference and Soviet-Western Relations, 1921-1922.* New York: Cambridge University Press, 1987.

WHITING, ALLEN S. *Soviet Policies in China, 1917-1924.* New York: Columbia University Press, 1954.

3

Soviet Expansion and the Coming of the Cold War, 1939–1946

At dawn on September 1, 1939, German legions rolled into Poland. Two days later, Britain and France declared war on Germany. World War II was a reality. Moscow expected the new "imperialist" war to be a replica of the first one, only this time the Soviet Union would be a spectator positioned to profit from the mutual exhaustion of the competing capitalist coalitions.

With the outbreak of war, the Soviet Union abandoned its professed policy of nonaggression for a course of territorial expansion. Exploiting the preoccupation of the other European powers elsewhere, it rationalized its actions in terms of national security. By whatever name and however legitimized, Soviet expansion was, with the subsequent defeat of Germany, to move Soviet power into the heart of Europe and thus give rise to the Cold War.

Stalin wasted little time in claiming his booty. On September 17 the Red Army occupied eastern Poland; soon thereafter Stalin pressured the Baltic states into permitting Soviet troops to be stationed on their territory, a prelude to their formal incorporation into the Soviet Union in August 1940, and he tried to intimidate Finland into surrendering territory that would strengthen the defensive position of Leningrad (concessions the Soviets had been seeking since April 1938). Upon the Finns' refusal, the Soviet Union unilaterally abrogated its treaty of nonaggression on November 28, 1939, and attacked the next day. Though resisting brilliantly, the Finns found themselves without help from the West and finally capitulated, signing a peace treaty on March 12, 1940. Thus ended the first wave of Soviet expansion.

Hardly had the Soviets begun to digest these territorial chunks than the Nazi blitzkrieg in April and May 1940 overran Norway, the Netherlands, Denmark, Belgium, and France. Britain stood alone and virtually defenseless. Stalin again availed himself of Hitler's absorption elsewhere, this time to wrench Bessarabia from Romania and make demands on Bulgaria and Turkey that would have resulted in the Black Sea's becoming a Soviet lake and Moscow's having control of the straits. With evident reluctance, Germany accepted the Soviet annexation of Bessarabia, at the same time taking measures to consolidate its own influence in the rest of Romania. The expansionist appetites of Germany and the Soviet Union sharpened their rivalry in the Balkans and in Finland. Stalin's covetousness was a match for Hitler's, and convinced Hitler that the USSR would have to be subjugated if his conquest of Europe was to be safeguarded.

Though officially neutral as far as the war in the West was concerned, the Soviet Union had a pro-German tilt: German naval vessels were outfitted in Murmansk (though after the German occupation of Norway, the Soviet port was not needed); crucial raw materials were supplied as part of overall Soviet-German economic agreements; foreign Communist parties opposed the war on orders from Moscow, thus weakening the home front in the Western countries and helping the Germans; and British ships were detained in Soviet ports because of the British blockade of Germany. Soviet deference to German needs in the prosecution of the war against the West did not, however, extend to the areas of overlapping Soviet and German ambitions.

By the fall of 1940, Germany's military power had assumed awesome proportions. Hitler negotiated a tripartite pact among Germany, Italy, and Japan on September 27, 1940. His efforts to link the Soviet Union to it failed, partly because of Soviet demands for concessions from Japan. In an effort to resolve some of the strains that were cropping up in German-Soviet relations, the two nations held talks in Berlin on November 12 and 13. The Germans asked "whether in the long run the most advantageous access to the sea for Russia could not be found in the direction of the Persian Gulf and the Arabian Sea, and whether at the same time certain other aspirations of Russia in this part of Asia—in which Germany was completely disinterested—could not also be realized."[1] They also indicated that they would support revision of the Montreux convention (governing access through the Dardanelles and the Bosporus) to make it more favorable to the Soviet Union. A secret protocol was drafted (but never signed) under which the USSR was to obtain recognition of its recent territorial acquisitions, a promise of peace with Japan, and a sphere of influence in the area "south of the national territory of the Soviet Union in the direction of the Indian Ocean." However, Molotov kept pressing for settlement of tensions arising from German troops in Finland, the German role in Romania and Bulgaria, and the disagreement on the straits. It is interesting to note that Molotov's demands were set forth in non-Marxist-Leninist, openly power-political terms and coincided with traditional czarist imperial objectives.

The limits of compatibility had been exceeded. On December 18, 1940, Hitler issued the order to prepare for the invasion of the USSR (Operation Barbarossa), with preparations to be completed by May 15, 1941. For the next six months Berlin fell ominously quiet.

For all his shrewdness, Stalin displayed a certain political obtuseness where Germany's military priorities were concerned. For example, on April 4, 1941, Molotov informed the German government of Moscow's intention to conclude a nonaggression pact with Yugoslavia the next day, even though German troops had outflanked Yugoslavia—occupying Romania in February and Bulgaria in March—and were preparing at that very moment to attack in order to extricate Mussolini, whose invasion of Greece had turned into a disaster for the Italian army. Instead of evincing imperial interest in areas that Germany had clearly staked out for itself, Stalin would have done better to digest what he had and bide his time.

In the Far East, Stalin secured his rear against attack by signing a five-year treaty of neutrality with Japan on April 13, 1941. He obtained Japan's recognition of the USSR's preeminence in the Mongolian People's Republic, its pledge to settle all outstanding Japanese claims for concessions in the northern part of Sakhalin Island, and an end to border clashes. The treaty was also intended to encourage Japan to strike south toward Southeast Asia rather than against the Soviet Union.

Thus, from September 1939 to June 1941, Stalin took advantage of a world at war to expand at the expense of weak neighbors. In the next four years, the Soviet Union was to pay a crushing price for his greed. But despite the enormous suffering of the Soviet people in that 1941-to-1945 period, Stalin's imperialism in 1939–1941 and 1945–1946 is no more to be condoned than is the crime of the man who murders his parents and then asks the court to excuse him because he is an orphan. In 1939 and 1940, Stalin deported and killed thousands of people from eastern Poland and the Baltic states for political and ideological reasons. This bloodletting was a prologue to what he was to do in Eastern Europe after 1945, and it contributed to the fear in the West and created the environment in which the Cold War was to develop. But this was still in the future.

On May 6, 1941, Stalin tightened his grip on party and government and assumed the post of chairman of the Council of People's Commissars (equivalent to premier). This, his first formal *government* position since his rise to undisputed leadership in the USSR, revealed the Kremlin's growing uneasiness over German intentions. Outwardly, German-Soviet relations remained unchanged as the Soviet Union tried in every way to mollify Hitler. Time, however, had run out on the unholy alliance.

The Wartime Alliance

Stalin's sense of accomplishment and security was short-lived. On June 22, 1941, the Nazi-Soviet honeymoon ended as German troops swept into the Soviet Union on an eighteen-hundred-mile front. So confident had Stalin been of Hitler's friendship that he refused to believe his own intelligence reports and Western warnings of an impending attack; he shied away from provocation, convinced that a German ultimatum would precede any attack. Not until eight hours after the Germans had crossed the frontier did Stalin accept the reality of the onslaught.

Twice within a generation Soviet leaders were engaged in a struggle for survival. This time, however, they were to have allies. A common cause—the destruction of nazism—submerged ideological antipathies and political antagonisms. Winston Churchill, long an avowed opponent of communism, offered the Soviets friendship and alliance. On July 12, the British and Soviet governments signed a protocol in which both agreed neither "to negotiate nor conclude an armistice or treaty of peace except by mutual agreement" and "to render each other assistance and support of all kinds in the present war against Hitlerite Germany." Thus began the forging of the Grand Alliance against Hitler.

On July 3, Stalin overcame his shock at what had happened and spoke to the Soviet people. With rare candor, no doubt dictated by the extreme gravity of the situation, he admitted that the country was in mortal peril, and that there was no time for comforting words. Sensing a need to justify his pro-Nazi policy orientation of 1939–1941, he said that it had given the Soviet Union time to strengthen its defenses. He made no mention of the territorial acquisitions of that period, emphasizing instead the initial German advantage from the treacherous attack and appealing to the people to unite to defeat the invader as their ancestors before them had triumphed over Napoleon and Kaiser Wilhelm II, both of whom had enjoyed a reputation for invincibility.

[Note: Stalin did not tell the Soviet people that he had erred in ignoring repeated warnings of the impending German invasion from his own intelligence community and from Winston Churchill, nor did he assume responsibility for the country's unpreparedness. According to Khrushchev's revelations about Stalin's shortcomings at the Twentieth Congress of the CPSU in February 1956, it was Stalin's refusal to heed well-founded and persistent reports of an imminent German attack that cost the Soviets so much and facilitated the rapid and extensive initial

Nazi advances. Khrushchev noted:

> Despite these particularly grave warnings, the necessary steps were not taken to prepare the country properly for defense and to prevent it from being caught unawares.
>
> Did we have time and the capabilities for such preparations? Yes, we had the time and capabilities. . . .
>
> Had our industry been mobilized properly and in time to supply the Army with the necessary material, our wartime losses would have been decidedly smaller. Such mobilization had not been, however, started in time. . . .
>
> When the fascist armies had actually invaded Soviet territory and military operations began, Moscow issued the order that the German fire was not to be returned. Why? It was because Stalin, despite evident facts, thought that the war had not yet started, that this was only a provocative action on the part of several undisciplined sections of the German Army, and that our reaction might serve as a reason for the Germans to begin the war. . . .
>
> As you see, everything was ignored; warnings of certain Army commanders, declarations of deserters from the enemy army, and even the open hostility of the enemy. Is this an example of the alertness of the Chief of the Party and of the State at this particularly significant historical moment?[2]]

As the Nazis penetrated deeper into Russia, even to the outskirts of Leningrad and Moscow, the Soviets relied on their traditional scourges for any would-be conqueror—the vastness of their country and the severity of its winters. They also adopted a "scorched-earth" policy, leaving nothing of use to the invader. The Germans were at first greeted as liberators in many non-Russian areas of the Soviet Union, such as the Ukraine—an illuminating comment on a generation of Communist rule. But the Nazis, themselves captives of their racist ideology, came as self-proclaimed conquerors intent upon colonizing the country and brutally exploiting its people and resources. They thus wasted, politically and psychologically, the strong vein of anti-Communist sentiment and by this blunder contributed greatly to their eventual defeat.

While the Nazis continued to advance into the Soviet Union, anticipating the victory that would make them masters of the Eurasian land mass, the newly formed Allied coalition sought to establish a firm basis for military cooperation. Churchill had promised to render all possible aid, but obviously only the United States could meet the enormous needs of the Soviet Union. In America, as in Great Britain, all hostility toward the Soviet Union was overshadowed by the determination to work together in the common interest. President Franklin D. Roosevelt moved to extend lend-lease aid. This aspect of cooperation with the Soviets proved successful, though not without frequent difficulties. Harry Hopkins, President Roosevelt's trusted adviser and troubleshooter, flew to Moscow in July 1941 to assess the Soviet capacity and will to resist Hitler. His favorable report convinced Roosevelt, and shipments to the USSR began almost immediately under an interim lend-lease agreement. In 1942, though eager to take the offensive against the Japanese after their attack on Pearl Harbor on December 7, 1941, the United States undertook to deliver more than $1 billion's worth of war material and supplies to the Soviet Union. Subsequently, other lend-lease agreements were concluded. (The USSR's contact with its allies was effected via Murmansk, Iran, and Vladivostok, particularly the first two.) America eventually supplied the USSR with approximately $11 billion in vitally needed goods of every description, from tanks and trucks to shoes and food. So grave was the danger that Stalin, according to a memoir published in 1978 by former Politburo member Anastas Mikoyan, at one time requested the presence of Western troops on Soviet soil.

British-Soviet cooperation first developed in Iran, where events impelled the two nations to act to forestall an imminent pro-Nazi coup in Tehran. They jointly occupied the country. In its note of August 25, 1941, the Soviet government justified the Allied action on the basis of the pertinent provision of its 1921 treaty with Iran, which held that

> if a third party should attempt to carry out a policy of usurpation by means of armed intervention in Persia, or if such power should desire to use Persian territory as a base for operations against the Russian Socialist Federal Soviet Republic, or those of its allies, and if the Persian government should not be able to put a stop to such a menace after having been once called upon to do so by the Russian Socialist Federal Soviet Republic, the Russian Socialist Federal Soviet Republic shall have the right to advance its troops into the Persian interior for the purpose of carrying out the military operations necessary for its defense. The Soviet Government undertakes, however, to withdraw its troops from Persian territory as soon as the danger has been removed.[3]

By mid-September 1941, the shah had capitulated and abdicated in favor of his son (who ruled until January 1979, when a revolution forced him to leave the country). The joint Allied occupation was followed by a treaty of alliance with Iran, signed on January 29, 1942, and Iran soon became a main Allied artery of supplies for the Soviet war effort. In addition to outlining Allied prerogatives, including the right to "maintain in Iranian territory land, sea, and air forces in such numbers as they consider necessary," the treaty assured Iran that the Allies would withdraw their forces "from Iranian territory not later than six months after all hostilities between the allied powers and Germany and her associates have been suspended by the conclusion of an armistice or armistices, or on the conclusion of peace between them, whichever date is the earlier." Soviet failure to abide by the terms of this provision precipitated one of the early crises of the postwar period—one involving Iran, the great powers, and the United Nations.

Meanwhile, the German advance overran the Soviet economic and industrial heartland. It failed, however, to attain its principal strategic objective: the destruction of the Red Army. Moscow and Leningrad held firm, and by the beginning of December it was apparent that Hitler would not winter in the Kremlin. As in 1812, winter providently came early. Furthermore, the Japanese surprise attack on Pearl Harbor meant that the Soviets no longer had to fear a two-front war. Nonetheless, the danger to the Allied cause was never greater than during the bleak winter of 1941–1942—a winter of successive defeats and disasters—and the summer of 1942. But when the Nazis and the Japanese had failed to attain victory by late 1942, their ultimate defeat was assured. Time and resources favored the Allies.

In November 1942, the British and Americans landed in North Africa while the Soviets engaged the Germans in the epic struggle for Stalingrad. The battle to the death for this vital industrial center on the lower Volga was a symbol of Soviet determination to retreat no further. The grim struggle for the city continued for weeks, fought street by street, house by house. On February 2, 1943, the Nazi forces surrendered. Stalingrad was saved. The defeat was one from which the Nazis never recovered, and the Allied cause received an incalculable boost of morale.

On all fronts, 1943 marked the turning of the tide. Now political differences within the strange alliance between the Soviet Union and the Western democracies assumed added dimensions. All had shared the resolve to defeat the Axis powers, subordinating other war aims to this overriding objective. However, as *military* victory approached, the *political* dilemmas and disagreements over the postwar settlement sharpened. The post-1945 Cold War was rooted in the incompatible objectives of the wartime Allies. Each sought security against a possible German revival, but this meant different and conflicting things to each. Subsequent Soviet maneuvering for power, position, and economic advantage and insistence on ideological conformity from the elites under its military control increased Washington's suspicion and rendered the task of shaping a congenial postwar settlement impossible. Thoughout the war, even during the darkest days of the Nazi advance, Stalin was more concerned with political issues than was Roosevelt or Churchill. Certainly he had a clearer idea of what he wanted as a victor, though for the time being military necessities superseded political differences.

From the first forging of the coalition, the Soviet Union pressed for the launching of a second front in Europe that would draw forty to sixty German divisions away from the east. Stalin broached the issue in his first direct communication to Churchill on July 18, 1941, and the oft-repeated demand was a constant source of discord. Stalin's xenophobia and memory of two trying decades of Soviet-Western relations were reflected in his complaints of Allied unwillingness to make military efforts comparable to those being made by the Red Army. More than any other single issue, this signified the uneasiness that existed within the alliance. The British tried to overcome such attitudes by signing a twenty-year treaty of alliance with the USSR on May 26, 1942. A vague promise by Churchill to expect a second front in France in 1942 was seized on by Molotov, who stated it as a promised certainty rather than an eventual intention, in his speech of June 18, 1942, which called upon the Supreme Soviet to ratify the Soviet-British treaty. (Churchill had compelling reason to promise all possible assistance to the Soviet Union, fearing that Stalin might make a separate peace with Hitler.)

Of the many political problems besetting Soviet-Western wartime relations, none assumed more dramatic proportions or proved more elusive of accord than that of the future of Poland. Since the Nazi-Soviet partition of 1939, there had been no diplomatic relations between the Soviet Union and Poland. As far as the Soviet government was concerned, Poland no longer existed. With the advent of the Nazi attack, however, Stalin adopted a conciliatory position with respect to the Polish question—a gesture designed to strengthen the newly formed bonds of friendship with the West. On July 30, 1941, an agreement was reached in London between the Soviet and Polish governments that was supposed to serve as a basis for future amicable relations. In a fundamental reversal of policy, the Soviets conceded that the territorial changes of 1939 were no longer valid. Diplomatic relations between Poland and the USSR were reestablished, and plans were made for training and equipping a Polish army on Soviet soil from among the thousands of Poles imprisoned after the 1939 partition.

Several days later, a portentous article appeared in *Pravda.* Though applauding the Soviet-Polish pact, it justified Soviet action in the 1939 partition on the grounds that Moscow was "duty-bound to give a helping hand to the Ukrainians and Byelorussians who made up most of the population in the Eastern regions of Poland."[4] *Pravda* also asserted that although the time was not suitable for discussion of final frontier lines, there was nothing "immutable" in the Polish-Soviet frontier as established by the 1921 Treaty of Riga: "The question of future Soviet-Polish borders is a matter for the future." Thus did the Soviets dilute the sense of their signed word even as the ink dried on the agreement. Similar occurrences were to mar future Allied unity.

During British Foreign Minister Anthony Eden's visit to Moscow in December 1941, Stalin insisted on recognition for the Soviet frontiers as they existed in June 1941, which would sanction all Soviet territorial acquisitions since September 1939. Though evaded at the time, this frequently repeated demand became, with the change in Allied fortunes, another source of discord. The Allies opposed Soviet claims to eastern Poland, as well as any prospective incorporation of the Baltic states into the Soviet Union.

Tension between the Polish government-in-exile and the Soviet government reached the breaking point over the Katyn Forest controversy. After the partition of Poland, the Soviets had interned, among others, some 15,000 Polish officers and men, the elite of the defeated Polish army. By the spring of 1940 the whereabouts of these men was a mystery. With the resumption of Polish-Soviet diplomatic relations in July 1941, the Polish government-in-exile repeatedly requested information concerning their fate. Soviet officialdom maintained an ominous silence. On April 13, 1943, the Nazis reported the "discovery" of the mass grave of the Polish officers in the Katyn Forest and blamed the Soviet Union for the atrocity. The Polish government-in-exile in London proposed an impartial investigation of this allegation. Stalin's reply was quick and harsh: he severed diplomatic relations with the Polish government, holding that Polish belief in the Nazi accusations indicated a lack of faith in the integrity of the Soviet government.

Though the ostensible cause of the breach was the Polish request for an investigation of the German charges, in the background was the continued insistence of the Poles upon a restoration of their 1939 frontier with the Soviet Union. The Poles refused to settle for territorial compensation at the expense of Germany. The Katyn incident was most convenient for Stalin. Eager to ensure a pro-Soviet (Communist) regime in postwar Poland, he announced the establishment of an organization known as the Union of Polish Patriots a few days later. This group subsequently served as the basis for the Soviet puppet Lublin government.

As a postscript to the Katyn Forest controversy, it may be noted that upon reconquering the area, the Soviets conducted their own investigation and "conclusively" placed the blame on the Nazis. The issue was again raised at the Nuremberg war-crimes trials, but the Soviet representatives chose neither to refute the German accusation of 1943 nor to take advantage of the opportunity to clear themselves in an open forum. Subsequent evidence proved that the Soviets had been responsible for the massacre.[5]

The Soviet-Polish rupture seriously tried Allied unity. The Allies—ever fearful of jeopardizing the alliance and pushing Stalin to conclude a sudden and separate agreement with Hitler, as in 1939; beset by continual Soviet demands for a second front; and increasingly indignant at Soviet disparagement of their own efforts on the battlefield—did not wish to make too much of the Polish issue. The tension eased noticeably when Moscow announced the dissolution of the Comintern on May 22, 1943. Replying to a question from a British correspondent, Stalin expressed the hope that this action would end all fears that the Soviet Union "intends to intervene in the life of other nations and to 'Bolshevize' them" and would demonstrate the USSR's interest in promoting the unity of all groups fighting Hitler. A psychologically dramatic gesture aimed at allaying Western suspicions and obscuring the Polish question, the announced dissolution of the Comintern purportedly meant that the Kremlin was disbanding its global apparatus for influencing and subverting foreign governments and promoting Soviet interests. We now know that Stalin did not have the slightest intention of shedding this multifaceted weapon of unconventional diplomacy. The Comintern was never dissolved; it merely relocated its headquarters in an undisclosed part of Moscow and functioned in secret.

The growing complex of political problems convinced the heads of state that a meeting was essential. Accordingly, at a preliminary conference of foreign ministers—Cordell Hull, Anthony Eden, V. M. Molotov—in Moscow from October 15 to 30, 1943, an agenda was prepared; and on November 28, 1943, Stalin, Churchill, and Roosevelt met at Tehran. A broad range of topics was discussed, but no final decisions were made, though Roosevelt did imply to Stalin that the United States would not challenge the Soviet position in Poland and the Baltic states.

Meanwhle, the military picture progressively brightened. Soviet offensives drained Nazi strength and drove the Germans from Soviet soil. By January 1944, the Red Army had crossed the former Polish frontier. On January 10, the Soviet news agency TASS contradicted Polish claims to the 1939 boundary and accused the Polish government-in-exile of deliberately aggravating the frontier question. No longer was Stalin prepared to accept only minor changes in the Soviet-Polish boundary as he had implied in 1941; now he demanded major territorial adjustment. The TASS statement declared that "the injustice committed by the [Soviet-Polish] Riga Treaty of 1921, which was imposed upon the Soviet Union," was rectified in 1939 (after the Nazi-Soviet partition of Poland) when "the territories of the Western Ukraine in which Ukrainians form the overwhelming majority of the population were incorporated with the Soviet Ukraine, and the territories of Western Byelorussia in which Byelorussians form an overwhelming majority of the population were incorporated with Soviet Byelorussia . . . the rebirth of Poland as a strong and independent state . . . must be . . . through the restoration to Poland of lands which belonged to Poland from time immemorial and were wrested by the Germans from her."[6]

The irreconcilability of Stalin and the Polish leaders, who rejected Churchill's suggestion that they accept territorial compensation at the expense of Germany, and the unwillingness of Western powers to jeopardize postwar cooperation with the Soviets prevented an acceptable settlement. At the urging of Churchill and Roosevelt, Polish Prime Minister Mikolajczyk journeyed to Moscow in a desperate effort to reach an agreement. He arrived on July 30, 1944, the eve of the tragic attempt by the Polish underground army to expel the Germans and liberate Warsaw before the entrance of the Red Army (then on the outskirts of the city) and thereby to gain control of the capital and force Soviet recognition of the Polish government in London, beneath whose banner the underground fought.[7] But four days before Mikolajczyk's arrival, the Soviet government had signed an agreement with its puppet creation, the Committee of National Liberation, which became the core of the postwar Communist Polish regime. Moscow declared that it had no desire to alter existing institutions and no territorial ambitions—by which it meant beyond the 1941 lines. Molotov had made a similar statement on April 2, 1944, as the Red Army approached the Soviet-Romanian frontier, and then, too, he had meant specifically the Soviet-Romanian frontier as it existed in 1941, thus making it clear that the 1940 Soviet annexation of Bessarabia was not open for negotiation.

A particularly embarrassing source of dissension among the Allies in the early days of the war was Finland. Finland had long had Western sympathy, and its joining the Nazi attack on the USSR placed American policymakers in a quandary. The Finns attempted to rationalize their behavior on the grounds that they only wanted to regain their lost land, but once America entered the war, it had to treat Finland as a belligerent. Efforts to induce Finland to disengage from Germany failed, and by the summer of 1944, Finland stood alone with no prospects of help from Germany. On September 19, 1944, it signed an armistice with the Soviet Union and was out of the war. (The terms of the peace treaty signed in 1947 were harsh, but they did ensure that Finland's independence would be preserved. They provided that Finland would withdraw to the Soviet-Finnish frontier line of March 12, 1940; this would continue as the boundary, except that in the far north Finland ceded the port of Petsamo to the Soviets and granted them a naval base at Porkkala-Udd, while in return the USSR agreed to relinquish its previously held lease on the peninsula of Hangoe; Finland would pay a $300 million indemnity in kind in six years; and Soviet forces would not occupy Finland.)

The year 1944 was one of Allied victories. On June 6, Anglo-American-Canadian forces landed in France and the long-awaited second front was a reality. By the end of the year, France had been liberated and the final preparations for the invasion of Germany itself were under way. On the eastern front, Soviet armies crossed the border into Germany. With the approach of victory, the unresolved political problems could no longer be evaded. Agreements had to be reached on the future of Poland and of all Eastern Europe, the division of Germany, the role of the Soviet Union in the war against Japan, the coordination of the final assault on Germany, and the preparations for the establishment of the United Nations.

Stalin thought in terms of spheres of influence. Security through expansion was a principle that had motivated the Kremlin for centuries; expansion entailed control, and control meant regimes that would unquestioningly toe Moscow's line. However rational and understandable Stalin's search for security was—after all, the Soviet Union had been devastated and lost more than twenty million people—what he did in the name of security in time triggered Western reactions that decreased his security and that of the West as well.

Stalin knew what he wanted and was open to a deal. In Moscow on October 9, 1944, Stalin and Churchill reached a secret understanding allocating spheres of influence. Under their so-called percentages agreement, Soviet influence in Bulgaria and Romania would be 90 percent as against 10 percent for Britain; in Hungary, 80/20; in Greece, 10/90; and Yugoslavia was to be divided on a 50/50 basis. This was Churchill's attempt to obtain the best possible deal for the West in an Eastern Europe that was already falling mainly to Soviet forces: Sofia, Bucharest, and Belgrade were then in Soviet hands. Because of the agreement, Stalin said nothing when the British suppressed an attempted takeover in Athens by the Greek Communists in December 1944. (But in a letter to Stalin on April 28, 1945, Churchill was to express dissatisfaction: "I must say that the way things have worked out in Yugoslavia certainly does not give me the feeling of a 50/50 interest as between our countries. Marshal Tito has become a complete dictator. He has proclaimed that his prime loyalties are to the Soviet Union."[8]) However, the United States was unwilling, for moral and domestic political reasons, to countenance politically what it was not prepared to resist militarily, namely, a cynical division of Europe into spheres of influence. This disagreement between Churchill and Roosevelt confused Stalin, who was eager for such an arrangement, and it was to be a source of future American-Soviet discord.

To reach agreement on plans for the final defeat of Germany and Japan and to establish a framework for a postwar settlement, the Big Three met in the Crimean resort of Yalta. The conference was held in the former czarist palace of Livadia from February 4 to 10, 1945.

Much has been written about the Yalta conference. Some insist that

Eastern Europe and China were here "sold out" to the Soviets; others argue that the agreements reached were the best possible given the military situation and political alternatives at the time. Any appraisal must consider that differences in the relative weights accorded the same "facts" will result in strikingly different final judgments. On the eve of the conference, most Western leaders firmly believed and hoped that it would be possible to extend the unity forged in wartime to the postwar period. Suspicion of Soviet intentions did exist among some professional diplomats, but popular sentiment in the West favored continued cooperation with the Soviet Union. Admiration for the courage displayed by the Soviet people and sympathy for their suffering and sacrifice were widespread.

Briefly, the military and political picture was this: Western troops were at the Rhine; Soviet forces were prepared to cross the Oder and launch the final attack on Berlin, some forty miles away. The Red Army already controlled most of Eastern Europe; Tito's pro-Moscow Communists dominated Yugoslavia. In the Far East, despite major victories over the Japanese at Iwo Jima and Okinawa, American military leaders expected a difficult fight before Japan's final surrender and urged that the USSR be brought into the final assault. In November 1944, the Joint Chiefs of Staff had weighed the pros and cons of Soviet participation and concluded that:

> (a) We desire Russian entry at the earliest possible date consistent with her ability to engage in offensive operations and are prepared to offer the maximum support possible without prejudice to our main effort against Japan.
> (b) We consider that the mission of Russian Far Eastern Forces should be to conduct an all-out offensive against Manchuria to force the commitment of Japanese forces and resources in North China and Manchuria that might otherwise be employed in the defense of Japan, to conduct intensive air operations against Japan proper, and to interdict lines of communication between Japan and the mainland of Asia.[9]

The discussions between Western and Soviet military staffs went smoothly in their planning for the final drive on Germany. However, the political issues affecting the fate of postwar Europe did not fare so well. The most important political discussions at Yalta focused on the Polish and German questions, the conditions under which the Soviet Union would later enter the war against Japan, and the voting procedures to be used in the United Nations Security Council. The Polish question figured in seven out of the eight plenary meetings. Attention centered on four key aspects of this, perhaps the most vexing of all pending questions: (1) a formula for establishing a single provisional government for Poland; (2) how and when to hold free elections; (3) possible solutions to the future of Poland's frontiers, both in the east and the west; and (4) steps designed to safeguard the security of the Soviet rear. The final communiqué issued on February 12, 1945, took note of these and other problems and sketched solutions that, if applied with fidelity and good faith, might have served the interests of all. But it was evident even before the war was won that Stalin intended to interpret the Yalta accords in a manner most apt to maximize Soviet security and power. A prime catalyst in the disintegration of the wartime alliance, the Polish question represented in a larger sense a barometer recording the perilous points of two incompatible conceptions of security.

Agreement on Germany's immediate future came more readily. All parties agreed that Germany must surrender unconditionally. Upon the termination of hostilities, an Allied Control Council was to serve as the top coordinating and policy organ of the occupying powers; three zones of occupation were established, a fourth later being allocated to France from the American and British zones; the Soviets agreed that the Western powers were to have free and unhampered access to Berlin, which was situated deep inside the Soviet zone of occupation; and the basic principles guiding reparations arrangements were reached. Accord was also achieved on the proposed organization of the United Nations and on the broad approaches determining future political actions in Eastern Europe and the Balkans. The stage was well set at Yalta to finish off Germany and manage its surrender.

The Far East played no part in the published formal deliberations at Yalta; it was the subject of a secret protocol. No mention of it, therefore, appeared in the public statement or the grandiloquent Declaration on Liberated Europe issued at the end of the conference. Throughout the war the Soviet Union had maintained formal relations with Japan in accordance with the 1941 neutrality pact. However, despite its official posture of neutrality, it associated itself with the Chinese government and signed the Four-Power Declaration of November 1, 1943, under which the United States, Great Britain, China, and the Soviet Union pledged themselves to cooperate against all their common enemies. More significant, as early as August 1942, Stalin privately assured U.S. Ambassador Averell Harriman of Soviet help in the war against Japan at the appropriate time, and he had specifically repeated this assurance in November 1943 and in September and October 1944. There had been some informal discussion at the Tehran conference of Soviet territorial objectives in the Far East, with Stalin expressing interest in a warm-water port and the return of southern Sakhalin and the Kuril Islands, but nothing definite was settled at the time. In October 1944, at the Moscow conference, Stalin reaffirmed to Churchill his willingness to enter the war against Japan three months after the defeat of Germany, subject to certain conditions, which were presented to the American government in December and served as the basis for the secret agreement on the Far East concluded at Yalta.

The agreement provided for (1) the preservation of the status quo in the Mongolian People's Republic; (2) the restoration of "former rights of Russia violated by the treacherous attack of Japan in 1904," namely, the return of southern Sakhalin, the internationalization of the commercial port of Dairen—"the permanent interests of the Soviet Union in the port being safeguarded and the lease of Port Arthur as a naval base of the USSR restored" (these were territories of China that were being disposed of)—and the restoration of former Russian economic privileges in Manchuria; and (3) the annexation of the Kuril Islands, which Russia had granted to Japan by the Treaty of St. Petersburg (May 7, 1875) in return for renunciation of Japanese claims to Sakhalin Island. These stipulations, made without Chiang Kai-shek's approval, were later accepted by China and incorporated into the Sino-Soviet Treaty of Friendship and Alliance, signed on August 14, 1945, which contained a Soviet promise "to render to China moral support and aid in military supplies and other material resources, such support and aid to be entirely given to the Nationalist government as the central government of China."

Was the price paid for Soviet participation excessive, considering the dividends expected? Would the United States government have accepted Stalin's conditions had it realized the imminence of Japan's surrender? Could it have prevented Stalin from seizing these territories on his own? Indeed, in view of traditional Russian Far Eastern objectives, would Stalin not have entered the war even without the Yalta concessions? Ironically, it was the American military—including Generals George C. Marshall and Douglas MacArthur and Admirals Ernest King and Chester Nimitz—with their estimates of another eighteen months of war after the defeat of Germany and anticipated heavy casualties in any invasion of the Japanese home islands, who convinced Roosevelt to grant Soviet demands. Three months later, the strategic position of the United States in the Pacific was so vastly improved that the Joint Chiefs of Staff felt less need for Soviet participation, but the die had been cast. The concessions gave Moscow a commanding position on the Asian mainland, far greater than that it had held in 1904, on the eve of the Russo-Japanese war.

The intricate story of all the controversies, discussions, and compromises that marked the Yalta deliberations, and their implications for the postwar period, will long be debated. We who examine the record in retrospect would do well to ponder the afterthoughts on Yalta so eloquently expressed by Sir Winston Churchill:

> It is not permitted to those charged with dealing with events in times of war or crisis to confine themselves purely to the statement of broad

general principles on which good people agree. They have to take definite decisions from day to day. They have to adopt postures which must be solidly maintained, otherwise how can any combinations for action be maintained? It is easy, after the Germans are beaten, to condemn those who did their best to hearten the Russian military effort and to keep in harmonious contact with our great Ally, who had suffered so frightfully. What would have happened if we had quarreled with Russia while the Germans still had three or four hundred divisions on the fighting front? Our hopeful assumptions were soon to be falsified. Still, they were the only ones possible at the time.[10]

On May 8, 1945, Germany surrendered unconditionally. Japan collapsed quickly thereafter. The dropping of the atomic bomb on Hiroshima on August 6 and the entry of the USSR into the war two days later—as Stalin had promised, though only by breaking his neutrality pact with Japan—sealed Japan's fate. It capitulated on August 14; the formal signing was aboard the battleship *Missouri* in Tokyo Bay on September 2.

The war was over. The challenge of the peace remained.

Cold War

The inability of the victors to maintain their wartime cooperation—and the consequent division of the world into two hostile camps—overshadowed all else in the immediate postwar period. Within months after the defeat of the Axis powers, this tragedy was revealed in the fundamental disagreements over Eastern Europe, Germany, Turkey, Iran, and the Far East. An investigation into the causes of the Cold War would take us far afield, and besides, an enormous literature on the subject does exist. However, to understand Soviet policy, we need to keep in mind a few relevant considerations.

First, there are these constants: the survival of Soviet-Western suspicion, only partially mitigated by wartime collaboration; the Soviet search for security, which involved not only an extension of military power westward into the center of Europe but also a radical transformation of the existing social, economic, and political order; the paranoia that led Stalin to regard the West as an enemy again; and, above all, territorial expansion, which went far beyond the demonstrable needs of national security and was manifest in czarist as well as in Stalinist foreign policy.

Second, we must consider the unpredictable chance actions and perceptions that shape historical events. Stalin viewed power in military terms, witness his depreciation of the Vatican's role in world affairs with the query, "How many divisions does the Pope have?" Considering remarks of American officials at Yalta, he may have expected a rapid

American military withdrawal from Europe and felt free to use the Red Army with impunity to bring about desired political outcomes in Eastern Europe. One may also muse on the Kremlin's view of the precipitate American decision, prompted by domestic politics, to end all lend-lease aid in May 1945, and on its view of Washington's silence regarding its request in January 1945 for a long-term reconstruction loan. The effect may have been to dispel any fleeting hopes Stalin had of basing Soviet recovery on continued American assistance. This in turn may have diminished his interest in a more conciliatory line toward the West and the problems it faced. Moreover, America's development of the atom bomb intensified Stalin's attention to military expenditures and modernization and to the urgency of overcoming the USSR's technological inferiority.

Finally, the inexorable drift in the 1945–1946 period toward the Cold War can also be discerned in the xenophobia, brutal domestic tyranny, and Great Russian chauvinism of Iosif V. Stalin and in his absolutist conception of security, which entailed total hegemony over all of Europe east of the Stettin-Trieste line. For example, the Soviet Union was of course entitled to firm guarantees against another attack through Poland. But Stalin treated Poland more as an accomplice of nazism than as its victim. He was no more considerate or generous toward Poland than he was toward the ex-enemy states of Bulgaria, Hungary, and Romania. Certainly, the expansion of Soviet power into the heart of Europe in 1945 exceeded the wildest dreams of the most imperialistic czar. For the first time in European history, one great power dominated the entire area between the USSR's western border and Western Europe, an area extending from the Arctic Ocean to the Black Sea (see map). This expansion of Soviet military power was seen by the Western nations as a permanent threat to their security. The roots of the Cold War lay in this fundamental conflict between incompatible conceptions of security and in the worst-case assessments that each side made of the other's moves and intentions.

Even before the war was over, Stalin showed signs of the implacable enmity that was to occasion a countervailing response of domestic anticommunism in the West. As soon as Stalin judged the defeat of Germany inevitable, he ordered Communist parties abroad to purge those who advocated continued "peaceful coexistence and collaboration in the framework of one and the same world." To convey the new line, he had published an article in April 1945 in a French Communist journal, *Cahiers du Communisme.* The Duclos Letter, so dubbed because the article was signed by the French Communist leader, Jacques Duclos, was the signal for party organizations to purge as unreliable those members who were not prepared to follow Moscow's twisting political line and wage political war against the policies of the Western governments. The "defunct" Comintern was soon to experience a public revival under a new imprimatur.

The Soviet Union in Europe

Why Stalin chose this moment to call attention to Moscow's control over foreign Communist parties, thereby inevitably raising Western suspicions of international communism again, is unknown. There are a number of possible explanations, none mutually exclusive. It could have been the counterpart of the move toward ending the relative relaxation of the wartime period and reimposing repressive measures at home. Perhaps it was deemed necessary in order to justify autocratic discipline over the Communist parties coming to power in Eastern Europe. Then again, Stalin may not have believed that the West would acquiesce to his conquests in Eastern Europe and wanted the extra margin of leverage over Western policies that indigenous Communist and Communist-front organizations provided. Or perhaps it was merely a reflection of his normal mode of political operation, one that he could comfortably revert to once the war was over.

Stalin's demands on Turkey were nothing but a blatant land grab, encouraged by the belief that Turkey could be pressured and that the West would not make an issue of the matter in the interest of agreement in Central Europe and the Far East. On March 19, 1945, the Soviet government informed Turkey, which had remained neutral throughout most of the war, that it would not renew the 1925 treaty of neutrality and nonaggression when it expired on November 7, 1945. As the price for a new treaty, Moscow insisted on the return of the northeastern districts of Kars and Ardahan, originally taken by Russia from the Ottoman Empire in 1877 but given up by the Bolsheviks in the 1918 Treaty of Brest-Litovsk, a loss they accepted in the Soviet-Turkish treaty of 1921; and on military bases in the straits and on the Aegean Sea. There was no Turkish provocation, no threat to the USSR, no insecurity to overcome. Stalin's territorial outreach heightened fears in Western circles that his aims in Central and Eastern Europe were not limited to the territory already under Soviet control. It also exemplified his persistence in pursuit of strategic advantage. Four months later, at the Big Three conference at Potsdam, he tried to persuade Churchill to agree to some foothold for Moscow at the expense of the Turks. At the final banquet, with the USSR's imminent entry into the war against Japan creating a heady mood of victory and camaraderie, Stalin went from table to table asking for autographs. When he came to Churchill, Winston obliged, then filled two glasses of brandy which they downed. After a pause, Stalin asked Churchill, "If you find it impossible to give us a fortified position in the Marmora, could we not have a base at Dedeagatch?" To this Churchill replied warily, "I will always support Russia in her claim to the freedom of the seas all year round."[11] It is intriguing that Stalin should have said, "Dedeagatch," which the Turks had lost for good in 1913, when Bulgaria seized Thrace, and which had subsequently been returned to its ancient Greek name of Alexandroupolis when most of Thrace was transferred to Greece. Perhaps Stalin, in maneuvering to get something at Potsdam, spotted it in perusing a pre-World War I map that also showed Kars and Ardahan as Russian territory, and got the idea that if nobody was about to give Russia Istanbul or a base right on the Bosporus or Dardenelles, a little neighboring seaport with a Turkish name might be a useful consolation prize.[12]

The postwar difficulties may conveniently be dated from the Potsdam conference of July 1945. Relations between the USSR and its Western allies had deteriorated noticeably since Yalta. Discord centered on the Polish issue, the heavy-handedness of Soviet rule in Bulgaria and Romania, the disposition of Trieste, the reparations question, and Allied administration of Germany. Stalin saw no reason to compromise. Behind his inscrutability and gruffness lay a disdain for discussions about principles and a confidence that whatever his artillery could reach was his to keep. In a conversation in the spring of 1945 with Milovan Djilas, an intimate of Tito's, Stalin described his attitude thus: "This war is not as in the past; whoever occupies a territory also imposes on it his own social system. Everyone imposes his own system as far as his army can reach. It cannot be otherwise."[13]

The West accepted the Oder-Neisse boundary between Poland and Germany, failed to insist on guaranteed land access to Berlin, and accepted Stalin's puppet creation in Poland. The conference reinforced the disenchantment that had followed Moscow's installation of coalition governments in which the Communists were assured control of the all-important ministries of interior and of the courts. In a moment of candor, Stalin admitted that a freely elected government in any of the East European countries "would be anti-Soviet, and that we cannot allow." While conflicting interpretations of what constituted "democratic" government aggravated relations, America's rapid demobilization encouraged Stalin to act without fear of effective countermeasures.

The foreign ministers of the big four powers met in the fall, primarily to draft treaties with Finland, Italy, and the Balkan countries. Old problems remained unsolved, and new ones appeared, such as Soviet demands for a trusteeship over one of the former Italian colonies and for the establishment of an allied control council in Japan comparable to the one operating in Germany, which would have given Moscow a veto over U.S. occupation policy.

Against the background of these protracted, stalemated negotiations, Stalin delivered a preelection speech on February 9, 1946, that signified repression at home and ideological and political conflict on the international level. He reaffirmed the fundamental postulates of Marxist-Leninist theory on the causes and nature of capitalist wars and blamed the West for World War II. He insisted that the defeat of Germany did not necessarily eliminate the danger of war and, lauding the superiority of the Soviet system, called for a "new mighty upsurge in the national economy" that would treble prewar production and guarantee the Soviet Union against another invasion.

The call for improving the standard of living could not disguise the implicit stress on developing the industrial strength on which military power was based. Stalin's gloomy outlook on relations with the capitalist world paralleled Moscow's toughness on the diplomatic front, and was interpreted in the West as an indication of Soviet hostility. The world was sliding toward bipolarity. One month later, on March 5, at Fulton, Missouri, Churchill called for a strengthening of Anglo-American ties in the face of growing Soviet expansion. Though no longer in power, Churchill was still a leader who commanded attention: "From Stettin in the Baltic to Trieste in the Adriatic an iron curtain has descended across the Continent. All these famous cities and the populations around them lie in the Soviet sphere and are subject, in one form or another, not only to Soviet influence but to a very high and increasing degree of control from Moscow." The Iranian crisis lent immediacy to his warning.

The Iranian Crisis

Iran was occupied by the USSR and Britain during the war in order to safeguard the flow of supplies to the Soviet Union. In early 1946 it could not obtain the promised evacuation of Soviet troops. During their occupation of northern Iran, Soviet authorities had denied the central government in Tehran access to the area and at the same time strengthened the local Communist (Tudeh) party. In September 1945, the Tudeh party sought increased autonomy for Azerbaijan, the Iranian province bordering on the Soviet Union. The central government refused Tudeh demands for fear of augmenting Communist influence elsewhere in Iran. In December 1945 the Communists announced the creation of a new government in Tabriz, capital of Iranian Azerbaijan, under Ja'far Pishevari, a veteran Communist and Comintern agent; they proclaimed a Kurdish People's Republic, with its capital in Mahabad, in western Azerbaijan; and they intensified their efforts to kindle an irredentist movement among the Kurdish tribes of northern Iraq and eastern Turkey, which further heightened Ankara's apprehensiveness. Meanwhile, Iranian troops seeking to reenter Azerbaijan were turned back by the Red Army.

Despite Stalin's assurance that the Soviet Union had no designs, territorial or otherwise, on Iran, Soviet troops continued to occupy the northern provinces. Iran appealed to the United Nations on January 19, 1946, charging the Soviet Union with interference in its internal affairs and with endangering the peace. American efforts to effect a withdrawal of all foreign troops by January 1, 1946, were rejected by the Soviet government, which maintained that under the Iranian-Soviet-British treaty of 1942, it was entitled to remain in Iran until March 2, 1946. During the often acrimonious negotiations in the UN Security Council, a cabinet crisis in Tehran led the shah to appoint Qavam Saltaneh, generally regarded by Western officials as pro-Tudeh, as premier. Qavam began direct talks with Soviet leaders and spent almost a month in Moscow attempting to negotiate a settlement. In the United Nations, Soviet tactics thwarted every effort at a solution—a portent of future Soviet behavior in the world organization. As the date for the departure of Soviet troops under the 1942 agreement came and went with no visible change in Soviet attitude, Western leaders grew profoundly disturbed, particularly in light of Stalin's February speech.

On April 4, the Soviet government agreed to evacuate Iran in return for Iranian concessions, including the formation of a joint-stock Soviet-Iranian oil company and a degree of autonomy for Azerbaijan. Westerners viewed this as a Soviet triumph and glumly awaited Iran's early disappearance behind the Iron Curtain. Though the final decision by the Soviet government to withdraw from Iran by May 9 is usually attributed primarily to President Harry S Truman's tough talk, pressure by the UN Security Council, and world public opinion, the credit, according to Richard N. Frye, should go mainly to the shrewdness of Premier Qavam.

> The Soviet evacuation of northern Iran was the result of a number of factors; probably the most important was the belief on the part of the Russians that Qavam had been won over to their side. He had suppressed the anti-Soviet elements and had agreed to a joint oil company, subject to ratification of parliament. The rebel government in Azerbaijan was growing in strength and there was every reason to suppose that it would maintain its position and even gain at the expense of the Teheran government. The pressure of world opinion and the debates in the United Nations, although they may have been responsible in influencing the Soviet government to evacuate Iran earlier than had been planned, were probably of much less significance than the factors mentioned above. When the Soviet government did announce that it had evacuated all its troops on May 9, 1946, it seemed as though Iran had fallen on the Soviet side of the curtain.[14]

Late that year, the Iranian parliament rejected the proposed economic treaty with the USSR. Qavam had outfoxed Moscow, and by the end of 1946, the danger of a Communist coup had passed. Azerbaijan was once again under the control of the central government. Shortly after, in an ironic twist, Qavam was dismissed and all but exiled because of palace intrigue.

The Iron Curtain Descends

Preparations for the conference to conclude peace treaties with the East European countries dragged on through the spring of 1946. Not until the end of July did representatives of twenty-one nations meet in Paris. Though no agreement was reached on Germany or Austria—both occupied by the four powers—the Soviet Union agreed to treaties with Italy, Finland, Hungary, and Romania in February 1947. The West had the treaties so coveted, but time quickly revealed how irrelevant they were. The Soviet government ignored the provisions guaranteeing democratic safeguards and entrenched its domination of Eastern Europe. Stalin pursued his principal political and strategic objectives in Eastern Europe with a singleness of purpose that became only too clear to the Western powers by early 1947. He sought to eliminate all Western influence from the area and concomitantly to establish Soviet hegemony.

The 1947 treaties legalized most of Stalin's territorial acquisitions in Eastern Europe: from Finland, the ice-free port of Petsamo and territory extending the Soviet frontier to Norway; seventy thousand square miles of eastern Poland, including the Vilno area which was ceded to Lithuania; the province of Ruthenia from Czechoslovakia; northern Bukovina and Bessarabia (and control of the Carpathian mountain passes into Central Europe and the Danubian plain) from Romania; and a common border with Hungary (see map, p. 71). The USSR advanced westward territorially by annexing land from each of the countries on its western border; indeed, its policy of expansion and annexation was designed specifically to give the Soviet Union a common border with every country in Eastern Europe, the easier to manage military and political control.[15] Moscow's annexation of Estonia, Latvia, and Lithuania (still not recognized by the United States) gave it control of the eastern shore of the Baltic Sea, and the incorporation of East Prussia from Germany was not recognized by the West until the Helsinki conference in 1975.

Of all the postwar problems, none contributed more to East-West hostility than that of the future of Germany. In a sense, the German problem is *the* European problem. Economic, political, strategic, and technological considerations all coalesce in the struggle over Germany; and the present unchallenged position of the Soviet Union in Eastern Europe cannot be permanently assured as long as Germany, with its reservoir of skilled manpower, scientific expertise, and industrial strength, remains a potential opponent.

The Soviets at first favored an exploitative policy to weaken Germany industrially. However, the Kremlin soon realized the folly of this course and shifted to a more conciliatory policy. This was first expressed by Molotov at the July 1946 Paris meeting of foreign ministers. Asserting that the spirit of revenge could not underlie negotiations with Germany, he acknowledged that it would be foolish to seek to destroy Germany as a state or to agrarianize her and deprive her of major industries. Molotov suggested instead that Germany be permitted to become "a democratic and peace-loving state . . . but [one] which would be deprived of the economic and military potentiality to rise again as an aggressive force." He proposed that the Ruhr, the key to German industrial power, be placed under inter-Allied control and that a single German government willing to fulfill all its obligations, particularly those concerning reparations to the USSR, be set up.

Secretary of State James F. Byrnes responded to this bid for German favor by making similar conciliatory comments in his Stuttgart speech of September 6, 1946. He also, significantly, threw American support behind Germany in the question of a return of the eastern territories. Before the Potsdam conference, the Soviet Union had unilaterally transferred all German territory east of the Neisse River to Poland, thus strengthening Poland's claim to the area that served to compensate it for the seventy thousand square miles of eastern Poland annexed by the USSR, and not unintentionally making Poland dependent on continued Soviet goodwill for preservation of its new territorial configuration. Byrnes's strategy forced the Soviets to side with the Poles against the Germans, thus deflating Soviet prestige in West Germany. Less than eighteen months after the defeat of Germany the victors had fallen out among themselves and were courting public opinion in the former foe.

The chill of Cold War, already perceptible in the middle of 1945, penetrated to the core of East-West relations by late 1946. The steel in Stalin's policy may be gleaned from a generally overlooked interview given to CBS correspondent Richard C. Hottelet in June 1946 by Maxim Litvinov, then a sidetracked, isolated, pessimistic deputy foreign minister, a holdover from the days when Moscow pushed collective security with the Western powers and he was its prime spokesman. When asked how he viewed prospects for East-West cooperation, Litvinov replied, "The outlook is bad. It seems as though the differences between East and West have gone too far to be reconciled. . . ." He gave two reasons: first, "there has been a return in Russia to the outmoded concept of security in terms of territory—the more you've got, the safer you are"; and second, "the root cause is the ideological conception prevailing [in Moscow] that conflict between the Communist and capitalist worlds is inevitable."[16]

By the beginning of 1947, Stalin's policy of imperial expansion had crested; he had what he wanted in the Baltic area, Eastern Europe, and the Far East. But his reach had exceeded his grasp in Iran and Turkey; his tyranny at home and exploitation of tensions abroad through foreign Communist parties had aroused a countervailing anti-Communist and anti-Soviet sentiment and policy; his obstructionism in the United Nations was interpreted as hostility to cooperation with non-Communist countries; and he faced the whirlwind of Western fears for the outcomes of the ongoing civil war in China and Greece (though in neither instance was Soviet assistance of any importance). The net result of all of this was a major transformation in the USSR's relations with the West.

Notes

1. Raymond James Sontag and James Stuart Beddie (eds.), *Nazi-Soviet Relations, 1939–1941: Documents from the Archives of the German Foreign Office* (Washington, D.C.: Department of State, 1948), 222.
2. Nikita S. Khrushchev, *Special Report to the Twentieth Congress of the Communist Party of the Soviet Union* (February 1956).
3. *USSR Information Bulletin,* No. 37 (August 26, 1941), 6–8, excerpts.
4. Pravda, August 4, 1941.
5. J. K. Zawodny, *Death in the Forest: The Story of the Katyn Forest Massacre* (Notre Dame, Ind.: University of Notre Dame Press, 1962).
6. *USSR Information Bulletin,* IV, No. 7 (1944), 1.
7. Samuel L. Sharp, *Poland: White Eagle on a Red Field* (Cambridge: Harvard University Press, 1953), 168–70.
8. *Sunday Times* (London), November 24, 1968.
9. U.S. Department of Defense, *The Entry of the Soviet Union Into the War Against Japan: Military Plans, 1941–1945* (Washington, D.C.: Government Printing Office, 1955).
10. Winston S. Churchill, *Triumph and Tragedy* (Boston: Houghton Mifflin, 1953), 402.
11. *Ibid.,* 669.
12. I am indebted to Professor Robert Osborn of Temple University for this insight.
13. Milovan Djilas, *Conversations with Stalin* (New York: Harcourt, Brace & World, 1962), 114.
14. Lewis V. Thomas and Richard N. Frye, *The United States and Turkey and Iran* (Cambridge: Harvard University Press, 1951), 239–40.
15. Huey Louis Kostanick, "The Significance of Geopolitical Changes in Eastern Europe," *Education,* Vol. 72 (February 1952), 381–87.
16. Quoted in Robert G. Kaiser, *Cold Winter, Cold War* (New York: Stein and Day, 1974), 12–13. For an overall evaluation of Litvinov's series of revealing discussions with Western journalists between May 1943 and February 1947,

see Vojtech Mastny, "The Cassandra in the Foreign Commissariat: Maxim Litvinov and the Cold War," *Foreign Affairs,* Vol. 54, No. 2 (January 1976), 366–76.

Selected Bibliography

ALPEROVITZ, GAR. *Atomic Diplomacy: Hiroshima and Potsdam.* Expanded and Updated Edition. New York: Penguin Books, 1985.

CHURCHILL, WINSTON S. *The Second World War.* 6 vols. Boston: Houghton Mifflin, 1948–1953.

CLARK, ALAN. *Barbarossa: The Russian-German Conflict, 1941–1945.* New York, Morrow, 1964.

DEANE, JOHN R. *The Strange Alliance: The Story of Our Efforts at Wartime Cooperation with Russia.* New York: Viking, 1947.

DJILAS MILOVAN. *Conversations with Stalin.* New York: Harcourt, Brace & World, 1962.

ELLIOT, MARK R. *Pawns of Yalta: Soviet Refugees and America's Role in Their Repatriation.* Urbana: University of Illinois Press, 1982.

ERICKSON, JOHN. *The Road to Stalingrad: Stalin's War with Germany.* New York: Harper & Row, 1975.

———. *The Road to Berlin.* Boulder, Col.: Westview Press, 1983.

EUBANK, KEITH. *Summit at Tehran.* New York: Morrow, 1985.

FEIS, HERBERT. *Churchill-Roosevelt-Stalin.* Princeton: Princeton University Press, 1957.

HERZ, MARTIN F. *Beginnings of the Cold War.* Bloomington: Indiana University Press, 1966.

IATRIDES, JOHN O. *Revolt in Athens: The Greek Communist "Second Round," 1944–1945. Princeton: Princeton University Press, 1972.*

INGRAM, KENNETH. *History of the Cold War.* New York: Philosophical Library, 1955.

KACEWICZ, GEORGE. *Great Britain, the Soviet Union and the Polish Government in Exile (1939–1945).* The Hague: Nijhoff, 1979.

KENNAN, GEORGE F. *Memoirs 1925–1950.* Boston: Atlantic-Little, Brown, 1967.

KIRK, GEORGE E. *Survey of International Affairs: The Middle East in the War.* New York: Oxford University Press, 1953.

KROSBY, H. PETER. *Finland, Germany, and the Soviet Union, 1940–1941: The Petsamo Dispute.* Madison: The University of Wisconsin Press, 1968.

LENSEN, GEORGE ALEXANDER. *The Strange Neutrality: Soviet-Japanese Relations*

During the Second World War, 1941-1945. Tallahassee, Fla.: Diplomatic Press, 1972.

LUKACS, JOHN. *1945: Year Zero.* New York: Doubleday, 1978.

MASTNY, VOJTECH. *Russia's Road to the Cold War.* New York: Columbia University Press, 1979.

MCCAGG, WILLIAM O., JR. *Stalin Embattled, 1943-1948.* Detroit: Wayne State University Press, 1978.

MCNEILL, WILLIAM H. *America, Britain, and Russia: Their Cooperation and Conflict, 1941-1946.* New York: Oxford University Press, 1954.

MOSELY, PHILIP E. *The Kremlin and World Politics.* New York: Vintage, 1960.

NAGAI, YONOSUKE, and AKIRA IRIYE (EDS.). *The Origins of the Cold War in Asia.* New York: Columbia University Press, 1977.

RIEBER, ALFRED J. *Stalin and the French Communist Party, 1941-1947.* New York: Columbia University Press, 1962.

ROZEK, EDWARD J. *Allied Wartime Diplomacy: A Pattern in Poland.* New York: Wiley, 1958.

SETON-WATSON, HUGH. *The East European Revolution.* New York: Praeger, 1956.

SHARP, SAMUEL. *Poland, White Eagle on a Red Field.* Cambridge: Harvard University Press, 1953.

STEPHAN, JOHN J. *The Kuril Islands: Russo-Japanese Frontiers in the Pacific.* New York: Oxford University Press, 1974.

STRIK-STRIKFELDT, WILFRED. *Against Stalin and Hitler, 1941-1945.* London: Macmillan, 1970.

THOMAS, HUGH. *Armed Truce: The Beginnings of The Cold War, 1945-46.* New York: Atheneum, 1987.

TOLSTOY, NIKOLAI. *Stalin's Secret War.* New York: Holt, Rinehart and Winston, 1981.

WHALEY, BARTON. *Codeword Barbarossa.* Cambridge: MIT Press, 1973.

YERGIN, DANIEL. *The Shattered Peace.* Boston: Houghton Mifflin, 1977.

4

Stalinization and Imperial Consolidation, 1947–1953

Stalin's policies gave rise to two developments—one American, the other Soviet—that institutionalized the Cold War and the division of East and West into mutually antagonistic blocs. The Truman Doctrine and the Zhdanov line were the formal expressions of the superpower impetus toward a bipolar world. The former led to an economic recovery program and military buildup and the latter to a closed ideological and political system, the consequences of which were to reinforce the trend toward bloc exclusiveness.

On March 12, 1947, President Truman announced the decision to extend economic and military assistance to Greece and Turkey, and "to support peoples who are resisting attempted subjugation by armed minorities or by outside pressure," i.e., international communism. The announcement was prompted by the inability of Great Britain to continue to bear the responsibility for defense of the eastern Mediterranean, and British power in the area was gradually replaced by that of the United States. Moscow branded the Truman Doctrine "a smokescreen for expansion." It described the policy as an example of America's postwar imperialism and circumvention of the UN, and dismissed the U.S. contention that the USSR threatened the Turkish straits or the provinces of Kars and Ardahan, insisting that "no one and nothing actually threatens Turkey's integrity. This 'assistance' is evidently aimed at putting [Turkey] also under U.S. control."

The Truman Doctrine was a watershed in U.S. postwar policy. Once committed to the proposition that no other European countries should be allowed to fall under Soviet control, the United States went beyond the Truman Doctrine with a more permanent and far-reaching program of economic assistance. On June 5, 1947, Secretary of State George C. Marshall, speaking at Harvard University, expressed America's willingness to help rebuild Europe and invited the European nations to draw up a list of their needs. Under the leadership of British Foreign Secretary Ernest Bevin and French Foreign Minister Georges Bidault, a conference of all European nations, including the Soviet Union, was convened in Paris on June 27. Discussions were at first secret. Then, on June 29, Moscow unexpectedly issued a statement denouncing the conference and the proposals. The thrust of the attack was to begin with largely economic, with Moscow alleging that the proposals entailed an integration of the various national economies that would require it to abandon its own plans for Eastern Europe's industrialization and incorporation into the Soviet five-year plans. It also intimated that the Marshall Plan, which provided economic assistance to promote Europe's recovery from World War II's destruction and dislocation, was intended to advance the economic, and hence political, expansion of American influence.

By July 2, Moscow had withdrawn from the conference and forced all the East European countries to follow suit. It is unlikely that the U.S. Congress would have appropriated any funds for the program had the USSR remained one of the possible recipients, and continued Soviet participation in the talks might well have sounded the death knell for the Marshall Plan and for European recovery, but Stalin was not prepared to run any risks where Soviet control of Eastern Europe was concerned.

The Soviet refusal to participate in the Marshall Plan program was a logical outcome of the crystallizing East-West estrangement and of Stalin's domestic priorities, which called for tightened controls, forced savings, cultural conformity, and isolation of the population from outside influences—in brief, a ruthless harnessing of the society for internal reconstruction and recompression. First, Stalin believed in an impending severe economic crisis in the United States, or at least he chose to commit the party to such a line. He had one month earlier denounced the prominent Soviet economist Eugene Varga, who wrote that a capitalist crisis was not imminent and that capitalism was entering a period of stabilization and growth.

Second, Stalin's interest in "Sovietizing" Eastern Europe made him doubly suspicious of any Western proposal that could interfere with this overriding strategic objective. To have permitted the East Europeans extensive economic access to the West would have politically strengthened the pro-Western elements still hanging on in the Moscow-managed coalition governments and complicated the process of full Sovietization. An authoritative Soviet study later wrote: "Washington devised the ambitious [Marshall] plan . . . as a means of . . . isolating from the USSR and returning to the capitalist fold all or at least some of the People's Democracies."[1]

Third, Stalin was not interested in all-European recovery unless there was immediate and significant advantage to the USSR. This was understandable economically, given the Soviet Union's need to tend its own wounds. It was also sound politically, since an unstable Western Europe decreased the likelihood of interference with Soviet policies in Eastern Europe. Indeed, instability might further strengthen Communist parties, particularly in Italy and France, where the Communists had emerged from the war with enhanced prestige and broad electoral support. Thus, impeding Western Europe's recovery would not only keep the West from challenging Soviet hegemony in Eastern Europe, but might even help the aggravation of internal turmoil in Western countries.

Fourth, Stalin mistrusted American motives. He assumed that the United States had imperial ambitions that mirrored his own and that the flag would follow the funds, with the U.S. influence and military control accompanying its aid. Moreover, in 1945, the USSR had approached the United States for a long-term credit and received no favorable response.

Finally, Soviet participation would have required Moscow to divulge statistical data revealing its economic weaknesses. A xenophobic and secretive Kremlin would hardly be receptive to such a requirement.

Whatever the compelling reasons, during the summer and fall of 1947, East-West relations sharply deteriorated as Soviet attacks on the Marshall Plan intensified. On September 18, 1947, Andrei Y. Vyshinsky, the Soviet delegate to the United Nations, set the general tenor for official policy in a speech before the General Assembly:

> As is now clear, the Marshall Plan constitutes in essence merely a variant of the Truman Doctrine adapted to the conditions of postwar Europe. In bringing forward this plan, the United States Government apparently counted on the cooperation of the Governments of the United Kingdom and France to confront the European countries in need of relief with the necessity of renouncing their inalienable right to dispose of their economic resources and to plan their national economy in their own way. The United States also counted on making all these countries directly dependent on the interests of American monopolies, which are striving to avert the approaching depression by an accelerated export of commodities and capital to Europe. . . .
>
> Moreover, this Plan is an attempt to split Europe into two camps and with the help of the United Kingdom and France, to complete the formation of a *bloc* of several European countries hostile to the interests of the democratic countries of Eastern Europe and most particularly to the interest of the Soviet Union.

Institutionalizing Sovietization

Stalin completed the breach by organizing his satellites into a formal grouping of states subservient to the Soviet Union. The Comintern was resurrected as the Cominform (Communist Information Bureau) at a special conference of Communist parties in Polish Silesia on September 22 to 23, 1947. Only nine parties—from Bulgaria, Czechoslovakia, France, Hungary, Italy, Poland, Romania, Yugoslavia, and the USSR—were invited because Stalin's primary aim was to consolidate Eastern Europe, not to promote international communism or the parliamentary prospects of Communist parties elsewhere in Europe.

By ending the policy that had encouraged West European Communist parties in the 1944-to-1947 period to enter into coalitions with bourgeois governments and by ordering them to oppose Marshall Plan programs, Stalin sought to intensify Western uneasiness over the revolutionary potential of their own Communist parties and thereby to divert the West's attention away from Soviet policy in Eastern Europe.[2] Besides, Stalin turned his regional need into an international advantage: Seeing that Communist movements in China, Vietnam, the Philippines, and Greece had already implicitly rejected Moscow's leadership by not waiting for the Red Army to "liberate" their countries, and by choosing the revolutionary rather than the evolutionary road to power, he used his about-face in Europe to reassert Soviet militancy and again place the USSR in the vanguard of world revolutionary activity.

To justify the establishment of the Cominform ideologically, the Kremlin formally revived the thesis of the capitalist menace and emphasized the enduring and irreconcilable antagonisms between the capitalist and Communist systems. Andrei A. Zhdanov's speech at the founding conference must be regarded as the most significant effort since the Comintern program of 1928 to formulate the position of international communism in the world and to integrate it into a unified whole. The importance of the speech lay not only in its ambitious scope, but in the powerful position of the man charged with its presentation. Zhdanov, who died the following year, was regarded as second only to Stalin.

Zhdanov began by announcing that the war had altered world power relationships:

> The fundamental changes caused by the war on the international scene and in the position of individual countries have entirely changed the political landscape of the world. A new alignment of political forces has arisen. The more the war recedes into the past, the more distinct become two major trends in postwar international policy, corresponding to the division of the political forces operating on the international arena into two major camps; the imperialist and antidemocratic camp, on the one hand, and the anti-imperialist and democratic camp on the other. The principal driving force of the imperialist camp is the USA. Allied with it are Great Britain and France. . . . The cardinal purpose of the imperialist camp is to strengthen imperialism, to hatch a new imperialist war, to combat socialism

and democracy, and to support reactionary and antidemocratic profascist regimes and movements everywhere.[3]

Clearly, he identified the United States as the principal antagonist and castigated the economic, ideological, and military bases of its foreign policy, claiming that its underlying motif was expansionism. Justifying Moscow's opposition to the Marshall Plan and its determination to control Eastern Europe, he at the same time dropped an olive twig along the way: "Soviet foreign policy proceeds from the fact of the coexistence for a long period of the two systems—capitalism and socialism. From this it follows that cooperation between the USSR and the countries with other systems is possible, provided that the principle of reciprocity is observed and that obligations once assumed are honored." But this hint that the Kremlin was open to a deal formalizing the division of Europe into spheres of influence was lost in the hostility that flowed from the rest of the speech and that characterized the behavior of the Soviet Union and its Communist agents in the months that followed. Zhdanov's call for all Communist parties to act in concerted opposition to the Marshall Plan was interpreted in the West as a declaration of permanent Cold War. The tactical consequences of this militant policy soon emerged in France and Italy, where in November 1947 general strikes accompanied by labor violence were instigated in an attempt to paralyze the nascent Marshall Plan program and in Southern Asia, where Communist parties split with bourgeois nationalist movements and attempted to subvert the newly independent governments in India, Burma, Indonesia, and the Philippines by direct revolutionary means.

In addition to mobilizing Communist parties against the Marshall Plan and Western policy in Europe, the Cominform had other, longer-term Soviet-bloc oriented purposes. Ideologically, it promulgated the line from Moscow and provided political guidance for foreign Communists. Organizationally, it facilitated the consolidation of Soviet power, ensuring Moscow's control over the various East European communist parties. Politically, as a focal point for international communism, it not only crystallized opposition to the West, but symbolized Communist unity and Soviet leadership of the international Communist movement. The establishment of the Cominform was a turning point for Stalin. Henceforth, accommodation and cooperation with the non-Communist world—the official line during the 1941-to-1947 period—was dropped, and the focus was on antagonism between blocs.

Soviet belligerency sharpened in the UN, in Germany, and in Austria, but it was in Czechoslovakia in February 1948 that Stalin showed his hegemonic absolutism and dropped the last fig leaf of democracy in Eastern Europe. The Communist takeover that ordained Czechoslovakia's disappearance behind the Iron Curtain shocked the West. After all, the Communists had been in control of most of the country's institutions since 1945; the first postwar elections in May 1946 had given them 38 percent of the vote (the largest percentage), and Czechoslovakia had pulled out of the Marshall Plan discussions on Stalin's orders. Moscow's preeminent and unchallenged influence was accepted as a fact of East European reality. Presumably, this should have satisfied Stalin's desire for a compliant imperial order in Eastern Europe that would assure the security of his western border. But Stalin would settle for nothing less than total domination. Perhaps more than any other single Soviet-inspired move, the fall of Prague dispelled remaining Western illusions concerning Soviet intentions, heightened fears of new Soviet thrusts, hastened Western rearmament, and froze the division of Europe. The disappearance of Czechoslovakia as a middle ground in which democratic socialist and Communist groups could coexist symbolized the end of possible cooperation between East and West.

Next, Stalin took steps to end the last vestiges of coalition government in Eastern Europe and to consolidate his empire—a process noticeably accelerated after the split with Tito. Through an intricate network of alliances, trade and economic agreements, joint-stock companies and Communist party and secret police connections, Soviet hegemony was entrenched throughout the region. Cultural and political ties with the West were eliminated, and economic transactions were reduced to insignificant levels. By June 1948, the Soviet Union had created a cowed empire from the Baltic to the Black Sea. To the West it seemed that only America's monopoly on atomic weapons barred Soviet domination of all Europe and prevented the Red Army from marching to the English Channel.

Two dramatic developments occurred in that month: the Berlin blockade and the expulsion of Tito from the Cominform. Each had an effect far beyond its immediate frame of reference. In retrospect, these were two of Stalin's major postwar miscalculations (the aggression in Korea might be considered a third), setting in motion a chain of events unfavorable to the consolidation of the Soviet empire and to the perpetuation of Stalinism as the modus operandi of Muscovite rule over Eastern Europe.

The Berlin Blockade

The Berlin crisis, the most dangerous crisis of the postwar Stalin period, was made possible only because of the Western powers' failure to insist on a land corridor to Berlin in 1944–1945. At the Tehran Conference in November 1943, Roosevelt, Churchill, and Stalin had agreed on a three-power occupation of Germany, but had left the final zonal divisions undefined. In April 1944, the Allied European Advisory Commission in London fashioned a general agreement on the boundary of the Soviet zone, and a formal protocol allocating the three zones was signed on September 12, 1944, three months after Western armies landed in France. It did not contain any specific provision for access to Berlin, which was located 110 miles inside the Soviet zone; nor did Roosevelt or Churchill consider the issues important enough to raise with Stalin. The details were left to the military. Prior to the Yalta Conference, the U.S. Joint Chiefs of Staff had proposed "that the general principle be accepted of freedom of transit by each nation concerned between the main occupied area and the forces occupying Berlin."[4] The Soviets were reluctant to discuss the matter and it was dropped, no doubt because the Americans wanted "to avoid raising any subject which might weaken Soviet desires to contribute to the overall Allied effort" or cause the Soviets to reconsider their promise to enter the war against Japan.[5]

On June 24, 1948, the Soviet Union imposed a blockade on the Western sectors of Berlin, saying that the Western powers were carrying out a separate currency reform in their sectors of the city without Soviet agreement. In the previous months, Soviet authorities had periodically interfered with Western access to Berlin, but had hesitated to impose a full blockade. Several considerations motivated their behavior. First, by forcing the Western powers out of Berlin and bringing the entire city under their control, the Soviets expected to gain added prestige that would improve their prospects of controlling Germany. Second, they hoped to undermine the efforts that were being made to establish West Germany as an independent country within the Western camp. Third, an Allied retreat in Berlin would have strengthened Communist party prestige elsewhere in Western Europe, further improving its electoral chances.

However, once the Berlin airlift started, the Soviets' decision in favor of a lengthy test of strength brought results that were almost diametrically opposite to their original expectations. The stakes were high, particularly for the United States. American willingness to pay the price of the airlift eventually convinced Stalin of the danger of his gambit, and a settlement was reached in May 1949, after months of trying negotiation. The blockade failed to drive the Western powers out of Berlin and also to prevent the establishment of the Federal Republic of Germany (FRG) on May 23, 1949. Moscow responded in kind by setting up the German Democratic Republic (GDR) in October 1949. This formalized partition of Germany is an everpresent reminder of the division between West and East and of the deep-rooted rivalry between them. As long as the West lacks guaranteed land access to West Berlin, it is captive to Soviet and East German squeezes. Berlin is a local sore in East-West relations, easily irritated and quickly swollen to international proportions.

In Berlin, however, the Kremlin had suffered its first postwar defeat in Europe. Whatever lingering hopes Stalin may have had for a withdrawal of U.S. troops from Western Europe were dashed, and he occasioned the acceleration of the West's rearmament and gave impetus and a stamp of permanence to the establishment in April 1949 of the North Atlantic Treaty Organization (NATO). In the Memorandum of the Government of the USSR on the North Atlantic Treaty of March 31, 1949, Moscow fulminated against the effort "to intimidate the states which do not agree to obey the dictate of the Anglo-American grouping of Powers that lay claim to world domination" and drew attention to its "real aggressive aims" and anti-Soviet character. Ideologically, Moscow's condemnation of NATO was another manifestation of the profound hostility between the Soviet Union and the West that had developed in less than four years.

We do not know what Stalin's aims were toward Germany. Experts disagree, and the evidence is episodic and fragmentary. It seems most unlikely, however, given Germany's humbling of Russia twice in a generation and Stalin's respect for German industry, technical skill, and energy, that he would have wanted a united Germany, especially one that was Communist and could become Moscow's rival for leadership in the Communist world. His probable preference, expressed in off-hand fashion to a group of visiting East European Communists in early 1948, was that Germany remain divided. "The West will make Western Germany their own, and we shall turn Eastern Germany into our own state."[6] In any event, Stalin's mishandling of the German question and misjudgment of U.S. resolve resulted in a return of U.S. military power to Western Europe and a major setback for his aim of making the Soviet Union the unchallenged power on the European continent.

As tensions mounted, Stalin strove to impede Western rearmament and check America's nuclear advantage. With the parlous state of East-West relations coming at a time of accelerating Sovietization of Western Europe, his fear was that the United States might use its nuclear weapons to demand political concessions. Accordingly, Soviet diplomacy directed considerable effort to mobilizing antiwar groups to foster Soviet policies. Specifically, the Peace Movement was manipulated "to reduce the danger of war during a period of maximum Soviet vulnerability; to neutralize the superior atomic capability of the West by building up popular feeling against the use of the atomic bomb; to reduce the political advantages to the West of its atomic monopoly; and to weaken the West's aircraft delivery system by rendering the overseas airbases politically insecure."[7] Stalin also desired an abatement of Cold War tensions in order "to buy time for a major Soviet technological-industrial effort aimed at producing a favorable long term shift in the balance of power"—that is, acquiring a credible nuclear deterrent of his own.[8] Though Soviet commentaries wrote of the need for "peaceful coexistence," relations between the Soviet Union and the West remained in deep freeze as long as Stalin lived.

Titoism: The End of the Muscovite Monolith

The world first learned of the deep fissure within the supposedly solid edifice of international communism on June 28, 1948, when the Cominform announced the expulsion of the Yugoslav Communist party for "anti-Party and anti-Soviet views, incompatible with Marxism-Leninism." The Yugoslavs were accused of having deviated from "the united socialist front against imperialism" and "taken up a position of nationalism." In a word, they were unwilling to turn their country into a colony of the Soviet Union.

Stalin would not accept Tito, his most faithful and "Stalinist" disciple in Eastern Europe, as an equal. He insisted upon unchallenged political and economic control by the Kremlin and a privileged position for Soviet diplomats and advisers stationed in Yugoslavia. Even when trying to curb Tito's militancy and revolutionary zeal, as when he told the Yugoslavs in early 1948 to stop supplying the Communist uprising in Greece lest it further complicate his relations with the West and "endanger his already-won positions" in Eastern Europe, he may well have reasoned that not only would "the creation in the Balkans of still another Communist state—Greece—" hardly be in his interest "in circumstances when not even the others were reliable and subservient," but that he could also use this issue as a litmus test of Tito's deference to his authority.[9] Irritated by his inability to bend the Yugoslav leadership to his will, Stalin invoked the ultimate weapon, excommunication, against his former protégé. He expected to overthrow Tito by waging an intensive propaganda campaign through the Cominform and by utilizing Soviet prestige to wean Yugoslav party members away from Tito, and he used every means at his disposal, short of military intervention. The result, Stalin assumed, would be to bring to power a pro-Soviet leadership prepared to do Moscow's bidding.

However, in positing that the highest loyalty of all good Communists must be to the Soviet Union as the "socialist motherland," Stalin underestimated the countervailing pull of nationalism (as had Karl Marx). He did not realize the broad basis of Tito's support or the force of Yugoslav nationalism. Aided by the fortunate circumstance of not sharing a common border with the Soviet Union, by the loyalty of party and military cadres whose bonds had been forged in the common struggle against Nazi overlordship and not in the bureaucratic intrigues of Kremlin-prescribed compounds, and by the undoubted popularity of Tito as a national hero, the Yugoslav leadership held firm. Stalin was to rue his boast that "I will shake my little finger, and there will be no more Tito. He will fall."

One may glean something of the way in which Stalin dealt with the East European and Baltic satellites from an account that the Yugoslav government, fearful of a Soviet attack and eager for international support, published in 1951:

> From the very moment inter-State relations were established, the Soviet Government began organizing espionage against the existing socialist order in Yugoslavia and against the independence of the Yugoslav peoples. The primary aim of these actions was to create a network of secret agents which would be a tool of the Soviet Government for undermining the Yugoslav Government. By a whole series of steps and acts which it undertook even before the Cominform Resolution of June, 1948, the Soviet Government attempted to impose unequal relations on Yugoslavia and to interfere in its internal affairs. . . .[10]

The Yugoslav white paper noted that "the Soviet Government considers that its diplomatic and other representatives [secret police agents] in a friendly country should have a special privileged status and that they have the right of prying into all State and Party affairs without the knowledge of the Government of that country." The Soviet government considered itself "a super-Government in another socialist country" and Soviet officials "did not hesitate to inveigle the citizens of that country into their intelligence service, taking as a point of departure the concept that Communists owe allegiance to the Soviet Government first and then to the leadership of their own socialist State." The Yugoslavs denounced the Cominform resolution of June 1948 as an open provocation to civil war:

> The Cominform Resolution was in effect a signal for the launching of the unprecedented campaign against Yugoslavia, aimed at forcing the Yugoslav Government and peoples, by way of political, diplomatic, economic, propagandistic, military and other kinds of pressure and threats, to renounce their rights to sovereignty and independence, their right to be the master in their own home. . . .
>
> The principle of economic cooperation with all countries, regardless of their internal systems, which the Governments of the USSR and the Eastern European countries support in words, has actually been transformed into an economic war which the Governments of those countries are waging against Yugoslavia in the most varied forms, including cancellation of regularly concluded contracts; the circumvention, violation and breach of trade agreements; the complete cessation and breaking off of all economic exchanges; the stoppage of reparations payments, issuing from the Peace Treaty, by Hungary; the obstruction and cessation even of transport and postal connections; the impeding of free navigation on the Danube, etc., etc.

Yugoslavia's resistance to Soviet domination was to have profound consequences for Soviet foreign policy after Stalin's death. Titoism, polycentrism, or national communism (as the phenomenon is most commonly called) is more than a reaction against Soviet domination; it represents a fusion of nationalism and communism into a doctrine and a movement having a variety of forms and signifying a measure of independence from Soviet control varying from complete opposition to significant autonomy in domestic matters. It represents the primacy of nationalism over communism and poses permanent dilemmas for Soviet leaders: Under what circumstances should the Kremlin use diplomacy and accommodation as opposed to compulsion and pressure in order to eliminate or moderate challenges to its established position and vital interests? How far dare Moscow go in acceding to demands for local autonomy in return for allegiance to the USSR, without jeopardizing its preeminent strategic and political position?

After 1948, Stalin initiated a series of purges of possible Titos and intensified the pace of Sovietization and Stalinization. He insisted on total subservience; leading Communists—Gomulka in Poland, Rajk in Hungary, Kostov in Bulgaria, Slansky in Czechoslovakia—were swept from power. The Stalinist pattern of organization was imposed upon Eastern Europe. Industry, foreign trade, and transportation were nationalized; centralized economic control and planning were introduced, and all economies were geared to servicing Soviet needs. Party organizations were purged and secret police ties with the Soviet KGB were expanded. To ensure the permanence and stability of his empire, Stalin sought to remake the economic, social, and political fabric of Eastern European societies.

This process, though piecemeal and wasteful, when combined with the Soviet pressure on Berlin and the rising threat from Communist revolutions in Asia, heightened Western feelings of insecurity and prompted the creation of NATO, which was intended to serve as a trip wire, a signal to the Soviet Union that any military move farther westward on its part would meet with an American nuclear response, which, at the time, was the West's only deterrent to a possible military attack. The West's sense of uneasiness over Soviet policy was aggravated in late 1949 by the USSR's detonation of its first atom bomb. As the lines of hostility and military wariness froze in Europe, events in the Far East attracted increasing attention.

A New Relationship with China

Soviet aims in the Far East had been realized at Yalta. Western agreement to restore the sphere of influence controlled by Russia in 1904, at the time of the Russo-Japanese war, fulfilled Stalin's ambitious territorial objectives; he had even improved on czarist Russia's patrimony in Asia.

Quite remarkably, Nationalist China quickly accepted the accords on Asia reached at the Yalta conference, to which it had not been invited. Like Sun Yat-sen in 1923, Chiang Kai-shek in 1945 was prepared to acquiesce to Soviet demands for hegemony over portions of imperial China that he then was unable to control in return for support against a domestic rival—in Chiang's case, Mao Zedong (Mao Tse-tung) and the CCP. Such was Chiang Kai-shek's eagerness that Washington on several occasions cautioned the Chinese against granting too many concessions, as, for example, agreeing to the unsupervised plebiscite in Mongolia in October 1945. Chiang recognized the "independence" of the Mongolian People's Republic and agreed to Soviet participation in the operation of the Chinese Eastern Railway (and the consequent privileged Soviet economic position), to joint Sino-Soviet use of the naval base of Port Arthur, and to the internationalization of Dairen. These Soviet gains were formally acknowledged in the Sino-Soviet Treaty of Friendship and Alliance, signed on August 14, 1945 (one day before the Japanese surrender). In return, the Soviet government recognized the government of Chiang Kai-shek as the legitimate government of China and pledged itself "to render to China moral support and aid in military supplies and other material resources, such support and aid to be entirely given to the Nationalist Government as the central government of China." But Mao's successful revolution was to change all of this.

After the Soviet and Chinese Communist debacle in 1927, Soviet control over the reorganized CCP had diminished, and Moscow's contact with it was rather limited in the 1935-to-1945 period, notwithstanding a common commitment to Marxism-Leninism. It is true that in the wake of the Japanese surrender, the Chinese Communists' takeover of major portions of Manchuria was aided by Soviet military authorities still occupying the area, who obstructed the easy deployment of advance elements of Chiang's army and who stacked quantities of captured Japanese weapons in places convenient for Mao's troops to collect them. Moscow had no interest in seeing a unified and strong China emerge too quickly. By covertly encouraging the rebel CCP, Stalin expected to acquire some added leverage on a Kuomintang (KMT) already dependent on Soviet goodwill and to obtain more time to consolidate Soviet acquisitions.

Stalin did not expect Mao to emerge the victor from the Chinese civil war, certainly not as quickly as he did. In late 1945, shortly before the CCP guerillas moved in, Soviet authorities stripped Manchuria of all usable industrial equipment, rolling stock, and valuables; they evidently did not foresee that within four years they would need to establish formal state-to-state relations with a fellow Communist and "fraternal" regime. Moscow was committed to Chiang's government; three times it agreed to his requests that Soviet troops remain in Manchuria until such time as the KMT could be present in sufficient force to forestall a Chinese Communist takeover of the area. (Soviet forces finally withdrew in May 1946). Stalin may have been as surprised as the West at the shocking disintegration of the well-equipped, well-supplied Kuomintang forces and at the dramatic Communist military advances in 1947 and 1948, and perhaps he feared U.S. intervention to prevent a CCP victory. According to a Yugoslav official, Stalin had recommended to Mao that he reach an agreement with Chiang and enter into a coalition government. Supposedly Mao agreed, but on returning home went his own way and won. Stalin is also alleged to have had doubts about the extent to which the Chinese Communists were genuine Communists—more than once referring to them as "radish Communists—red on the outside but white on the inside."

The outcome of the Chinese civil war was not determined in Moscow. At best, Soviet leaders contributed only marginally to Mao's victory. The CCP's reputation for reform and efficiency, the purposefulness and honesty of Mao and his associates, and the appeal that a strong and united China had for all strata of Chinese society contrasted vividly with the Kuomintang's failure to cope with China's inflation, poverty, and socioeconomic collapse; the venality of KMT officials; and Chiang Kai-shek's insensitivity to the peasants' profound desire for an end to war.

American efforts to mediate the civil war proved futile. It is doubtful that they ever enjoyed the faintest prospect of success. Moscow pursued a policy of outwardly correct diplomatic relations with the KMT while taking tentative steps to strengthen the position of what it considered to be the most pro-Soviet factions in the CCP. For example, without consulting Mao, Stalin invited Kao Kang, who was the Communist in charge of Manchuria, to Moscow in July 1949 to sign a trade agreement.[11]

On October 1, 1949, the People's Republic of China (PRC) was proclaimed in Beijing. An era of Far Eastern history had come to an end. China's destiny was no longer decided in Europe or Japan. For the first time in more than a century, all of mainland China was ruled by one Chinese elite. The century of weak central authority, civil wars, unequal treaties, economic subordination to foreign powers, and military helplessness was now past. Out of this crucible emerged a ruthless, dedicated, disciplined leadership—the Calvinists of Asia—intent on creating a powerful, industrialized, independent China. This development inevitably affected Soviet foreign policy and great-power relationships in Asia, relationships already greatly altered as a consequence of World War II and the unstable 1945-to-1949 interregnum.

For Moscow, a replacement for the Sino-Soviet treaty of 1945 was necessary. In December 1949 Mao went to Moscow and for two months negotiated a new political and military relationship between China and the Soviet Union. Though distrustful of Stalin on the basis of their previous dealings, Mao decided against a Titoist alternative, which might well have created problems for him in the CCP, and succeeded in exacting significant concessions from the Soviet leadership. After tough bargaining, three agreements were signed on February 14, 1950. First, a thirty-year treaty of alliance directed against the United States (though formally it was directed against "Japan or any other State which should unite with Japan, directly or indirectly") was concluded. Second, an agreement was reached on Manchuria, whereby the Chinese Changchun Railway and the naval base at Port Arthur were to be returned to China "immediately upon the conclusion of a peace treaty with Japan, but not later than the end of 1952," and the commercial port of Dalny (Dairen) was recognized as China's though its disposition was left in abeyance pending a peace treaty with Japan. (In case of war, Port Arthur was to be jointly operated; because of the Korean War, its final transfer to China was postponed until 1955.) Third, the Soviets agreed to a $300 million credit, a niggardly amount that sealed Mao's coolness toward Moscow and prompted Khrushchev's observation in 1956 that "Stalin treated Mao Tse-tung like a beggar."

These agreements were modified in 1954 to the further advantage of China, but even in 1950 they reflected the Kremlin's awareness that Mao, like Tito, had come to power under circumstances completely different from those that had led to Soviet hegemony over Eastern Europe. Historically, Russian policy had dealt with a weak, divided China, but Stalin recognized that new conditions necessitated concessions. He decided to pursue a "correct," if hardheaded, policy toward Beijing. He did force Mao to accept the independence of Mongolia and joint exploitation of Xinjiang's mineral resources, but he was careful not to overreach himself. Mao, commanding his own army and controlling a vast land mass, was accorded a basic equality vis-à-vis the Soviet Union. Stalin had learned the lesson of Tito well: once bitten, twice shy.

Within a few months, the Sino-Soviet alliance was tested by conflict in Korea. The Korean War, like the Berlin blockade and the excommunication of Tito from the Cominform, was to have far-reaching significance for Soviet relations with the Western world and was profoundly to affect its dealings with other Communist countries, though not until after the tyrant's death did the seeds that he had sown yield bitter fruit.

The Korean Adventure

Stalin's interest in neighboring Korea was strategic. Like "Russian policymakers in the late nineteenth and early twentieth centuries," he recognized the importance of Korea, "with its warm-water ports in the southern part of the peninsula and its strategic location vis-à-vis both China and Japan."[12] Moreover, he aimed to undo the 1911 Japanese annexation of Korea, thereby reversing one result of Russia's defeat in 1904–1905 and ending the Japanese threat to the USSR.

During the Allied conferences in World War II, Stalin maintained a strategic silence on his aims in Korea, shrewdly permitting the absence of concrete arrangements to allow him maximum military and diplomatic flexibility. It was to his advantage that neither at Yalta, in the secret agreement on the USSR's entry into the war against Japan, nor at Potsdam in July 1945 were specific dispositions made for Korea. The Soviet Union entered the war against Japan on August 8, 1945, "contrary to what Stalin and other Soviet spokesmen had been consistently saying about the need to conclude an agreement with China before Soviet entry into the Pacific War."[13] But Stalin was not one to be hobbled by consistency.

Soviet troops could have occupied all of Korea, because U.S. forces were nowhere in the vicinity and in no position to establish a foothold. However, Stalin was not looking for a quarrel with the United States. Therefore, on August 15, when in General Order Number 1 the United States proposed a temporary U.S.-Soviet occupation of Korea divided along the 38th parallel, Stalin acquiesced. He did so in part to avoid a confrontation with the United States; in part because he hoped Washington would agree to his request for a Soviet zone of occupation in Japan (in cabling his acceptance on August 16, Stalin asked that Soviet troops also be permitted to occupy the northern half of Hokkaido Island); and in part because he assumed that an early withdrawal of U.S. and Soviet forces would leave political control of the Korean peninsula in the hands of well-organized Soviet-trained Korean Communists. Under the pro-Moscow faction of the Korean Communist party (renamed the Korean Workers' party in August 1946), headed by Kim Il-sung, North Korea was quickly built up militarily and industrially. In contrast to what occurred under Soviet occupation of Manchuria, North Korea was not ravaged economically, since it was in Communist hands from the very beginning;[14] and in contrast to U.S. policy toward South Korea, Soviet policy in North Korea was a model of clarity, determination, and rationality.

With the onset of the Cold War in Europe, Moscow blocked UN efforts to effect a peaceful reunification, and the division of Korea took on an appearance of permanence. American and Soviet troops withdrew, leaving the country divided at the 38th parallel "between two rival authorities, each bent on the elimination of the other and on unification of Korea after its own pattern."[15] All prospects for a peaceful reunification vanished on June 25, 1950, when North Korean Communist troops invaded South Korea in a calculated attempt to settle the issue by force. Well equipped, having the advantage of surprise, and encouraged by the evident U.S. lack of interest and the widespread discontent with the Syngman Rhee regime that had appeared in the May elections, they came very close to victory.

The UN Security Council convened in emergency session on the very day of the invasion in response to a request by the United States government. The Soviet Union was not represented at this or any of the subsequent meetings of the council, having undertaken a boycott of the United Nations in January 1950 in protest against its failure to recognize the PRC as the legitimate government of China. The Soviet delegate did not return until August 1. With the USSR absent, the Security Council passed a resolution calling for the immediate cessation of hostilities and the withdrawal of the North Korean forces to their side of the border. It also requested all UN members to help in implementing this resolution. President Truman immediately committed U.S. forces, abruptly reversing his previous view that Korea was indefensible and beyond the area strategically necessary for America's own defense.

Soon afterward, the Soviet government set its vast propaganda apparatus in motion and, relying heavily on foreign Communist front organizations, condemned the United States for allegedly intevening in a civil war, carrying on an aggressive war, practicing bacteriological warfare, and perpetrating assorted atrocities. By October 1950, U.S. forces (fighting under the UN banner) counterattacked, crossed the 38th parallel, and advanced northward toward the Yalu River—and the Manchurian border. Once across the 38th parallel, they were no longer merely repelling agression; they were seeking to unify all Korea by force of arms. This decision by General Douglas MacArthur was never explicitly sanctioned by the UN. The Chinese, apprehensive over the approach of a hostile army and insecure enough to fear invasion of the mainland by Kuomintang troops who had fled to the island of Taiwan, sent in "volunteers" in early November. The war took on a new dimension. After much bitter fighting, a stalemate developed, roughly along the 38th parallel. Truce negotiations and hard fighting dragged on for almost two years. An armistice agreement was finally signed in July 1953, and today an uneasy truce prevails in a divided Korea.

What were Stalin's motives in approving the invasion of South Korea? In the absence of archival materials, all explanations must be tentative. The impending return of Port Arthur and Dairen to the PRC, agreed on in the 1950 Sino-Soviet treaty, must have lent added importance to the warm-water ports in South Korea and prompted Stalin to gamble on what seemed like a reasonably sure thing. Two persistently argued hypotheses have generally been discredited: first, the revisionist New Left contention that South Korea started the war (an aggressor always has the advantage initially, and it was North Korean forces that swept rapidly into South Korean territory in the early weeks of the war), and second, the conspiracy theory, that the attack was planned by Stalin and Mao in early 1950. Both are overly simplistic and based on distorted data, derived more from partisan bias than solid evidence. Most observers no longer assume that Moscow imperiously ordered the invasion. Soviet leaders knew what was in the offing and approved—witness the elaborate preparations that were required for the attack and the Kremlin's undeniable influence at the time in Pyongyang.

A more intricate variant suggested by Khrushchev's memoirs and linked to political rivalries within the North Korean Communist movement, holds that Kim Il-sung convinced Stalin that the fighting would be an internal affair involving only the Koreans themselves, that the South Koreans would turn against Syngman Rhee's dictatorship once the invasion began, and that the civil war would end quickly, precluding any outside intervention.[16] Seeing an opportunity for seizing prime real estate at little risk, Stalin gave the go-ahead. After all, he had good reason to believe that the United States would accept a *fait accompli* and do nothing to save Korea. America's apparent lack of interest in South Korea had been dramatically highlighted by Secretary of State Dean Acheson's failure to include it in the U.S. "defense perimeter" in a major speech on January 12, 1950; and Kim Il-sung's persuasive assurance that the forcible reunification of Korea could be accomplished swiftly and by North Korean forces alone whetted Stalin's strategic appetite. Nor did Stalin expect that the UN would do anything other than pass some resolutions of admonition, as the League of Nations had done in similar circumstances in the 1930s—hence the continued Soviet absence from Security Council deliberations. Even though he expected a quick victory, Stalin took elaborate precautions to keep Soviet advisers away from the fighting, so as not to give the United States an excuse for intervening. Ultimately, he was betrayed by Washington's unpredictability—by Truman's decision to fight for what Washington had previously declared not to be a vital interest for the United States.

Though thwarted militarily, Stalin benefited politically in two important ways. First, the United States was required to commit a large part of its limited existing strength to a remote area, thereby rendering it impotent in frustrating the establishment of the Soviet imperium in Eastern Europe. Second, the Korean War made Mao more dependent on Soviet weaponry and assistance, and thereby widened the split between the PRC and the United States. For the next fifteen years or so, the existence of a common enemy—the United States—induced the PRC to stay (roughly until the mid-1960s) on reasonably close terms with the Soviet Union and enabled Moscow to strengthen its position in Europe and expand in the Third World.

Stalin's Policies in Retrospect

Stalin pursued the Sovietization of Eastern Europe and its economic subordination to Soviet interests, operating through the Council for Mutual Economic Assistance (Comecon)—the Soviet counterpart of the Marshall Plan—and through an elaborate network of interlocking bilateral military treaties. Whereas in the Far East he could count on disciplined revolutionary proxies to advance communism and Soviet interests, in Europe he had to rely primarily on the Red Army and the KGB. He even went so far as to place a Soviet marshal in command of the Polish army in order to ensure its reliability.

Soviet military domination, the extensive purges, and the concomitant Soviet-type restructuring of the sociopolitical systems in Eastern Europe greatly vitiated Stalin's campaign to promote a relaxation of tensions between the two Europes. Following the failure of his policies in Berlin and Korea, Stalin sought to ease tensions in Europe sufficiently to "check the adverse trend in the world power position of the Soviet Union by removing the stimulus to Western cohesion and mobilization, and by encouraging divergent trends within the Western alliance."[17] Specifically, he groped for a policy that would stabilize the situation in Europe at a time of military engagement and volatility in Asia. In order to check the Western military buildup that had begun in earnest in 1950, he played on French-German animosities and deep-rooted uneasiness over West German rearmament, and he exploited "the peace issue, neutralism, trade, and other forms of collaboration with elements of the bourgeoisie."[18] Above all, he wanted to forestall the effective integration of the Federal Republic of Germany into NATO and its attendant remilitarization.

In retrospect, we can discern Stalin's innate conservatism in foreign policy. Though his policies were imperial—that is, though they took advantage of Moscow's victory in World War II to advance Soviet power in Europe and the Far East and thereby improve the USSR's strategic line of defense—they were also pragmatic, limited, and geared to the avoidance of war with the United States. The price of Stalin's gains in Eastern and Central Europe was better relations with the West, which viewed with deepening concern each entrenchment of Soviet power and influence on the doorsteps of Western Europe. Stalin did not try to overwhelm the West by force. His aim was to undermine its security and cohesion, and correspondingly to enhance the strength and stability of the imperial system he had created in Eastern Europe. Under this system, each country in Eastern Europe was permitted to retain its form as a nation-state (in contrast to the fate of Estonia, Latvia, and Lithuania, which in 1940 were incorporated into the USSR itself) but each was to be Communist in character, which for Stalin meant that its leadership was to do exactly as Moscow ordered and that its institutions and developmental pattern were to be an imitation of the USSR's. To Stalin, security was synonymous with a permanent Soviet military presence, unquestioned political control, ideological conformity, and economic subordination to Soviet needs. His imperial system (the "socialist camp") was an uninterrupted land mass extending from the Baltic Sea to the Black Sea.

Stalin was no openhanded patron of revolutions. He was fully prepared to exploit them where feasible, but stayed clear of committing Soviet forces to their advancement. He was not averse, as in Greece, to scuttling a Communist leadership if he thought its actions might jeopardize Soviet interests elsewhere in the region, and in Western Europe he sacrificed the prospects of the Italian and French Communist parties by ordering them to take active measures against the delivery of Marshall Plan economic aid. His decision not to extend to Finland the Sovietization imposed everywhere else in Eastern Europe was surprising. He may have had second thoughts about the implications of further aggravating tensions with the United States or about the difficulties that would have been encountered in the absence of a strong Communist party that could pave the way for a takeover; or, very possibly, he misplayed a strong hand, witness Andrei Zhdanov's remark to Djilas in 1946, "We made a mistake in not occupying Finland."[19]

Though Europe was the scene of the greatest expansion of Soviet military power and political influence, Stalin appreciated the importance of the Far East and did well in advancing Soviet national interests there, specifically, by obtaining handsome dividends at Yalta for Soviet participation in the war against Japan and by reaching an early accommodation with Mao Zedong's new Communist regime. Where Stalin erred, however, was in not keeping the North Koreans on a tighter leash. As in Europe in the case of Berlin, his misjudgment in the Far East resulted in a return of American military power that was to have enormous significance, if not for Stalin then certainly for his successors.

Overall, Stalin had a sound grasp on the realities of the postwar international system and used ideology to serve his ends. Ideology is by its very nature ambiguous and malleable. The Bolsheviks had come to power believing that the capitalist world was uniformly hostile and that "imperialism" was dedicated to the destruction of "socialism." However, they quickly learned to differentiate among the imperialists, some being more threatening than others, though all being targets for exploitation, one against the other. After the Bolsheviks were in power and had established the first Communist state, Leninist scripture referred to the irreconcilability of capitalism and socialism (that is, communism) and the inevitability of "frightful collisions"; but it was Stalin in the late 1920s and 1930s who developed the theory of "capitalist encirclement," partially out of a genuine sense of insecurity, but primarily to justify the suffering and sacrifice demanded of the Soviet people by his decisions to industrialize, collectivize, and transform Soviet institutions and society radically.

In doctrinal terms, this theory reflected the pervasive fear of an imperialist attack against the Soviet Union and implied a type of war quite distinct from Lenin's "inevitable" *intercapitalist* wars, which would stem from the nature and contradictions of capitalism, impelled to expand abroad in search of markets and raw materials (that is, imperialism). No systematic attempt was ever made to link Lenin's theory of these inevitable competitive intercapitalist wars with the subsequent Stalinist corollary of the "inevitable" capitalist war against the Soviet Union. Thus there were, in fact, two distinct Communist doctrines on war, though the impression that they were one and the same was encouraged. First came the Leninist theory of imperialism, with its focus on war and rivalries between capitalist countries, and second was the theory of capitalist encirclement, with its focus on the inevitability of war between the capitalist and Communist camps.

Shortly before the nineteenth congress of the CPSU in October 1952, Stalin published his *Economic Problems of Socialism in the USSR,* which contained an astute diagnosis of the international scene and of Soviet relations with the non-Communist world. He held that as an aftermath of World War II, capitalism had suffered grievous wounds and no longer ruled the world. Economically, the world had split into two parallel and self-contained trading systems. Politically, the capitalist countries had lost much of their former awesome power and therefore were not likely to attack the Soviet Union, although the contradictions and antagonisms between the two systems would continue to exist. A capitalist attack on the Soviet Union was unlikely because "war with the USSR . . . is more dangerous to capitalism than war between capitalist countries; for whereas war between capitalist countries puts in question only the supremacy of certain capitalist countries over others, war with the USSR must certainly put in question the existence of capitalism itself." He perceptively foresaw the reemergence of Germany and Japan as powerful nations and their competition with the United States for shrinking world markets. (Remember, this was said at a time when the United States was preeminent in the world, and both its allies and its former enemies Germany and Japan were weak and very much under its influence.) Finally, while emphasizing the continued and fundamental ideological and political hostility between the Communist and capitalist systems, Stalin carefully implied that *armed* conflict between them was not probable. In this way he kept alive the possibility of a measured relaxation of tensions, though it remained for his successors to give substance as well as form to the policy of peaceful coexistence.

The year 1953 was a fateful one. Stalin had ruled the Soviet Union for a generation. One of history's most ruthless tyrants, he was, in the words of France's General Charles de Gaulle, "possessed by the will to power. Accustomed to a life of machination to disguise his features as well as his inmost soul, to dispense with illusions, pity, sincerity, to see in each man an obstacle or a threat, he was all strategy, suspicion and stubbornness. His fortune was to have found a people so vital and so patient that the worst servitudes did not paralyze them, a soil full of such resources that the most terrible destruction and waste could not exhaust it." Undistinguished as a theorist, Stalin was seldom deluded by the orthodoxy that he imposed in ideological and party affairs. He placed no store in the imminence of world revolution, but was quite willing to use revolutions abroad to improve the international position of the Soviet Union. He understood the nature of power and used it to advantage to expand the Soviet empire, in the process fusing the needs of national security with his imperialist ambitions. He modernized the country's economy and institutions, and transformed a backward nation into one of the world's greatest industrial-military powers. Stalin ruled in the autocratic tradition of the harshest and most expansionist of the czars.

On March 5, 1953, Moscow announced the death of Stalin. An era had come to an end.

Notes

1. B. Ponomarov, A. Gromyko, V. Khvostov (eds.), *History of Soviet Foreign Policy 1945-1970* (Moscow: Progress Publishers, 1973), 162.
2. William O. McCagg, Jr., *Stalin Embattled 1943-1948* (Detroit: Wayne State University Press, 1978), 261-84.
3. Andrei Zhdanov, *The International Situation* (Moscow: Foreign Languages Publishing House, 1947), excerpts.
4. Jean Edward Smith, *The Defense of Berlin* (Baltimore: The Johns Hopkins Press, 1963), 31.
5. *Ibid.*, 32.
6. Milovan Djilas, *Conversations With Stalin* (New York: Harcourt, Brace & World, 1962), 153.
7. Marshall D. Shulman, *Stalin's Foreign Policy Reappraised* (Cambridge: Harvard University Press, 1963), 80-81.
8. Thomas W. Wolfe, *Soviet Power and Europe, 1945-1970* (Baltimore: Johns Hopkins Press, 1970), 25.
9. Djilas, *op. cit.*, 182-83.

10. Ministry of Foreign Affairs of the Federal People's Republic of Yugoslavia, *White Book on Aggressive Activities by the Governments of the USSR, Poland, Czechoslovakia, Hungary, Romania, Bulgaria, and Albania Towards Yugoslavia* (Belgrade, 1951), 14–37, excerpts.
11. Nakajima Mineo, "The Sino-Soviet Confrontation in Historical Perspective," in Yonosuke Nagai and Akira Iriya (eds.), *The Origins of the Cold War in Asia* (New York: Columbia University Press, 1977), 210.
12. Robert M. Slusser, "Soviet Far Eastern Policy, 1945–50: Stalin's Goals in Korea," in Nagai and Iriya (eds.), *ibid.*, 127.
13. *Ibid.*, 136.
14. Joungwon Alexander Kim, "Soviet Policy in North Korea," *World Politics*, Vol. 22, No. 2 (January 1970), 237–54.
15. Peter Calvocoressi, *Survey of International Affairs, 1949-1950* (London: Oxford University Press, 1953), 466.
16. Edward Crankshaw (commentary), Strobe Talbott (trans. and ed.), *Khrushchev Remembers* (New York: Bantam, 1970), 400–402.
17. Marshall D. Shulman, "Some Implications of Changes in Soviet Policy Towards the West: 1949–1952," *Slavic Review*, Vol. 20, No. 4 (December 1961), 630.
18. *Ibid.*, 631.
19. Djilas, *op. cit.*, 155.

Selected Bibliography

ADLER-KARLSON, GUNNAR. *Western Economic Warfare 1947-1967: A Case in Foreign Policy.* Stockholm: Almquist & Wiksell, 1968.

BADER, WILLIAM B. *Austria Between East and West, 1945-1955.* Stanford: Stanford University Press, 1966.

BELOFF, MAX. *Soviet Policy in the Far East, 1944-1951.* New York: Oxford University Press, 1953.

DAVISON, W. PHILLIPS. *The Berlin Blockade: A Study in Cold War Politics.* Princeton: Princeton University Press, 1958.

DEDIJER, VLADIMIR. *The Battle Stalin Lost: Memoirs of Yugoslvaia, 1948-1953.* New York: Viking, 1971.

HAHN, WERNER G. *Postwar Soviet Politics: The Fall of Zhdanov and the Defeat of Moderation, 1946-53.* Ithaca, N.Y.: Cornell University Press, 1982.

HALLE, LOUIS J. *The Cold War as History.* New York: Harper & Row, 1967.

HELLMANN, DONALD C. *Japanese Foreign Policy and Domestic Politics: The Peace Agreement with the Soviet Union.* Berkeley: University of California Press, 1969.

KAPLAN, MORTON. *The Life and Death of the Cold War.* Chicago: Nelson-Hall, 1977.

KORBEL, JOSEF. *The Communist Subversion of Czechoslovakia.* Princeton: Princeton University Press, 1959.

LATTIMORE, OWEN. *Pivot of Asia: Sinkiang and the Inner Asian Frontiers of China and Russia.* Boston: Little, Brown, 1950.

NAGAI, YONOSUKE and AKIRA IRIYA (EDS.). *The Origins of the Cold War in Asia.* New York: Columbia University Press, 1977.

SETON-WATSON, HUGH. *The East European Revolution.* New York: Praeger, 1956.

SHULMAN, MARSHALL D. *Stalin's Foreign Policy Reappraised.* Cambridge: Harvard University Press, 1963.

TAUBMAN, WILLIAM. *Stalin's American Policy: From Entente to Detente to Cold War.* New York: Norton, 1982.

ULAM, ADAM B. *Titoism and the Cominform.* Cambridge: Harvard University Press, 1952.

WHITING, ALLEN S. *China Crosses the Yalu: The Decision to Enter the Korean War.* New York: Macmillan, 1960.

II

Regional Dimensions of Soviet Foreign Policy

5
The Soviet Union and Eastern Europe

Since 1945, the lodestar of the Soviet Union's European policy has been strategic control of Eastern Europe in order to prevent that territory from ever again serving as a springboard for an invasion of the Soviet Union. Stalin's postwar objectives were relatively clear-cut: to eliminate Western influence from Eastern Europe and concomitantly establish Moscow's hegemony, and to develop a belt of submissive Communist regimes whose leaders governed at Moscow's discretion and depended for their survival on Soviet troops. From 1945 to 1953, the Soviet Union's Draconian policy toward Eastern Europe was unmistakably Stalin's handiwork.

His successors, however, were faced with more subtle challenges: to preserve yet decentralize their empire; to obtain Western acceptance of the permanence of Soviet domination over Eastern Europe; and to expand Soviet power without jeopardizing the security of the USSR or its imperial system. They soon discovered that preserving an empire is more difficult than acquiring one. Not only do the techniques of rule differ from those of revolution, but the price of empire may prove so high that it weakens the structure of power within the metropolitan country itself. Over the years, Stalin's successors alternated reform and repression in a never-ending search for a mix that extended the range of permissible autonomy within a framework that ensured loyalty, stability, and strategic control.

The Soviet leaders, eager to establish the legitimacy of their rule and effect an orderly transition of power, revived the principle of collective leadership. Except for the purge and execution in the summer of 1953 of Lavrenti Beria, the head of the secret police, who posed a physical threat to their survival, shifts at the top were managed without recourse to the terror of the Stalin period; and the struggle for power has remained bloodless, a reflection of the changing, more sophisticated nature of Soviet autocracy. In addition to reassuring the various privileged groups (such as the party, the military, and the technocracy) whose support is essential for the maintenance of the regime, the leadership—impelled by a series of unfavorable economic, demographic, social, and political trends—has divested itself of the more oppressive and inefficient aspects of the Stalinist legacy.

During the period from 1953 to 1956, decompression in the Soviet Union produced a ripple effect in Eastern Europe that resulted in three major upheavals—in East Germany, Hungary, and Poland. The first satellite eruption broke out in June 1953, four months after Stalin's death. A wave of strikes and riots swept East Berlin and parts of Soviet-occupied Germany in protest against increased production quotas and police repression. The Soviet army quickly and brutally suppressed the outbreaks. Though the West had stayed out of the crisis, the danger of the situation, and of inadvertent escalation, was not lost on Soviet leaders. They understood that in the GDR, as elsewhere in Eastern Europe, the task was to chart a course between the Scylla of Stalinism and the Charybdis of runaway relaxation of controls.

Throughout most of 1953 and 1954 the Kremlin was occupied with intra-Communist–world problems, in Eastern Europe, in China and within the Soviet Union itself. To decrease the likelihood of intrusive pressure from the West, Soviet leaders held out prospects of an easing of Cold War tensions, most immediately by accepting an armistice agreement in Korea on July 27, 1953. Thus began the effort to liquidate the liabilities bequeathed by Stalin. The armistice enabled the Soviet government to reduce the military drain on its economy, return the East-West conflict to the political and diplomatic arenas, and provide the Chinese Communists with time to consolidate their hold on the mainland; and it gave them more leeway in tackling the succession problem and in meeting the expectations of the Soviet people for a better life.

De-Stalinizing the Empire

On August 9, 1953, Premier G. M. Malenkov spoke of the government's intention to allocate more resources to satisfy consumer needs. He alluded to a departure from the previous hostility toward the West, though simultaneously he used the occasion to inform the world that the United States was "not the only possessor of the hydrogen bomb."

The "de-Stalinization" process that reached its apogee at the CPSU's twentieth congress in February 1956 developed slowly, varying in degree and scope from country to country but following a common pattern. Amnesties were proclaimed, forced collectivization was halted, price cuts on consumer staples were instituted, the more oppressive features of the labor and criminal codes were changed, and the arbitrary power of the secret police was curbed. The aim was to "return to Leninism." In Eastern Europe, those who were too closely identified as Stalinists were gradually replaced by national Communists, that is, those Communists who were popularly regarded as defenders of the country's interests against unreasonable exploitation by and abject subservience to the Soviet Union. Party and government apparatuses were separated, and economic reforms were introduced.

In another major policy reversal, Moscow decided on a reconciliation with Tito. The USSR and Yugoslavia concluded a barter agreement in September 1954, ending the Cominform's economic blockade. In May 1955, party leader Nikita S. Khrushchev and other top Politburo members went to Belgrade and did penance for Stalin's sins against Yugoslavia. They signed a joint government declaration endorsing the principle of nonintervention in domestic affairs and tacitly recognizing Yugoslavia as a socialist state, although it is significant that a comparable accord on party-to-party reconciliation was not agreed upon until Tito's visit to the USSR in June 1956. At that time Moscow formally acknowledged the principle of "many roads to socialism," which was to serve as the doctrinal basis for granting greater measures of autonomy to the members of the Soviet bloc.

Moscow hoped the reconciliation with Tito would be a first step toward the reconstitution of the formal unity of the Communist world. It sought thereby to stem the appeal of Titoism—that is, full independence and equality for all Communist states—and to reconcile loyalty to the Soviet Union with acceptance of the national autonomy allowed by Moscow. The Soviet leadership also hoped that the rapprochement would weaken Yugoslavia's ties with the West and diminish the value of the Balkan pact that Belgrade had signed in 1954 with Greece and Turkey. Improved Soviet-Yugoslav relations "harmonized with the then current Soviet policy of attaining cooperation with the respectable socialist parties of the West, demonstrating to the world Moscow's reasonableness and flexibility, and of encouraging neutralist tendencies in the free world by demonstrating that the USSR was not a threat against which an unaligned country needed to seek protection by joining the other bloc."[1] The Soviet-Yugoslav second honeymoon, however, lasted only until late 1956, when, in the aftermath of the Hungarian revolution, Moscow's temporary turn from diversity to bloc unity and neo-Stalinism alienated Belgrade. But this time, in contrast to 1948, the quarrel did not result in a rupture.

Khrushchev's determination to carry out far-ranging reforms at home and to place Soviet–East European relations on a more truly fraternal basis required improved relations with the Western countries. Accordingly, in the spring of 1955, over the objections of Molotov and others, Khrushchev agreed to a peace treaty with Austria, thus reversing Moscow's previous insistence on linking the treaty with a settlement of the German problem. The state treaty ending the four-power occupation was signed on May 15, following Austria's pledge, written into its constitution, of perpetual neutrality, comparable to that of Switzerland and Sweden. It was significant because it marked the first voluntary Soviet withdrawal from an entrenched position in the center of Europe (in May, the USSR also officially returned Port Arthur to the CPR, and in September, it withdrew from the military base that it had been granted in 1947 at Porkkala-Udd, only twelve miles from Helsinki in Finland). Moscow's surprising amiability extended to other areas as well. For example, in 1953 the Soviet Union renounced all claims against Turkey, made overtures for closer relations with Greece and Iran, and began to participate actively in the economic development and technical assistance programs of the various UN organizations.

Moscow's previously unchallenged authority in the Communist world was seriously shaken as a consequence of what was perhaps the most spectacular event in Soviet politics of the post-Stalin period: Khrushchev's secret speech at the CPSU's twentieth congress in February 1956, denouncing Stalin's crimes and self-deification. An outgrowth of the struggle for power among the Kremlin oligarchs, the speech had a powerful effect on the course of developments in Eastern Europe, China, and the world Communist movement. It immediately set in motion in Eastern Europe additional pressures for changes that gathered momentum and threatened to unhinge the Soviet empire.

Even without Khrushchev's speech against Stalin and the impetus that it gave to de-Stalinization, the twentieth congress would have been important because of the significant doctrinal innovations that reflected the Kremlin's approach to and apparent perception of world affairs. First, Khrushchev declared that "war is not fatalistically inevitable," thereby revising Lenin and Stalin. He acknowledged the Marxist-Leninist precept that wars are inevitable as long as imperialism exists, but noted that it was formulated at a time "when 1) imperialism was an all-embracing world system, and 2) the social and political forces which did not want war were weak, poorly organized, and hence unable to compel the imperialists to renounce war." What was "absolutely correct" in that period was no longer true because of the radically changed international system. According to Khrushchev, "Now there is a world camp of socialism, which has become a mighty force. In this camp the peace forces find not only the moral, but also the material means to prevent aggression." In other words, the emergence of the Soviet Union (and by implication its possession of nuclear weapons) enabled the forces for peace in the world to find a champion and to rebuff would-be aggressors; the USSR's possession of nuclear weapons would deter any would-be capitalist aggressor. Moreover, if "all anti-war forces" cooperated with the Soviet camp, "the greater the guarantees that there will be no new war."[2]

Second, Khrushchev formally embraced the Titoist thesis that there are many roads to socialism, thereby providing doctrinal approval for diversity in the Soviet bloc and the theoretical basis for closer cooperation not only with Yugoslavia but also with the socialist parties of Western Europe. To lend authority to this ideological change, he cited something that Lenin had written on the eve of the Bolshevik Revolution:

> All nations will arrive at socialism—that is inevitable, but not all will do so in exactly the same way, each will contribute something of its own in one or another form of democracy, one or another variety of the dictatorship of the proletariat, one or another rate at which socialist transformations will be effected in the various aspects of social life.

Noting that alongside the Soviet form of socialist transformation distinctive forms were evolving in the People's Democracies of Eastern Europe, in China, and in Yugoslavia, he acknowledged that "it is probable that more forms of transition to socialism will appear."

Third, Khrushchev held that under certain circumstances socialism (that is, Communist parties) could come to power "by using parliamentary means." This possibility, he stressed, had not been available to "the Russian Bolsheviks." Now it existed, as a consequence of the USSR's success and establishment of People's Democracies in Eastern Europe, the growth of "the forces of socialism" and the weakening of capitalism, and the opportunity for "the working class in a number of capitalist countries to unite the overwhelming majority of the people under its leadership." But Khrushchev declared one condition to be essential:

> Whatever the form of transition to socialism, the decisive and indispensable factor is the political leadership of the working class headed by its vanguard [that is, the Communist party]. Without this there can be no transition to socialism.

Finally, Khrushchev drew attention to the growing importance of the newly independent countries of the Third World and provided the ideological rationale for the emerging Soviet involvement there (see Chapter 8).

In bringing Soviet foreign-policy perceptions and guidelines into line with emerging international realities, Khrushchev greatly disturbed the Chinese, who saw in his stress on peaceful coexistence and efforts to effect a limited détente with the United States a downgrading of the Sino-Soviet alliance, a shift in Soviet foreign-policy priorities and methods, and a possible shelving of Beijing's quest for international recognition and for the overthrow of the Kuomintang regime on Taiwan. But the disruptive effects of de-Stalinization were most apparent in Eastern Europe. An unwary Kremlin had unwittingly released turbulent anti-Russian, anti-Communist, and nationalist currents. The result was the most substantial uprising against Soviet rule ever witnessed. Shaking the very foundations of the Soviet empire, it led to a Stalinist revival and to serious reconsiderations of ways in which to ensure the permanence of Soviet strategic gains in Eastern Europe and avoid the perils of liberalization.

Riots broke out in Poznan, Poland, in June 1956. Sparked by Khrushchev's revelations, smoldering resentment of a decade of economic exploitation and Soviet domination flared into open denunciations of the Moscow-controlled government. The Poles' traditional hatred of Russia made for a volatile political situation. The Kremlin, realizing the gravity of the situation, grudgingly made concessions. It permitted the ouster of many known pro-Moscow Communists from the Central Committee of the Polish United Workers' (Communist) party and in October 1956 accepted the elevation of Wladyslaw Gomulka, who had spent several years in prison for supposed Titoist tendencies, to the post of party secretary. Moscow also publicly reaffirmed Poland's sovereignty and independence, agreed not to interfere in its domestic affairs, and withdrew Soviet Marshal Rokossovsky as head of Poland's armed forces. Trade and financial relations were adjusted to Poland's advantage, and the number of Soviet troops permitted by special agreement to remain in Poland pending a settlement of the German question was sharply reduced. (Notwithstanding its greater independence in internal affairs, Poland remains inevitably influenced in important foreign-policy decisions by its powerful Communist neighbor, if only because friendship with the USSR is Poland's ultimate guarantee against the possibility of another Soviet-German "understanding" at its expense, as in 1939. Soviet troops in East Germany and in Poland, as well as Poland's deep-rooted fear of the claims of a revived, united, expansionist Germany to the territories east of the Oder-Neisse line that are now incorporated into Poland, are Moscow's levers to assure that nation's continued adherence to the Soviet bloc.)

Events in Hungary took a violent and tragic turn. Matyas Rakosi, a confirmed Stalinist and longtime party boss of Hungary, was deposed in June 1956, and his successor, Ernö Gero, was not up to the challenge of mounting popular pressure for change. On October 23, revolution erupted in Budapest. Anti-Communist and anti-Soviet, it threatened the entire Soviet position as it had in Poland because the Hungarians wanted full independence and their party leadership had lost control of the situation. The rebels wanted to disband the Communist party, leave the Warsaw

Pact organization, and liquidate all vestiges of Soviet rule. Confronted with the imminent loss of Hungary and possible disintegration elsewhere in Eastern Europe, Moscow hurled 250,000 troops and 5000 tanks against the Hungarians on November 4, after it violated a truce that betrayed key Hungarian military leaders and delivered them into Soviet hands. Where negotiation had failed, brute force and deceit succeeded.

The UN General Assembly called upon the Soviet government "to desist from its intervention in the internal affairs of Hungary, to withdraw its forces from Hungary, and to cease its repression of the Hungarian people." Aided by the coincidence of the Suez and Hungarian crises, the Soviets ignored UN and Western protests. Whereas through the temporary coalescence of Soviet and American policy on Suez the UN was able to end the Middle Eastern hostilities, no similar congruence of power could be marshalled on behalf of Hungary. As the Soviet steamroller crushed the Hungarians, the West watched, helpless to intervene for fear of precipitating World War III. This moment of truth for the West tragically confirmed what Raymond Aron has described as "the unwritten law of the atomic age": that the Soviet Union can do as it pleases within its sphere of influence without fear of retaliation. And Hungary is part of that sphere.

But the Kremlin learned several bitter lessons. First, Soviet control in Eastern Europe can be preserved *only* if backed by the Red Army. Military force, not ideology, is the effective cement for cohesion. Second, nationalism remains strong, even among avowed Communists, and in Eastern Europe it is permeated with an anti-Russian tinge. Third, authority once weakened cannot easily be reimposed. Fourth, a prerequisite for the continued political and military adherence of East European countries to the Soviet-dominated Warsaw Pact military alliance is Soviet acceptance of a substantial measure of economic, cultural, and political autonomy for those countries.

Strategically, control of Eastern Europe plays a key role in Soviet military thinking about the defense of the USSR, and Moscow will undoubtedly resist any attempt, either by the West or by the region's members, to dislodge its military influence and control. Khrushchev implied as much when he castigated "some comrades" for opposing the decision to intervene and noted that "the saliva of the imperialists was running in their mouths at the prospect of Hungary's leaving the Socialist camp. They thought that one by one they could sever the Socialist countries from their united base."[3] His successors have been no less decisive and are always on guard lest diversity lead to disaster.

On the other hand, Eastern Europe can no longer be considered an unquestioned asset to the Kremlin. The area represents a material drain on Soviet resources; the reliability of East European troops remains a continual question; and East European nationalism, a force too often slightened in the West, greatly complicates the process of Soviet rule. The intervention in Hungary cost Moscow heavily among influential West European intellectuals and in the consequent agonizing reappraisals that occurred in Western Communist parties. African and Asian leaders expressed varying degrees of disappointment, but the remoteness of Hungary to them blunted their concern and indignation. They were far more outraged over the British, French, and Israeli attack on Egypt, a country only recently emerged from colonialism and one with which they felt intimate emotional ties. Moreover, Soviet leaders, unlike their Western counterparts who must contend with an influential public opinion, could simply ignore the protests. What the 1956 crises in Eastern Europe (and the 1968 crisis in Czechoslovakia) have shown is that the Soviet Union regards Eastern Europe as vital to its national security and that it is prepared to use force if necessary to preserve its hegemony there.

In November 1957, on the occasion of the fortieth anniversary of the Bolshevik Revolution, the leaders of international communism met in Moscow to repair the damage of 1956. They issued a "declaration of unity" reaffirming the solidarity of the Communist camp "headed by the Soviet Union." This declaration implicitly acknowledged the disruptive consequences of national communism, emphasized the unity of the Communist world, and attacked "revisionism" (the sin of going further than Moscow in doctrinal, internal, or international innovation). The Chinese gave lip service to Moscow's leadership for the last time and tried to nudge the Soviet Union back to Stalinism, especially as it related to Moscow's policy toward the United States and Western Europe. Throughout the meeting, Moscow groped for a way of reinstituting the Cominform, which had been disbanded in the heady days of de-Stalinization in 1956, and of reimposing bloc unity, particularly in Eastern Europe. But like Humpty-Dumpty, the Cominform could not be put back together again, largely because of Yugoslav and West European Communist opposition to Chinese efforts on behalf of a forceful reassertion of Soviet political and ideological authority within the bloc.

Courting Belgrade

Tito, who absented himself from the gala get-together, refused to sign the Moscow declaration—an indication of the brittleness of the 1955-to-1956 Soviet-Yugoslav reconciliation. He had supported Khrushchev's intervention in Hungary out of fear that the "counterrevolutionary fever" might spread elsewhere in Eastern Europe, even to Yugoslavia; out of a desire to bolster Khrushchev in curbing the Stalinists in the Kremlin; and in order to retain a degree of influence on Soviet policy in Eastern Europe. But the declaration made him uneasy. Soon after the conference, the Soviet press launched an intensive antirevisionist campaign. The Yugoslavs bore the brunt of direct criticism when, in April 1958, they published their new party program, which read like a codification of revisionism that "contradicted point by point the programmatic directive for the bloc and the world communist movement" issued the previous November.[4]

During the years 1958 to 1961, the Soviet-Yugoslav controversy centered on four main points. First, the Yugoslavs maintained that the USSR as well as NATO was responsible for the Cold War and the division of the world into rival blocs. Second, they insisted on the unqualified right of each Communist state to determine its own course toward socialism. Third, they accused Moscow of continuing Stalinist practices and of having developed into a bureaucratic state that kept "strengthening in all fields of social life" instead of withering away in accordance with Marxist-Leninist theory. And fourth, the League of Yugoslav Communists' party program claimed for Yugoslavia a democratic and socialist evolution that Moscow could not accept or allow to go ideologically unchallenged. The Soviet leadership denounced the Yugoslavs for "assisting imperialism" and deviating from the position taken by the Communist parties of other socialist countries; they applied economic and political pressure, but stopped far short of military threats or another break.

In November 1960, at another international Communist conference in Moscow, Khrushchev failed to heal the growing disunity in the Communist world, most prominently the Soviet problems with Beijing. The continuing deterioration of Soviet relations with China in the 1960s gave impetus to better relations with Yugoslavia. However, the Soviet invasion of Czechoslovakia in August 1968 triggered Yugoslavia's deepest anxieties over Soviet intentions in Eastern Europe, and the Soviet-Yugoslav relationship has fluctuated ever since. Moscow has found the Yugoslav position congenial on many issues, such as the convening of the Conference on Security and Cooperation in Europe (CSCE), the establishment of a nuclear-free zone in the Balkans, the admission of the two Germanies to the United Nations, the condemnation of U.S. policy in Southeast Asia and the Middle East, and the need for disarmament. However, on other issues of core concern to each—for example, on the issue of Soviet authority in Eastern Europe and the world Communist movement, on the policy of nonalignment, and on nonintervention in the internal affairs of socialist countries—their disagreement persists.

Throughout the 1970s, Soviet-Yugoslav relations were generally good: Tito and Brezhnev exchanged visits; disagreed without rancor on bloc politics, Eurocommunism, and China; and encouraged expanded economic ties. Moscow carefully avoided overt threats, though after the 1968

Czechoslovak crisis Belgrade took firm steps to improve its defenses against attack from the east. During his visit to Belgrade in November 1976, Leonid Brezhnev came with an ambitious agenda for drawing Yugoslavia into more intimate ties with the Soviet bloc, including "closer cooperation with Comecon on Yugoslavia's part, Yugoslav involvement in Warsaw Pact 'ideological activity,' closer cooperation in foreign policy, the establishment of a Soviet-Yugoslav friendship association, permanent flight-route rights for Soviet military and civilian aircraft . . . and a disclaimer that the Soviet Union supports anti-Tito groups or plays a role in the Yugoslav-Bulgarian dispute over Macedonia."[5] However, not only did Tito, in a significant symbolic assertion of his country's independence, not go to meet Brezhnev at the airport, but he stressed that any improvement in Soviet-Yugoslav relations could be based only on principles of independence, equality, noninterference in internal affairs, and respect for the freedom to choose one's own road to socialism. For the remaining years of Tito's rule, Moscow did nothing that would heighten existing differences, contenting itself with Yugoslavia's growing economic dependence on Soviet–East European trade, legalization of carefully circumscribed berthing and repair facilities for foreign warships, and expanded high level exchanges.

Since Tito's death in May 1980, Soviet-Yugoslav relations have entered a period of new uncertainty and wariness. A Soviet invasion is always a possibility that cannot be dismissed, since the Kremlin covets permanent military access to the Mediterranean and an end to Yugoslavia's irritating type of national communism, which remains a perennial challenge to the reimposition of its full authority over the bloc. But Moscow is unlikely to take on such a tough protagonist. Through a combination of pressure and accommodation, it will attempt to nudge the Yugoslav leadership closer to the Soviet position on bloc and world issues. Soviet temptation will be a function of Yugoslavia's internal cohesion: the more satisfactorily the post-Tito republic party oligarchs negotiate their differences, tackle economic problems, and sustain national unity, the less the Kremlin will be tempted, or able, to intervene, and vice versa. For the foreseeable future, amity is Moscow's aim. During his visit to Yugoslavia in March 1988, Gorbachev publicly acknowledged the Soviet Union's culpability for the split in 1948. The unsigned declaration issued by Gorbachev and the Yugoslav president was a model of accommodation. It stated that "no one has a monopoly of the truth" and the sides declared "their lack of any claim to impose their ideas about social development upon anyone else whomsoever." Moscow's implicit eschewal of force against recalcitrant communist leaderships was welcomed in Belgrade; its broader implications for Eastern Europe, however, remains to be tested.

For their part, the Yugoslavs resist Moscow's efforts to reestablish a single center of authority for the world communist movement. They opposed the attempt of Fidel Castro, when he was chairman of the nonaligned movement (1979–1982), to gain acceptance for the thesis that the Soviet bloc is a "natural ally" of the nonaligned; and they are quick to reject Soviet and East European suggestions that Tito was in any way responsible for the conflict of 1948 or that Yugoslavia is part of "the socialist [Soviet] camp." On the core issues, Moscow finds Belgrade as Titoist as ever.

Interregnum 1956–1968

In the decade or so after the tumultuous events of 1956, Moscow's policy toward Eastern Europe underwent a number of important changes. First, Moscow accommodated to East European nationalism by granting substantial domestic autonomy to indigenous Communist elites. In Hungary, Janos Kadar, who came to power under the worst possible circumstances (he was installed by the invading Red Army in November 1956), was still able to implement far-reaching economic reforms and political liberalization and in the process gain general acceptance—even popularity—in the country. In Poland, Gomulka defused Polish rebelliousness and de-Stalinized the economy and social life. He got along well with the USSR until he was forced by labor unrest and inflation to resign in December 1970. There have been no serious problems with Bulgaria, the most pro-Soviet of the East European countries, or with East Germany (GDR), which is a bulwark of orthodoxy. In Romania and Czechoslovakia, however, Moscow encountered difficulties with national Communist leaders.

Second, the USSR readjusted its economic relations with Eastern Europe. It gave the East Europeans concessionary rates on imports of some Soviet raw materials and extended long-term credits without visible political strings. Third, it accepted expanded economic and cultural links between Eastern Europe and the West, though it did caution bloc members against using "their relations with capitalist countries at the expense of other fraternal countries."

By the time Khrushchev was deposed in October 1964, Soviet policy toward Eastern Europe had changed considerably. From the one-sided and callous exploitation of the Stalin era, it had moved to a more businesslike and sophisticated economic give-and-take. From day-to-day control by pro-Moscow satraps and resident KGB procurators, it had changed to allow considerable autonomy to national Communists in managing their internal affairs, as long as there was no threat to the communist character of the regime or its loyalty to the USSR. And from imposed conformity to

Soviet norms in all things, Soviet policy had grown to tolerate diversity in most areas. From a classic type of colonial system, the Soviet–East European bloc evolved into an imperial system, in which the center placed preeminent importance on strategic and military control rather than on economic exploitation or cultural conformity. As long as each country remained Communist and a member of the Warsaw Pact, and local power was exercised by a Communist leadership that did not challenge Soviet strategic hegemony, Moscow tolerated experiments with the limits of diversity.

The duumvirate of Leonid Brezhnev and Alexei Kosygin altered the style—the ebullience of Khrushchev was replaced by the deliberateness of Brezhnev—but not the substance of Khrushchev's policy. They followed the trail he marked to preserve Soviet hegemony in Eastern Europe. Confronted with intensifying nationalism in Eastern Europe, worsening relations with China, and the end of the myth of international Communist solidarity, the Soviet leaders tried to improve relations with the West and find a formula for asserting their authority within the bloc.

Intervention in Czechoslovakia

In January 1968 a combination of disgruntled Stalinists and reformers ousted Antonin Novotny, Moscow's man in Prague, as general secretary of the Czechoslovak Communist party, and brought in Alexander Dubček. Long a loyal party bureaucrat, Dubček became the rallying figure for all factions and groups seeking to liberalize Czechoslovak society and to assert a greater autonomy in domestic affairs. By mid-February, liberalization was occurring so rapidly that the skepticism among the population at large changed to hopeful anticipation. By late spring, the air of freedom intoxicated the country. Dubček and the reformers spoke of a parliament free from party control; they rehabilitated the victims of the Stalinist past, began to rid the party and trade unions of the front men for Moscow, and eliminated censorship. Ludvik Svoboda replaced Novotny as president. In the Central Committee, the Dubček group was in control. Democratization flowered. From early February to August 1968, Czechoslovakia experienced a rebirth of political, cultural, and social freedom. The secret police were stripped of their arbitrary powers, and links to the Soviet KGB apparatus were exposed, and criticisms of the past and proposals for the future were aired with a candor and passion that disturbed the oligarchs of Byzantine communism in Moscow.

The "Prague spring" lasted until August 21. In the early hours of that day, Soviet troops invaded Czechoslovakia. As with Hungary in 1956, Moscow responded with overwhelming force to a perceived threat to its strategic military position in Central Europe. Joined by Polish, East German, Hungarian, and Bulgarian (but not Romanian) troops in order to give the intervention a Warsaw Pact imprimatur, the Red Army quickly occupied the country.

The Soviet justification for the invasion of Czechoslovakia appeared in *Pravda* on September 26, 1968. Quickly dubbed the *Brezhnev Doctrine,* it proclaimed the inherent right of the Soviet Union to be the sole judge and jury of when the limits of permissible autonomy in the socialist world had been exceeded and to intervene as it saw fit to preserve socialism. While reaffirming the principle of "many roads to socialism," it insisted that no action "should do harm either to socialism" in the country or party involved . . .

> or to the fundamental interests of other socialist countries and of the entire working-class movement which is striving for socialism. This means that each Communist party is responsible not only to its own people but also to all the socialist countries and to the entire Communist movement. . . . Just as, in V.I. Lenin's words, someone living in a society cannot be free of that society, so a socialist state that is in a system of other states constituting a socialist commonwealth cannot be free of the common interests of that commonwealth.

The article warned that though every Communist party is free to apply the basic principles of Marxism-Leninism, it is not free to depart from those principles or to adopt a nonaffiliated attitude toward the rest of the socialist community:

> It should be stressed that even if a socialist country seeks to take an "extrabloc" position, it in fact retains its national independence thanks precisely to the power of the socialist commonwealth—and primarily to its chief force, the Soviet Union—and the might of its armed forces. The weakening of any link in the world socialist system has a direct effect on all the socialist countries, which cannot be indifferent to this. Thus, the antisocialist forces in Czechoslovakia were in essence using talk about the right to self-determination to cover up demands for so-called neutrality and the C.S.R.'s withdrawal from the socialist commonwealth. . . . The Communists of the fraternal countries naturally could not allow the socialist states to remain idle in the name of abstract sovereignty while the country was endangered by antisocialist degeneration.

Castigating those who "disapprove" of the actions taken by the Soviet Union, the article declared that world socialism "is indivisible and its defense is the common cause of all Communists and all progressive people on earth, first and foremost the working people of all the socialist countries."

Two months later, speaking in Poland, Brezhnev declared:

> affirmation and defense of the sovereignty of states that have taken the path of socialist construction are of special significance to us Communists. . . . And when external and internal forces hostile to socialism try to turn the development of a given socialist country in the direction of restoration of the capitalist system, when a threat arises to the cause of socialism in that country—a threat to the security of the socialist commonwealth as a whole—this is no longer merely a problem for that country's people, but a common problem, the concern of all socialist countries. . . . Let those who are wont to forget the lessons of history and who would like to engage again in recarving the map of Europe know that the borders of Poland, the GDR and Czechoslovakia, as well as of any other Warsaw Pact member, are stable and inviolable. These borders are protected by all the armed might of the socialist commonwealth.

In proceeding as they did, Soviet leaders demonstrated the paramountcy of Eastern Europe in their thinking about the defense of the Soviet Union. They used force even at the risk of jeopardizing many of their policy goals—for example, détente with the United States, including prospects for an agreement limiting strategic delivery systems; the weakening of NATO; and the support of foreign Communists, many of whom publicly condemned the Soviet aggression against an ally and fellow-Communist country.

Most Western analysts believe that the choice of specific foreign options is generally affected by domestic political considerations, be they lack of consensus in the Politburo, rivalry among different bureaucratic elites, pressure from the military or economic constraints, or something else. Czechoslovakia offers a strong case for the contention that domestic determinants are of central importance. Examination of the probable reasons for the invasion may help us understand the factors governing Soviet policy in the region.

What may have been the most important single determinant was the Kremlin's fear that the virus of Czechoslovak liberalization would find a congenial breeding ground in the national consciousness of the Ukrainians and stimulate demands in the Ukrainian SSR for extensive reform and relaxation of Muscovite domination. After all, if the Slavs and fraternal Communists of Czechoslovakia were permitted democratization, why not those of the Soviet Union? This line of analysis assumes that the ethnic and racial diversity of the USSR has a profound effect on Soviet politics and policymaking, though given the secrecy shrouding Soviet foreign policy decision-making, it is difficult to adduce this in specific instances. The Russians, who constitute no more than 52 percent of the approximately 286 million Soviet people, have had trouble for more than 300 years with the 50 to 55 million Ukrainians, the second-largest nationality group. Of all the peoples in Eastern Europe, the Czechs and Slovaks are regarded by Ukrainians as the nearest to them in tradition and culture.

Ethnic nationalism is a perennial and intensifying nightmare for Moscow. Soviet leaders proclaim abroad the notion of "proletarian internationalism" (that is, unswerving acceptance by all Communists of the primacy of defending the homeland of socialism—the Soviet Union) to justify Soviet claims to leadership of the world Communist movement; but they may be even more concerned with its acceptance *internally* as ideological justification for Great Russian domination over the non-Russian nationalities of the Soviet Union.

A second major consideration in the Soviet decision to invade Czechoslovakia was the pressure of the military to safeguard the Soviet position in Central Europe against possible erosion; strategic imperatives transcended political risks. The Czech suggestion in July 1968 that the Warsaw Pact be revised raised the specter of another Hungarian crisis. The military argued that Czechoslovakia was too centrally placed geographically for Moscow to let it go neutralist or succumb to instability. As it was, Warsaw Pact maneuvers in 1966 had exposed glaring weaknesses along the Czechoslovak–West German border; and Prague's unwillingness to agree to the permanent stationing of Soviet troops on Czech soil was an objection the Soviet high command wished to override. Soviet marshals saw an opportunity to station troops permanently in Czechoslovakia, at that time the only Warsaw Pact member on the central front without such a deployment. The Kremlin's desire to fill this gap elicited the mordant comment that the Russian invasion (its first) filled a gap of 600 years of Czech history! Czechoslovakia's importance in Soviet strategy in Europe had been described by one analyst thus:

> Not only does it share a long border with the West, but it also occupies a central position linking the northern and southern sectors of the Warsaw Pact. The loss of Czechoslovakia, either through its voluntary reorientation or its occupation in the event of a Western invasion, would isolate Soviet forces in Hungary from those in the GDR and Poland and would expose the Soviet Union's "iron triangle" in Western Russia, the Baltic Republics and the Ukraine. Equally, Comecon's Comprehensive Programme for Integration, favored by the USSR since the early 1960s, with its joint railway stock system, criss-crossing oil and gas pipelines and shared electricity grids, simply would not have been feasible without full Czechoslovak participation. Add to this the fact that Czechoslovakia in 1968 was a major supplier to the USSR not just of defense-related advanced technology but, more significantly perhaps, also of uranium, and a fuller picture of Czechoslovakia's strategic importance to the Soviet Union begins to emerge.[6]

East German leaders strongly supported the Soviet military, arguing that if Czechoslovakia continued to liberalize, to open her economy to Western investment, and to follow her own way in dealing with the Federal Republic of Germany, as Romania had, the net result would be a severe weakening of the GDR, Moscow's ally in orthodoxy and most important economic partner. Finally, it is also possible that Soviet intelligence had assured the Politburo that the Czechs would not fight and that the incident could be handled swiftly and satisfactorily if massive power was applied.

A final consideration may have been the Politburo's sense that, as in Hungary in 1956, the Czechoslovak Communist party leadership had lost control and that there was no alternative to a military intervention, if the USSR's strategic interests were to be safeguarded. The Czechoslovak reform movement had raced beyond the party's rein.

Thus for domestic, strategic, and ideological reasons, Moscow acted in Czechoslovakia as it had in Hungary twelve years earlier. The USSR showed that control over East European real estate is nonnegotiable—that its policy is based on the axiom "What's mine is mine; what's yours is negotiable." It will use force to preserve its imperial system intact. Though seeking better relations with Western Europe, it will not tolerate any erosion of its strategic hold over a contiguous Communist country, nor will considerations of prestige among foreign Communist parties deter it from expeditiously suppressing national Communists who exceed Moscow's guidelines for autonomy.

In Moscow's behavior we see again the dominance of Russian national and imperial interests over the needs and wishes of Communist parties abroad. Different political constellations in control in the Kremlin at any given time may be prepared to accept lesser or greater parameters of autonomy, but the ultimate determination of what is permissible is Moscow's prerogative. Eastern Europe cannot divest itself completely of Soviet influence; geography, the reliance of the "new class" in Eastern Europe on the protective power of the Red Army, growing dependency on imports of Soviet energy, and the realities of international relations preclude such a divestiture. By keeping fears of a West German revanche alive, particularly among the Poles and East Germans, Moscow ensures their military dependence. Should any of the East European regimes show signs of assuming an anti-Soviet, anti-Communist stance, Moscow would presumably feel impelled to act militarily once again to preserve its perceived vital interests. Its velvet glove contains an iron fist. To paraphrase what the Mexican dictator Porfirio Diaz once said of Mexico and the United States: "Poor Eastern Europe, so far from God, so close to the Soviet Union."

Moscow's toleration of polycentrism in Eastern Europe also received an assist in the 1960s and 1970s from the deepening Sino-Soviet rift. In addition to the rapprochement with Yugoslavia, the quest for a rationalization of economic relationships, and the spillover from its own internal decompression, Moscow sought Eastern Europe's support for its position in the quarrel with Beijing. Especially after the rupture with Albania in 1961, it permitted larger doses of autonomy in return for adherence to the Soviet line against China. Thus desatellitization has accompanied the end of monolithism in the bloc. The degree of polycentrism has varied from country to country, with Romania's assertiveness in foreign policy perhaps representing the most dramatic example of the utility of the Sino-Soviet rift to the emergence of nationalism and political assertiveness. In August 1980, another and potentially far more dangerous and complicated threat to the Soviet imperial system erupted in Poland.

Crisis in Poland

Events in 1956 had placed Soviet-Polish relations on a sound basis, but by the late 1960s, Gomulka's failure to generate economic growth and his crackdown on cultural and intellectual freedom led to new unrest. Steep increases in the price of food just before Christmas 1970 triggered a wave of strikes and violence at the Lenin shipyard in Gdansk and elsewhere. Edward Gierek took over, as Moscow watched but did nothing because Soviet-Polish relations were not affected, the party (Polish United Worker's Party or PUWP) remained in control, and discontent was directed inward and not against the Soviet Union or Poland's role in the Warsaw Pact.

Gierek kept power for a decade. His economic policy was to raise wages to mollify the workers, borrow heavily abroad to finance huge industrial projects that he hoped would produce goods for export to repay foreign loans, and tinker with cosmetic reforms in management-labor relations but retain firm party rule. By the mid-1970s, however, escalating costs of oil imports worsened the balance-of-payments situation; party privilege, corruption, and mismanagement of public enterprises alienated the working class; and poor grain harvests resulted in higher prices and a lower standard of living. In June 1976, strikes protesting the hike in food prices, especially of meat, resulted in arrests, repression, and further alienation of the proletariat from the party and government. Tensions simmered as the economic situation worsened. In mid-August 1980 price increases for meat again precipitated a wave of strikes, this time leading to major concessions—notably the government's agreement with the Gdansk shipyard workers led by Lech Walesa, an unemployed electrician who helped create Solidarity (the Independent Self-Governing Trade Unions) on August 31, 1980. In September, Stanislaw Kania, a moderate committed to "socialist renewal"[7] and a political solution "because no other means are available," replaced Gierek; in February 1981, General Wojciech Jaruzelski, the defense minister, was made prime minister. As the party lost ground to Solidarity, Jaruzelski gradually emerged as the regime's strongman.

Moscow viewed Solidarity as a threat. For the first time since 1956 it worried that Polish domestic turmoil might disrupt the Red Army's lines of communication to East Germany, spread to other parts of Eastern Europe, lead to escalated demands for reform and wrest control away from an indecisive party leadership, and even occasion serious disagreements in the Politburo over how best to proceed. At first, Moscow adopted a critical but cautious and multifaceted approach to Solidarity. Warning against "antisocialist" elements, it supported Kania's policy and extended more than $1 billion in credits and commodities, while taking steps within the bloc to pressure the Poles to keep their house in order. At the 26th congress of the CPSU in February 1981, Brezhnev cited Poland as an example of how "mistakes and miscalculations" in domestic policy give rise to conditions in which "opponents of socialism, supported by outside forces are, by stirring up anarchy, seeking to channel events into a counterrevolutionary course." But he gave no prescription for a solution, and the possibility of a Soviet military intervention loomed large, as the parallel between Poland in 1981 and Czechoslovakia in 1968 seemed self-evident.

Throughout the spring and summer, Soviet and Polish officials met frequently amidst increasing strains during which Solidarity and the Roman Catholic Church coalesced into a national force for democratization and for national as opposed to "socialist" renewal. While the Soviet media denounced Solidarity and Western "interference" and called on the PUWP to take a firm position, Warsaw Pact maneuvers along the Polish border intensified and signaled Moscow's possible resort to a military option. On May 13, 1981, an escaped Turkish criminal attempted to assassinate the Polish-born and immensely popular Pope John Paul II in front of the Vatican. Subsequent investigations have implicated the KGB, operating through Bulgarian officials.[8] The incident reflected the Kremlin's growing fear that an alliance between the working class and the Church would cripple party efforts to regain control of a deteriorating situation.

Before the PUWP congress in July 1981, held against Moscow's wishes, the central committee of the CPSU warned:

> As a result of the manifold activities of revisionists and opportunists and enemies of the Polish party, experienced activists fully dedicated to the party's cause and endowed with impeccable reputation and morality are being shunted aside. . . .
>
> We wish to say, in particular, that in recent months the forces of counterrevolution are actively disseminating anti-Sovietism of all kinds to

> wipe out all the results of the activity of our two parties and to revive nationalist and anti-Soviet feelings at various levels of Polish society. . . .
>
> Respected comrades, in addressing this letter to you, we are not guided solely by our concern over the situation of fraternal Poland, or the conditions and future prospects for Soviet-Polish cooperation. To no less an extent, we, like the other fraternal parties, are disturbed by the fact that the offensive by antisocialist enemy forces in Poland threatens the interests of our entire commonwealth, its cohesion, its integrity and the security of its borders—yes, our common security. Imperialist reaction is supporting and stimulating Polish counterrevolution. It does not hide its hope of thus changing in its favor the balance of power in Europe and in the world.[9]

At the congress, Kania changed personnel, introduced reforms to revamp the party, and gave repeated assurances of Poland's fealty to the Soviet Union and the socialist community.

In early September, at its national congress, Solidarity infuriated Moscow with a series of bold resolutions, especially one calling on the working class in other socialist countries to establish free trade unions. This resolution was passed by the militants who ignored pleas for restraint from moderates such as Lech Walesa. A few days later, the Polish government made public an ominous Soviet note saying that anti-Sovietism had reached "dangerous limits," that its main aim was to incite among Poles "hostility and hatred" of the Soviet Union, and that Solidarity "has become in effect a permanent tribune from which slanders and insults sounded against our state. The so-called message to the working people of Eastern Europe has become a revolting provocation."[10] On October 18, General Jaruzelski replaced Kania as first secretary of the PUWP. The penultimate step toward banning Solidarity had been taken. On the very next day, Jaruzelski convened the Military Council at the Ministry of Defense and instituted measures that deployed military units throughout the country to cope with the threats "to the country's internal life." On December 13, 1981, martial law was proclaimed, and Solidarity banned.

Moscow surmounted the dangerous Polish crisis, skillfully avoiding an open military intervention and forestalling a complete breakdown of civil order. Its undoubted connivance and cooperation facilitated Jaruzelski's well-planned and surgically executed police operation. Strategic control and the integrity of its imperial system were preserved, but the price has been high: a sullen population, which is hardly the stuff of which dependable allies are made; indeterminate subsidies for Poland's ailing economy; perennial nervousness over a possible spread of Polish disaffection; economic bottlenecks elsewhere in Eastern Europe because of reduced Polish exports of coal, sulfur, and selected industrial goods; and reliance for the first time on a military, rather than a party, leadership, which could itself become a problem if it looks more to Polish nationalism and a hybrid pluralism than to Soviet-approved "scientific socialism."

Poland remains a problem for Moscow. However, it has become manageable and far less dangerous in its potential for bloc disruptiveness than it was at the beginning of the 1980s. General Jaruzelski has stabilized his rule and has even acquired a measure of national acceptance, especially since the sweeping amnesty of September 1986. He has divided the opposition, permitted cultural liberalization, and improved relations with the Catholic Church, though not with the outlawed and much-weakened Solidarity movement. Still eluding him is a formula for revitalizing the economy and overcoming the widespread dispiritedness that permeates Polish society. Internationally, by 1987, he had normalized relations with the West (the United States lifted economic sanctions in February 1987) and gained admission to the International Monetary Fund, an important step toward reestablishing creditableness and rescheduling Poland's hard currency debt of more than $35 billion.

All this has been balm to Gorbachev, whose relationship with Jaruzelski is better than it is with any other bloc leader. Gorbachev's efforts to change Soviet society are followed very closely by the Poles, who vacillate between fears that the failure of his program could mean a return to a period of harsh controls and that its success might entail greater Soviet domination over Poland's stagnating economy. Symptomatic of Gorbachev's policy of *glasnost* (openness) and desire to place Soviet-Polish relations on a firmer footing is his willingness to deal more honestly with the seamy side of Stalin's treatment of the Poles in the 1937–1945 period. Gorbachev agreed to establish a joint commission that is to examine, among other events, the massacre in 1940 of Polish officers in the Katyn Forest, outside Smolensk. On the occasion of the 48th anniversary of the Nazi invasion of Poland, Jaruzelski—no doubt with Gorbachev's knowledge—criticized the USSR's collusion with Germany to partition Poland and its subsequent repression and deportation of thousands of Poles. The review of these searing emotional issues may be essential for Moscow's prospects of long-term reconciliation with Poland, an objective that is crucial for Gorbachev's success in fostering better relations within the bloc.

Gorbachev: A Study in Caution

Within months after Gorbachev came to power, two "debates" surfaced, reflecting uncertainty in the Kremlin over how to deal with Eastern Europe; one related to nationalism versus proletarian internationalism and the other to the Brezhnev Doctrine and future intrabloc discords.

On June 21, 1985, an article in *Pravda* by O. Vladimirov (a pseudonym for a high-ranking party official) deplored the persistence with which the nationalism and national interests of individual East European states complicated the joint struggle against imperialism, which, he said, is attempting "to weaken the alliance of fraternal countries, to alienate and isolate them from the USSR, and ultimately to attempt to secure an erosion and even a change of social system."[11] It stressed the need for bloc unity, which requires "a coordinated course" and "vigorous political cooperation," euphemisms for Soviet-preferred options.

A month later, *Kommunist,* the official party journal, published a virtual rejoinder by Oleg Bogomolov, a leading economist and director of a major research institute, whose views reflect Gorbachev's. Bogomolov argued the need for a differentiated approach. He noted that the individual socialist countries "are at different stages of economic development; have differing economic and political structures and traditions. As a result, the sum of their national and state interests cannot be completely identical."[12] Each country's own specific interests and priorities must be respected.

An even touchier problem was raised in September by Yuri Novopashin, a colleague of Bogomolov's. Writing in the journal *Rabochii klass i sovremennyi mir* (The Working Class and the Modern World), he questioned the validity "of the so-called Brezhnev Doctrine of the 'limited sovereignty' of the members of the Socialist community," noting that there is "no magic wand" that can eliminate "national egoism," on the one hand, or "great-power ambitions," on the other.[13] Three months later, on December 14, *Pravda* countered this view by drawing attention to the fifteenth anniversary of the Czechoslovak Central Committee's adoption of a document criticizing the "revisionist" and "counterrevolutionary" evils of the "Prague Spring" and upholding the principles underlying the Brezhnev Doctrine. The document, it noted, "reflects experience that goes beyond the bounds of what is specific and national," and is still valid.

Gorbachev did not address the issue at the CPSU's twenty-seventh congress in February 1986, but in late June, at the Polish party's congress, he sounded a familiar Brezhnevian refrain: Asserting that socialism is irreversible, he said, "it manifests itself as an alliance of countries closely linked by political, economic, cultural, and defense interests. To threaten the socialist system, to try to undermine it from outside and wrench a country away from the socialist community means to encroach not only on the will of the people, but also on the entire postwar arrangements and, in the last analysis, on peace."[14] In his speech on November 2, 1987, commemorating the 70th anniversary of the Bolshevik Revolution, Gorbachev lauded the socialist camp "in all its national and social variation" as "good and useful," and stressed that "we have become convinced that unity does not mean being identical or uniform." He set forth five principles for regulating relations among socialist countries:

> These are unconditional and total equality; the responsibility of the ruling party for affairs in its state, and for patriotic service to its people; concern for the general cause of socialism, respect for one another, a serious attitude toward what has been achieved and tried out by friends; voluntary and varied cooperation; and the strict observation by all of the principles of peaceful coexistence. The practice of socialist internationalism rests upon these.[15]

No crisis threatening Soviet military-political hegemony over the bloc has yet faced Gorbachev, so it remains unknown how he would translate these principles into practice. For the moment, he has permitted each leadership to chart its own path toward economic reform and, more importantly, to determine the outcome of the succession struggles underway among the aging generation of Eastern European leaders without direct interference from Moscow.

The first turnover of power occurred in Czechoslovakia in December 1987, when Gustav Husak, who was installed after the Soviet invasion in August 1968, stepped down at age 75 in favor of his deputy, Milos Jakes, who is a decade younger and reputed to be just as orthodox in outlook. In Hungary, the 76-year-old Kadar presides over an economy that, once the envy of the bloc, is now in deep trouble. With a massive foreign debt, growing difficulty in selling its industrial products in Western markets, sagging agricultural prices, and flagging innovation and efficiency, the economic and political liberalization of the 1970s ("Kadarism") seems to have reached the limits of what the system will tolerate. In the worst plight is tightly-controlled, Stalinist Romania, where the maverick Nicolae Ceauşescu shows no interest in reform, notwithstanding rapidly deteriorating economic conditions and spreading unrest, the bitter harvest of grandiose, unproductive industrial investments in the 1970s. The cool reception accorded Gorbachev's call for reform when he visited Bucharest in April 1987 attested to Ceauşescu's intention of carrying on as usual, if his circumstances permit. Even Bulgaria and East Germany, both relatively prosperous and loyal to Moscow, are chary of reform. Their septuagenarian rulers—Todor Zhivkov and Erich Honecker, respectively—fear *perestroika's* unanticipated consequences and prefer to wait until more is known about its effects in the Soviet Union. None of the foregoing suggests that Gorbachev is ready to force the pace of change in Eastern Europe.

Institutionalizing Soviet Hegemony

To promote bloc cohesion and integration, the Soviet Union relies on a number of multilateral institutions, most notably the Warsaw Treaty Organization (WTO; more commonly referred to as the Warsaw Pact) and the Council for Mutual Economic Assistance (Comecon). The Warsaw Pact was created on May 14, 1955, the day before the signing of the Austrian state treaty. Moscow decided that it needed a formal alliance binding the bloc together. In shifting from an exclusive reliance on bilateralism to a heavy emphasis on multilateralism, it was motivated by several aims. The first and most immediate, given the imminence of the treaty with Austria, was to find a way to legitimize the continued presence in Hungary and Romania of the Soviet troops, until then justified on the basis of assuring lines of communication for Soviet occupation forces in Austria. The second, after Moscow had failed to prevent the FRG's rearmament and formal entry into NATO on May 9, 1955, was to carry through on its previously announced intention to have Soviet-bloc countries "take common measures for the organization of armed forces and their commands," and to create a counterpart to NATO. Third, Moscow wanted an effective instrument for safeguarding its interests in the area.

From the beginning, political objectives were paramount—witness that the first joint military exercises were not held until late 1961. The WTO's Political Consultative Committee, responsible for coordinating all but purely military matters, was inactive in the early years, but took on added importance after the 1968 Czech crisis, since which time Moscow has kept more than 80,000 troops in the country. In November 1976, it established a Committee of Foreign Ministers and a Unified Secretariat in order to improve "the mechanism of political collaboration."

Though formally a military alliance protecting the bloc against external threats, the Warsaw Pact mainly serves an intrabloc policing function. It is also used by Moscow to pressure a reluctant member to go along with the consensus view, to persuade bloc members to join with it in isolating a dissident member (for instance, excluding Albania from participation because of its pro-Beijing policies from 1961 to 1978), to rebut Chinese accusations that the USSR is a disintegrating rather than integrating influence within the Communist world, to keep East European ethnic tensions in check, and to encourage a sense of common interest among the members.

The military objectives of the Warsaw Pact, though subordinate, are substantial. They include organizing Eastern Europe as a defensive buffer zone against a possible invasion from the West, extending the Soviet air defense system as far west of the Soviet homeland as possible, serving as an offensive prod against NATO in the event of a war in Europe, creating military forces loyal to the Communist regimes, and promoting bloc unity through standardization of weaponry, tactical coordination, and interlocking command structures. A considerable professional interaction among the officer corps also reinforces their sense of community as members of an alliance system.

In recent years, however, some Western assessments have questioned the extent to which the Warsaw Pact has evolved into a conventional alliance or can be considered by Moscow as a reliable instrument of policy. The erosion of Soviet authority, the use of the alliance to suppress the reform movement in Czechoslovakia in 1968 and to threaten an intervention against Poland in 1980–1981, the greatly diminished perception in Eastern Europe of threat from NATO, and the growing Soviet pressure for increased defense expenditures at a time of economic austerity all have contributed to a sense of "bloc fatigue" and have complicated Soviet management of the Warsaw Pact.

In its quest for improved military effectiveness and integration, the Soviet Union finds Romania a persistently troublesome stumbling block. Since 1966, when he proposed that the position of commander-in-chief of Warsaw Pact forces be rotated and that the East European members be consulted on decisions affecting the use of nuclear weapons, Ceauşescu has opposed larger military spending and argued that it would adversely affect his country's socioeconomic development; and he has moved steadily to reduce Romania's military participation. Not only did Ceauşescu refuse to join the invasion of Czechoslovakia and publicly condemn the action as a "flagrant transgression" and contradiction "to the fundamental standards concerning relations that must reign among socialist countries and among Communist parties and of generally recognized principles of international law," but since 1972 he has withdrawn from joint military maneuvers and has had Romanian representatives at WTO meetings maintain a relatively inactive role. Since 1978 the Romanian leadership, while reaffirming its adherence to the Pact's defensive purposes, has not allowed Romanian troops to be used outside of the territory of the Romanian state. Furthermore, there have been no major Warsaw Pact maneuvers on Romanian territory for a number of years.

Moscow has so far acted with remarkable restraint. It permits Romania to prevent full military integration because there is no serious NATO force on the "southern tier" Balkan flank and also because it has no fear of liberalization occurring in Romania. For the moment, imposing a greater degree of military cohesion would only jeopardize the long-term viability of the alliance. So Moscow continues to be patient.

The Pact was renewed in April 1985 for twenty years on the same terms as before, ensuring continued Soviet hegemony. Notwithstanding periodic strains with the East Europeans over such issues as burden-sharing, weapons development, and alliance cohesion, Moscow considers WTO's very existence effective in putting members on notice of the Soviet Union's determination to remain in the region indefinitely. The ultimate question concerning the Warsaw Pact is how reliable would the East European forces be in the event of a war in Europe? A great deal would depend on the kind of war and the circumstances under which it began. However, judging by the USSR's difficulties in fashioning agreement on basic issues, the thin crust on which the legitimacy of Communist regimes stands, the pervasive suspicion of Moscow that permeates public perceptions in Eastern Europe, and the unwillingness of Soviet leaders to decrease their force levels significantly in the area, the Pact's future must be a matter of continuing concern in the Kremlin. One is reminded of Winston Churchill's prophetic comment to de Gaulle in November 1944: "At present, Russia is a great beast which has been starved for a long time. It is not possible to keep her from eating, especially since she now lies in the middle of the herd of her victims. But after the meal comes the digestion period. When it is time to digest, the Russians will have their difficult moments. . . ."[16]

Moscow has used Comecon to promote economic integration and thereby political stability and institutionalization of its authority in the bloc. Originally established in January 1949 as a symbolic facade to parallel the Marshall Plan and as an instrument of boycott against Yugoslavia, Comecon was for many years a moribund organization. Under Stalin, there was no necessity for an effective regional organization; the USSR was in physical control and preferred to maximize its exploitation on a bilateral basis. It felt no need to rationalize the Soviet–East European economic relationship.

Starting under Khrushchev in 1955, Comecon went through a period of gradual upgrading: information was pooled, economic agreements were placed on a five-year instead of a one-year basis, and an atmosphere of bargaining replaced that of acquiescence. On December 14, 1959, Comecon adopted a charter (heavily amended in December 1962 and June 1974) defining its purposes and organizational structure. Standing commissions deal with a wide range of subjects, from electric power and nuclear energy to financial problems and transportation. In institutional terms, Comecon came of age in the 1960s, but actual integration has proceeded very slowly.

At Khrushchev's behest, in June 1962 a programmatic document, "The Basic Principles of the International Socialist Division of Labor," was adopted. In November Khrushchev pushed for a supranational entity capable of rationalizing and transforming the economies of the bloc:

> We must move more boldly toward establishing a single planning agency for all countries that belong to the Council for Mutual Economic Assistance. This planning agency should be empowered to draw up joint plans and settle organizational questions so as to coordinate the development of the countries of the socialist system.[17]

But his optimism and drive were not enough to overcome the legacy of autarky-oriented economies that Stalin had imposed on the East European countries, or the opposition of the Romanians, who did not want to abandon major industrial projects. The technological backwardness that made most East Europeans feel that the plan for division of labor was intended to keep them in an inferior position to the Soviet Union was also a stumbling block. The kind of cooperation that Khrushchev envisaged implied a sense of genuine community, which did not exist.

There were many other reasons for Khrushchev's failure. First, the idea of a supranational organization was perceived in Eastern Europe as entailing a surrender of newly regained national prerogatives to the USSR. The countries of the area were still in the early stages of their existence as nation-states, and for them, nationalism was (and is) a positive force. Second, bureaucratic vested interests resisted the retooling and dismantling of national economic institutions. Further, they lacked the sense of shared trust and commitment to rely on their counterparts for fulfillment of national economic targets. The East Europeans mistrusted not only the Soviet Union, but each other. There is no love of neighbors in the area, which remains a cauldron of ethnic animosities. (The West's common suspicion of the USSR tends to make them overlook this aspect of East European reality.) Finally, the heterogeneity of Eastern Europe, with its different levels of economic, industrial, technological, and educational development, heightened protectionist attitudes and militated against meaningful multilateralism.

After several years of drift, Moscow's determination to promote economic interdependence in the "socialist commonwealth" (a concept popularized by Khrushchev) was renewed. Comecon has had some successes—the Druzhba (Friendship) oil pipeline, an electrical power grid system, and a pool of rolling stock—but basic planning, investment, production, and pricing patterns have not easily been reshaped. In derision of integration, this Hungarian joke made the rounds: The Comecon countries, wanting a common emblem to signify their unity and fraternity, adopted a flag with a red field in which there were seven lean cows milking one another.

In July 1971 Comecon adopted a twenty-year blueprint for integration, albeit within the existing sovereign nation-state system. Moscow was serious about the Comprehensive Program and insisted that it be accorded the status of a multilateral treaty. The Program postulates cooperation in drafting five-year economic plans, joint planning, a convertible ruble for making commercial transactions in the bloc easier, pooling of research and productive capacities, cost-sharing for the development of energy resources, and raising the standard of living of less-developed members. However, fundamental problems continue, such as the absence of a supranational authority, the reliance on consensus-building, and the indefiniteness in the statutes about implementing recommendations.[18]

In June 1984, at the first summit since 1969 of Comecon members (the USSR, Bulgaria, Czechoslovakia, the German Democratic Republic, Hungary, Poland, Romania, Cuba, Mongolia, and Vietnam), Moscow indicated a continued willingness to meet members' needs for imported energy and raw materials, but, in return, it stipulated that they provide consumer goods and machinery "of a high quality and world technical level"; and that they contribute more investment and labor for the development of Soviet resources. It called for greater coordination of economic plans, especially in the fields of microprocessors, robotics, and energy conservation. Gorbachev wants the East European countries to live up to their economic commitments—repaying debts and expanding exports to the USSR, thereby redressing the chronic imbalance that has existed in their trade relationships since the mid-1970s. The promotion of multilateral enterprises, which began late in the Brezhnev era, is still inhibited by interference from central administrative bodies. Accordingly, the ambitious multilateralization implicit in the 1971 Comprehensive Program has given way to greater reliance on traditional bilateral relationships. Before Soviet-bloc integration can match Western Europe's, Moscow will have to overcome, (1) Eastern Europe's suspicion that integration will weaken their national sovereignties and bring a new, disguised form of Soviet interference; (2) regional differences in levels of economic development and each country's desire to industrialize; (3) the desire to insulate national economies from disruptive price competition; and (4) the persistence of political over economic factors in shaping policies toward Comecon.

How stable is Soviet rule in Eastern Europe? Notwithstanding the impressive array of military, economic, political, and ideological arrangements that Moscow uses to perpetuate its strategic control, it must remain very watchful. As one wit observed, the Soviet Union is the only Communist country surrounded by hostile Communist states. The centrifugal forces—nationalism, neorevisionist national communism, slothful economies that consume more than they produce, sociocultural alienation, demands for human rights in accordance with the provisions of the 1975 Helsinki Conference on Security and Cooperation in Europe, and the weakening ideological vigilance of increasingly nationalistic party elites—

are a constant worry. On the other hand, Moscow can look with some confidence to the centripetal forces to keep Eastern Europe securely in the Soviet orbit.

First and most unequivocally, the presence of approximately thirty Soviet divisions in East Germany, Poland, Hungary, and Czechoslovakia acts as a constant reminder of Moscow's limited tolerance for dissidence and of its capacity to settle any crisis with dispatch. Not only has the USSR shown its readiness to use force to suppress threats to "socialism", but the nations of Eastern Europe know that no help will come from the West. Militarily, Moscow has a free hand to maintain hegemony over the bloc. The constraints on its use of force are internal and bloc-derived.

Second, and of growing importance, Eastern Europe's dependence on Soviet energy and raw materials has increased enormously, and its more active participation in Comecon may well be the sine qua non for continued Soviet assistance. Ever since the energy crisis exploded on the international scene in the mid-1970s, Eastern Europe's economic situation has worsened. Except for Romania, the area is energy poor. By contrast, the USSR is the world's largest producer of oil and natural gas. Since 1975, Moscow has begun to raise the prices of oil and raw materials; it is no longer willing to give its East European partners concessionary benefits. Moscow has told the East Europeans that if they want assured supplies in the future, they must invest in the development of Soviet resources or look elsewhere. No longer will the Soviet Union play the role of a colony to Eastern Europe. This has led the East Europeans to invest in some Soviet projects: the 1800-mile Bratstvo (Brotherhood) natural-gas line from Orenburg in the Ural Mountains to Uzhgorod on the Czech border; a huge cellulose plant in Siberia that will provide paper; an asbestos complex at Kiyembayevski; and a large nuclear power station in the Ukraine, planned to have four 1000-megawatt plants. In addition, rising energy costs mean that many East European manufactures are even less competitive than before on world markets, making sales to the USSR imperative; and Moscow is beginning to balk at the shoddy goods that it freely accepted in the past. Economic necessity may well prompt the East Europeans to reassess more favorably the definite advantages that they derive from Comecon, and from the Soviet Union in particular. If they wish to receive continued preferential treatment—especially in the energy field (even Romania now has to import crude petroleum from the USSR)—and cushion the projected downturn in their rate of growth, they will have to accede to Soviet insistence on closer coordination of the planning process, increased specialization, greater investment in the Soviet energy sector, and expanded transfers of technology.

Third, the fears of the individual East European leaderships bind them to a policy of friendship with the Soviet Union. The Poles' phobia is of another Soviet-German deal at their expense, the GDR worries about a Rapallo-type accord between Moscow and Bonn, Romania dreads an imposed return of its part of Transylvania to Hungary, and so on. Discord among nationalities, a potentially explosive brew, lends credence to the Soviet Union's claim that its policy contributes to the maintenance of peace and stability in Eastern Europe.

Fourth, a generation of party—military—secret police cadres has acquired a stake in the political status quo. They know their regimes ultimately depend on Moscow's friendship, and therefore they pay ritualistic tribute to Marxist-Leninist internationalism to mollify the Kremlin. At the same time, they try to mobilize popular support in order to obtain internal acceptance of their authoritarian regimes.

Finally, there is that least reliable unifying cohesive, ideology—or Moscow's interpretation of what it is at any given moment. It legitimizes Soviet policies, but cannot be counted on for inoculative potency against the virus of nationalism or polycentric communism. When applied to domestic issues, ideology is in many respects nothing more than a fig leaf, a flimsy cover for pretended unity, not a guide to problem-solving or political bargaining within the bloc.

Eastern Europe is destined to remain the USSR's Achilles' heel. Soviet leaders would prefer to prevent crises and not have to suppress them. While recognizing and wishing to avoid the prohibitive costs of a return to Stalinist methods, they must at the same time minimize the contradictions of policies established by Khrushchev—decentralization, diversity, and consumerism, which contain within them the seeds of rampant nationalism, incipient anticommunism, and cynicism toward ideology. Their policy is geared toward reinforcing mutual dependencies and transmuting them into a genuine interdependency that will assure Soviet strategic interests and promote bloc cohesion. Barring serious instability in the USSR, there is no real threat on the horizon to the preeminent Soviet position in Eastern Europe. Moscow is willing to bear the costly burdens of its imperial system because the uncertain consequences of any significant pullback or restructuring of the relationship with Eastern Europe are regarded as far more dangerous to the Soviet Union itself than muddling along.

Notes

1. Department of State, *Soviet Affairs Notes,* No. 224 (July 28, 1958) Washington, D.C.), 3.
2. N. S. Khrushchev, Report of the Central Committee of the Communist Party

of the Soviet Union to the 20th Party Congress (Moscow: Foreign Languages Publishing House, 1956), 41–42, excerpts.

3. *New York Times,* December 3, 1959.

4. Department of State, *Soviet Affairs Notes,* No. 224, 4.

5. Pedro Ramet, "Soviet-Yugoslav Relations Since 1976," *Survey,* Vol. 26, No. 2 (Spring 1982), 68–69.

6. Karen Dawisha, "Soviet Security and the Role of the Military: The 1968 Czechoslovak Crisis," *British Journal of Political Science,* Vol. 10 (1980), 343.

7. Martin Myant, *Poland: A Crisis for Socialism* (London: Lawrence and Wishart, 1982), 141.

8. Two well-documented studies implicating the KGB are Paul B. Henze, *The Plot to Kill the Pope* (New York: Scribner's, 1983) and Claire Sterling, *The Time of the Assassins* (New York: Holt, Rinehart & Winston, 1983).

9. *New York Times,* June 11, 1981.

10. *New York Times,* September 19, 1981.

11. *Pravda,* June 21, 1985.

12. Elizabeth Teague, "*Kommunist* Speaks Out in Defense of East Europe's National Interests," *Radio Liberty* RL 262/85 (August 12, 1985), 5.

13. Elizabeth Teague, "Soviet Author Repudiates 'Brezhnev Doctrine,'" Radio Liberty RL 4/86 (December 20, 1985), 1.

14. *New York Times,* July 2, 1986.

15. FBIS/SOV, November 3, 1987, 60.

16. John Lukacs, *A History of the Cold War,* 3rd ed. (New York: Doubleday, 1966), 250.

17. *Pravda,* November 20, 1962.

18. George Ginsburgs, "Unification of Law in the Socialist Commonwealth: The Implications of the 20-Year Comprehensive Programme of Economic Integration," in Donald D. Barry et al. (eds.), *Codification in the Communist World* (Leiden: A. W. Sijthoff, 1975), 123–44.

Selected Bibliography

BRZEZINSKI, ZBIGNIEW K. *The Soviet Bloc: Unity and Conflict,* Rev. ed. Cambridge: Harvard University Press, 1967.

DAWISHA, KAREN. *The Kremlin and Prague Spring.* Berkeley: University of California Press, 1984.

DAWISHA, KAREN. *Eastern Europe, Gorbachev and Reform: The Great Challenge.* New York: Cambridge University Press, 1988

GATI, CHARLES. *Hungary and the Soviet Bloc.* Durham: Duke University Press, 1986.

HOLLOWAY, DAVID and JANE M. O. SHARP (EDS.). *The Warsaw Pact: Alliance in Transition?* Ithaca: Cornell University Press, 1984.

HUTCHINGS, ROBERT L. *Soviet-East European Relations: Consolidation and Conflict, 1968–1980.* Madison: University of Wisconsin Press, 1984.

JONES, CHRISTOPHER. *Soviet Influence in Eastern Europe.* New York: Praeger, 1981.

MIĆUNOVIĆ, VELJKO. *Moscow Diary.* Garden City, N.Y.: Doubleday, 1980.

REMINGTON, ROBIN A. *The Warsaw Pact.* Cambridge: MIT Press, 1972.

STEHLE, HANAJAKOB. *Eastern Politics of the Vatican, 1917–1979.* Athens: Ohio University Press, 1981.

TERRY, SARAH (ED.). *Soviet Policy in Eastern Europe.* New Haven: Yale University Press, 1984.

VALENTA, JIRI. *Soviet Intervention in Czechoslovakia, 1968.* Baltimore: Johns Hopkins University Press, 1979.

VALI, FERENC. *Rift and Revolt in Hungary.* Cambridge: Harvard University Press, 1961.

VAN BRABANT, JOZEF M. *Socialist Economic Integration.* New York: Cambridge University Press, 1980.

VOLYGES, IVAN. *The Political Reliability of the Warsaw Pact Armies.* Durham: Duke Press Policy Studies, 1982.

WETTIG, GERHARD. *Community and Conflict in the Socialist Camp: The Soviet Union, East Germany and the German Problem 1965–1972.* New York: St. Martin's Press, 1975.

WOZNIUK, VLADIMIR. *From Crisis to Crisis: Soviet-Polish Relations in the 1970s.* Ames: Iowa State University Press, 1987.

6
Soviet Policy Toward Western Europe

find finlandization

For generations, Russian leaders have seen Europe as "the most important peninsula in the Eurasian continent" and believed that it is their continent and "that they have the right to be politically predominant in the European area."[1] The expansion of Soviet military power into the center of Europe after 1945 gave rise to the Cold War and a permanent threat to the nations of Western Europe. Yet despite the USSR's sustained military buildup and forward deployment of conventional forces far beyond what might be presumed necessary to assure control of Eastern Europe or deter an attack by NATO, Moscow is not aiming at an all-out war. Its sights are on hegemony in Eastern Europe and influence in Western Europe.

In the early post–World War II years, Moscow's objectives in Western Europe were subordinated to its East European policy and the demands of internal reconstruction, even though in the process Stalin aroused a sorely weakened and vulnerable Western Europe and an America intent on a return to normalcy to undertake a collective defense that he had hoped to forestall. Stalin was especially interested in the future disposition of Germany. The Soviet Union initially favored an exploitative and Carthaginian solution to the German problem: extensive reparations; the cession of territory east of the Oder and Neisse rivers to Poland as compensation for the USSR's absorption of eastern Poland; the expulsion of twelve million Germans from Eastern Europe; and the establishment of a Moscow-controlled Communist party in the Soviet-occupied part of Germany. However, by mid-1946 it had adopted a more conciliatory position, seeking to obtain a choice in the management of the Ruhr and to disrupt the West's decision to include Germany's economy in its effort to promote overall West European recovery.

During the tense years of 1947, 1948, and 1949, Stalin's imperial strategy crystallized in the establishment of the Cominform, the Communist takeover of Czechoslovakia, the Berlin blockade, and the Sovietization of Eastern Europe. Unable to prevent the creation of NATO, Moscow played on European fears of a militaristic and revanchist Germany, hoping to forestall the Federal Republic's rearmament under U.S. auspices. In a diplomatic note to the Western powers on March 10, 1952, Stalin went so far as to propose a peace treaty and Germany's reunification as a neutral state; but this was very likely a ploy to kill West Germany's integration into the Western military alliance rather than a serious proposal for fundamentally restructuring the polarized alignments that gave Moscow a hegemony in middle Europe. The proposal implied that Moscow had "doubts about the long-term viability of the East German regime" and hoped to be "compensated for the loss of East Germany with a greater Soviet voice in the affairs of a united Germany—in short, the advantage of what later came to be called 'Finlandization'"; Moscow hoped to ease tensions, but within a framework that would at the same time assure Soviet military preeminence on the continent.[2] Even in retrospect it is difficult to take Stalin's proposal seriously: a unified—possibly Communist—Germany could only be a Soviet planner's nightmare, a threat not only to the imperium in Eastern Europe but also to the USSR itself.

Under Khrushchev, the Soviet leadership ushered in an era notable for its flexible and differentiated approach to Western Europe. A mixture of blandishment, pressure, bargaining, and growing military power, Soviet policy has shown remarkable persistence and continuity in its tactically versatile pursuit of key objectives. In general, the USSR seeks (1) to sow and exploit discord between the countries of Western Europe and the United States and among NATO members, and not to dominate Western Europe as it does Eastern Europe; (2) to foster its security, which it believes lies in a weakened West and retention of a favorable balance of power, rather than physical expansion of Soviet power beyond the present confines of the Warsaw Pact; (3) to improve relations with the Federal Republic of Germany, while maintaining control over the German Democratic Republic; (4) to increase the political, economic, and military leverage that it can bring to bear on concrete issues; and (5) to induce docility rather than strike for dominion.

If Moscow does indeed have a long-term political strategy for an ideal relationship with the countries of Western Europe, it could be that frequently referred to as "Finlandization."[3] With due apologies to the Finns, the term is commonly understood to signify a process whereby the Soviet Union influences the domestic and foreign policy behavior of non-Communist countries so that they voluntarily follow policies congenial to or approved by the Soviet Union. It is a policy of special constraints where

Soviet interests and preferences are involved, in which governments are overly careful beforehand in dealing with the Soviet Union and in acting on issues of special interest to Moscow. Specifically, Finlandization may be said to have a number of characteristics: (1) responsiveness—in foreign policy to Soviet preferences and concerns; (2) avoidance of alliances with countries the Soviet Union deems to be competitors or rivals, or restrictions on the policies of the alliance to become what is considered nonprovocative to the USSR; (3) acceptance of Soviet interpretations of neutrality in peace or war; (4) accommodation to Soviet power that limits one's response to threatening Soviet policies; (5) restraint over the media in one's country to muffle or minimize criticism of the USSR, so as to avoid provocation; and (6) openness to penetration by Soviet ideas and media. Over the years, Moscow has cited the "broad international significance" of Soviet-Finnish relations, but the essence of what constitutes a "Finlandized" state varies from relationship to relationship.

Moscow and the FRG

For more than a century, Moscow has alternated between fascination with and fear of German discipline, drive, efficiency, and technology. The revival of German military power is a cause of constant Soviet concern. In 1954, an article in *Kommunist,* the journal of the CPSU, charged that to realize its "aggressive plans," the United States needed "a powerful, well-trained land army in Europe equipped with the latest weapons" and therefore had initiated German rearmament in order to make West Germany "into an obedient instrument of its aggressive policy, into a mailed fist that would be directed against the Soviet Union and the People's Democracies and at the same time be used to subject NATO to United States control." This Soviet interpretation had not changed fundamentally.

From 1955 on, the Soviet Union sought Western acceptance of the territorial status quo in Europe, recognition of the division of Germany and the legitimacy of the GDR, a weakening of ties between West Berlin and the FRG, and a minimal level of rearmament by the Federal Republic. To prod the West on these issues, Khrushchev decided to aggravate the Berlin problem. On November 27, 1958, he provoked a minicrisis, insisting that West Berlin be set up as a "free" city, guaranteed by the four occupying powers and the two existing German states, and that the Western powers withdraw from the city. Khrushchev's pseudoultimatum was extended for almost three years, as the Soviet government avoided any precipitous action; there was petty harassment of traffic from the Federal Republic to West Berlin, but no repeat of the 1948 blockade as the West held firm. Frustrated and in need of some visible sign of achievement to still his critics in the Kremlin—and to help East Germany party boss Walter Ulbricht, whose regime was hemorrhaging from the flight of refugees, most of whom were skilled workers essential to economic development—he agreed to a politically humiliating but extremely effective move. On August, 13, 1961, without warning, workers put up the Berlin wall, physically sealing off the two sectors of the city. A monument to Communist weakness, it helped Ulbricht and permitted Khrushchev to save face. The crisis petered out, especially after the upturn in Soviet-American relations that followed the Cuban missile crisis of October 1962, and ended on June 12, 1964, when the Soviet Union and the GDR signed a twenty-year treaty of friendship. The treaty was reassurance for Ulbricht, who had feared a Soviet deal with Bonn at his expense. But more important, by ending the Berlin crisis, Moscow was able to proceed on a new tack toward Western Europe.

Within hours after Ulbricht had signed the treaty and left Moscow, Khrushchev held a talk with the ambassador from the Federal Republic to discuss a new Soviet policy and a proposed visit to Bonn. Aware of the advantages of improved bilateral relationships with key Western countries, Khrushchev aimed for greater influence on FRG politics, particularly for arms limitation and nuclear abnegation. He believed that a major Soviet initiative could aggravate intra-NATO tensions and prevent the FRG from acquiring control of or developing nuclear weapons, and he hoped to use the specter of Rapallo to extract concessions from the FRG's allies, particularly France. His son-in-law, Alexei Adzhubei, traveled to Bonn in July, and in the following month Khrushchev announced his intention to visit. However, two months later he was deposed by his closest associates—some speculate because of his German policy, though more likely it was because of domestic issues.

By 1966, after having assessed the situation themselves, Khrushchev's successors adopted his line and explored ways of improving Soviet-FRG relations. They dropped the "demand" for a German peace treaty, kept Berlin quiet, stressed the need for a European security treaty without offering details, and permitted the repatriation of many Soviet citizens of German origin (a decision that had been made by Khrushchev). At the twenty-third congress of the CPSU in March and April 1966, Foreign Minister Andrei Gromyko declared that "the normalization and improvement of relations with the Federal Republic of Germany" depended, in effect on the Bonn government's renouncing nuclear weapons and accepting the existing frontiers of all states in Europe. He also called for a European security conference. The matter dragged on inconclusively until after the Soviet occupation of Czechoslovakia in August 1968, when polemics in the Soviet media against the Federal Republic dropped sharply as Moscow hinted at a desire to continue the talks. The discussions were given new impetus in March 1969, when the Soviet ambassador in Bonn pointedly briefed the government about the Chinese "aggression" on the Ussuri River; faced with tension in the East, Moscow again signaled that it desired normalization in the West.

Soviet overtures received a welcome reception in Bonn with the coming to power of the Social Democratic party (SPD) in October 1969. SPD Chancellor Willy Brandt's *Ostpolitik* meshed with Brezhnev's *Westpolitik*. Convinced that reunification was unlikely in the foreseeable future and desirous of easing the situation of West Berliners, reducing the hostility between the FRG and the GDR, and opening the way for better relations with Eastern Europe, Brandt abandoned Bonn's previous insistence on reunification and expressed a willingness to recognize the territorial and political status quo in Europe. On November 28, 1969, the Federal Republic signed the nonproliferation treaty, renouncing any right to acquire, develop, or use nuclear weapons. On December 7, 1969, at Brandt's initiative, talks opened in Moscow on renouncing the use or threat of force between the two countries; and on February 1, 1970, the FRG and the Soviet Union reached a major economic agreement under which the FRG agreed to provide 1.2 million tons of large-diameter pipes on favorable terms financed by a consortium of German banks, in return for which the Soviet Union was to deliver natural gas over a twenty-year period starting in 1973. Key Soviet military, political, and economic objectives were within reach.

The capstone of the Soviet diplomatic strategy was the treaty signed in Moscow on August 12, 1970, in which the USSR and the FRG agreed to settle their disputes by peaceful means. The treaty further stipulated that the two parties (1) "undertake to respect without restriction the territorial integrity of all States in Europe within their present frontiers"; (2) "declare that they have no territorial claims against anybody nor will assert such claims in the future"; and (3) "regard today and shall in future regard the frontiers of all States in Europe as inviolable such as they are on the date of signature of the present Treaty, including the Oder-Neisse line which forms the western frontier of the People's Republic of Poland and the frontier between the Federal Republic of Germany, and the Democratic Republic." For Moscow, the treaty meant that the Federal Republic accepted the division of Germany, the reality of the GDR, and the renunciation of nuclear weapons; it was the augury—and essential precursor—of what Moscow was to achieve at Helsinki five years later, namely, Western recognition of Soviet hegemony in Central and Eastern Europe; and it accelerated the acquisition of advanced technology and extensive credits from the FRG—an objective that was increasingly important for Moscow.

Brandt's only condition for satisfying Soviet desires was an acceptable arrangement for West Berlin. After very difficult negotiations lasting from March 1970 to August 1971, the four powers—the Soviet Union, the United States, France, and Britain—signed an agreement that went a long way toward improving the condition of the West Berliners. Unimpeded civilian transit traffic to West Berlin, which is situated 110 miles inside the GDR, from the Federal Republic by road, rail, and waterways was assured; West Berlin could maintain its special relationship with, but not be part of, the FRG; and the West Berliners were to be granted easier access to visit family in the GDR.

That Moscow was keen on Brandt's *Ostpolitik* was evident; in May 1971, it forced the old-guard and antiaccommodationist Walter Ulbricht to resign from the party secretaryship (he died on August 1, 1973) and replaced him with the more compliant Erich Honecker, who was prepared to subordinate the GDR's long-term aims and make concessions to Bonn's demands on the West Berlin issue. By implication, the USSR eschewed the use of the city's vulnerability as a lever against the FRG. However, between treaties and practices there is many a slip. In miniviolations of the 1971 four-power agreement, East Germany has made frequent demonstrations of military power in East Berlin, with Soviet approval. It has elected representatives from East Berlin to the GDR parliament, and it has periodically interfered with transit traffic between the FRG and West Berlin. The Cold War rivalry over Germany has not ended; it has merely become more subtle. For the foreseeable future, we can expect that Moscow will continue to downgrade the GDR's political goals in order to increase its standing in Bonn and to exploit intra-NATO conflicts.

Economic cooperation with the Federal Republic is also important to the Soviet Union (as well as to the GDR, which received about $4 billion from Bonn during the 1971-to-1982 period for the construction of new roads and bridges on the transit route from the FRG through East German territory to West Berlin). By 1978, the FRG had become the USSR's leading non-Communist trading partner and source of high-technology imports. Soviet imports include a vast iron and steel complex, turbines and large-diameter pipe for the 3500-mile natural-gas pipeline from the Yamal Peninsula of Western Siberia to Eastern Europe and the FRG, electronic equipment for petrochemical plants, trucks, and heavy machinery. Most of this has been financed by long-term German credits, estimated at upwards of $10 billion, and cemented by economic agreements that run to the end of the century. During Brezhnev's visits to the Federal Republic in 1973, 1978 and 1981, discussions of economic relations figured prominently.

A harsh tone entered the political relationship in December 1979, when Bonn agreed to the stationing of Pershing-II and cruise intermediate range missiles as part of the two-track decision adopted at the NATO ministerial meeting. The Soviet invasion of Afghanistan that month and the eruption of the Polish crisis the following summer exacerbated the situation. However, Bonn resisted U.S. pressure to curtail economic ties, rejecting "the use of negative levers—particular sanctions—against the USSR. This is partly the result of German historical experience, which suggests that the USSR is unlikely to alter its political behavior on significant issues."[4] The Germans remain skeptical of the notion of linkage on substantive issues.

The political bitterness increased when the social democratic coalition of Helmut Schmidt, whose party had ushered in the Soviet–West German détente of the 1970s, was toppled in late 1982 by a center-right coalition headed by Helmut Kohl and his Christian Democratic Party; and when Moscow blatantly though unsuccessfully tried to affect the outcome of the March 1983 general elections by siding with the social democrats and the peace movement in an attempt to derail the scheduled delivery of the first contingent of missiles, which started arriving on schedule in December 1983. Moscow pulled out all the propaganda stops to help the peace movement, stoking old fears of German militarism and revanchism, raising the spectre of a new arms race, and playing on West European uneasiness about West Germany's growing power—all to no avail. The failure to prevent the deployment was a major setback for Yuri Andropov, who had succeeded Brezhnev on the latter's death in November 1982.

The chill that permeated Soviet–West German relations did not end until July 1986, when Gorbachev received FRG Foreign Minister Hans-Dietrich Genscher. Moscow's renewed courtship of Bonn took on particular policy significance following Gorbachev's decision in March 1987 to accept Reagan's "zero option," which called for the elimination of all Soviet and American intermediate range missiles. The conciliatory efforts that sought Chancellor Kohl's support for the dismantling and destruction of the recently deployed missiles also included a state visit in July 1987 by West Germany's president and Moscow's granting permission (after several humiliating postponements) to Erich Honecker to proceed with a visit to the Federal Republic of Germany in September—the first by an East German leader. Improved relations with Bonn would further Moscow's current priority of securing treaties banning chemical weapons and short-range, nuclear-capable missiles (those with a range of less than 300 miles that were not covered by the intermediate range missile accord—generally referred to as the INF treaty—signed by Gorbachev and Reagan in Washington in December 1987).

While Gorbachev may encourage neutralist sentiment in West Germany, he is not likely to permit reunification, even if it would entail the neutralization of a united Germany. On a number of occasions, he has expressed himself as being strongly committed to the existence of the two

German states. The division of Germany helps Moscow to ensure and justify the Soviet position in Eastern Europe and precludes the emergence of a powerful European rival. Like his predecessors, his strategy will be minimalist—promoting mutually advantageous economic ties, keeping the FRG nonnuclear, and exploiting FRG-U.S. (and West European–U.S.) disagreements over how to deal with the Soviet Union. In a profound sense, the two countries are locked into a status quo security situation that has little prospect for basic change and that may be likened to the condition of an old couple who dance a waltz, no matter what the music calls for.

The Courtship of France

After assuming power, the Brezhnev-Kosygin leadership continued Khrushchev's "opening to the West" with its attention to France. The Soviet media had long castigated French colonialism in Southeast Asia and North Africa, and when Charles de Gaulle returned to power in 1958, Moscow attacked him for seeking to establish a military dictatorship and for refusing to grant independence to Algeria. But this changed as Khrushchev saw opportunities to exploit French differences with Bonn, London, and Washington. He did not permit the Soviet interest in penetrating the Third World to interfere with his European policy.

Perhaps nowhere is the complexity and often indeterminate character of Soviet policy toward Western Europe more apparent than in Moscow's attempt to court the Federal Republic and France simultaneously. When it tries to attract the one, it often dismays the other. With the FRG, the USSR suggests the mutual benefit of a relationship reminiscent of Rapallo, leaving vague the issues of unification and the military power that such a German state would require to pursue an independent policy, all of which is anathema to Paris. With France, Moscow stresses the Franco-Russian alliance in two world wars and the dangers of German militarism. Its effectiveness in dealing with both is limited because the French and Germans compare notes on what Soviet officials say, and act accordingly.

De Gaulle's grant of independence to Algeria was welcomed in Moscow, but his dissatisfaction with NATO, his rejection of the U.S. proposal for a multilateral nuclear force, his opposition to Western European economic and political integration, his quest for a reduced American role in Europe, his acceptance of the Oder-Neisse boundary, and his readiness to improve relations with Moscow unilaterally accounted for the Kremlin's interest in the French connection. It saw France as the odd-member-out of NATO and was pleased with the Gaullist preference for a Europe of cooperating but nationalistic and independent sovereignties, which conflicted starkly with the "Atlanticist" formulations so favored by American and British officials. As one Soviet writer noted, "A powerful France holds no menace for the Soviet Union or its interests. On the contrary, the more France asserts her great-power independence, the easier it will be for us to work in common for solution of the pressing problems of Europe and the world." De Gaulle's distinctive blend of unsentimental realism and striking purposiveness intrigued Moscow, so much that it was not deterred from pressing for closer bilateral relations by his *force de frappe* (independent nuclear force), refusal to sign the nuclear test ban treaty or discuss arms control, tenacious opposition to Soviet pressure durng the Berlin and Cuban crises, and cultivation of a special relationship with Bonn.

President de Gaulle visited the Soviet Union during the halcyon stage of the Soviet courtship, in June 1966, scarcely three months after he had informed NATO of his intention to withdraw France's participation in the integrated military commands and indicated the desirability of a shift of venue for NATO's headquarters from Paris to Brussels. Soviet leaders sought to encourage de Gaulle's weakening of NATO and urged more intimate Franco-Soviet ties. The Moscow declaration of June 30, 1966, announced the plan of the two governments "to continue regular consultations." Moscow persisted in its efforts to strengthen the relationship, but after the Soviet invasion of Czechoslovakia, which coincided with the twilight of de Gaulle's political career, a certain disenchantment and constraint developed in Paris. Succeeding French Presidents Georges Pompidou and Valéry Giscard d'Estaing continued high-level visits and Soviet leaders regularly returned them, but the mood was not quite the same as it had been in de Gaulle's time.

By the early 1970s, France edged back toward some military cooperation with NATO and dropped the acid exchanges with its allies that were so characteristic of the de Gaulle era. Moscow is under no illusions that France can disengage itself from the Atlantic alliance and play a completely independent role in Europe, but it finds enough promise in the neo-Gaullist propensities that shape the outlook of French leaders and the tenor of French domestic politics to seek agreement with France on the convergent strands of the two countries' foreign policy. Moscow, like Paris, supports the preservation of the territorial status quo in Europe, a non-nuclear FRG, a diminished role for the United States in Europe, a NATO of modest size, and expanded East-West economic cooperation. Both retain vestigial uneasiness over the danger of a resurgent German nationalism and militarism. Overall, France is useful to the Soviet Union in the ongoing process of détente, which is favored by each country. France's demands are few, and its contributions are important to the advancement of Soviet aims.

In the economic and technological realm, France has led the way to the Soviet market. In October 1964, it extended the USSR a seven-year credit for $356 million, which was used to finance chemical plants and equipment; this action made France the first member of the European Economic Community (EEC) to break with the community's previous five-year limit on credits to the Soviet Union. A ten-year Franco-Soviet trade agreement was concluded in October 1971, during the first of Brezhnev's visits to France. In January 1982 the two governments signed an agreement calling for France to purchase about 280 billon cubic feet of Siberian natural gas every year for twenty-five years, starting in 1984, and for large-scale Soviet imports of French equipment. With this agreement—which France signed notwithstanding the crackdown on Solidarity in Poland the previous month, the continued Soviet occupation of Afghanistan, and President Ronald Reagan's imposition of sanctions on companies selling the Soviet Union equipment for the natural gas pipeline—French President François Mitterrand affirmed his belief that expansion of East-West trade ought not become hostage to the vagaries in political relations between the USSR and the West. In the 1980s, France has been the USSR's second most important West European trading partner—a distant second to the Federal Republic.

In Mitterrand, a socialist who was elected in May 1981, and again in 1988, Moscow has had a stern critic, who is difficult to woo. It is annoyed by his sale of modern arms to China, opposition to Soviet-subsidized clients in Africa, outspokenness on human rights issues, and staunch support of Atlantic solaridity. Relations have also been plagued by disputes over trade and espionage. Soviet purchases of French capital goods have not been enough to offset massive French imports of Siberian natural gas, and the trade imbalance has become a sore point in the political realm. Even more divisive has been the wave of Soviet industrial espionage, focused on the field of space technology. The uncovering of Soviet agents triggered a series of expulsions that prompted Moscow to charge the French government with "anti-Soviet hysteria."

Nevertheless, the Soviet leadership seems determined that friendly relations with France be promoted. The first visit that Gorbachev paid to a Western country in his capacity as head of the CPSU was to France in October 1985. Moscow values "the special dialogue with France in its own right for the simple reason that it interferes with U.S. attempts to coordinate Western policies. Hence, the Soviets place highest value on France's independence from the United States, but probably entertain few illusions about the likelihood of establishing French dependence on the Soviet Union."[5] Moscow also appreciates the French attitude toward détente and Mitterrand's frequent stress on "traditional" Franco-Russian friendship.

Gorbachev and Thatcher

One of the interesting features of Gorbachev's diplomacy in Western Europe is his attention to relations with Prime Minister Margaret Thatcher, Britain's "iron lady." Except for the period of wartime alliance against Hitler, Anglo-Soviet relations have been adversarial in nature. Britain has been seen as a close ally of the United States and an advocate of a strong NATO.

In December 1984, when still a junior member of the Politburo, Gorbachev visited Britain and impressed Prime Minister Thatcher, whose observation that she thought "we can do business" took on significance a few months later on his elevation to the summit of Soviet power. For the past few years, even during intermittent periods of tension (for example, in September 1985, when the defecting head of the KGB in Britain turned out to have been a British double agent for almost two decades), Gorbachev has worked to improve relations, expanding trade and settling mutual financial claims dating to 1917. He hopes that Thatcher's receptivity to arms control can be enlisted to persuade the United States to agree to a program of verification and confidence-building measures that will ensure continued adherence to the 1972 antiballistic missile (ABM) treaty combined with restraint in deploying the space-based system of defense against missiles—in much the same way that her support helped secure Western Europe's approval for the INF accord. However, none of this prevented his hoping (vainly) for her defeat in the June 1987 British elections. Just a few months earlier, during a visit to the Soviet Union, Mrs. Thatcher had openly told Soviet audiences that she believed a strong NATO and possession of nuclear weapons were essential to counter the Soviet Union's military buildup in Central Europe and to maintain the peace. Thus, Gorbachev prefers the anti-nuclear, anti-American, less pro-NATO orientation of the Labour Party.

It is evident that in Moscow's policy toward the key European members of NATO (the Federal Republic of Germany, France, and Britain) the Soviet theme is peaceful coexistence and détente. The attitude Moscow seeks to convey is one of reasonableness, accommodation, and limited goals, certainly for the immediate future. What Moscow seldom mentions, though it is crucial to the political reality that it seeks to fashion, is the role of military power in shaping policy responses and public perceptions. The Soviet military buildup along NATO's central front causes considerable uneasiness and is widely discussed in Western Europe because a Soviet strike across the North German plain would threaten the nerve centers of the alliance; but what is less known is the awesome power and diplomatic pressure that Moscow directs along the northern tier of Western Europe.

The Nordic Sector

Short on population but long on strategically prime real estate, Scandinavia constitutes about one-third of non-Communist Western Europe. Its political and military roles are of crucial importance to the Soviet Union. On the Baltic side, Scandinavia controls the approaches to Leningrad and the Baltic republics of the USSR; on the Atlantic side, Norway sits astride the approaches to the Kola peninsula, where the Soviet network of military installations is considered by Western intelligence analysts to be the most heavily concentrated system of air, naval, and missile bases in the world. The Kola Peninsula offers the Soviet Union the shortest trajectory route over the top of the world to targets in the United States and safeguards the sea and air lanes to key military and industrial sites in the Soviet north; it is also the base for two-thirds of the Soviet submarine fleet.

The Soviet Union desires the neutralization of the Nordic area: Finland, Sweden, Norway, and Denmark. Finland's neutrality and policy of deferring to Soviet wishes on most foreign-policy issues was introduced in 1944 by former Prime Minister J. K. Paasikivi, and has been the centerpiece of Finnish statecraft ever since. For 800 years a dukedom of Sweden and then part of the Russian Empire for more than a century, Finland acquired independence only after World War I. After 1945, having sided with Germany, it was forced to cede, in the southeast, the entire Karelian Isthmus and the second largest city of Viipuri (Viborg), thus enabling Moscow to thicken Leningrad's defensive buffer from 20 to 120 miles from the Soviet-Finnish border; and in the north, the district and ice-free port of Petsamo (Pechenga) to the USSR. In total, Finland surrendered about 12 percent of its territory. Under the 1948 Soviet-Finnish treaty of friendship, cooperation, and mutual assistance, the Finns agreed to consult with the Soviet government if Moscow should feel threatened by Germany or any country that is allied with it—that is, any member of NATO. These constraints severely limit but do not eliminate Finland's possible initiatives in foreign policy. For most of the post-1955 period, Moscow has pursued a moderate policy toward Finland, a reward for that nation's accommodation to the USSR's position in foreign affairs.

Sweden followed a policy of neutrality in the two world wars, but it is well armed and would presumably resist any invasion. It has never seriously considered joining NATO and argues for keeping the Nordic area nuclear-free, a policy that sits well with Moscow and reassures it on the security of its Baltic flank. Soviet provocations, however, have introduced hitherto unknown stress into Soviet-Swedish relations.

In late October 1981, a Soviet nuclear-armed submarine ran aground within the prohibited zone near the Swedish naval base at Karlskrona.

That this was part of a pattern of Soviet submarine intrusions was made clear by a Swedish parliamentary commission of inquiry, which made its report public in April 1983. Behind Moscow's repeated violations of Swedish territorial waters are probably a combination of factors: aggressive intelligence-gathering by a strong Baltic fleet that includes more than twenty attack submarines; probes to test Sweden's coastal defenses on the assumption that it is a potential enemy, notwithstanding its proclaimed policy of neutrality; confidence that the Swedes will not sink any Soviet ships for fear of triggering a stiff counterreacton; and a strengthening of the pacifist case against expenditures on high-tech weapons, by revealing the "deficiencies of the Swedish Navy, coastal defence and surveillance system" and thus demonstrating the futility of trying to develop an effective counter to the USSR's military capability.[6] The Finlandization of Sweden would be a signal achievement and would enormously enhance Soviet leverage against Norway, Moscow's main target in the Nordic region.

Moscow's awareness of Norway's strategic importance was an outgrowth of World War II, when German submarines operated out of occupied Norway to interdict the American lend-lease aid that was shipped to Murmansk. After the war, a slice of territory taken from Finland made the Soviet Union Norway's neighbor in the far north, along 110 miles of bleak, frozen wasteland that Norwegians say is land the strategist remembered but God forgot. To the east of Norway's northernmost district of Finnmark, the Soviet Union has the three ice-free ports of Petsamo, Severomorsk (a new naval base), and Murmansk, located fifteen, sixty, and one hundred miles, respectively, from the Norwegian frontier. Their security is a prime Soviet concern.

Norway is a staunch member of NATO, but it has no desire to fuel Soviet apprehensions or precipitate trouble through any misperception of its behavior. Therefore, Norway (and Denmark) announced in 1961 that no nuclear weapons would be introduced on its territory, that no NATO bases would be housed, and that no large-scale NATO exercises would be permitted near the Soviet border. Nor, it announced in early 1978, would large numbers of West German forces participate in NATO exercises on Norwegian soil. Norway has also kept force levels in Finnmark at a low threshold and has been slow to develop radar facilities and military bases there to avoid arousing undue Soviet alarm over its defensive and missile capabilities. Moscow would prefer that the Nordic countries officially agree to the establishment of a nuclear-free zone in the area, but neither Norway or Sweden is prepared to foreclose the possible option of acquiring nuclear weapons should they ever deem that necessary.

While suspicious of Norway's membership in NATO and the silent war of electronic eavesdropping and intelligence surveillance that continually goes on, Moscow has accepted Norway's self-imposed limitations as evidence of a desire not to threaten Soviet security, and in all likelihood will continue to do so as long as no power other than Norway controls the approaches to the Kola Peninsula. But since all Soviet ships and submarines must pass through the Norwegian Sea en route to the Atlantic Ocean, Moscow cannot be happy at the monitoring of Soviet naval deployments. Control of Finnmark would, of course, seal this gap in Soviet military secrecy.

Though Soviet policy toward Norway is overwhelmingly strategic, economic considerations in the Svalbard archipelago that commands the approaches to the Kola Peninsula foreshadow future tensions. In 1920, Norwegian sovereignty over Svalbard (which includes the island of Spitzbergen) was internationally recognized, but the archipelago was demilitarized and the forty signatories to the treaty—including the Soviet Union—were granted most-favored-nation status, allowing them the same rights as the Norwegians for fishing, mining, and other commercial ventures. In addition to Norway, only the Soviet Union has so far been active in the region, maintaining a coal-mining concession. (The approximately 2000 Soviet miners do not produce as much as the 1000 Norwegians, but that may be due to the inclusion of a large component of intelligence agents in the Soviet community.) The discovery of offshore oil has greatly enhanced the area's importance, some estimates holding that 40 percent of the world's reserves of oil may exist in the Arctic region. The prospect of having international oil companies drilling in their backyard makes the Soviets very nervous, and Moscow may decide to press for an exclusive Soviet-Norwegian sovereignty in the area. Moreover, the Barents Sea is a rich fishing area. Negotiations between Norway and the Soviet Union for delineating national jurisdictions over the continental shelf "in the Barents Sea have proceeded intermittently since 1970 without success": whereas Norway rests its position on the generally recognized median line principle, the USSR contends that the Arctic Ocean has unique characteristics of both land and sea and thus requires special legal adaptations, which accord with its claim in 1926 to all lands and islands within a vast triangular area, or sector, extending a line from the Kola Peninsula to the North Pole and from there to a line through the Bering Strait between Alaska and the USSR.[7] At stake are 83,000 square miles of continental shelf in the area between Svalbard and the Soviet island of Novaya Zemlya.

The Norwegians are under no illusions about Moscow's ultimate strategic objectives on Svalbard; they remember Molotov's ham-handed approach with members of Norway's government-in-exile in Moscow in late 1944, during the German occupation. "The Soviets then demanded a rewriting of the Svalbard treaty of 1920, claiming that the new Soviet government has signed it because it was politically and militarily weak at the time, but that it did not correspond to Soviet interests. Molotov wanted removal of the clause that expressly prohibits military installations and military forces on Svalbard."[8] The Norwegians resist Soviet pressure for revision of the treaty, but they go out of their way to permit the Russians to operate easily under its present terms. Soviet long-term intentions toward Norway should emerge from the lengthy legal discussions now underway.

Moscow believes in continually testing an adversary's determination, in probing its political will. Therefore, the growing Soviet military boldness in the area has to be of concern: "Naval and air exercises move westward into the Norwegian Sea. The number of reconnaissance flights over Finnmark and adjacent districts increases. Unidentified submarines are detected in the fjords."[9] In August 1978, the Soviets on Spitzbergen built a radar station at their helicopter landing strip near the Soviet-run town of Barentsburg, without informing Norwegian authorities. Soviet ships frequently violate Norwegian territorial waters, testing alertness and gathering intelligence on the Allied radio navigational stations used by Polaris submarines and on electronic capabilities, especially the cable at Gamvik on the Nordkinn Peninsula, which links submarine-listening equipment on the seabed between Norway proper and the island of Spitzbergen. The USSR also testfires ICBMs into the contested area of the Barents Sea.

On the other hand, according to one Norwegian defense analyst, Johan J. Holst, "the rudiments of a pattern of mutual restraint may be emerging":

> Soviet ground forces on the Kola peninsula are limited in size compared to requirements for a major offensive against central portions of North Norway. Their numbers have been fairly stable for two decades, although marginal changes have taken place in connection with the restructuring of Soviet army units. . . . No fighter-bomber aircraft are deployed to airbases on the Kola peninsula. . . . With respect to operations, major Soviet exercises . . . in recent years apparently have not included maneuver forces such as airborne troops and marine infantry units. It also seems that the practice of including the embarkation of motorized infantry units in the exercise pattern had been de-emphasized. These are the elements in the Soviet pattern of exercises which had been causing the most public concern in Norway.[10]

In a speech in the Arctic port city of Murmansk on October 1, 1987, Gorbachev called for making Northern Europe a nuclear-free zone, limiting naval activity, and cooperating to exploit the region's resources, "for example, we are interested in enlisting Canada and Norway in the creation of joint firms and enterprises for extracting oil and gas on our northern sea shelf." Thus far, there has been no sign that any of these issues are being seriously discussed by the two countries. Moscow's aims in the Nordic region seem unchanged: to foster neutralism; to create nuclear-free zones; to pry Denmark, Norway, and Iceland away from active involvement in NATO; and to strengthen the domestic left and pacifist/peace groups.[11]

Iberia

In contrast to Scandinavia, the Iberian Peninsula attracted Soviet attention relatively recently, only after the revolution in Portugal in April 1974 and the death of Francisco Franco in Spain in November 1975, which ended decades of right-wing dictatorships. Both countries are classic Marxist examples of societies ripe for Communist revolutions. They have strong, well-organized Communist parties, tempered by decades of survival underground and led by able, experienced Communists, and weak bourgeois parties; they have troubled economies beset by intensifying "contradictions"; they have a politicized working class; they have archaic, rigid social structures in need of modernization and rising mass expectations; and Spain has discord among nationality groups.

The Communists, and the diverse coalition of peasants and workers they tried to manipulate, came very close to seizing power in Portugal in the 1974-to-1975 period, but they overplayed a strong hand. Two aspects of Soviet policy require consideration. First, the Soviet Union could do very little to affect the outcome of Alvaro Cunhal's bid for power directly beyond helping the Portuguese Communist party (PCP) by covertly channeling funds for organizational and electoral activities. Other than that, it maintained a correct attitude at the government-to-government level to avoid straining Soviet–U.S. relations, then in difficulty because of competitive policies in the Middle East and Vietnam. Second, Moscow's policy of détente in no way impelled it to restrain Cunhal, the most pro-Soviet and unregenerate Stalinist among the West European Communists and presumably highly responsive to Kremlin "advice." Had Cunhal succeeded in his strategy of infiltrating and polarizing the armed forces movement, in which pro-Communists and pro-Marxists held key positions, Portugal would most likely have drifted toward a neutralist stand in NATO and would have terminated U.S. military bases. It might even have withdrawn from NATO and provided basing privileges for Soviet ships. Soviet foreign policy stood only to gain, and Moscow would have denied playing any role and credited the development to the Portuguese people. A Communist success without avowed Soviet participation would have left the United States upset but paralyzed. Despite an inevitable increase in tensions between the Soviet Union and the United States, the strategic setback to NATO would have been a significant gain for Soviet policy in Europe. As it was, even Cunhal's failure benefited Moscow, allowing it to parade its adherence to the principle of nonintervention in the domestic affairs of West European countries and its concern for détente.

In June 1974, the USSR and Portugal established diplomatic relations and agreed to an exchange of ambassadors for the first time since 1917. In October 1975, Soviet leaders received the Portuguese president, and the two governments negotiated an expansion of commercial and cultural ties. But by 1980 a chill had set in, the result of the decline of the PCP's electoral fortunes, the Soviet moves in Afghanistan and Poland, and the government's desire to play a more active role in NATO.

Relations with Spain proceeded more slowly. Commercial ties resumed in 1971, but not until February 1977 did the two governments establish diplomatic relations, ending a hiatus of thirty-eight years. Gromyko's visit to Spain in November 1979 was the first ever by a Soviet foreign minister. Moscow has been critical of Spain's entry into NATO in 1982 and its expulsion of Soviet diplomats for espionage and alleged involvement with the Basque terrorist organization ETA, a Marxist-Leninist group whose stated aim is to gain independence for the Basque region of Spain. Nonetheless, despite continuing tensions, diplomatic normalization between the USSR and Spain may be considered to have come of age in May 1984, with the visit of King Juan Carlos—the first by a Spanish head of state. Since then, high-level visits have become regular occurrences, and there is a possibility of a state visit by Gorbachev.

Moscow's aim is political—to encourage Spain's neutralism within NATO now that it is a member. The Soviet Union has a good image in Spain, perhaps better than it has anywhere else in Western Europe, and enjoys considerable prestige with the left, which remembers the support that Moscow gave the Republican cause in the 1935–1938 civil war; accordingly, it is not likely that any Spanish government will ask it to return the 40 tons of gold that the Republican government sent to the USSR for safekeeping in 1937–1938, but that the Soviets insist was given in payment for weapons and supplies. Fueling opposition to U.S. bases and to military integration in NATO lies at the core of Soviet interest in Spain.

Attitude Toward European Unity

A major hurdle for Moscow's promotion of détente and normalization of relations in Europe has been its opposition to West European integration and unity. Ideologically, Moscow is hostile to the idea, in accordance with the canons of Marxist-Leninist scripture, which hold that the drastic and desperate measures of "monopoly capital" may temporarily stave off the inevitable collapse of capitalism but will ultimately lead to increased international tensions and a further deterioration in the condition of the working class. At the operational level, "the Europe of Trusts" (as the edifice of supranational institutions is called) politically limits the Soviet Union's freedom of diplomatic maneuver, ability to play one capitalist country against another for maximum commercial benefit, and economic penetration of that part of the Third World that fashioned a special relationship with the EEC. Though preferring bilateral diplomacy, Moscow could not indefinitely ignore the EEC, which came into being with the Treaty of Rome in March 1957.

The subject of considerable discussion in Moscow, the EEC was acknowledged to have brought an accelerated rate of economic growth and unexpected stability to member countries. Khrushchev publicly denounced it in May 1962, but this capitalist creation forced him to offer proposals for strengthening the economic structure of Comecon. Paradoxically, in order for his "socialist commonwealth" to compete and deal with its capitalist counterpart, he had to allow the nations of Eastern Europe greater measures of autonomy, thus further complicating Soviet hegemonic ambitions.

When de Gaulle vetoed Britain's application for membership in the EEC in Janaury 1963, Moscow was elated, seeing this as vindication of Leninist expectations. However, propaganda aside, the Kremlin could not ignore the Common Market's vitality. The Soviet policy of détente in Europe; the eagerness of the Soviet bloc for expanded economic relations with Western Europe; the pressure from West European Communist parties, who sensed the general support that the EEC enjoyed in their respective countries; the interest of the East Europeans in more economic, technical, and cultural "windows to the West"; and the desire for a status quo *cordiale* with Western Europe to offset the widening rift with Beijing wrought a subtle change in Soviet perceptions and attitudes and posed a dilemma for Kremlin policy makers.

In March 1972, in a speech marking the subtle evolution in Soviet policy from unrelenting hostility to incipient accommodation, Brezhnev implicitly recognized the EEC:

> The USSR is far from ignoring the actual situation in Western Europe, including the existence of such an economic group of capitalist countries as the "Common Market." We attentively follow its evolution and its activities. Our relations with its members, naturally, will depend on the extent to which they, on their part, recognize the realities existing in the socialist part of Europe, in particular the interests of Comecon countries. We are for equality in economic relations and against discrimination.[12]

However, exploratory talks between the two economic communities did not begin until early 1975 and yielded little. In 1977, however, when the EEC imposed a 200-mile limit on North Sea fishing, Moscow for the first time sent an official delegation to Brussels; to obtain fishing privileges in the territorial waters of member states, it had to accord de facto recognition to the EEC.

Despite having taken the initiative in proposing that official relations be established between Comecon and the EEC, the Soviet Union was a reluctant suitor. The talks did not assume a serious character until Gorbachev, impelled by economic necessity (trade, investment, and technology), reversed Soviet policy in June 1985 and accepted as a basis for negotiations the EEC's position that any agreement must permit it to deal with individual Comecon countries (as it presently does with Hungary and Romania) and not be tied to agreement between the two organizations. Gorbachev seems bent on reaching an agreement with the West Europeans, though unwillingness to recognize West Berlin as part of the Western trade group has thus far held up a joint declaration of mutual recognition by the two communities. As part of a strategy of greater participation in the world trading system, Gorbachev is also seeking to affiliate with the General Agreement on Tariffs and Trade (GATT); however, this may be difficult, since the centralized nature of foreign trade in the Soviet Union contravenes the concept of free trade and market competition that underlies GATT's philosophy.

CSCE

The central political objective permeating almost all Soviet diplomatic moves after 1945 was Western recognition of the post–World War II territorial and political status quo in Europe. To this end, and to forestall the European Defense Community and West German rearmament, Moscow started to lobby for a European security conference as early as 1954. It raised the idea often in the 1960s, but the Western powers gave it a cool reception.

By 1970, the mood had changed in the West; interest in an accommodation with the Soviet Union and improved East-West relations was strong. The USSR was now acknowledged to be a superpower in every military sense of the term: it enjoyed essential equivalence with the United States in nuclear weapons and delivery systems and a numerically commanding advantage in conventional forces. Moreover, though the Soviet Union remained solidly entrenched in Eastern Europe, it was allowing increasing measures of autonomy and its own sociopolitical system had relaxed since the Stalinist period. Washington's interest was evident in the unseemly haste with which it swept under the rug the Soviet invasion of Czechoslovakia and the Brezhnev Doctrine and urged the Strategic Arms Limitation Talks (SALT), no doubt also hoping that Moscow's interest in a limitation on strategic weapons would have a salutary effect on U.S. efforts to reach an agreement with Hanoi for an end to the American involvement in Vietnam. With the 1970 Soviet-FRG treaty, the 1971 quadripartite agreement on Berlin, and the Soviet acceptance of American and Canadian participation, Western opposition to the Conference on Security and Cooperation in Europe (CSCE) weakened. Moscow overcame what was perhaps the last hurdle when in May 1971, Brezhnev challenged the West to judge the Soviet Union's peaceful intention by "tasting" the wine of negotiations, offering to meet NATO's demand for parallel but interrelated talks on the reduction of forces in Central Europe.

Deliberations on CSCE started in Helsinki on November 22, 1972. When the Final Act was signed by the heads of state of thirty-five countries on August 1, 1975, the Soviet Union realized a thirty-year ambition. Though officially only a political statement of intent and not a treaty or a legally binding document, the Final Act in effect ratified the existing frontiers in Europe. It was a political settlement of World War II and recognized Soviet hegemony over the Communist half of Europe. Still, the Soviet triumph was not unmixed. The Helsinki Conference may have given the East Europeans ammunition to use against Moscow in their struggle for greater autonomy and expanded contacts with the West, though the suppression of Solidarity in Poland currently contravenes such speculation. The Final Act reiterated those general principles that are the staples of international summitry: sovereign equality of states, inviolability of frontiers, territorial integrity of states, nonintervention in the internal affairs of other countries, renunciation of force or the threat of force to change existing frontiers, and so on.

There are three sections, or "Baskets," to the Final Act. Basket 1, as the set of principles on security, confidence-building measures (CBMs), and disarmament is called, was of most interest to Moscow. By noting that the "participating states regard as inviolable all one another's frontiers as well as the frontiers of all states in Europe, and therefore they will refrain now and in the future from assaulting these frontiers," it affirmed the present division of Europe. The Western powers contented themselves with CBMs such as prior notification of major military maneuvers and of smaller military exercises, and invitation on a voluntary basis for the exchange of observers at maneuvers. While voluntary in nature, the CBMs were operating often enough to merit further exploration as a technique of arms control. Basket 2, which is also of interest to Moscow, deals with economic and technological cooperation. However, Basket 3, which constitutes a potpourri of political principles on the freer flow of people, ideas, and information, was included at the dogged insistence of the West Europeans and contains the fly in the CSCE ointment Moscow so eagerly sought to avoid. It serves as the basis for criticizing the Soviet record of human rights violations in a multilateral forum.

On balance, Moscow considers CSCE useful. The first review conference (the Helsinki Final Act calls for the periodic convening of such evaluative meetings), which met in Belgrade from October 1977 to March 1978, was marked by acrimony and ended with no action on any issue. The second conference, held in Madrid from November 1980 to September 1983, with lengthy recesses occasioned by Western ire over events in Poland, subjected Moscow to sharp criticism for its failure to live up to the provisions of Basket 3—that is, for its jamming radio broadcasts, imprisoning Soviet citizens who tried to monitor the USSR's violation of human rights, tightening bars to emigration, and so on. However, the Soviet leadership was willing to endure this in order to obtain agreement for a Conference on Confidence and Security-building Measures and Disarmament in Europe, which began in Stockholm in January 1984 and concluded on September 19, 1986, with adoption of a document that creates procedures for verifying a variety of military activities in Europe, the hope being that these will foster a climate conducive to the reduction of conventional force levels.

The third Helsinki review conference opened in Vienna in November 1986, shortly after the conclusion of the Stockholm conference. Like the previous ones in Belgrade and Madrid, it will meet periodically over several years and will cover a range of issues, with special attention to human rights and humanitarian concerns. Progress here will be a function of the general state of East-West relations. Gorbachev's policy of *glasnost,* with its sweeping cultural liberalization and more measured handling of dissidents, offers hope of continued progress. However, the Vienna venue is not, as one Western observer cautioned, intended as a specialized conference:

> Of necessity, therefore, detailed negotiations on such subjects as conventional stability, confidence and security building measures, trade, the environment, science and culture, to name but a few, will have to take place in negotiating fora to be established by the Vienna meeting. . . .
>
> Progress to date has, however, been remarkably slow. Only a few sentences of relatively modest significance have been provisionally agreed. The position of the Soviet delegation with regard to Western priorities within the human dimension of the CSCE process has remained ungenerous.[13]

Deranging NATO

Of far greater potential importance for Soviet policy than the current CSCE meetings are the talks that began officially in Vienna on October 30, 1973. Originally termed Mutual and Balanced Force Reduction (MBFR), the official title is the Conference on Mutual Reduction of Forces and Armaments and Associated Measures in Central Europe, commonly referred to as MFR. MFR was the price Moscow paid to obtain CSCE. Its outcome will determine the military component of détente in Europe. Ironically, just as Moscow's harvest from Helsinki may prove to be smaller than Moscow originally anticipated, so NATO may find MFR more of a problem for the Atlantic alliance than for the Soviet Union.

MFR reveals the multiple and adaptive nature of Soviet policy. Though not at all enthusiastic in the beginning, Moscow has used MFR to stabilize its present favorable military advantage in Europe. It seeks to weaken NATO through MFR, not merely militarily, but politically as well. Though Moscow considers NATO to be dominated by the United States, it recognizes the existing differences in national positions and exploits them, playing off one member or faction against another. NATO's failure to resolve essential policy questions on strategy, interoperability and standardization of weapons strengthens the Soviet belief in the divisive propensities inherent in relations among capitalist countries and lead Moscow to wait for the right time and circumstance to capitalize on the disagreements. Thus ideological predilections and perceptions are reinforced by political phenomena, in this case the MFR negotiations.

Perpetuation of a favorable military balance depends on checking the growth of the Bundeswehr; through arms reduction and limitation, Moscow hopes to place ceilings on the military forces of the Federal Republic. One wedge in this drive was the Warsaw Pact proposal submitted on June 8, 1978, in which the Russians agreed for the first time that the two sides should have an equal number of troops in Central Europe and that no country would be permitted to increase its forces above present levels. The joker in this game is the number of Soviet troops in Central Europe, the Kremlin's figures being significantly lower than NATO's. This data issue has anesthetized MFR talks.

Other issues that Moscow has raised are the limitation of NATO forward-based systems (FBS), a treaty on the renunciation of the first use of nuclear weapons, and a limit on the size of military maneuvers. Disengagement as a way of encouraging a withdrawal of U.S. forces crops up repeatedly; for example in the late 1950s, Moscow proposed a demilitarized zone of four hundred kilometers on either side of the Elbe. Among other Soviet proposals has been one for the establishment of a nuclear-free zone that would include Poland, Czechoslovakia, and the two Germanies. Though there have been hints that Gorbachev may announce token unilateral troop reductions, it will not be easy to break the stalemate in the MFR talks—to develop reliable verification procedures and to reach agreement on how deep the cuts in Soviet force levels must be in order to rectify the current imbalance that favors the Warsaw Pact.

The characteristics of Soviet military policy in Europe are important to any consideration of the range of Moscow's probable and possible political objectives. Briefly, these characteristics are high conventional force levels and their strong forward deployment; a commitment in military doctrine "to wage and to win a campaign" with *all* available weapons, including nuclear arms; and impressive buildup of mobile battlefield cover for moving combat forces; a substantial numerical advantage over NATO forces in tanks, motor-rifle divisions, armored personnel carriers (half of which have amphibious capability), and artillery; improved and highly effective logistical support; and the buildup of aircraft and missiles capable of carrying nuclear weapons with great accuracy against targets in Europe but not included under SALT II because they lack an intercontinental capability. Soviet forces maintain a high level of combat readiness, and they are consistently modernized and given deeper penetration capability.

Nonetheless, NATO officials do not believe that Moscow intends an all-out aggression against Western Europe, and implementation of the INF treaty eliminating an entire category of offensive nuclear missiles would reinforce this judgment. Several explanations may help illumine the purposes prompting the Kremlin's military buildup in Central Europe.

First, massive military power is perceived as the best defense, not only against any NATO attack or attempt to intervene in Eastern Europe, but also against attempted national Communist defections or uprisings.

Second, the Soviet leadership, like its czarist predecessor, values redundancy. As the saying goes, "Russians feel more comfortable with three armies too many than with three divisions too few." Overinsurance is axiomatic in Soviet military doctrine.

Third, if war comes, Moscow wants an overwhelming retaliatory capability. In recent years, it seems to have shifted from the expectation that the next European war would be nuclear to predicate a war-winning strategy on the forward deployment of massive conventional forces, which are expected to neutralize the nuclear option. Some British analysts contend the Soviet troops are being trained to live off the land, carry sufficient ammunition with them during rapid forward thrusts, and achieve a decisive victory before NATO can react. The ability to strike suddenly, with minimal reinforcements, is expected to provide the clout either to deter or to demolish, as need requires.[14]

Fourth, by forward deployment, the Soviet Union seeks a critical edge over NATO and the eventual acquiescence to Soviet military superiority in Central Europe. Expecting that in the short run NATO may react with intensification of its military buildup and modernization (and this is a matter of concern to Moscow), the Soviets think that the West has a short memory and will in time accept the forward Soviet deployment as the norm for a tolerable balance of power in Europe.

Finally, since the mid-1970s, Soviet commentators have called attention to NATO's growing modernization program. When they "quantify the NATO threat, normally they use a method similar to Western worst-case analysis. Seldom does one see qualitative distinctions made among various NATO members' weapons or divisions."[15] They fear the trend in NATO is toward increased defense budgets and weapons modernization; hence their own sustained programs.

Politically, the Soviet Union prefers an orderly and stable environment in Western Europe. It does not like changes that might complicate the realization of its specific objectives: a nonnuclear Federal Republic of Germany and a modest U.S. presence, both of which are keys to keeping NATO minimally potent; a Western Europe of nation-states at a low level of integration; worsening West European–U.S., and especially FRG–U.S., relations; assured access to West European Communist parties, whose ideological assertiveness and prospects for sharing power are beginning to complicate Soviet hegemony in Eastern Europe and leadership of the world Communist movement. Moscow aspires to be security manager of Europe and assumes that the position can best be attained in an atmosphere of détente and through expanded bilateral relations with the existing capitalist governments.

Occasionally, its realization of these political goals is jeopardized by its relentless force modernization and quest for military advantage. The resulting action-reaction syndrome in the military sphere heightens political tensions. Thus, starting in 1977, the Soviet leadership began to deploy the SS-20, an advanced, solid-fuel mobile missile, which carries three nuclear warheads and is capable of hitting targets anywhere in Western Europe. In December 1979, NATO responded with a decision to deploy 108 new Pershing-II missiles and 464 ground-launched cruise missiles by 1988: unlike previous intermediate-range ballistic missiles (IRBMs, or theater nuclear forces [TNF], as they are also called), these weapons have 1200-mile and 1500-mile ranges, respectively. Realizing that the modernized Pershing-IIs had the ability to hit command and control targets in the western part of the Soviet Union, including Moscow, and therefore constituted a formidable first strike weapon, and seeing that the intensive propaganda campaigns and sizable antinuclear protests failed to sow disunity in NATO and block the Pershing-II deployment, Moscow changed course. It embraced Reagan's zero option and signed the INF treaty in Washington in December 1987. What is evident throughout is the nexus between military considerations and political tactics in Soviet attempts to limit Western Europe's military buildup and political cohesion.

Reality is more complex than the theories or conceptual formulations that we use to explain it. The NATO countries may disagree on many issues, but they are far from exhibiting fatalistic acceptance of Soviet military superiority. They do not manifest the telltale signs of Finlandized states, though most of them are beset by strong domestic pressures to accept some such variant. If the Finlandization of the West should come to pass, it would be a consequence not just of Soviet strength but also, and perhaps mainly, of Western weakness—debilitating domestic politics, intra-alliance dissonances, a contraction of power under the guise of advancing détente, and a lack of commitment to professed ideals and institutions. Naturally, Moscow will try to exploit the disarray in the West and induce a lowering of its guard. As it looks to the 1990s, the Kremlin seems wedded to the same general policy that brought it such handsome benefits in the 1970s. Although it is heir to constraints, dilemmas, and miscalculations that frustrate and complicate its diplomatic efforts, Moscow seems in recent decades to have always been attentive to longer-range calculations for the attainment of key objectives and the ordering and management of European affairs. Soviet pragmatism should not obscure Moscow's steady outlook and well-structured ambitions.

Notes

1. Malcolm MacKintosh, "Future Soviet Policy Toward Western Europe," in John C. Garnett (ed.), *The Defence of Western Europe* (London: Macmillan, 1974), 39.
2. Victor Baras, "Stalin's German Policy After Stalin," *Slavic Review*, Vol. 37, No. 2 (June 1978), 262–63.
3. For a discussion of this concept, see George Ginsburgs and Alvin Z. Rubinstein (eds.), *Soviet Foreign Policy Toward Western Europe* (New York: Praeger, 1978), Ch. 1.
4. Angela E. Stent, "Accommodation: The USSR and Western Europe," *The Washington Quarterly*, Vol. 5, No. 4 (Autumn 1982), 96.
5. Michael J. Sodaro, "Moscow and Mitterrand," *Problems of Communism*, Vol. XXXI, No. 4 (July–August 1982), 33.
6. Erling Bjol, *Nordic Security*, Adelphi Paper No. 181 (London: International Institute for Strategic Studies, Spring 1983), 17–18.
7. Clive Archer and David Scrivener, "Frozen Frontiers and Resource Wrangles: Conflict and Cooperation in Northern Waters," *International Affairs*, Vol. 59, No. 1 (Winter 1982–83), 70–71.
8. Per Egil Hegge, "The Soviet View of the Nordic Balance," *The Washington Quarterly*, Vol. 2, No. 3 (Summer 1979), 66.
9. *New York Times*, June 20, 1977.
10. Johan J. Holst, "Norway's Search for a Nordpolitik," *Foreign Affairs*, Vol. 60, No. 1 (Fall 1981), 70–71.

11. Trond Gilberg et al., "The Soviet Union and Northern Europe," *Problems of Communism,* Vol. XXX, No. 2 (March–April 1981), 5–6.
12. *Pravda,* March 21, 1972.
13. William Friis-Møller, "CSCE Follow-up Meeting—West Hopes for Successful Outcome," *NATO Review,* Vol. 35, No. 5 (October 1987), 24, 26.
14. For example, P. H. Vigor, *Soviet Blitzkreig Theory* (New York: St. Martin's Press, 1983).
15. Keith A. Dunn, "Soviet Perceptions of NATO," *Parameters,* Vol. 8, No. 3 (September 1978), 59–60.

Selected Bibliography

ALLISON, ROY. *Finland's Relations with the Soviet Union, 1944–84.* New York: St. Martin's Press, 1985.

BERGESEN, HELGE OLE, ARILD MOE, and WILLY ØSTRENG. *Soviet Oil and Security Interests in the Barents Sea.* New York: St. Martin's Press, 1987.

ELLISON, HERBERT J. (ED.). *Soviet Policy Toward Western Europe.* Seattle: University of Washington Press, 1984.

GILBERG, TROND. *The Soviet Communist Party and Scandinavian Communism: The Norwegian Case.* Oslo: Universitatsforlaget, 1970.

GINSBURGS, GEORGE, and ALVIN Z. RUBINSTEIN (EDS.). *Soviet Foreign Policy Toward Western Europe.* New York: Praeger, 1978.

KORBEL, JOSEF. *Détente in Europe, Real or Imaginary?* Princeton: Princeton University Press, 1972.

LAIRD, ROBBIN F. *France, the Soviet Union, and the Nuclear Weapons Issue.* Boulder: Westview Press, 1985.

MYAGKOV, ALEKSEI. *Inside the KGB.* London: Foreign Affairs Publishing Company, 1977. Provides an account of KGB operations to take France out of NATO.

NERLICH, UWE (ED.). *Soviet Power and Western Negotiating Policies.* 2 vols. Cambridge: Ballinger, 1983.

PIPES, RICHARD (ED.). *Soviet Strategy in Europe.* New York: Crane, Russak, 1976.

PISAR, SAMUEL. *Coexistence and Commerce: Guidelines for Transactions Between East and West.* New York: McGraw-Hill, 1970.

SLUSSER, ROBERT M. *The Berlin Crisis of 1961: Soviet-American Relations and the Struggle for Power in the Kremlin.* Baltimore: Johns Hopkins University Press, 1973.

STENT, ANGELA. *From Embargo to Ostpolitik: The Political Economy of West German–Soviet Relations,* 1955–1980. New York: Cambridge University Press, 1981.

TIERSKY, RONALD. *French Communism, 1920–1972.* New York: Columbia University Press, 1974.

VIGOR, P. H. *Soviet Blitzkrieg Theory.* New York: St. Martin's Press, 1983.

VLOYANTES, JOHN P. *Silk Glove Hegemony: Finnish-Soviet Relations, 1944–1974.* Kent, Ohio: Kent State University Press, 1975.

WOLFE, THOMAS. *Soviet Power and Europe, 1945–1970.* Baltimore: Johns Hopkins University Press, 1970.

7 Moscow's Cold War in the Far East

Security considerations transcend expansionist ambitions in Soviet Far Eastern policy. The relative stability and continuity of the Soviet Union's European policy contrast with the major accommodations to unforeseen difficulties that have been required of its policy in the Far East (China, Japan, Mongolia, the two Koreas) during the past few decades. In retrospect, the Stalin era looms as the apogee of Sino-Soviet accord. Stalin found dealing with Chiang Kai-shek easy and advantageous, and when the Communists took power in China, Mao Zedong was prepared to accept a junior partnership and follow the Soviet lead in world affairs. All of this changed rapidly in the post-Stalin period.

In October 1954 Nikita Khrushchev led a Soviet delegation to Beijing to negotiate a series of political and economic agreements that would more accurately reflect China's independence and growing stature within the Communist world. Under the agreement of October 11, 1954, Moscow made a number of concessions, indicative of its desire to eliminate obvious past inequities and possible sources of future friction. The naval base of Port Arthur was returned (formally in May 1955), in accordance with the 1950 treaty; the Soviet share in the four joint-stock companies that had been set up in 1950 and 1951 (to mine nonferrous and rare metals, to extract and refine petroleum, to build and repair ships, and to develop civil aviation) was transferred to the PRC, with appropriate compensation to be paid in goods over a number of years; and the USSR provided an additional long-term credit of $230 million and agreed to help build fifteen additional industrial projects and participate in the construction of a railway line from Lanchow through Urumchi (in Xinjiang) to Alma Ata, on Soviet territory, and of another line between Timin in Chinese Inner Mongolia and Ulan Bator in the MPR to the USSR's Trans-Siberian Railroad. Moscow would not, however, return Tanu-Tuva, which had been detached from Chinese Turkestan during a time of maximum Kuomintang weakness and incorporated into the Soviet Union in 1944; nor would it agree to any questioning of Mongolia's independence or weakening of Soviet-MPR ties. Finally, it resisted Beijing's effort to convert North Korea into a Chinese satellite, but agreed to a compromise whereby the Yenan (Chinese) faction of the Korean Workers' (Communist) party was assured of suitable minority representation.

This was the high-water mark of Sino-Soviet amity and cooperation in the post-Stalin period. From 1955 on tensions mounted and relations deteriorated, as national interests overshadowed Communist ecumenism.

The Sino-Soviet Conflict: Origins

The catalysts for Sino-Soviet disagreements came from Europe. Khrushchev's reconciliation with Tito, his acceptance of the principle of "many roads to socialism" and his interest in better relations with the United States, Beijing's main enemy, alienated the Chinese. His attack on Stalin at the twentieth party congress and subsequent de-Stalinization policy was the final shock to Mao. An implicit criticism of his own rule in China, this policy forced Mao to launch his own equivalent of de-Stalinization—the very short-lived policy in 1956–1957 of "let a hundred flowers bloom, let a hundred schools contend." Mao used this bogus liberalization to draw opponents into the open, destroy them, and reassert his authority against leading rivals (Marshal Peng Teh-huai, purged in 1959, and Liu Shao-chi, purged in 1966). Mao's perceived need to respond to Khrushchev's disruptive policy initiatives may have forced him on to ideological and economic paths that hastened the separation from Moscow. The animus between Khrushchev and Mao was profound, as Khrushchev suggests in his memoirs and as their acrimonious exchanges confirm.

There was a lull in the gathering storm in late 1956, when, in the wake of the Soviet repression in Hungary, Khrushchev assured the Chinese that "We are all Stalinists . . . "; and at the November 1957 Moscow conference of Communist parties, when Mao backed Khrushchev's antirevisionist line, which was directed against Tito and other national Communists. (The supreme irony was that Mao himself had been communism's first "Titoist" in departing from reliance on Moscow in the 1930s and fashioning his own strategy for making a revolution.) But as Soviet policy explored the path of détente with the United States, Moscow's relations with Beijing took a turn for the worse. The adhesive of Marxism-Leninism (and the sharing of a common enemy) that had bound the Soviets and the Chinese in the Stalin period loosened under the strain of divergent national interests. Khrushchev's ideological innovations and his stress on peaceful coexistence with the West contrasted with Mao's preference for doctrinal orthodoxy and monolithism, and the polarizing strategy epitomized by the 1947 Zhdanov line.

The tensions increased with Moscow's criticism of the ideological pretensions that underlay Mao's "Great Leap Forward" campaign in 1958 to bypass socialism and move directly to communism through a system of communes, mass mobilization, and do-it-yourself backyard industrialization. At the 1956 party congress, Khrushchev superseded Stalin's "two-camp" thesis with his "zone of peace" concept, which gave ideological sanction to the USSR's courtship of bourgeois Third World governments and movements (and this at a time of serious Chinese tensions with India and Indonesia). He maintained that as a result of the emergence of the Communist camp and the weakening of colonialism, "a vast 'peace zone,' including both socialist and nonsocialist peace-loving states in Europe and Asia, has emerged in the world arena" and that these new nations could play a "progressive" role in weakening "imperialism" (that is, the United States) and strengthening the Communist world.

The resulting clash with Mao's revolutionary line took place on the Third World stage. Mao saw Khrushchev's formulation that war was no longer "fatalistically inevitable" as the ideological rationale for Moscow's reluctance to use its putative missile superiority, represented by the launching of Sputnik in October 1957, on China's behalf. In August and September of 1958, during the crisis between China and the United States that had been triggered by the Communists' bombardment of the Kuomintang-held offshore islands of Quemoy and Matsu, Moscow's restraint emphasized that it would not risk nuclear war with the United States in order to help Beijing liberate Taiwan. The Quemoy crisis demonstrated that neither the Sino-Soviet alliance nor the shared commitment to Marxism-Leninism was sufficient to overcome diametrically opposed national interests in a concrete situation.[1]

Whatever chances there were for a reconciliation probably vanished with Mao's mastery over his rivals, many of whom favored better relations with Moscow (and a more pragmatic approach to domestic problems) because they wanted to modernize the Chinese army with Soviet assistance or develop China's nuclear capability with Soviet expertise and have a common front in Asia against the United States.[2] Khrushchev's unwillingness to provide more substantial economic assistance and his refusal in 1959 to help China acquire a nuclear capability undermined the anti-Mao faction in the CCP. Adding insult to injury, Khrushchev expanded his relations with the United States, and his visit there in 1959 showed that he had no intention of helping China regain Taiwan. Nor was he going to play nuclear brinksmanship to please Mao. In response to Mao's derisory description of the United States as a paper tiger, Khrushchev retorted, "The United States may be a paper tiger, but [it is] a paper tiger with nuclear teeth."

At a meeting of ruling Communist parties in Bucharest in June 1960, Moscow made a number of concessions in an effort to find a formula for bridging the rift. In return for Beijing's acceptance of Khrushchev's 1956 doctrinal innovations—the possibility of many roads to socialism and the nonevitability of war—Moscow agreed that armed revolutions as a way of bringing about change should be accorded ideological equality with the thesis that the working class could come to power through parliamentary means. In November 1960, at the Moscow conference of eighty-one Communist parties, Khrushchev again looked for a course through the troubled sea of differences with Mao over revisionism and dogmatism (the latter being the charge leveled by the Yugoslavs against the Chinese position that war was inevitable and cooperation with capitalism impossible). However, no amount of ideological circumlocution could resolve the concrete policy differences that divided the two colossi of communism. Khrushchev's peremptory withdrawal in the summer of 1960 of all Soviet technicians (and their blueprints) from China, leaving dozens of incomplete Soviet-assisted projects, intensified Beijing's hostility. If Khrushchev's purpose was to pressure Mao into submission, he failed dismally.

By 1961, the seriousness of the rift had become a matter of public record, as Moscow and Beijing hurled charges and countercharges at one another. The kid gloves came off at the CPSU's twenty-second congress in October of that year. Khrushchev declared that the line established in 1956 was correct and would not be altered to suit the "Albanian leaders," who were not invited to the congress and were regarded by Moscow as Chinese clients, or "anyone else." The Chinese, who had sent a delegation headed by a moderate, Premier Zhou Enlai, were surprised by Khrushchev's open attack on Albania. To the indirect but evident castigation of Beijing, Zhou responded, "If there are quarrels in the socialist camp, we consider that they should be settled through bilateral contacts and that a public denunciation does not contribute to the cohesion of the socialist camp," and then he walked out of the meeting.

The condemnatory attacks crescendoed throughout the remaining years of the Khrushchev period. Moscow called Mao "a megalomaniac warmonger," "an irresponsible scribbler," and "a dogmatist" of whom it could truly be said, "Blessed is he who chatters about war and does not understand what he is chattering about." It labeled the Chinese "imitators of Trotsky" (the most serious charge that can be leveled by one Communist against another). Beijing responded with comparable venom and vigor, referring to Khrushchev as "a Bible-reading and psalm-singing buffoon."

A high-level meeting of Soviet and Chinese party officials was held in Moscow from July 5 to 20, 1963, in an effort to mediate the dispute, but like previous attempts it failed. Each side printed lengthy charges and rebuttals. In March 1964, for example, *Kommunist,* the journal of the CPSU's Central Committee, whose articles are intended primarily for Soviet party cadres, printed a lengthy assessment and indictment of Chinese behavior.[3] It accused the "Chinese deviationists," whose "nationalistic vanity" had forestalled all Soviet attempts at reconciliation, of disrupting the unity of the socialist camp and instilling in the Chinese people a feeling of hostility toward the USSR. Behind Chinese slander is the desire to pose as "supreme arbiter" of socialist ideology. Beijing calls disarmament an illusion, deliberately distorting the Soviet position and denouncing nuclear nonproliferation and efforts to improve relations with the West while "trying feverishly to set right" its own relations with Britain, France, Japan; it obviously would improve relations with the United States, too, if only it could find the opportunity. The Chinese think that the central question in revolution is whether socialist countries will lead it, but this is secondary to the problem of choosing the correct path leading to revolution and power for the working class. All good Communists today should know that a country may become socialist irrespective of its economic development. The Chinese attack the creature comforts of the USSR, but we must fulfill our obligations to our own people. Trotsky had factionalism in his soul, plus willfulness and bourgeois attitudes. The Chinese have stolen many of their ideas from his baggage. They echo him, in both his "no war, no peace" and "permanent revolution" formulations. Despite the concluding call for reconciliation, the tenor of the article and Khrushchev's attempt to convene an international Communist meeting evinced the depths of the chasm separating Moscow and Beijing.

In July 1964 the CPSU sent an invitation to twenty-five Communist parties to attend a conference in Moscow on December 15. Moscow and Beijing seemed on the brink of a formal and irrevocable rupture when Khrushchev was deposed on October 14, 1964. By that time, the specific reasons for the rift had been well documented.

Issues

Though the Sino-Soviet dispute is often cast within an ideological framework, it is fundamentally a rivalry over power and mirrors the divergent strategies, interests, and objectives of the two countries. Briefly, the main source of discord were five broad issues.

First, Moscow believed that as the senior and most powerful member of the international Communist community, it should be accorded the authority to interpret Marxist-Leninist doctrine and establish basic strategy for the bloc, in particular to decide on the best way to deal with the capitalist world. It resented Chinese pretensions to leadership and felt that the Chinese, as newcomers, were not familiar with global realities and did not appreciate the extent to which imperialism could be weakened by nonmilitary means.

Second, the two nations disagreed over priorities: the areas and issues that were most important to Moscow were least important to Beijing, and vice versa. For example, if for no other reason than that the main military threat to the USSR came from the West, Moscow's primary political interest was drawn to European developments, to centrifugal tendencies in Eastern Europe, to the resurgence of West Germany, and to the impact of the Common Market. A satisfied power territorially, the Soviet Union was not prepared to go to war against the United States over the Taiwan question, an issue that was paramount in Chinese thinking. Thus did geography, history, and economics shape national priorities.

Third, Moscow and Beijing differed in their approach to developing countries. While their differences were not as clear-cut as many in the West sometimes imagined, they did connote China's readiness to advocate militant policies that would have interfered with Moscow's courtship of key Third World countries and exacerbated relations between the Soviet Union and the United States. The Chinese sought to profit politically from the failure of Khrushchev's Cuban gamble, but they themselves did not, in practice, precipitate any such dramatic showdowns with the "paper tiger," the United States. A major source of discord between Moscow and Beijing was Soviet assistance to India, particularly the military help given after the Sino-Indian war of 1962. Another was Moscow's program of extending extensive economic and military assistance to non-Communist non-aligned countries, whereas aid to China was brusquely terminated in 1960. By emphasizing the revolutionary path to power and opposing (more in principle than in practice) cooperation between local Communist parties and bourgeois-nationalist parties, China directly challenged the Soviet strategy for spreading Communist influence in the Third World.

Fourth, Moscow's unwillingness after 1959 to help China to develop a nuclear capability and its signing of the limited nuclear test ban treaty in 1963 signified to China a Soviet desire to keep its Communist ally a second-rate military power dependent on Moscow's nuclear shield. Ironically, the Chinese detonated their first nuclear explosion literally within hours of Khrushchev's fall from power.

Fifth, China had long-standing border grievances against the USSR. Under treaties imposed on imperial China by czarist Russia in 1858, 1860, and 1881, China was forced to cede almost one million square miles of territory in central Asia and the maritime provinces of Sibera (see map). Beijing argued that these "unequal treaties" should be renegotiated, a demand rejected by Moscow.

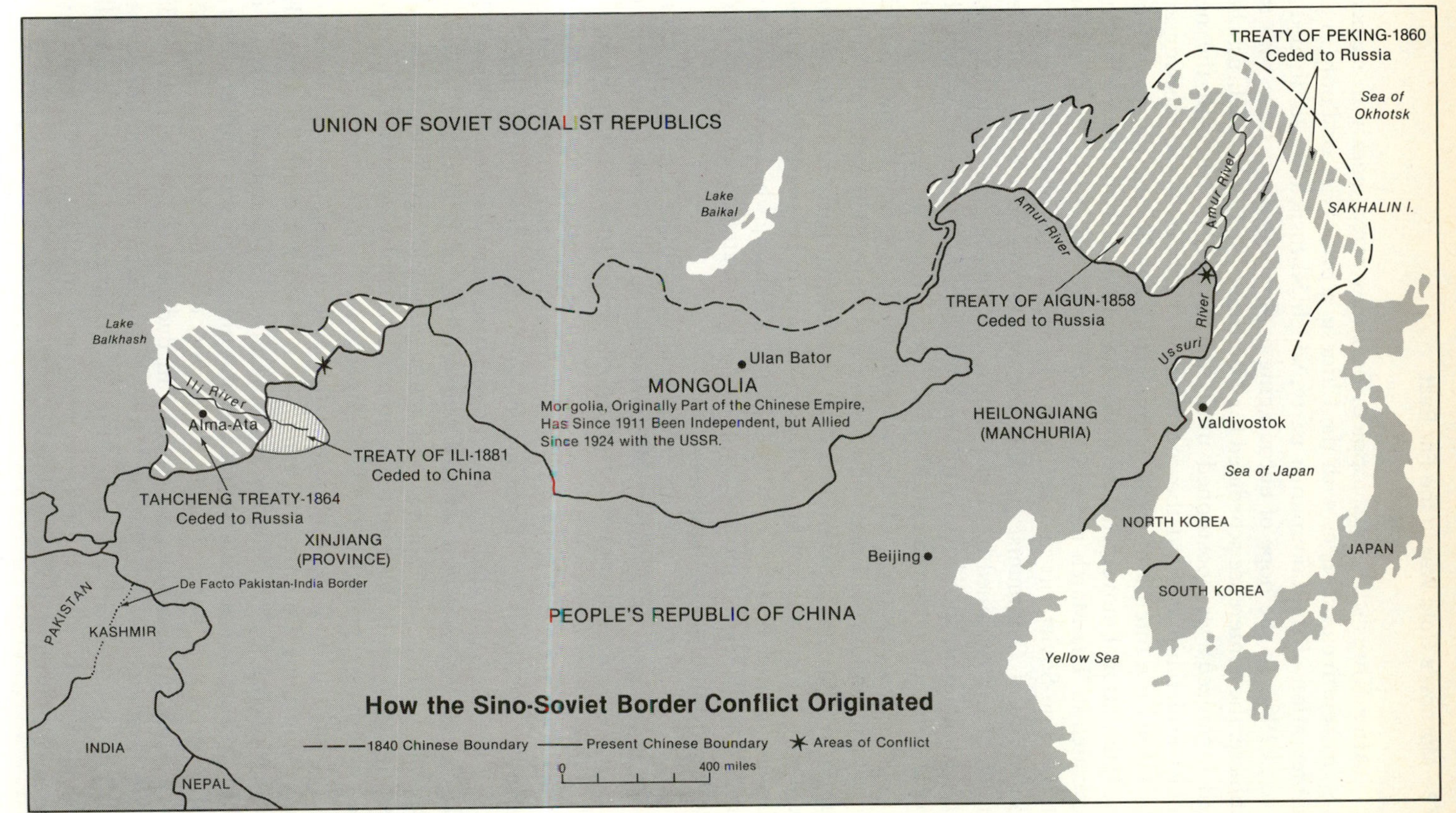

How the Sino-Soviet Border Conflict Originated

After Khrushchev was toppled, Brezhnev acted quickly to suspend the vituperative exchanges with the Chinese, a priority second only to the reintegration of the Communist party, which Khrushchev had divided in two in 1962. In the hope of encouraging exploratory discussions with the Chinese, the conference scheduled for December 1964 (which Khrushchev had organized) was postponed until March 1, 1965. Though the new Soviet leadership stressed the consultative character of the meeting and disclaimed the intention of excommunicating any Communist party from the international movement, the Chinese Communists and their adherents boycotted it. The March meeting did little more than highlight the depth of the Sino-Soviet rift and reaffirm the desirability of holding a world conference of Communist parties. For a time the Soviets shelved their polemics and refrained from responding to Chinese gibes that they were practicing "Khrushchevism without Khrushchev." However, within the world Communist movement, Moscow strengthened its ties. For example, it concluded a new treaty of alliance with the Mongolian People's Republic, which had long depended on Moscow and feared Beijing's ambitions; it supported the establishment of a rival Communist party in Japan to compete with the entrenched pro-Chinese one; and in February 1965, Premier Kosygin visited North Korea and North Vietnam, which generally followed China's lead in intrabloc politics for geostrategic reasons but which were noncommittal in the dispute itself.

By late 1966 the grievances between the Soviet Union and China were unchanged. In October, Moscow ordered all Chinese students to return home, in retaliation for expulsion of Soviet students from China. In November, it resumed open attacks on Beijing, charging that "experience shows that success is achieved by Communist parties that guide themselves unswervingly by Marxism-Leninism, while those espousing pseudorevolutionary phraseology and dogmas inevitably suffer a fiasco." In March 1967, *Kommunist* accused Mao Zedong of following a policy of "splittism" that "undermined the unity of world revolutionary forces, greatly damaged the liberation movement, and is playing into the hands of the imperialists, primarily the U.S. imperialists."

Events in Eastern Europe and the Middle East, the restiveness of many nonruling Communist parties over Moscow's centralist aims, the jubilee celebration in Moscow in November 1967, and the turmoil in China arising out of the Cultural Revolution (which was neither cultural nor a revolution, but a struggle for power) diverted Moscow's attention for a while. At a consultative meeting in Budapest in late February 1968, again boycotted by the Chinese, Moscow engineered enough support to convene an international conference of Communist parties (originally scheduled for November 1968, but postponed until June 1969 because of the Soviet invasion of Czechoslovakia).

On March 2, 14, and 15, 1969, border clashes erupted at the confluence of the Amur and Ussuri rivers below the Soviet city of Khabarovsk in the vicinity of a swampy, uninhabited, vaguely delineated area known as Damansky Island. For the first time, regular military units of one Communist country fought against those of another. A common adherence to Marxism-Leninism was no automatic bar to conflict. Skirmishes in this area had been going on since 1959, and each side had cited thousands of violations by the other. As the result of a Soviet initiative on May 17, 1963, discussions on a wide range of border questions had been started in Beijing in February 1964, but broke off soon thereafter. The two governments agreed to resume the talks in Moscow on October 15, 1964, but the overthrow of Khrushchev resulted in an indefinite postponement. The Damansky affair symbolized a dangerous deterioration in diplomatic relations;[4] it was followed in late spring and early summer by border clashes in Xinjiang and veiled Soviet threats of a preemptive strike against China's nuclear installation at Lop Nor. Realizing the gravity of the situation, Beijing reopened talks on October 20, 1969.

Brezhnev used the Moscow conference of world Communist parties in June 1969 to condemn and try to isolate China (which did not attend), and China was conspicuously excluded in his proposal to create a "system of collective security in Asia." (Soviet diplomacy has worked ever since to conclude friendship treaties with the countries bordering China: Afghanistan, Pakistan, India, Burma, Laos, Vietnam, Mongolia, and North Korea.) However, the blandness of the conference's final document, which made no explicit mention of China (or Czechoslovakia), indicated that Moscow was not able to censure—much less excommunicate—Beijing without risking a serious split and wider challenge to its authority within the world Communist movement.

In other spheres Moscow could proceed more forcefully against China. To make sure that the ideological militancy and economic disruptiveness of the Cultural Revolution would not tempt Mao to start new border incidents, *Pravda* issued a stern warning on August 28, 1969. Observing that "given goodwill, the necessary conditions can and must be assured to guarantee normal relations between the Soviet Union and the People's Republic of China," it called on China to cease "its absurd territorial claims on the Soviet Union" and warned that if a war broke out, "with the existing weaponry, lethal armaments, and modern means of delivery, it would not spare a single continent." This is as close as the Soviet Union has ever come to threatening the use of nuclear weapons against China. There is conjecture that Moscow was not only warning China but also trying to sound out Washington's reaction to a possible strike against the nuclear facility at Lop Nor in Xinjiang.[5]

For a time, government-to-government relations showed some

improvements. In September 1969, after attending Ho Chi Minh's funeral in Hanoi, Premier Kosygin made a quick visit to Beijing where he and Zhou Enlai agreed that the two countries would start negotiating the boundary issues to improve relations, that the disagreement on principles should not interfere with the normalization of state relations, that talks would begin on the dispute along the Amur and Ussuri rivers, and that the negotiations would be conducted without threat and with every effort to maintain the status quo.[6] In October the border negotiations were resumed; in late 1970, after a hiatus of three years, ambassadors were exchanged and new trade agreements were signed.

Nevertheless, the Soviet leadership's growing perception of implacable Chinese hostility prompted a major military buildup. Beginning in the mid-1960s, even before the Damansky Island crisis, Moscow increased the number of divisions in the Far East from fifteen in 1967 to twenty-one in 1969, thirty in 1970, and forty-five in 1980—about 25 percent of the entire Soviet army (to which should be added 200,000 well-armed KGB border guards)—an unmistakable sign that diplomatic efforts to bridge the chasm have been less than successful. The Soviet army is well equipped, possessing commanding superiority in tanks, artillery, combat aircraft, and, of course, nuclear-capable missiles. The 4500-mile border is heavily fortified. The superior system of Soviet communications allows for rapid reinforcement; for example, in the sparsely settled Xinjiang region (Chinese Turkestan), the Soviets have a railroad line running from Alma Ata in Soviet Kazakhstan to the border at Druzhba, whereas the Chinese are poorly situated for serious fighting in this predominantly non-Chinese, Muslim area. As a result of the Soviet-Mongolian treaty (as renewed on October 19, 1976), Moscow has significantly increased its combat forces in the MPR. Militarily, the Soviet army is more than a match for the numerically larger Chinese forces, whose level of modernization and firepower is perhaps ten to twenty years behind the USSR's. Moreover, the Soviet naval buildup in the Far East in the late 1970s, though an additional source of tension with Japan, serves as a constant reminder to China of its vulnerability to Soviet military power.

Sino-Soviet tensions festered on after the dramatic announcement in mid-August 1971 that Secretary of State Henry Kissinger had arrived secretly in Beijing and arranged for President Richard Nixon to visit China the following year. This completely new variable, a stunning turnabout, fueled Soviet paranoia over possible U.S.-Chinese collusion against the USSR. For Moscow there was bitter irony in Beijing's startling policy reversal, which was in its own way every bit as politically momentous as Moscow's deal with Berlin in 1939 had been.

Moscow's détente toward the West having failed to perpetuate the isolation of China, the Kremlin's policy of containing China had to be adapted to the new political situation. Soviet leaders declared that they were not in principle against the Sino–U.S. normalization of relations, provided that it was not used as a lever against other parties. Their worst fears were of secret arrangements designed against the USSR. After Nixon's visit to China in February 1972 (he was also scheduled to go to Moscow in May), Brezhnev continued to work for the containment of China through a combination of military and diplomatic means, while holding out the offer of improved ties and hoping that when Mao died his successors would prove amenable to a Sino-Soviet reconciliation. Thus, in March 1972, at the All-Union Trade Union Congress, Brezhnev expressed readiness for improved relations on any basis:

> Official Chinese representatives tell us that the relations between the USSR and the People's Republic of China must be built on the basis of the principles of peaceful coexistence. [*Note:* In the Communist lexicon, "peaceful coexistence" refers to relations between a Communist and a non-Communist country.] Well, if Beijing does not think it possible to have more than this in relations with a socialist state, then we are ready to build Soviet-Chinese relations at the present time on such a basis.[7]

For the next few years, Soviet policy in the Far East sought to offset Beijing's opening to the West with a campaign to strengthen Moscow's own ties with Mongolia, North Korea, and Japan; to undercut Chinese standing in the Third World by exposing its negligible ability to help national liberation movements or governments in need of military or economic assistance; to play on the fears of Southeast Asian countries, including Vietnam, of Chinese ambitions; and to enhance the USSR's prestige through projection of its formidable military power. Like much of the world, Moscow became an inveterate Mao-watcher.

The Post-Mao Situation

The death of Mao in September 1976, however, brought little substantive change in Beijing's policy, though the polemics somewhat abated. Indeed, the new Chinese leadership went out of its way to downgrade Soviet overtures. For example, Brezhnev's message the following month addressing Hua Guofeng as "comrade" and congratulating him on his appointment as chairman of the CCP was returned by Chinese officials, who noted that "we have no party-to-party relations with them [the Soviets]."[8] Even the messages of condolence on the death of Mao Zedong from Soviet-bloc party leaders were rejected, for the same reason.

Soviet criticisms of China were halted to test Beijing's receptiveness. Then, on April 22, 1977, at a celebration marking Lenin's birth, a member of the CPSU Secretariat accused Beijing of fomenting "international tensions" and of "striking alliance with the most reactionary forces"; and on May 14, *Pravda* warned that "China is today the only country in the world whose official circles advocate publicly and without any camouflage a new world slaughter" and cautioned the West and Japan against arming China or allowing themselves to be used by "the Maoists and other provokers of war."

A technical agreement in October 1977, to which both sides deliberately gave no publicity, resulted in the lifting of the ten-year Soviet blockade of Chinese shipping at the heavily trafficked junction around Bear Island (Hei Hsia-tzu, in Chinese), situated just below Khabarovsk. New navigation rules for this very limited sector of the Amur-Ussuri basin were negotiated as a matter of mutual convenience, to prevent recurring incidents that could create more difficulties than either country would like. They in no way affected the general boundary problem, which seems likely to remain unresolved as long as the USSR rejects the idea that "disputed territories" exist on the grounds that the very use of the phrase implies acceptance of the legitimacy of Chinese claims to some Soviet territory. Moscow refuses also to concede Beijing's claim that the treaties of Aigun (1858), Beijing (1860), and Ili (1881) were "unequal" and should be renegotiated. Therefore, notwithstanding the Bear Island agreement, the persistence of widely divergent points of view on how to proceed with the boundary talks suggests that progress in this sector depends on an a priori improvement in overall Sino-Soviet relations, and such a change does not seem in the offing.

The essentials of the Sino-Soviet rift are as complex today as they were at the time of Mao's death. In the late 1950s, when the split was developing and before Westerners were even aware that there was a problem, esoteric doctrinal exegeses obscured policy differences. These emerged full-blown in the 1960s. The root cause remains nationalism, and precisely because the split derives from rival national interests and conceptions of security, each side views the other as a long-term threat, which geography has confirmed in perpetuity. In international relations, neighbors are rarely friends. Political and ideological considerations are more significant than military ones, though both the USSR and China fear that their geographic and economic vulnerabilities may tempt the other. Each seeks to enhance its prestige by denigrating the backsliding of the other. The Soviet Union sees China as a competitor for leadership in the international Communist movement and among radical groups. The two seek influence in the Third World, though for different reasons—Moscow to undermine the United States, Beijing to undermine the USSR. They have serious border problems. It is probable, too, that continuation (or termination) of the dispute has become enmeshed in the internal struggle for power in the party-military elite of each country. Finally, both the Russians and the Chinese have long historical memories, and the deeply ingrained psychological, cultural, and racial (particularly on the Russian side) antagonisms inevitably make reconciliation more difficult.

Since 1979, Sino-Soviet talks aimed at improving government-to-government relations have been held intermittently, thus far without any notable effects. The few cosmetic improvements have not changed the basic political complexion of a troubled relationship, though they have moved the dialogue beyond the level of "mutual scolding." There are border talks dealing with minor boundary problems concerning jurisdiction over islands in the Amur and Ussuri Rivers; protocols examining the use of water resources of the Argun and the Amur Rivers; increased trade; modest student and scholarly exchanges; a round robin of diplomatic discussions to normalize relations; and the USSR's agreement to modernize a number of the industrial plants that it had built in China in the 1950s.

The Sino-Soviet dispute is a dynamic one, constantly changing its contours in response to the international developments and new power-political and economic considerations. When Soviet leaders, seeking to contain China and promote Soviet security in the Far East, anticipate dealing with Beijing in the decade ahead and coping with its multidimensional challenges, they face a relationship that is significantly different from what it was in, say, the last years of Mao's rule. In the changes one can discern the evolving and interrelated range of issues and concerns that now confront Soviet leaders.

First, the Sino-Soviet alliance established in February 1950 is dead. On April 3, 1979, Beijing informed Moscow that the treaty would not be renewed when it expired in April 1980. Though long regarded as an anachronism, the alliance did signify a certain ideological kinship and sense of shared antagonists. To Moscow, China's renunciation of the alliance, coupled with its rapprochement with the United States and Japan, leaves no doubt that in Beijing's eyes the Soviet Union is the main enemy in Asia, and the Kremlin has acted accordingly.

Second, China is more of a nuclear threat now than it was a decade ago. The time for nuclear preemption has passed. China has a slowly growing stockpile of nuclear weapons and a mix of short- and intermediate-range missiles that can hit Soviet targets east of the Ural Mountains; moreover, it is developing an ICBM capability as well (Beijing tested its first one in May 1980). In anticipation of China's acquisition of a credible nuclear force by the 1990s, Moscow is expending an ever-increasing portion of its military budget for defense. In addition to having shifted sizable naval forces to the Pacific fleet in late 1978, the USSR deployed more than 200 SS-20s to augment its military capability in the Far East, although these are to be destroyed under the provisions of the 1988 U.S.-Soviet INF treaty.

Third, the USSR faces a China that is no longer diplomatically isolated. The normalization of Sino-American relations, the signing of the Sino-Japanese treaty of friendship and cooperation in August 1978, the seating of the PRC in the United Nations in 1971, and the ever-widening range of contacts with Western and Third World countries all mock the Soviet effort to isolate China and give Beijing greater authority in its dealings with Moscow. China's opening to the West in particular necessitates continual Soviet reassessments of Beijing's military, economic, and political options, since the modern technology and expertise that China imports will make it a more formidable adversary and its diplomatic flexibility has in the main limited Soviet maneuverability. The Soviet-Vietnamese friendship treaty of November 1978 provided the USSR with some middle range options for frustrating China's policies in Cambodia, Laos, and Vietnam, but at the same time it strained relations with the United States and forced Moscow to react to Chinese thrusts instead of making its own. To the extent that the USSR exercises its privileges in Vietnam against China, Moscow risks arousing U.S. and Southeast Asian fears of Soviet expansion and a consequent deterioration in relations with these countries, whose instinctive response will be to draw closer to China—a prospect Soviet leaders seek to prevent.

Fourth, every projection of Soviet power adds credence to Chinese accusations of Soviet moves toward hegemony. Politically, Moscow is on the defensive and in the position of having to deny that it is ambitious, provocative, or covetous. It is a truism that in almost any confrontation between a stronger and a weaker power, the former has the greater difficulty in justifying its actions to interested regional and international onlookers, as China found out when it attacked Vietnam in March 1979 to punish it for having invaded Kampuchea (Cambodia) to unseat a pro-Chinese but exceptionally bloodthirsty and belligerent Communist leadership.

Fifth, the competition for authority in the world Communist movement that loomed large in the 1950s and 1960s has become far less of a factor in the determination of Soviet policy toward China. Doctrinal disquisitions are less common, if only because fewer of the faithful regard them as anything other than verbal rituals to justify what was done for other quite tangible, nonideological reasons. The acentric character of international communism is accepted, and Moscow's search for supporters relies more on demonstrating the advantages of association than on its skill at dialectical hair-splitting.

Sixth, the USSR's position in the Third World is vastly superior to that of the PRC's. The appeal of the Yenan way, of Mao's strategy for waging a people's war, has palled. As the target areas of Sino-Soviet competition have spread, the Soviet Union's advantage has become pronounced. Moscow simply commands enormously greater resources for an ambitious imperial policy in the Third World and possesses a credibility in crises for prospective clients that Beijing lacks. It is increasingly evident, too, that the Chinese model of development, about which so much was written in the 1960s and early 1970s, is unsuited to most Third World countries, which lack the organization and total control necessary to exact sustained sacrifices on a mass scale; which see the model being discarded in China itself as the post-Mao leadership unabashedly introduces bourgeois reforms and seeks aid from abroad; and which can obtain the military assistance they need to stay in power and fight their enemies from the USSR by eschewing a Maoist line. And too, simply stated, such countries lack the cultural cohesion, drive, and discipline of the Chinese.

Moreover, whereas Moscow proclaims a principled purpose in extending support to Third World countries—that is to help them either to overthrow "reactionary" governments or to defend themselves against external threats from "aggressors" (pro-Western rivals)—Beijing no longer disguises the anti-Soviet animus that motivates its policy. This was clearly apparent when China withdrew support in 1973 from the Dhofari rebels in Oman and drew closer to the shah of Iran, when it supported anti-Communist nationalist groups in southern Africa in the 1970s because the Communists mostly looked to Moscow, and when it approved of Egyptian President Anwar Sadat's decision to sign a peace treaty with Israel in 1979. By consistently supporting Third World governments or movements that are pursuing a line that places them in opposition to the United States, Moscow has effectively undercut Beijing's diplomacy in the Third World.

Seventh, the Soviet Union has reason to be concerned in the 1990s about the possible formation of an anti-Soviet constellation. Beijing has normalized relations with the United States and Japan and obtained extensive credits from Britain, France, and the Federal Republic of Germany. Moscow fears that the transfer of advanced weapons and technology from the West and the know-how to accelerate industrialization from Japan will transform China into a superpower within a decade or two, and that such a transformation could tempt the United States to play the so-called China card, joining forces with China in order to challenge Soviet interests in the northwest Pacific, Southern Asia, and possibly even in Eastern Europe. Admittedly a worst-case scenario, it is one that Soviet planners do not dare to ignore.

Eighth, the Chinese factor in particular and Far East considerations in general demand a bigger chunk of Soviet military power. The permanent deployment of sizable military contingents in the Far East is costly and requires the diversion of already scarce pools of labor, capital, and materials from the civilian to the military sector and from the European to the Asian part of the Soviet Union. A decade ago, a troublesome China was relatively easy to handle militarily; a decade hence, the problem will be magnified many times over.

Ninth, Moscow can no longer look forward to a post-Mao period bringing with it a return to the halycon days of the Sino-Soviet relationship. That period has come and the new Chinese leadership under Deng Xiaoping—the octogenarian victor in the post-Mao succession struggle—has opted for the Maoist attitude toward the Soviet Union. During his last year, Brezhnev tried to exploit frictions in Sino-American relations over the Taiwan issue to improve Sino-Soviet relations. And whereas at the Twenty-fifth Congress in February 1976 he had said that "Maoist ideology and policy are incompatible with Marxist-Leninist teaching," and indeed, that "they are directly hostile to it," in March 1982 he noted, among other conciliatory comments, that notwithstanding China's alignment with the imperialists in world affairs, "we have not denied and do not deny the existence of a socialist system in China." At Brezhnev's funeral in November 1982, Yuri Andropov singled out Foreign Minister Huang Hua for special atention, but that gesture led nowhere. Indeed, at Andropov's funeral in February 1984, no comparable overture was made by the Kremlin leadership. Mao may have aggravated the dispute in the 1960s and early 1970s out of personal pique, but the essentials of his far-ranging hostility are apparently shared by his successors.

Finally, the Soviet leadership is unlikely to make any major concessions to the Chinese on the territorial issue, especially in the Amur-Ussuri river basin, which may contain rich coal and mineral deposits. As the global competition for raw materials intensifies, Moscow will have even less reason to relinquish control of potentially valuable pieces of real estate. The more uncompromising the Soviets are on the border issues, the less likely they will be to find the Chinese prepared for a genuine reconciliation.

In a major speech delivered in Vladivostok on July 28, 1986, Gorbachev spoke of "the need for an urgent, radical break with many of the conventional approaches to foreign policy."[9] Comparing the situation in the Far East with that in Europe—clearly, with the Soviet Union's two-front problem in mind—he noted that "the Pacific region as a whole is not yet militarized to the same extent as the European region," but the potential for this happening "is truly enormous and the consequences extremely dangerous." For the first time, he addressed directly "the three obstacles" raised by the Chinese as preconditions for an improvement in Sino-Soviet relations: Mongolia, Afghanistan, and Kampuchea. Gorbachev held out three conciliatory olive twigs, saying that "the question of withdrawing a considerable number of Soviet troops from Mongolia is being examined" by Moscow and Ulan Bator; that the Soviet Government would withdraw six regiments from Afghanistan by the end of the year; and that the Kampuchean issue [that is, the USSR's subsidizing of Vietnam's occupation of Kampuchea] "depends on the normalization of Chinese-Vietnamese relations." He also called for expanded trade and hinted at concessions on long-festering border issues and the construction of a railroad linking the Xinjiang Uygur Autonomous region of China and Soviet Kazakhstan. He said all the right things, but one swallow does not a spring make. Still, although Moscow has been slow to meet Beijing's conditions for better relations, there has been some movement under Gorbachev.

All in all, the USSR's failure to maintain the alliance with China was a major diplomatic setback that inevitably colors any assessment of Soviet policy in the Far East. In the case of China, Moscow certainly fared poorly in the matter of advancing Soviet ambitions and safeguarding essential national interests. Never mind who was responsible for the turn of events—the net result was to change China from an ally to an adversary. Coping with this new leadership and the challenge it poses to Soviet interests will place great demands on Soviet diplomacy.

Apart from the absorption with China, the USSR has also conducted an active policy toward the other regional actors in northeast Asia—Japan, Mongolia, and North Korea—with which it has some accomplishments to its credit. A few comments about each are appropriate.

Soviet-Japanese Relations

At the time of the Korean War, Moscow regarded Japan as "the main American bridgehead in the Far East." Japan was the staging area from which the United States mounted its military operations in Korea and threatened the Soviet Union and China with long-range air power. The United States used the war to accelerate the transition of Japan from occupied ex-enemy state to passive participant and incipient ally. In September 1951, at the San Francisco conference convened to sign a peace treaty with Japan, Soviet aims toward Japan emerged in the open. The Soviet delegate proposed Japan's neutralization: that Japan agree "not to enter into any coalitions or military alliance directed against any Power which participated with its armed forces in the war against Japan," and that it not permit any foreign power to have its troops or military bases on Japanese territory. There were other proposed amendments as well, including limits on Japanese rearmament, demilitarization of all straits leading into the Japan Sea, and acknowledgment of Soviet title to all the northern islands under Soviet occupation. The Soviet proposals were rejected; the peace treaty was signed, though not by the Soviet Union (or China), and Japan concluded a mutual security treaty with the United States.

After Stalin's death, Soviet leaders desired to establish diplomatic ties with Japan but were unwilling to accede to Japan's demand for the immediate return of Shikotan and the Habomai Islands off northern Hokkaido. They persuaded a weak Japanese government to agree to the Adenauer formula, which had led to the reestablishment of diplomatic ties between the USSR and West Germany, namely, "restoring diplomatic relations before the differences between the two countries were resolved"; and to accept the promise of the return of the above-mentioned islands "under certain conditions" after the signing of a formal peace treaty.[10] In the declaration signed on October 19, 1956, leading to the resumption of bilateral relations, Moscow recognized the right of Japan to enter into diplomatic and military agreements with any country and disengaged itself from a common approach with Beijing to Japan, thereby angering Mao. It saw normalization as essential for further Soviet influence over the Japanese and for helping the domestic effectiveness of the various Japanese organizations—cultural, political, and commercial—that favored closer ties with the USSR.

Over the years, there has been a remarkable continuity in Soviet objectives: to undermine the U.S.–Japanese mutual security pact; to keep Japan from acquiring nuclear weapons or rearming on a major scale (which would be contrary to a provision in the U.S.–imposed Japanese constitution limiting Japan to "self-defense" forces); to see the U.S. military presence in Japan reduced; and to expand economic relations.

A major impediment to better political relations has been Moscow's unwillingness to return what Japan calls the northern territories, which include Shikotan and a group of five islands called Habomai (all of which Moscow in 1956 agreed to return) as well as Iturup and Kunashir, both of which Moscow insists Japan renounced in 1951 at San Francisco. In a reversal of its promise of 1956, the USSR has repeatedly linked the return of Shikotan and Habomai to Japan's renunciation of the U.S.–Japanese security pact. In November 1967 Politburo member Mikhail Suslov told a visiting Japanese Socialist party delegation that the USSR would never return any former Japanese territory as long as Japan's military pact with the United States was in effect.

Throughout the 1960s Moscow saw no reason for softening its position. Skillfully exploiting the strong antimilitary, pacifist sentiment in

Japan and the growing opposition to U.S. control of Okinawa (which was returned to Japanese jurisdiction in 1970), it watched the pressures of domestic Japanese politics force a diminished American military presence. The antinuclear movement also made it politically difficult for U.S. nuclear submarines to have easy access to Japanese ports.

In the early 1970s Soviet leaders found it expedient to hint at a possible compromise, without ever being really specific. This attitude was motivated by the beginnings of a Sino-Japanese rapprochement, which led China to support the Japanese claim to the northern territories as Sino-Soviet relations worsened, and by the Nixon visit to China in February 1972, which aroused Soviet fears of U.S.–Chinese–Japanese collusion against the USSR. High-level exchanges all faltered on the inability to reach agreement on a peace treaty, which in turn foundered on the territorial dispute. Moscow is reported to have offered, on occasion, the return of Shikotan and Habomai in exchange for a treaty, but Tokyo insisted on all four territories, a reflection of the growing inflexibility of all Japanese political parties on this issue.[11] Not only have the two northernmost, larger islands become Soviet military bases, but Moscow fears that the surrender of what it has regarded as Soviet territory since 1945 would establish a precedent that could be exploited by Beijing.

The issue was further complicated in December 1976 when the Soviet government announced the establishment of a 200–nautical mile fishing zone, effective March 1, 1977, that makes the ability of Japanese fishermen to operate in Soviet waters and in the vicinity of the disputed islands hostage to Soviet goodwill.[12] Ever since the Soviet Union and Japan established diplomatic relations in 1925, Moscow had used the fisheries issue to obtain diplomatic and political concessions from the Japanese government. Paradoxically, however, with the proclamation of the 200–nautical mile fishing zone, it has lost much of its former leverage, because in reaction to restrictions placed on its own catches by other countries, Moscow reduced Japanese quotas.

> Based on the so-called "principle of equal quota," what Moscow and Tokyo have agreed upon since 1979 are total fishing quotas of 750,000 and 650,000 tons, respectively for Japanese and Russian fishermen within the other's 200-mile zone. Whereas the Japanese quota became about half of the previous one of 1,220,000 tons, the Soviet quota has remained the same or even increased above the former level of 500,000–600,000 tons. Furthermore, in an exchange of a 100,000 ton difference, the Japanese side has been paying the USSR a fee in foreign currency, which the Soviet Union badly needs. As these quotas have become a stable standard acceptable for both the USSR and Japan, the Japan-Soviet negotiations on fishing rights have recently become *pro forma,* almost ceremonial, lasting only about ten days. Thus, the fishing issue has ceased to be a serious source of dispute or a resource for manipulation by the Soviets.[13]

One of the USSR's important objectives in recent years has been to enlist Japanese industry and expertise to aid in the economic development of Siberian resources. Serious talks began in January 1966 with the establishment of the Joint Japan-Soviet Economic Committee. But not until 1974 was any significant agreement concluded. Japan invested $450 million for the purchase of equipment abroad to develop the coalfields in the South Yakutian Basin of Siberia, in return for which it will be repaid over a twenty-year period with 100 million tons of coking coal. (The coal mines are located at Neryungri, one of several sites being developed in conjunction with the new 2000-mile-long Baikal-Amur Mainline [BAM] railroad.) Another agreement, the Tyumen oil project, fell through at the last minute; the Japanese backed out because costs were prohibitive and because Japan still exports far more than it imports from the USSR.

The economic potentialities of Soviet-Japanese trade have been limited by Japan's political dissatisfaction, even though economic considerations generally play a very important role in Japanese foreign policy. Moscow courts Japanese investment to develop its rich oil, natural gas, and mineral deposits in Siberia and to discourage Japan's keen interest in the Chinese market. It hopes that a combination of economic inducements and pressure will influence Japanese foreign policy and that an innate pragmatism on both sides will keep economics fairly separate from politics (much more than in Soviet-American relations). In this, however, its thinking may be out-of-date. Japan's increasingly labor-intensive, high-tech economy "has resulted in a greatly reduced level of demand for Soviet raw materials, particularly in the energy, steel, and construction sectors that once absorbed the vast majority of Soviet exports to Japan."[14] Prospective Japanese investors are not as attracted to the proximity of Soviet resources in Siberia as they were in the 1970s. Moscow wants Japan's high technology equipment; some it can purchase, and some it tries to obtain by means of espionage and bribery (as in the mid-1980s when Toshiba and the Kongberg Vaapenfabrik of Norway surreptitiously sold computer controls for Japanese milling machines that were used by the Soviet military to manufacture better propellers for nuclear submarines). For the foreseeable future, Soviet-Japanese trade is unlikely to exceed the current level of less than two percent of total Japanese trade; moreover, "not since 1976 have the two countries agreed to a single new joint project, in contrast with three agreements in 1965–1969 and four in 1970–1975."[15]

Moscow views with suspicion the improvement in Sino-Japanese relations, epitomized by the peace treaty signed on August 12, 1978. It has repeatedly expressed displeasure and warned that it would have to reconsider its efforts to conclude a peace treaty with a state pursuing a policy hostile toward the Soviet Union. In 1975 and 1976, it proposed a Soviet-Japanese treaty of amity that would sidestep territorial issues—as did the prospective Sino-Japanese treaty that avoided any mention of the disputed Senkaku Islands—but the Japanese replied that the Soviet-Japanese territorial issue involved vital national interests. The Soviet government regards the Sino-Japanese treaty as anti-Soviet, first, because of inclusion, at Beijing's insistence, of the antihegemony clause, which states that "the contracting parties declare that neither of them should seek hegemony in the Asia-Pacific region or in any other region and each is opposed to efforts by any other country or group of countries to establish such hegemony"; and second, because it reinforces Moscow's fear of a Beijing-Tokyo-Washington military alliance being formed against the USSR. The treaty has intensified Moscow's diplomatic efforts to obtain Japan's agreement to a comparable document.

Ever since the late 1970s the Soviet Union has strengthened its military installations and presence on the northern islands of Etorofu and Kunashir off Hokkaido, a move the Japanese termed "a very unfriendly gesture." The buildup may be only part of the general augmenting of Soviet force levels in the Far East, or it may signify the USSR's disapproval of the Sino-Japanese treaty, be a warning against Japan's providing China with advanced military technology, or manifest opposition to Japan's budding remilitarization. Also worrisome is Moscow's deployment of SS-20s (although these will be phased out and dismantled now that the INF treaty is operative), and perhaps even more so is the rapid expansion of conventional forces, especially the Soviet Pacific Fleet (the largest of its four fleets) of about 100 major surface combat ships and a larger number of attack submarines, and the more than 2000 combat aircraft, including recently deployed long-range bombers.

Thus far, Gorbachev's overtures have failed to dispel the growing Japanese perception of the Soviet Union as Japan's principal security threat. The visit by Eduard Shevardnadze in January 1986, the first in ten years by a Soviet foreign minister, was a disappointment, because he brought no concessions on the military and territorial issues. Nor did Gorbachev make a state visit, as then–Prime Minister Yasuhiro Nakasone had expected. Continuity best describes Gorbachev's policy toward Japan.

The massive expansion of Soviet military power in the Far East is part of Moscow's policy of containment of China and deterrence against Japan. Integral to this regional strategy is friendship with the Mongolian People's Republic and North Korea, both of which are front-line pieces on the Sino-Soviet chessboard.

The USSR and the MPR

With an area of 604,000 square miles and a population of about two million, Mongolia shares a 1500-mile border with the USSR and a 2500-

mile border with China. Landlocked as it is between the USSR and the CPR, the MPR could not help being influenced by the wishes of its stronger neighbor, that is, the USSR. Under effective Soviet tutelage since 1921, it is solidly in Moscow's camp. China (under the Kuomintang) formally recognized Mongolia's independence on January 5, 1946, in accordance with the public preference expressed in a Soviet-controlled plebiscite held on October 20, 1945. When the Communists came to power, they too recognized the MPR's independence, in a 1950 treaty. However, after Chiang Kai-shek was chased from the mainland, he reversed the Kuomintang's recognition of MPR independence, and for more than twenty years the U.S. government ignored Mongolia out of deference to Taiwan; not until January 1987 did the MPR (with Moscow's approval) agree to reestablish diplomatic ties with the United States.

Mongolia's pro-Moscow position on the Sino-Soviet dispute was confirmed by the Soviet-Mongolian twenty-year treaty of mutual assistance of January 15, 1966, which replaced the treaty of February 1946 and authorized the stationing of Soviet troops in the country to deter any probes from the Chinese autonomous region of Inner Mongolia. Mongolia fears absorption by the Chinese, which it sees occurring in Inner Mongolia. A thick network of fortifications has been constructed on the MPR side, and the civilian population has been largely relocated away from a sixty-mile belt along the border. In contrast to North Korean leader Kim Il-sung, Mongolia's party boss, Yumjagiin Tsedenbal, who stepped down for reasons of health in August 1984 (when he was succeeded by Jambyn Batmonh), openly took the Soviet side in the Sino-Soviet dispute and frequently criticized Mao and other Chinese leaders. Agreements in the mid-1950s and early 1960s permitted Chinese laborers to enter the country to work on various construction projects, but these have long since expired, and Soviet economic influence predominates. Indeed, in mid-1983, Mongolia expelled several thousand of the 8000 long-time Chinese residents from the capital, Ulan Bator, possibly as a Moscow-inspired move "to convey an impression that the Mongolians act independently and cannot be taken for granted in the talks on normalizing Chinese-Soviet relations."[16] (In discussions with Beijing, Moscow has argued that third parties should not be included in their negotiations.) Ulan Bator's economy is closely tied to the USSR and the once discreet Sino-Soviet competition for Mongolia's allegiance has been supplanted by an obviously commanding Soviet presence. (Mongolia became a full member of Comecon in 1962.) Though its economy is enmeshed with that of the USSR, on whose power it relies for preservation as an independent state, the MPR manages to maintain its cultural distinctiveness and internal autonomy. Moscow's interest is strategic, and its policy has been to strengthen the MPR's status as a buffer state. Within this context, but also in keeping with the conciliatory measures mentioned by Gorbachev in his July 1986 Vladivostok speech, the USSR announced in June 1987 the withdrawal of some Soviet contingents—according to Western sources, about 11,000 troops, or between 20 and 25 percent of its total forces in the country. The move is a gesture toward Beijing, intended to accelerate the normalization process.

The Korean Triangle

Soviet relations with the Democratic People's Republic of Korea (DPRK) are more complex. Since the end of the Korean War, Kim Il-sung has gained control of his internal affairs, skillfully playing off Moscow and Beijing.[17] The modernization of the DPRK's substantial armed forces has been accomplished primarily with Soviet assistance and weapons; and Pyongyang's assertive foreign policy, aimed at Korea's reunification under Communist rule, depends in large measure on Soviet and Chinese forebearance and implicit support.

By virtue of U.S. support for and military presence in South Korea, the Soviet Union has leverage over the DPRK, which it uses to prevent Pyongyang from slipping closer to China and to ensure that it does not start a war to reunify Korea. Moscow expects the status quo to persist for the foreseeable future and wants to restrain Kim Il-sung without edging him toward Beijing, as happened in January 1968, after the crisis occasioned by the DPRK's seizure of the U.S. intelligence ship *Pueblo*. At the time, Moscow saw in Kim's action a bellicosity and unpredictability that could prove dangerous; it feared that Pyongyang might invoke the security provisions of the Soviet-DPRK military treaty if the United States retaliated.

On a number of occasions in the 1960s and 1970s—for example, during President Nikolai V. Podgorny's visit to Pyongyang on the eve of the 1969 conference of Communist parties in Moscow, and during Mao's meeting with Nixon in 1972—the Soviet leadership tried to bring the DPRK more into harmony with its tune on China, with limited success.

In the early 1980s, Moscow was annoyed by Kim Il-sung's periodic praise of Eurocommunism, preference in Kampuchea for the Khmer Rouge guerillas against the Vietnam-backed regime of Heng Samrin that the USSR supports, and coolness toward Soviet policy in Afghanistan.

There has been, however, a marked change in Soviet–North Korean relations since May 1984, when Kim Il-Sung made his first official visit in twenty-three years to the Soviet Union. The reasons underlying the latest rapprochement are complex and related to broader Soviet objectives in Northeast Asia. Whereas Kim Il-Sung seeks to obtain Moscow's recognition of his son, Kim Jon-Il, as successor-designate, Soviet economic assistance for his sluggish economy, Soviet weapons to upgrade his army and keep abreast of the increasing military capability of South Korea, and Soviet diplomatic suspport to offset the diplomatic isolation that has come with North Korea's involvement in international terrorism, Gorbachev would like a friendly North Korea for the access to ports and sea lanes that it provides the Soviet navy, for a counter to a possible anti-Soviet, Sino-Japanese-American entente, and for leverage against China.[18] The delivery in 1985 of advanced Soviet aircraft represented tangible proof of Moscow's deepening commitment to North Korea.

In this environment of intricate and carefully calculated diplomatic moves, Moscow watches warily as the DPRK, with a population of only about twenty million, builds a formidable military force that is reputed to have the fifth largest army in the world, improves economic ties with China and Japan, and goes its own way in the Third World. In the main, Moscow (and Beijing) understand the nationalism that underlies the DPRK's attempt to maintain a balanced position between its two giant Communist neighbors and benefactors. With great-power relationships taking so many unexpected twists, Moscow prefers its Korean flank to remain quiet and stable; as Gorbachev indicated during Kim Il-Sung's visit in October 1986, it favors "a peaceful democratic unification" of North and South Korea. As if to underscore this point to Kim, Moscow decided to participate in the 1988 Olympics in Seoul, thus distancing itself from Pyongyang in a highly symbolic way.

The Balance Sheet

Any assessment of the strengths and weaknesses, the accomplishments and failures, the prospects and dilemmas that have characterized Soviet policy in the Far East over the past few decades is complicated and must at best be an approximation. The unequivocal accomplishments have been remarkably few.

The USSR has become the preeminent military power on the mainland of Asia, but in the process it has aroused the fears of its neighbors. It does not face, as it did in the 1930s, a dangerous and expansionist Japan, but it has more independent-minded actors to contend with.

China is still more a nuisance than a military threat, but it is not thoroughly anti-Soviet. Moscow's deep-rooted fears of China stem from China's *potential* to develop into a genuine superpower and from Moscow's own *actual* weaknesses—shortages of labor and capital that may reduce the USSR's rate of growth; ethnic diversity, which may place in question the reliability of non-Russian military contingents; the need to import advanced technology; the enormous economic inefficiency and waste that plague the Soviet system; and so on.

Moscow can derive satisfaction from the role that it played in bringing about a thinning-out of American power in Asia. In contrast to the decade after World War II, in the 1990s the United States will not be in a position to project significant military power (conventional, not nuclear) in the Far East in a way that could threaten Soviet clients or interests. The United States may be able to deter Soviet expansion, but its capacity for generating threats to the USSR is limited.

Finally, the USSR has excellent relations with Mongolia, and its relations with Japan, which admittedly leave much to be desired, are nevertheless closer than they were in the 1950s.

Against this modest list of achievements can be set developments that call into question the wisdom and farsightedness of Soviet policymakers.

First and foremost, there is the Khrushchev-Brezhnev squandering of Stalin's legacy of close relations and alliance with China. No possible improvement of relations on the state-to-state level is likely to restore the relationship that existed at the signing of the 1950 treaty of alliance. The next generation of Soviet leaders will have to divert significant resources away from economic growth to beef up the defenses along the rimland of Sino-Soviet confrontation.

Second, Brezhnev's proposal for an Asian collective security system has been a dud in the Far East. As a device for containing China, it never worked—which means that Soviet diplomacy must continue to stress bilateralism if it is to make any headway on this aim.

Third, the Soviet courtship of Japan has stumbled badly. Moscow had hoped to secure much greater Japanese participation in the development of Siberia. Moreover, the Japanese have rejected the Soviet proposal for an Asian version of the Conference on Security and Cooperation in Europe and have seen fit to draw closer to China, over strenuous Soviet objections.

Looking back at the record of Soviet diplomacy in the Far East since the death of Stalin, one must conclude that, with the exception of its important contribution to the defeat of the United States in Vietnam, Moscow had little effect on the major developments and new trends that are emerging in the area. The 1990s may provide some clues to the fundamentals on which future Soviet policy is to be conducted: whether the Soviet Union will become more interested in projecting its growing military power in order to influence the course of events, or whether it will adhere to a cautious, essentially status quo policy, reacting to opportunity and striving to associate more closely with the economic dynamism that is making the Pacific Basin a leading center of world industrial and technological development.

Notes

1. See John R. Thomas, "Soviet Behavior in the Quemoy Crisis of 1958," *Orbis,* Vol. 6, No. 1 (Spring 1962), 38–64.
2. See Donald S. Zagoria, "Mao's Role in the Sino-Soviet Conflict," *Pacific Affairs,* Vol. 47, No. 2 (Summer 1974), 146–48. See also Gerald Segal, "Chinese Politics and the Soviet Connection," *The Jerusalem Journal of International Relations,* Vol. 2, No. 1 (Fall 1976), 96–128.
3. "For the Unity of International Communist Activity on the Principles of Marxism-Leninism," *Kommunist,* No. 5 (March 1964), 13–52, excerpts.
4. For example, see George Ginsburgs, *The Damansky/Chenpao Island Incidents: A Case Study of Syntactic Patterns in Crisis Diplomacy,* Asian Studies Occasional Paper Series, No. 6 (Edwardsville: Southern Illinois University, 1973); and Thomas W. Robinson, "The Sino-Soviet Border Dispute: Background, Development, and the March 1969 Clashes," *American Political Science Review,* Vol. 66, No. 4 (December 1972), 1175–1202.
5. Victor Louis, a foreign journalist alleged to have close ties to the KGB and Soviet officials, caused shock waves when he suggested that whether the Soviet Union attacked Lop Nor or not was only "a question of strategy," and that if the Soviet Union had intervened in Czechoslovakia to defend socialism, why should it not also apply the Brezhnev Doctrine to China? See *New York Times,* September 18, 1969. The Soviet government also circulated a note to its East European allies asking whether the USSR should launch a preemptive strike against China.
6. Zhou Enlai told this to Audrey Topping at a dinner in Beijing in May 1971. See *New York Times,* May 21, 1971.
7. *Pravda,* March 21, 1972.
8. *New York Times,* October 29, 1976.
9. The quotes from Gorbachev's Vladivostok speech are taken from the text translated by *FBIS/USSR National Affairs,* 29 July 1986, R11–R18.
10. James William Morley, "Soviet-Japanese Peace Declaration," *Political Science Quarterly,* Vol. 72, No. 3 (September 1957), 373–74.
11. *New York Times,* January 11, 1976.
12. Robert Rand, "Sonoda's Visit to Moscow," Radio Liberty Research Paper (January 17, 1978), 2.
13. Hiroshi Kimura, "Soviet Policy Toward Japan," Working Paper No. 6 (Providence, R.I.: The Center for Foreign Policy Development, Brown University, August 1983), 17–18.
14. Gordon B. Smith, "Recent Trends in Japanese-Soviet Trade," *Problems of Communism,* Vol. XXXVI, No. 1 (January–February 1987), 58.

15. Kenichi Ito, "Japan and the Soviet Union—Entangled in the Deadlock of the Northern Territories," *The Washington Quarterly,* Vol. 11, No. 1 (Winter 1988), 38.

16. *New York Times,* June 5, 1983.

17. After 1956, Kim effectively purged the pro-Soviet faction in the Korean Workers (Communist) party. Since Kim's opponents "were inspired by the de-Stalinization campaign in the Soviet Union and the Soviet representative in Pyongyang was sympathetic to their cause, Kim had little choice but to denounce them. Obviously, both Kim Il-song and Mao Tse-tung had reasons to resent Khrushchev's unilateral decisions of 1956. The outcome, particularly the removal of the Russian faction men, was a consolidation of the position of Kim Il-song." Kim emerged as the undisputed leader in North Korea. "The events in 1956 also stimulated the North Korean regime to adopt a more nationalistic line of policy and to assert independence within the international Communist camp. Having eliminated the moderating influence of the Soviet faction men, the party also veered to the left in ideology and in economic policies, paralleling the steps taken by Peking." See Chong-sik Lee and Kiwan Oh, "The Russian Faction in North Korea," *Asian Survey,* Vol. 8, No. 4 (April 1968), 287–88.

18. Lee Suck-Ho, "Evolution and Prospects of Soviet-North Korean Relations in the 1980s," *Journal of Northeast Asian Affairs,* Vol. V, No. 3 (Fall 1986), 23–27.

Selected Bibliography

AN, TAI SUNG. *The Sino-Soviet Territorial Dispute.* Philadelphia: Westminster Press, 1973.

BRZEZINSKI, ZBIGNIEW K. *The Soviet Bloc: Unity and Conflict.* Cambridge: Harvard University Press, 1967.

CHUNG, CHIN O. *Pyongyang Between Peking and Moscow.* University: University of Alabama Press, 1978.

DALLIN, ALEXANDER, JONATHAN HARRIS, and GREY HODNETT (EDS.). *Diversity in International Communism: A Documentary Record, 1961–1963.* New York: Columbia University Press, 1963.

ELLISON, HERBERT J. (ED.). *The Sino-Soviet Conflict: A Global Perspective.* Seattle: University of Washington Press, 1982.

GINSBURGS, GEORGE, and CARL F. PINKELE. *The Sino-Soviet Territorial Dispute 1949–64.* New York: Praeger, 1978.

GITTINGS, JOHN (ED.). *Survey of the Sino-Soviet Dispute.* New York: Oxford University Press, 1968.

GRIFFITH, WILLIAM E. *The Sino-Soviet Rift.* Cambridge: MIT Press, 1964.

JAIN, RAJENDRA K. *The USSR and Japan: 1945-1980.* Atlantic Highlands, N.J.: Humanities Press, 1981.

MEHNERT, KLAUS. *Peking and Moscow.* New York: Putnam, 1963.

NORTH, ROBERT C. *Moscow and Chinese Communists.* 2nd ed. Stanford: Stanford University Press, 1963.

PARK, JAE KYU and JOSEPH M. HA (EDS.). *The Soviet Union and East Asia in the 1980s.* Boulder: Westview Press, 1983.

ROZMAN, GILBERT. *A Mirror For Socialism: Soviet Criticisms of China.* Princeton: Princeton University Press, 1985.

SOLOMON, RICHARD H. and MASATAKA KOSAKA (EDS.). *The Soviet Far East Military Buildup.* Dover, Mass: Auburn House, 1986.

STEPHAN, JOHN J. *The Kuril Islands.* New York: Oxford University Press, 1974.

SWEARINGEN, RODGER. *The Soviet Union and Postwar Japan: Escalating Challenge and Response.* Stanford: Hoover Institution Press, 1978.

ZAGORIA, DONALD S. *The Sino-Soviet Conflict, 1956-1961.* Princeton: Princeton University Press, 1962.

8
Moscow's Forward Policy in the Third World

The emergence of the Soviet Union as a superpower was marked by its shift from a continental-based strategy to a global one. This development, a function as much of military capability as of diplomatic opportunity, is most evident in the USSR's penetration of the Third World. It is in this arena, made up of two-thirds of the world's nations, that the Soviet Union engages the United States in a low-cost, relatively low-risk, highly intensive pattern of classical imperial competition.

For reasons that have become more rather than less compelling in an age of nuclear stalemate, the regions of the Third World have taken on special importance for Soviet strategists. Whereas Europe and the Far East have relatively stable political and military constellations that coincide generally with established territorial boundaries and spheres of influence shielded by security agreements, Southern Asia, the Middle East, Latin America, and sub-Saharan Africa are characterized by transient alliances and systemic instability and so have attracted superpower attention and rivalry. Gains or setbacks in these areas of contention are not likely to have a significant effect on the fundamental balance of power in the short run. Yet the implications for the long term are enormous; and for ideological and strategic reasons, Moscow considers the prizes worth the effort and the possible jeopardy to the Soviet-American relationship.

Lenin's Theory of Imperialism Lives On

Third world countries have long occupied an important place in Soviet ideological formulations and long-term projections. The essentials upon which Soviet strategy is predicated were set forth first by Lenin in his theory of imperialism: a belief that capitalist countries, impelled by their economic and government systems to seek cheap sources of raw materials and labor as well as outlets for their surplus production and capital, expanded into Africa, Asia, the Middle East, and Latin America in order to stave off their own decay and disintegration; and that this expansionistic compulsion bred wars among capitalist countries that were competing for choice colonies and markets. Originally published in Switzerland in 1916, Lenin's *Imperialism: The Highest Stage of Capitalism* attempted to extend Marx's concept of the class struggle from the domestic to the international arena and to show thereby that World War I had stemmed from the avarice of monopoly capital and the big financial interests. Whereas Marx predicted that the downfall of capitalism would be brought about by the proletariat of the industrialized nations, Lenin's thesis was that this process could be hastened and the capitalist countries could be undermined and eventually toppled by detaching the colonies from the control of the capitalist rulers—that "the road to Paris and London lies through Calcutta and Bombay," an apt phrase erroneously attributed to Lenin.

Lenin, the revolutionary, advocated national self-determination. As a concept meaning "the political freedom of a people to establish and to function as an independent nation," national self-determination had but a brief and almost exclusively tactical significance in Russia during the period of War Communism, when some non-Russian peoples took advantage of the Bolsheviks' weakness to gain their independence. Once secure in power, the Bolsheviks interpreted national self-determination in such a way as to preclude any further secessions from the Soviet Union. However, *outside* of the Soviet Union, the concept has been used to portray the Soviet Union as a champion of the liberation of all peoples from colonial rule and as an opponent of imperialism.

In the early years, the Soviets were engrossed with survival in European Russia, but as the situation stabilized, Lenin shrewdly perceived that the East could be used to improve Russia's military and political situation. Accordingly, he assigned colonial areas a more significant role in Soviet strategy. In July 1920, at the second Comintern congress, Lenin's "Preliminary Draft of Theses on the National and Colonial Questions" stressed the division of the world into oppressing and oppressed nations and enjoined the Comintern to promote the alliance between the proletariat of the advanced industrialized countries and the peoples of the economically backward colonial areas. As natural allies, the two would work toward the defeat of capitalism, the proletariat by weakening imperialist power at its home base and the colonial peoples by driving out the European rulers and thereby creating social and economic unrest in their home bases. Lenin acknowledged that nationalist movements in colonial areas would usually have a bourgeois character initially. Nevertheless, he endorsed temporary cooperation with them, provided that the Communist movement, however rudimentary, maintained its sense of identity and independence of action. (The first Soviet experiment with such a coalition was in China in the 1923-to-1927 period and had disastrous results.) Lenin also stressed the need "to fight against the clergy" and against "Pan-Islamism and similar tendencies which strive to combine the liberation movement against European and American imperialism with the strengthening of the position of the Khans, the landlords, the mullahs, etc."

In April 1924, as part of the quest for Lenin's mantle of legitimacy, Stalin embraced his position of the intimate connection among the vitality of national-liberation movements, the success of the proletarian revolution in Europe, and the preservation of socialism in the Soviet Union. Stalin lauded Lenin for expanding the national question to include all the oppressed peoples of Asia and Africa, and he expressed the view that, though it was but one aspect of the world proletarian revolution, "the road to the victory of the revolution in the West lies through the revolutionary alliance with the liberation movement of the colonies and dependent countries against imperialism."[1]

Four years later, at Stalin's command, the Comintern abandoned the "united front from above" strategy—characterized by a friendly attitude toward bourgeois-nationalist movements seeking independence from imperialist rule. The new line—the "united front from below" or anticapitalist strategy—regarded these groups as "lackeys" of imperialism who had sold out and deserted the revolution. Therefore, the Comintern now held that only Communists could lead the liberation movements. All cooperation with the non-Communist nationalists was abandoned, and the Communists sought to build up their following at the expense of cooperation with the bourgeois-nationalist elements.

Events elsewhere, however, soon left Stalin with little time for the colonial question. During the period from 1934 to 1945, with the excepton of the brief Nazi-Soviet honeymoon, he sought to develop better relations with the ruling imperialist powers and hence was quite circumspect about Comintern activities in colonial areas. Soviet national interest demanded accommodation and cooperation with the West. Generally speaking, the entire 1922-to-1945 period was one in which Soviet diplomacy centered on European and Far Eastern developments. The paramount problem was ensuring the security of the Soviet Union. Internal troubles (such as the intraparty struggle for power after Lenin's death, the agricultural crisis occasioned by Stalin's decision to accelerate industrialization and the collectivization of agriculture, and the bloody purges of the mid-1930s) further diminished Soviet interest in the colonial world. Even after 1945, when the Cold War chilled the relations of the former allies, Stalin's priorities—the reconstruction of a nation devastated by war, the consolidation of Soviet rule over Eastern Europe, the rivalry with the United States over Germany, the challenge of the Titoist heresy, the adaptation required by the triumph of the Communists on the Chinese mainland, and the Korean War—still kept the Soviet purview localized.

Whether it was through ineptitude or inadvertence, Moscow's application of the Zhdanov line (the unremitting hostility to the West and capitalism proclaimed at the founding conference of the Cominform in September 1947) to newly independent India, Burma, Indonesia, and the Philippines spelled disaster for almost a decade. It resulted in the decimation of local Communist parties, whose abortive coups against the infant bourgeois nationalist governments isolated them from the mainstream of indigenous national liberation movements, and in the increased suspicion of the Soviet Union among Third World countries and elites. After 1945, Stalin's policy made the Middle East also a wasteland for Soviet diplomacy. Relations with Iran and Turkey were severely strained as a consequence of his attempt to force Iran to accept puppet status and to blackmail Turkey into granting concessions on the straits that would have preluded its becoming a Soviet satellite. In addition, Moscow's support for the partition of Palestine and the creation of the state of Israel alienated the Arab world.

Stalin's death came at a time when a series of imperatives demanded far-reaching changes in Soviet society and foreign policy. Had Stalin lived for another decade he might well have implemented some of the innovations introduced by his successors; at the 1952 party congress, for example, hints that war between capitalism and communism was not inevitable and that war between capitalist countries was more probable were already discernible. However, there is no gainsaying that Stalin's demise enabled the new Soviet leaders to move more rapidly at home and abroad.

The Leninist legacy of exploiting the Third World to advance Soviet security and strategic interests found a kindred heir in the ideological revisions of Khrushchev. Starting from the fundamental Leninist assumptions concerning the vulnerability of the Western capitalist countries to pressure from colonial and developing areas, the universal urge of national liberation movements toward independence from their colonial rulers, the irresistible attraction to capitalists of the markets and resources of the Third World, and the inevitability of competition among capitalist countries and groups, Khrushchev modernized Marxist-Leninist thought on Third World developments and gave it an optimism characteristic of his own nature. He substantially modified Stalin's two-camp thesis and, at the twentieth congress of the CPSU in February 1956, proclaimed the existence and growing role of a "zone of peace," which gave ideological recognition to the independent role in world affairs of the former African and Asian colonies that Moscow had already begun to appreciate.[2] Khrushchev also revised Lenin's thesis that the contradictions arising out of the rivalry for the spoils of colonial expansion would drive the capitalist nations to war, maintaining instead that decolonization and the disintegration of Western overseas empires had gone too far to be reversed and that the "camp of socialism" acted as a restraint on old-fashioned imperialism. Therefore, he said, in order to preserve their foothold in the Third World, the Western powers now cooperate through multinational corporations and various associations whose intent is to disguise neocolonialism, that is, the preservation of Western influence through economic leverage. On February 26, 1960, during a visit to Indonesia, Khrushchev coined the phrase "collective colonialism" to describe the process.

Khrushchev also devised an ideological justification for differentiating among developing countries and for offering assistance to some non-Communist developing countries but not to others. The concept of the national democratic state was originally advanced at the November 1960 Moscow Conference of Communist and Workers' Parties and later modified in the party program adopted at the twenty-second congress of the CPSU in late 1961. It referred to radically oriented non-Communist developing countries that adhere to nonalignment in world affairs, adopt anti-Western foreign policies, and pursue domestic programs aimed at building socialism through a "noncapitalist path of development." These national democracies are promising candidates for eventual transition to the status of people's democracies. The "national democratic state" is seen as a stage in the consolidation of the anti-imperialist, antifeudal, democratic revolution, as a temporary, transitional form for developing countries desiring to move toward socialism. In 1963, a refinement, "the revolutionary democratic state," was added—apparently to distinguish the radical Third World regimes that implemented many of the programmatic demands of the local Communist party and tolerated its active functioning from the ones that persecuted Communists.

Khrushchev's effort to devise ideological typologies for categorizing developing countries according to their pro-Soviet affinities was not continued by Brezhnev, who was generally less interested in doctrinal exegesis. But if Soviet writings and official pronouncements contain any clue at all to understanding the leadership's perception of Third World developments, it is the bedrock belief in Lenin's theory of imperialism. This, coupled with the pervasive optimism that says that the world trends favor the advance of socialism, is evident in Soviet explanations of Third World alignments, policies, and developments. It may not be the entire truth behind Moscow's way of seeing and responding to reality, but it provides the Soviets with an outlook, a way of organizing and weighing the importance of events, and a useful road map for traversing the changing international system. Whether it be the Congo in 1960, Cuba and the Bay of

Pigs in 1961, Chile in 1973, southern Africa or the Persian Gulf currently, Soviet assessments of key Third World developments are Leninism made modern. In recent decades, firsthand experience with the Third World has dictated modifications of Lenin's theory of imperialism, in conformity with the historical forces at work there, but always within its overall framework.

Strategic Impetus for the Forward Policy

A combination of strategic, political, ideological, and marginally economic considerations ushered in Moscow's "forward policy" in the Third World (see map). Ironically, it was Washington's deterrent policy during the pre-missile age when U.S. nuclear superiority was paramount that facilitated the USSR's entry into and courtship of Third World countries. The Soviet leadership perceived the U.S. defense strategy of ringing the Soviet Union with military and refueling bases in neighboring states in order to enhance the nuclear strike effectiveness of the Strategic Air Command's (SAC) long-range bomber force as a threat to their national security; even more important, the polarization this engendered ran counter to the thrust of the forces of nationalism and nonalignment in the Third World, which aimed at discarding all traces of former Western overlordship and at steering an independent course in world affairs.

Strategically, Soviet leaders sought to eliminate, neutralize, or at least weaken the U.S. military presence in the countries lying south of the USSR, to deprive SAC of potential refueling facilities, and to end the intelligence flights over the Soviet heartland. Accordingly, starting in 1954 with Afghanistan, they gave varying degrees of encouragement to the policies of Third World elites who found military alliance with Western countries difficult to sustain domestically and who therefore opted for foreign policies ranging from coolness to outright hostility toward the West.

Politically, Moscow sought diplomatic normalization, not communization. Its overtures and aid were intended to dispel the suspicion of the Kremlin that was inherent in the attitudes of many of the ruling elites in less developed countries. Some of this anti-Communist sentiment derived from the Western European education of the elites, but a deep animus against communism also existed in Muslim countries, and Southern Asia clearly remembered Communist attempts at armed revolution in the late 1940s.

Notwithstanding this legacy from the Stalinist period, Moscow's proclaimed anticolonialism, its expert application of olive branch and checkbook, and its shrewd diplomatic maneuvering began to show results; in 1955 readiness to build a major steel-producing plant in India and the

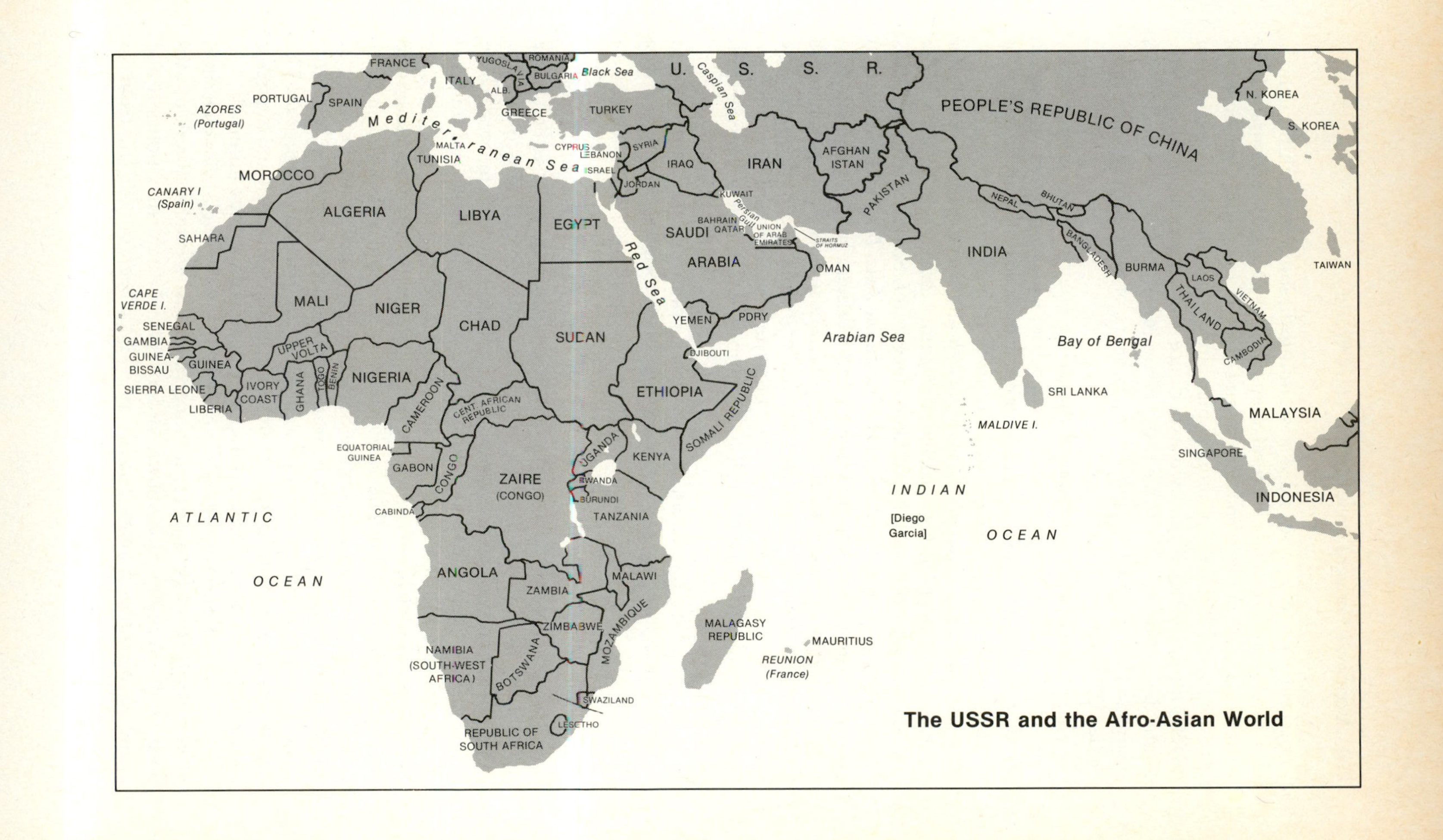

The USSR and the Afro-Asian World

arms deal with Egypt heralded a stunning diplomatic breakthrough. In UN forums and through bilateral relationships, Moscow encouraged the nationalization of key industries and resources, heavy public-sector investment, and central economic planning, stressing the relevance for developing countries of its own experience with modernization and economic development. All of this had a favorable impact upon socialistically inclined elites, at least during the early years of courtship by the "new" Soviet Union.

Proceeding on the age-old dictum "The enemy of my enemy is my friend," Moscow courted those regional actors who were most opposed to the U.S. policy of global containment, which led to the pressing of military pacts everywhere in the Third World, often in countries that were not directly threatened by Soviet attack and that agreed only in order to obtain U.S. weapons for possible use against local rivals. In 1955, India and Egypt were the two most likely targets of Soviet attention: India opposed the U.S. organized SEATO (Southeast Asia Treaty Organization) pact, which provided military assistance to Pakistan, India's regional archrival; and Egypt opposed the Baghdad pact, whose only Arab member was Iraq, Egypt's principal competitor for leadership in the Arab world. The result of the U.S. "pactitis" was to polarize regional conflicts and give Moscow an incentive for discarding its outmoded ideological baggage from the Stalin era.

Ideologically, the Kremlin's "forward policy" in the Third World reflected the optimism of Khrushchev and his associates. Having survived the terror of Stalin's last years, they emerged now for the first time as leaders in their own right. They saw the forces of history as favoring the advance of socialism and the final destruction of capitalism and colonialism. To them, a powerful and economically expanding Soviet Union was a natural ally of the new nations, which basically shared Moscow's anti-imperialist, anticolonialist, anticapitalist outlook. It was a time, too, when Soviet leaders believed that their model of development and internal transformation held great interest for new nations.

Economic considerations were least important to Soviet leaders in the mid-1950s to 1960s. The raw materials of the developing countries could, of course, be utilized by the Soviet economy, but they were not of crucial importance. As Nikita Khrushchev declared in 1955: "We value trade least for economic reasons and most for political purposes." The USSR was, and remains in the 1980s, an essentially planned and autarchic society in which dependence on imported materials is kept minimal.

Two broad purposes initially underlay the emerging Soviet courtship of key Third World countries: to undermine the Western system of alliances and international economic order, and to establish a political and economic presence in areas that had previously been outside the realm of

Soviet capabilities. In the 1960s two other broad objectives crystallized: to offset the Chinese challenge for leadership in the Communist world; and to acquire naval and air facilities that would provision the USSR's blue-water fleet, keep close tabs on and counteract U.S. forces operating in strategically important areas, protect clients threatened by their pro-Western rivals, and enable Moscow to project military power more expeditiously into politically promising situations.

Examination of the Soviet record in four key geographic regions—Southern Asia, sub-Saharan Africa, Latin America, and the Middle East (see Chapter 9)—may enhance understanding of the nature and effectiveness of Soviet policy, the range of Soviet objectives, and the dilemmas and difficulties that Moscow faces in its efforts to acquire influence and affect developments in the Third World.

Southern Asia

The shift in Soviet policy toward India may be dated from September 1953, when the Kremlin appointed a personable ambassador who immediately initiated discussions aimed at closer economic relations. The first success was a dramatic agreement, signed on February 2, 1955, under which the Soviet government undertook to finance and construct a million-ton steel plant in the public sector in the Bhilai region of central India. By the time of the visit of Party Secretary Khrushchev and Premier Nikolai Bulganin in December 1955, Soviet-Indian friendship had become important for both countries. For the Soviet Union, it meant a link with the region's leading power and nonaligned country and a safeguard against India's membership in any anti-Soviet military alliance; it offered a showcase for Soviet assistance—a demonstration to the new nations of the tangible benefits to be derived from improved relations with the USSR; it brought the USSR respectability right at the takeoff stage of its courtship of African and Asian nations; and it served as a marked contrast to the military-minded, Cold War–oriented policy of the United States. For India, the relationship served as a potentially significant counterpart to U.S. support for Pakistan. It brought much-needed investment for public-sector industries, which the United States was ideologically leery of supporting, and it led quickly to Moscow's support in the United Nations for India's position on Kashmir. Moscow's penetration of the "zone of peace" was off to an impressive start. Similar agreements with other nonaligned countries were concluded in the decades that followed.

Under Khrushchev, the USSR sided with India in its dispute with Pakistan. It upheld India's policy of nonalignment and opposition to U.S. military alliances in the area, to western colonialism in Africa, and to U.S.

involvement in Vietnam. During the Goa affair of December 1961, the Soviet Union alone among the great powers fully upheld India's use of force to liquidate the Portuguese enclave on its west coast. Moscow's judicious neutrality on the Sino-Indian border dispute was especially appreciated.

However, when China attacked India in October 1962, Moscow uncomfortably straddled the fence; it was unwilling to condemn its Communist ally and thereby foreclose all possibility of a reconciliation, yet it wanted to retain its expensively cultivated stake in Asia's leading non-aligned nation. Luckily for the Soviets, the Chinese did not press their advantage, and the Western powers came to India's defense with military assistance. The crisis passed, and Moscow reingratiated itself with offers of MiG fighter aircraft, SAMs (surface-to-air missiles), warships, and other military equipment. In 1964 Khrushchev agreed to sell India a factory for producing MiGs, on license; Brezhnev reaffirmed this commitment with ancillary agreements. The first MiGs built in India were delivered to the air force in the early 1970s.

During the undeclared war that erupted between India and Pakistan in September 1965, Moscow was instrumental in persuading the two disputants to cease hostilities and sign the Tashkent declaration of January 1966. This was the first time that the USSR had played the role of peacemaker in a Third World conflict. Its aims were to prevent China's involvement in the region and to improve relations with Pakistan as well as with India. The Soviets' longer-range goal in drawing closer to Pakistan and encouraging a gradual normalization of relations between India and Pakistan was to realize their dream of a land route that would link Soviet Central Asia to India via Afghanistan and the Khyber Pass and would enormously expand their economic penetration of the subcontinent. A more prominent Soviet role on the subcontinent would thwart China and provide greater support for Soviet naval activities in the Indian Ocean and Arabian Sea.

Soviet prestige in India soared on August 9, 1971, with the signing of a twenty-year Soviet-Indian treaty of friendship and cooperation, which India wanted as a deterrent to possible Chinese intervention on behalf of Pakistan. India's need for the treaty had arisen five months earlier out of the Pakistani government's suppression of the separatist movement in East Pakistan. As millions of refugees fled to India, tensions built-up, exploding into war in December 1971. The treaty proved its worth: China stayed out, limiting itself to diplomatic support of Pakistan, while India, well supplied with Soviet weapons, crushed Pakistani forces. In the UN Security Council, the Soviet Union vetoed all resolutions calling for an immediate cease-fire, thus enabling India to complete its military campaign in east Pakistan and help create the independent nation of Bangladesh in its stead.

But prestige is not tantamount to influence, nor can it necessarily be translated into secure military advantage, as Moscow discovered again in its relations with Egypt and Iraq, both of which also signed friendship treaties with Moscow, in May 1971 and April 1972, respectively. These treaties, which loom so prominently in Western assessments of the putative Soviet stranglehold on Third World countries, *must* be analyzed in the context of the domestic political situation of the courted countries; otherwise, it is impossible to appreciate the extent to which the Soviets, far from ensnaring the client, were themselves ensnared by the native leadership for internal or regional political reasons. The answer to the question, "Who is influencing whom?" does not lie in the uncritical assumption that the USSR is always, or even usually, in command of the events when it is dealing with a Third World country. India's use of its treaty with the USSR to humble and partition Pakistan and become the undisputed dominant power on the subcontinent was a development Moscow had not foreseen. Neither had Moscow anticipated that lessened military dependence on the Soviet Union would result in New Delhi's feeling no compulsion to respond to repeated Soviet allusions to desired naval privileges at Visakhapatnam, a major port on India's southeastern coast.

The Soviet Union did everything to foster intimate ties. For example, in 1973 it signed a fifteen-year economic accord on terms advantageous to India and lent India two million tons of wheat; it put two scientific space satellites in orbit for India and agreed to make the countries' five-year economic plans complementary. In late 1976, when oil was difficult to obtain at prices India could afford, Moscow proposed a barter deal on favorable conditions, and it offered a $450 million credit in September 1976 to enable India to expand steel-making capacity in the public sector. Soviet-Indian relations remained close under Prime Minister Indira Gandhi (1966 to March 1977) but Moscow did not receive what it really wanted: naval facilities for its Indian Ocean flotilla; support for Brezhnev's plan, floated in June 1969, for an Asian collective security system; and a special relationship that would keep India at a distance from China. Brezhnev had to settle for Mrs. Gandhi's understanding attitude toward the Soviet invasion of Czechoslovakia, criticism of U.S. policy in Vietnam and the Middle East, and general support on issues that were of little direct interest to India, such as SALT, Berlin, and CSCE. The USSR did not obtain the privileged strategic foothold it coveted.

Under the Janata coalition government, which took office after defeating Mrs. Gandhi in March 1977, India looked increasingly to the West for economic assistance. (By the late 1970s, taking into account debt repayments, Soviet net economic aid to India was less than $50 million a year; the Western aid consortium provided ten to twenty times more assistance.) New Delhi normalized its relations with Beijing in 1977 and was unwilling to condemn China's attack against Vietnam in February 1979. In January 1980, Mrs. Gandhi returned to power in a stunning electoral triumph. Gromyko came in February to strengthen Soviet-Indian ties and obtain her support for the USSR's military intervention in Afghanistan the previous December. She did not endorse its action and urged a withdrawal of "foreign" troops, but neither did she criticize Moscow publicly, which suited Soviet purposes. In December 1980, amid sharply worsening U.S.–Soviet relations over Afghanistan, Poland, and SALT, Brezhnev visited India. Playing on its disquiet over the U.S. rearming of Pakistan and a possible disruption of Persion Gulf oil arising from a spread of the Iran-Iraq War that had broken out three months earlier, he put forth a five-part proposal for a nonaligned and peaceful Gulf region and strongly defended the Soviet position on Afghanistan. To mollify the Indians, who were unresponsive to his vague and self-serving formulations, and remind them of the value of friendship with the Soviet Union, Brezhnev left agreements on continued Soviet economic assistance (particularly in the energy sector), arms sales, and expanded trade. During Mrs. Gandhi's visit to Moscow in September 1982, these extensive relationships were cemented.

The USSR continues to accord pride of place to India. Gorbachev's visit in November 1986, his first to a Third World country, was intended to convey a sense of India's importance internationally and to the Soviet Union; he has met often with Prime Minister Rajiv Gandhi (who succeeded his mother, Indira Gandhi, when she was assassinated by Sikh extremists in November 1984). Although Moscow has used its nuclear umbrella to protect India from China, supplied the most advanced conventional weaponry in the Soviet arsenal (for example, starting in January 1987, the MiG-29 fighter aircraft, heretofore available only to members of the Warsaw Pact), and sold oil and vital nonferrous metals at bargain prices, it is without tangible dividends to show for its lengthy courtship and enormous investment: no naval facilities for its Indian Ocean flotilla, no privileged access, and no particular popularity in the country at large.

Indeed, looking to the 1990s, Moscow has cause for concern over simmering tensions that have prompted Gorbachev to bring to bear the full panoply of public diplomacy in order to strengthen private and informal understandings. First, it worries about the improvement in U.S.–Indian relations that has been nurtured by the Reagan administration and is exemplified by its sanction of the sale of high-tech equipment to India. Second, Moscow is running a substantial adverse balance in its nonmilitary trade with India, with little prospect of any change given India's reluctance to increase its imports from the USSR. Though extending substantial economic credits, Gorbachev finds the Indians reluctant to turn to the Soviet Union for modernization of their industrial infrastructure or for new technology. What keeps an approximate symmetry in the balance-of-payments account are the arms that India buys. If India were to turn to the West for the next generation of weapons, Moscow would lose much of its leverage in New Delhi and find itself unable to tap into India's sophisticated electronics and computer industry.

Third, Gorbachev knows that his quest for better relations with China makes India nervous—and all the more interested in cultivating closer ties to the West and Japan. His hints of neutrality on Sino-Indian border problems and calls for extending the nuclear-free zones to include the Indian Ocean region are upsetting to New Delhi, which worries that Moscow is looking ahead to a time when it might downgrade relations with India in the interests of détente with China.

Finally, Gorbachev must find a way to allay Indian suspicions of Soviet interference in its domestic politics. This is an old source of tension. Moscow uses the rupees it earns in trade to subsidize the activities of the pro-Soviet Communist Party of India and to persuade businesspeople with a stake in commercial contracts with the USSR to lobby in favor of expanded trade. Rajiv Gandhi learned from his mother to keep a wary eye on Moscow's relations with the CPI. By now, the view is widely accepted in New Delhi that the CPI is a way of both signaling and subverting, and it is jested that half of the party is in the pay of Moscow, the other half in the pay of the Indian government. In the years ahead, Moscow will have to work hard to maintain its close relationship with India.

A different set of priorities shaped Moscow's policy toward Vietnam. America's major intervention after 1964 prompted extensive Soviet economic and military assistance to enable Hanoi to prosecute its war: aid rose from approximately $40 million in 1964 to almost $1 billion annually from 1967 to 1972. At stake was not only Soviet credibility as an ally and Soviet rivalry with China for influence among Asian Communists, but also a desire to embroil the United States in a quagmire that would reduce its capacity for decisive action in areas of greater concern to the USSR.

Soviet aims in Vietnam were ambivalent in the years after 1945 when Stalin refused to support Ho Chi Minh's bid for Vietnamese independence in order to avoid antagonizing France and compromising the strong position of the French Communist party. Moscow established diplomatic relations with Ho Chi Minh's Democratic Republic of Vietnam (DRV) on January 30, 1950, soon after the Communist triumph in China, but gave Hanoi little attention or aid. It served as cochairman of the 1954 Geneva Conference, which formally ended French rule in Indochina and recognized the two Vietnams, but despite a limited involvement in the

1962 Laotian crisis, Moscow did not urge intensification of "wars of national liberation" by Vietnam: it regarded Vietnam as a sideshow and did not want a Communist insurgency in Laos or Cambodia to hamper its efforts to improve relations with Indonesia, Burma, India, Malaysia, Thailand, and Ceylon. However, Ho Chi Minh had his own ambitions, which inexorably drew Moscow into the Vietnam conflict, as much because of its rivalry with China as because of that with the United States.

In the early stages of the American military escalation in 1965, Soviet leaders may have been concerned over the United States's intentions, the DRV's capability, and China's response. But the ineffectiveness and cost of American policy soon revealed unanticipated benefits for Moscow. Nurtured by Soviet propaganda, anti-Americanism rose sharply in the Third World and Western Europe. Domestic strife intensified in the United States and bred an incipient neoisolationism. America's economy was beset by serious inflation and a growing deficit in the international balance of payments, leading to a de facto devaluation of the dollar in August 1971. All of this exacerbated strains in the Western alliance and reinforced American domestic pressures for a retrenchment of foreign-policy commitments. U.S. military power was squandered in a war that the United States could not win and that was strategically peripheral to the global superpower rivalry.

During the late 1960s and early 1970s, both Moscow and Beijing, though increasingly at odds on a wide range of issues, lent support to Vietnam. For its part, Hanoi sought to preserve an essential neutrality on the Sino-Soviet dispute. It benefited from the rivalry that impelled each party to accede to Hanoi's requests lest it be labeled defeatist and seem overly concerned about the United States. In 1972, when both Moscow and Beijing were courting Washington—the USSR in order to reach an agreement on SALT I and promote détente in Europe, and China in order to have the Nixon visit lead to diplomatic normalization—they still met the DRV's economic and military needs. Neither Communist power was willing to pressure Hanoi to agree to a negotiated settlement, even in the interests of better relations with the United States.

Hanoi's victory in 1975 brought Moscow new problems. Now a unified nation of more than 62 million people, Vietnam has expanded into Laos and Kampuchea. Moscow's support of this expansionism has made the other nations of Southeast Asia leery of Soviet overtures for closer ties, which are intended to offset China's diplomatic efforts in the region.

Vietnam's economic and military reliance on the Soviet Union has become even more pronounced since 1975 because of Vietnam's deteriorating relationship with China and erratic progress toward normalization with the United States: in December 1975, Le Duan, the general secretary of the Vietnamese Communisty party (Ho Chi Minh died in 1969) signed a long-term economic agreement with the USSR; in June 1978, Vietnam joined Comecon as a full member; and on November 3, 1978, the USSR and Vietnam signed a twenty-five-year treaty of friendship and cooperation. Although not a formal military alliance, the treaty calls for mutual consultations in the event of a military threat—an obvious allusion to China. It presented Moscow with an opportunity to close the ring around China and acquire important military privileges at the Cam Ranh Bay naval base and the Da Nang airfield, one of the largest in the region. When Vietnam overthrew the pro-Beijing Pol Pot regime in Kampuchea in January 1979, it could count on the USSR's support. When the Chinese launched a punitive expedition against Vietnam the following month, Moscow warned Beijing not to press too hard; the Chinese pulled back, and the Moscow-Hanoi treaty passed its first test.

The Soviet Union has benefited in a number of ways. Its military relationship with Vietnam enables it to fly reconnaissance missions throughout Southeast Asia, virtually to double the length of time that the Soviet Pacific Fleet spends at sea, to encourage Vietnam to pursue a foreign policy that perpetuates Sino-Vietnamese tensions, and to complicate China's security problems. Moscow uses Vietnamese migrant labor to help offset its severe manpower shortage. Under an agreement concluded in 1981, Vietnam sends upwards of 7000 workers each year (some estimates range as high as 100,000), using part of their wages to help it repay its growing indebtedness to the USSR. Reinforcing the USSR's effort to establish a long-term presence in the country is a sizable aid package, which exceeds $2 billion annually—one half economic, and one half military.

Support for Vietnam's occupation of Kampuchea has hampered Moscow's attempt to improve relations not only with China but also with the ASEAN countries (the Association of South-East Asian Nations, whose members are Indonesia, Malaysia, the Philippines, Singapore, Thailand, and Brunei). Shevardnadze's extensive promotional tour of the region in March 1987—the first by a Soviet foreign minister in almost three decades—was multipurposed: to show the flag, to convey the desire of both Moscow and Hanoi for a peaceful resolution of the Kampuchean problem, and to encourage trade and establish "a regular dialogue" with the vibrant, free-market ASEAN economies. The Soviet quandary seems resistant to early resolution. Improved relations with China depend on reconciling Chinese and Vietnamese interests in Kampuchea, but Gorbachev is reluctant to pressure Vietnam very much for fear of jeopardizing the military privileges that Moscow has enjoyed since the late 1970s; to complicate matters still further, their continuation intensifies ASEAN's suspicions of Soviet-Vietnamese ambitions in the region. Moreover, in the case of Kampuchea, Moscow's concern is that the alternative to the pro-

Vietnamese regime of Hun Sen "would be reinstatement of the pro-Chinese Khmer Rouge, a prospect the Soviet Union would avoid at all cost."[3]

Sub-Saharan Africa

Soviet interest in Africa, though low-keyed in the early years of Moscow's policy in the Third World, nonetheless has been persistent. By the 1960s Moscow recognized the significance of sub-Saharan Africa's emergence upon the international stage. At first the Soviet operations were heavy-handed and they were bungled egregiously: in the Congo in the early 1960s, in Guinea in late 1961, and in Kenya in 1965. Soviet diatribes against Western power and declarations of support for decolonization and for African development were seldom followed up by meaningful deeds, and preoccupation with tactics to outmaneuver the Chinese Communists often left the Africans confused and with unfulfilled needs. Initially, too, an unsophisticated tenor was apparent in most Soviet writing on Africa, which rigidly applied a Marxian class analysis to tribal and cultural animosities and mistook economic dependency for political subservience. Nevertheless, the Soviet Union did in time demonstrate a sound appreciation of political realities and strategic possibilities, and its policy in Africa has been relatively effective.

A few generalizations about Soviet behavior between 1957 and 1974—before the takeoff stage—may help to keep in focus the scope and character of the USSR's aims and policies in Africa. With the surge of decolonization seemingly capable of shaking the foundations of the Western international system, the anticolonialism and radical nationalist outlook of Kwame Nkrumah and Sekou Touré drew Moscow to Ghana and Guinea and boosted Khrushchev's doctrinally inspired expectations. A key objective was the normalization of diplomatic ties. Though most African governments of the times were innately conservative and suspicious of communism and kept the USSR at a distance, Moscow persisted and eventually did establish diplomatic ties with most of black Africa. Its network is now very active.

These ties were partly made effective through an economic program applied with erratic success; its incremental nature suffered because of the encumbrance of experts who could communicate only with difficulty, because of faulty equipment and tardy delivery schedules, and because of a Soviet inability to offer adequate assistance where it was needed most, in agriculture and in light industry. The principal recipients of economic assistance were Guinea, Ghana, Ethiopia, Mali, Somalia, Nigeria, and Sierra Leone; commitments were made mostly during the Soviet-African honeymoon of the late 1950s when, expecting to acquire prestige, Moscow complied willingly with sometimes vainglorious requests from indigenous elites for showpiece projects and instead wasted resources and reaped disenchantment. It has since preferred small-scale practical investments in which development loans are supplemented by trade credits to promote imports of Soviet equipment. In the late 1960s, the USSR began to concentrate on Nigeria, where it has been aiding in the development of the petroleum and the iron and steel industries. Although Soviet-built projects now dot Africa—an oil refinery in Ethiopia, a dairy farm in Guinea, a hydroelectric power station in Ghana, a cannery in Kenya, a spinning mill in Uganda—Soviet impact on the economies of courted African countries has been marginal, mainly because of an unwillingness to transfer substantial economic resources to the continent. In fact, until the Angolan episode, the Soviet Union had been almost niggardly: from 1957 to 1974, it provided more economic credits (approximately $850 million) to Afghanistan than to all of sub-Saharan Africa, which received about $780 million.

In the military sphere, the record is quite different. Arms helped widen and ease Soviet political access to Africa. Realizing that no African proletariat, no well-organized Communist parties, and no divisive class antagonisms existed, and that African states were heavily rural, often rent by tribal and ethnic feuds and as often dissatisfied with colonial territorial divisions, the Soviet Union has been ever ready over the years to exploit local rivalries, secessionist impulses, and national liberation movements seeking the end of European colonialism and, more latterly, of white supremacist regimes, by assuming a major role as supplier of weapons and advisers. Though it spreads its stake thinly over a number of actors on the African stage, the USSR has usually gravitated toward those elites who are particularly receptive to Soviet ideas and who are anti-Western not because of Cold War preferences, but for reasons relating to inter-African rivalries—for example, to tensions between Somalia and Ethiopia or Congo-Brazzaville and Zaire (formerly the Belgian Congo). As in the economic sphere, these efforts to influence the outcome of internal struggles for power have met with mixed fortunes. The Soviet government was stymied in the Congo in 1960, and again in 1964—1965 when it backed an attempt by Algeria and Egypt to maintain a rebel group in Stanleyville (now Kisangani). But its support for the central government in the Biafran civil war vastly improved its relations with Nigeria. Arms supplies have also been helpful in establishing closer ties at various times with Guinea, Ghana, Malia, Benin (formerly Dahomey), Burkina Faso (formerly Upper Volta), Burundi, and Uganda (until Idi Amin was toppled in 1979).

The attention of Soviet strategic planners has been focused increasingly upon the Horn of Africa. In both cases, the impetus is strategic and political rather than ideological or economic. Moscow's interest in the Horn is an outgrowth of its Middle East policy and its ambitious construction of a blue-water fleet.

The prospect of a foothold in Somalia, which dominates the entrance to the Red Sea and the northwest littoral of the Indian Ocean, led in 1969 to a significant flow of military and economic aid and in 1974 to a multifaceted treaty of friendship and cooperation. In a gesture unprecedented in Soviet diplomacy, Moscow cancelled Somalia's foreign-aid debt, which amounted to about $45 million (or 16 percent of Somalia's gross national product for one year). In return, the Somali connection brought Moscow naval and communications facilities at Berbera on the Gulf of Aden (which dominates access to the Red Sea) and at Mogadishu on the Indian Ocean, and privileges at the Soviet-modernized airfields at Berbera and Uanle Uen. Somalia became the most important Soviet client in sub-Saharan Africa.

But privileges and a major presence do not make a satellite. What led to the toppling of the infrastructure that Moscow had built in Somalia was Soviet strategic covetousness and political myopia. Tempted by the revolution that followed the overthrow of Emperor Haile Selassie in 1974 and the anti-Western policies of the self-proclaimed "Marxist-Leninist" military leadership in Addis Ababa, the Soviet Union agreed after two years of hesitation to Ethiopia's requests for arms. In December 1976, against the backdrop of deteriorating Somalian-Ethiopian relations, the Soviets started to supply small arms, and by April 1977, they raised their ante, furnishing Ethiopia with heavy weapons (including tanks and aircraft), Soviet military advisers, and Cuban myrmidons. Moscow tried to keep a foot in both warring camps, hoping to mediate the conflict and emerge with its Somalian facilities more or less intact and with a vastly improved position in populous, large, politically radical, and potentially important Ethiopia.

Soviet leaders fully expected Somalia's complete dependency on Soviet weapons to constrain President Mohammed Siad Barre's independence of action. Instead, in July 1977, Somalia invaded Ethiopia in an attempt to annex the Somali-populated Ogaden province. In November, Siad Barre chose to foreclose the Soviet option, renouncing the 1974 treaty of friendship, expelling Soviet military personnel, and withdrawing the use of all facilities enjoyed by the USSR in Somalia. This led Moscow to make a major diplomatic realignment. In late 1977–early 1978, a massive Soviet and Cuban military intervention on behalf of Ethiopia's ruling Dergue, headed by Mengistu Haile Mariam, drove back the Somalis. The new Soviet-Ethiopian relationship was capped, on November 20, 1978, by a twenty-year treaty of friendship. Soviet military assistance was essential for Mengistu's efforts to crush the separatist movements in different parts of the country. In 1988, Soviet and Cuban forces were still in Ethiopia, more to prop up the regime than to protect it from Somalia, whose military threat has diminished significantly. After years of cajoling, Moscow finally persuaded Mengistu to create in 1984 a vanguard Marxist-Leninist party, the Workers' Party of Ethiopia. This made Ethiopia the first Communist country on the African continent, at least nominally, because power is still held by the military and is not shared with previously-known Communists. Moscow's strategic needs have been satisfied since 1980 by its privileged use of Ethiopia's Daklak Islands and some airfields for reconnaissance activities. In return, it meets Mengistu's military needs but not his economic ones. For help in coping with the periodic droughts that have devastated the countryside and in generating essential development projects, it encourages him to look to the West and the World Bank, whose emergency assistance in the period since 1984 has averaged more than $1 billion annually.

By contrast, the scale and character of Soviet commitments to southern Africa suggest that until 1974 the region was considered relatively unimportant. It was dominated by South Africa, Portugal, and Rhodesia (Zimbabwe); the independent black African states were weak, and the prospects of the various liberation movements based in Zambia, Tanzania, and Zaire were unpromising. Moscow kept its economic assistance to a minimum, although from the early 1960s, the Soviet Union and its eastern-bloc associates helped to train (and presumably to indoctrinate) guerrillas and to channel a trickle of weapons to favored national liberation groups, often through second parties such as Algeria and Egypt and occasionally through the Liberation Committee of the Organization of African Unity, which was created shortly after the OAU's establishment in 1963.

However, Moscow preferred bilateral contacts. In the Portuguese colonies, its matériel went to Marxist-oriented movements—the Popular Movement for the Liberation of Angola (MPLA) and the Front for the Liberation of Mozambique; and in the Zimbabwe, after its unilateral declaration of independence from Britain in 1965, assistance went to the politically more congenial Zimbabwe African People's Union, which proved to be far weaker than its rival, the Zimbabwe African National Union. Except for the MPLA, however, whose Communist antecedents and pro-Moscow orientation date back to 1955, most of the liberation movements in southern Africa seemed able to work better with the Chinese, so Moscow did not press its affiliations with them and until 1974 wielded little clout in the region. Since southern Africa was not a centerpiece of Soviet global strategy, the main Soviet objectives there were to use the simmering situation to exacerbate the West's relations with African countries by polarizing alignments and issues, and to counter the challenge of China's activism.

The overthrow of the decades-old military dictatorship in Portugal on April 25, 1974, transformed the political situation in the region with dramatic suddenness and led Moscow to intensify arms shipments, especially to the MPLA. Portugal's decision to pull out of Africa after more than 500 years of colonial rule accelerated the decolonization process. In Guinea-Bissau, the Cape Verde Islands, and Mozambique, power was transferred smoothly. Only in Angola did the absence of an undisputed indigenous leadership result in civil war and a superpower contest of wills. The massive influx of Soviet arms and Cuban troops in mid-1975 and 1976 brought victory to the MPLA and demonstrated the readiness of Moscow to take bolder risks in promoting strategic goals. (The MPLA controlled the capital of Luanda when independence was formally proclaimed on November 11, 1975. In the civil war that followed, the overwhelming Soviet military hardware—armored cars, tanks, jeeps, small arms, and batteries of 122-mm ground-to-ground rockets—manned by approximately 20,000 Cuban troops proved decisive. This same mix of Soviet and Cuban aid was also to prove effective in Ethiopia in 1977–1978.)

The success of the MPLA in Angola was a welcome antidote to the Kremlin's setbacks in the Middle East. In exercising its greatest show yet of resoluteness in sub-Saharan Africa, Moscow calculated that there were few risks and many prospective gains, not the least of which was exposure of China's inability to act in critical periods on behalf of liberation movements and its backing of groups that were also the protégés of Western countries. Soviet intervention also highlighted the United States' unwillingness to use force to help its clients, and demonstrated to friendly states what Moscow could do in Africa on behalf of prospective clients. In the words of *Pravda,* the MPLA's success would prove "a stimulus for the development of the liberation struggle of the peoples of Namibia [South-West Africa], the South African Republic and Zimbabwe."

Admittedly, Angola is a tempting plum. Abundantly endowed with oil, untapped mineral resources, and fertile land, it is potentially one of the wealthiest countries in Africa. Moreover, air and naval facilities there would position the Soviets to interdict the sea route around the Cape of Good Hope. But a scenario in which Angola becomes a Soviet satellite and the Soviets build a naval base to rival the South African base at Simonstown, though theoretically possible, is most improbable in the foreseeable future. To press now for military privileges would lend credence to China's charges of Soviet imperialist designs, which could prove embarrassing to the USSR and to the MPLA (still in a politically precarious position and subject to harassment by the rival UNITA guerrilla group operating in southern Angola) and which in the long term could prove counterproductive to Soviet aims of undermining South Africa.

Soviet and Cuban military power (an estimated 30,000 troops) keep the MPLA in power. In October 1976, Angolan President Agostinho Neto (who died in September 1979) signed a friendship treaty with Moscow, which has become increasingly important as the South Africa–backed UNITA insurgency has grown in effectiveness. Repeated Soviet-Cuban-led military campaigns in 1985, 1986, and 1987 failed to defeat UNITA. The rising military costs, now in excess of $1 billion a year, may prompt Gorbachev to look to diplomacy for some tolerable compromise. Meanwhile, Neto's successor, José Eduardo dos Santos, tries to broaden contacts with the West, which accounts for the bulk of Angola's trade and which could contribute to a diplomatic solution to the knotty political-military problems in Southern Africa.

Mozambique, also, is linked by a friendship treaty to the Soviet Union. But little has been done for this Marxist regime militarily or economically, in part because of Moscow's unwillingness to tackle neighboring South Africa head-on and in part because the probable costs of major involvement so far from any center of Soviet power far outweigh any possible gains. Backward, resource-poor Mozambique is more a long-term problem than a strategic prize.

On this issue, and on opposition to the apartheid regime in South Africa, Moscow is content to follow the line laid down by the so-called front-line African states, prominent among which is the Marxist regime in Zimbabwe, headed by Robert Mugabe. Soviet-Zimbabwean relations, chilly during the struggle for Zimbabwean liberation, when Moscow had backed Mugabe's non-Marxist rival, have improved in recent years. Gorbachev has welcomed Mugabe to Moscow on several occasions, and there are recurring reports of impending economic and even military accords.

The manifestations of Soviet interest in sub-Saharan Africa are widespread and unambiguous. What remain very much subjects of speculation and disagreement, however, are the motives that prompted this imperial outreach and what it has achieved. Here I offer some tentative observations on the impact of Soviet policy in the African milieu and the way in which developments on the African continent are in turn shaping that policy. These observations may be pertinent also to Soviet policy in southern Asia, the Middle East, and Latin America, and thus in a sense serve as a set of capsule assessments of the achievements and disappointments of Moscow's forward policy.

First, there are still no Soviet satellites in Africa. Moscow has not succeeded in drawing any African state into the kind of relationship that it has with the East European members of the Warsaw Pact. During the past two decades, it has found that the African countries that have sought

Soviet aid are not so weak that they cannot determine their own policies. Some countries may be beholden for military and economic favors, as in the cases of Angola and Ethiopia, and they may even grant Moscow air and naval privileges, as did Somalia and Guinea; but as has been seen in Ghana, Mali, and Somalia, the evanescence of privileges makes reliance upon these countries for the conduct of an imperial policy difficult.

Obviously, Moscow gives in expectation of a return. It covets special favors, and when they are proffered, accepts them with the clear realization that they may be abruptly withdrawn. These unpredictable hazards are a new feature of the changing international order, but in terms of its philosophy of incrementalism, the USSR is prepared to take the risks; in its view, the main advantages it stands to gain from aiding African countries and movements are those that place it in an improved strategic and military position vis-à-vis the United States. Any improvement in the strategic and military context within which the Soviet Union regionally and globally operates justifies the outlay. The USSR is less impelled by the uncertain increments in leverage that it may acquire over developments within a recipient country, but if local advantages also accrue, so much the better.

Second, there is little evidence that in pursuing their forward policy, Soviet leaders have been unduly concerned about the financial and military costs of involvement in Africa, or that the Kremlin has made an agonizing reappraisal over any damage that may have been done to the U.S.–Soviet détente by its intervention in Angola and Ethiopia. Still, Soviet activism does not necessarily foreshadow the adoption of an adventurist or high-risk policy. The Soviet and Cuban involvement in Angola and Ethiopia rested on political principles that evoked a sympathetic African reaction: defense of regimes recognized by Black African states; upholding of the territorial inviolability of an existing nation (Ethiopia); and cooperation in response to specific requests for military assistance. While Moscow demonstrated an impressive military capability and a willingness to project its power on behalf of prospective clients, it depended for its efficacy upon landing and staging facilities from sympathetic governments whose immediate aims were congruent with its own.

A politically congenial set of circumstances is prerequisite for the projection of military power in the Third World. For this reason alone, Moscow may be expected to tread gingerly in its behavior toward African states. Despite the varied Soviet military privileges in Guinea, Angola, Ethiopia, and Mozambique, the threat posed by the Soviet naval presence in southern Africa and the Indian Ocean has been exaggerated. Moscow does not possess the fully controlled land-based support facilities so vital for a politically significant projection of military power. Therefore, its naval forces must rely on local goodwill, which is an ephemeral phenomenon in Third World politics.

Third, Moscow responds to local initiatives in its pursuit of limited objectives. Whatever the strategic rationale and objective for its far-ranging policy may be, each particular move is a result of an African need and an invitation to cooperate and not of Soviet pressure (though the Soviet hand may well be involved in local intrigues that result in the coming to power of elites predisposed to Moscow, as in Angola). The application of infinitely malleable ideological criteria (exemplified by Soviet support for such bloody tyrants as Idi Amin of Uganda and Bokassa of the Central African Republic), the downgrading of expectations for a rapid transformation of African economic and social institutions, and the readiness to absorb setbacks (witness the acceptance of the deposals of Kwame Nkrumah in Ghana and Modibo Keita in Mali) show that Moscow puts a premium on pragmatism and prompt adaptation to political realities and is demonstrably able to find its way in the labile African political environment.

Fourth, Sino-Soviet rivalry is not the prime catalyst of Moscow's African policy. Western analysts have made too much of this as a policy determinant, with the consequent tendency to underestimate the centrality of the global rivalry with the United States in Soviet thinking. Moscow knows that China lacks the resources, military capability, and political urgency to intervene effectively on behalf of vulnerable clients and that in the unfolding struggle for southern Africa, Moscow—not Beijing—holds most of the trumps. Only in Southeast Asia is China a credible competitor.

Finally, Africa's resentment of the West provides Moscow with its greatest asset. Residual regional and ethnic rivalries, economic dislocation and dissatisfaction, and Black Africa's shared animosity toward South Africa are the stuff on which the Soviet future in Africa is predicated. Moscow can contribute relatively little to the tasks of nation-building, modernization, socioeconomic transformation, and integration into the world economy; the Soviet Union is no model for Africa, though there are those who persist in arguing that it is. Resolution of the Namibian crisis and an evolution acceptable to the outside world in South Africa's policy toward its black people could cut the ground from underneath the USSR's policies, but since this is not likely to happen soon, the USSR finds itself welcome for the political-military aid that it renders.

The Soviet Union came to Africa with clean hands—without the taint of a colonial legacy. It experienced an intoxicating initial accumulation of prestige. But Moscow is no longer unknown or unblemished, and in the coming decades Soviet diplomacy will be forced to adapt to an environment more complex and demanding than the one into which it adroitly moved in the 1960s and 1970s. The next stage—the preservation and extension of influence and the transference of economic and military assistance into political advantage—is a more trying, uncertain enterprise, as Moscow has already learned.

Latin America

Of all the regions of the Third World, none seemed to the post-Stalin Soviet leadership a less promising target for penetration and influence-building than Latin America. Prior to 1959 Soviet writings reflected an assumption of U.S. overlordship. However, the success of Fidel Castro's guerrilla-generated revolution in 1959 and his early self-proclaimed "conversion" to communism opened up new vistas to Soviet leaders. In particular, Castro's successful defiance of the United States alerted Moscow to the general revolutionary potential of the entire region.

Moscow became Castro's arms supplier soon after the formal establishment of diplomatic relations between the Soviet Union and Cuba in May 1960, with shipments expanding greatly after the abortive American-sponsored attempt to overthrow him in April 1961. In the summer of 1962, the Soviet leadership made a bold bid to deploy offensive missiles on the island and thereby to effect a major change in the U.S.-Soviet balance of power. Though failing in this, the aftermath of the Cuban missile crisis of October 1962 brought Moscow two important chips in the ongoing superpower game: a U.S. pledge not to invade Cuba and an enormously closer relationship with Cuba.

The Cuban connection is expensive, but worth the price to Moscow. Economically, the Soviet Union makes up the large Cuban trade deficit by buying Cuban sugar and nickel at above world market prices and by selling oil at concessionary prices. The overall subsidy (in the 1980s) is estimated to exceed $4 billion annually. In addition, Soviet arms, amounting to another $1 billion a year, are provided lavishly and almost free of charge. From this basic investment, Moscow reaps a rich strategic harvest. Militarily, it obtains substantial privileges, which include the largest intelligence collection of its kind in the world, a twenty-eight-square-mile facility that has expanded by more than 60 percent in size and capability during the past decade or so. In addition to this installation, which is manned by 1500 Soviet technicians in Lourdes in western Cuba, the USSR has an airfield that it can freely use for its own reconnaissance and antisubmarine-warfare missions. Its naval ships use Cuban ports, thus increasing their time on-station off the U.S. coast and in the Caribbean. Politically, Cuba serves as a constant irritant to the United States, a base for anti-American propaganda throughout the Western Hemisphere, and a conduit for supplies and advisers to revolutionary movements and regimes that are opposed to U.S. "imperialism." Moreover, it has proved to be a useful surrogate for projecting power in the Horn of Africa and Southern Africa.

Although Moscow has avoided making any formal commitment to come to Castro's defense in the event of attack—Cuba is the only one of the USSR's prime Third World clients without a friendship treaty—Soviet leaders regularly affirm the USSR's readiness to help defend Cuba, though not at CPSU congresses. On other occasions, however, they speak out as staunch supporters.

Even prior to Castro's advent to power, the USSR had diplomatic relations with Mexico, Argentina, Brazil, Chile, and Uruguay. By the late 1960s, it had exchanged diplomatic representatives with five Andean countries: Bolivia, Colombia, Ecuador, Peru, and Venezuela; and in the 1970s, with a number of Caribbean countries: Costa Rica, Grenada, Guyana, Jamaica, and Nicaragua.[4]

In Latin America, as elsewhere in the Third World, Moscow has relied on a combination of subregional rivalries, anti-American sentiments, and the ambitions of local dictators to help it establish a presence, touch-off arms races, and exploit consequent polarizations. For example, in the mid-1970s, the USSR extended $650 million to the radical military regime in Peru, which harbored irredentist resentment toward Ecuador and Chile, enabling it to purchase advanced MiG aircraft, tanks, and other weapons; in the early 1980s, Moscow wooed the brutal right-wing military junta in Argentina, purchasing large quantities of beef and more than 60 percent of Argentina's grain exports in order to offset the partial embargo imposed by the Carter adminstration after the invasion of Afghanistan. In appreciation for the junta's business-as-usual policy, Moscow sold Argentina five tons of heavy water and twelve tons of enriched uranium for nuclear reactors, upheld Argentina's position against Britain in the war over the Falklands/Malvinas in April–May 1982, and even blocked discussions of the junta's human rights violations in UN bodies. In both cases, however, the restoration of democracy (1980 in Peru, 1983 in Argentina) limited Soviet prospects for diplomatic gain. Such turnabouts have also occurred in Soviet relations with Chile, Brazil, Uruguay, and Grenada.

In July 1979, the success of the Sandinista Revolution drew the USSR's attention to Nicaragua. Diplomatic relations were established three months later, and the first Soviet ambassador arrived in January 1980. Since signing an economic agreement in Moscow in March 1980, the Soviet government has extended the Sandinistas considerable economic and military assistance (much of it via Havana). As U.S. economic and military pressure on the Sandinista regime increased, so, too, did Soviet bloc support. Although estimates vary, the amount of $300 to $400 million a year since 1983 is usually cited. Moscow has provided the weaponry needed to keep the regime in power, the bulk of its oil requirements (upwards of 400,000 tons a year), and enough foodstuffs and equipment to keep Nicaragua's economy functioning. Sensing the risks of provoking a sharp U.S. response that might trigger a full-fledged invasion, Moscow has proceeded carefully. It has lauded the efforts of Latin American leaders to find a political solution that would end U.S. support for the anti-Communist insurgents (the Contras) and enable the Sandinistas to institutionalize their rule. One thing it assuredly does not want in the region is another costly client to subsidize.

Since Gorbachev took office, there also has been an increased interest in improving relations with leading Latin American countries—Argentina, Brazil, and Mexico. In October 1986, Shevardnadze became the first Soviet foreign minister to visit Mexico; and in October 1987, he traveled to Argentina, the USSR's largest trading partner in South America; to Uruguay, where Moscow seeks expanded trade and access to ports for its merchant ships; and to Brazil, a distant second to Argentina in trade, with whose impressive computer industry Moscow would like to develop closer ties. Despite reports that Gorbachev might visit the region in the near future, there is little likelihood of an imminent expansion of Soviet–Latin American trade, certainly not until these countries can bring their international debt problem under control.

In the final analysis, Moscow's interest in Latin America is preeminently political. It has no need to acquire tangible advantages: U.S. estrangement from important Latin American countries and diminished influence in an environment of rising anti-Americanism, mounting Third World criticisms of U.S. policy, and American domestic factionalism over issues that are not of primary concern to the Kremlin are reward enough to sustain the present strategy.

Notes

1. Joseph Stalin, *Works,* Vol. VI (Moscow: Foreign Languages Publishing House, 1953), 144–46.
2. N. S. Khrushchev, *Report of the Central Committee of the CPSU to the Twentieth Party Congress* (Moscow: Foreign Languages Publishing House, 1956), excerpts.
3. Leszek Buszynski, *Soviet Foreign Policy and Southeast Asia.* (New York: St. Martin's Press, 1986), 251.
4. Cole Blasier, *The Giant's Rival: The USSR and Latin America* (Pittsburgh: University of Pittsburgh Press, 1983), 19–20.

Selected Bibliography

BLASIER, COLE. *The Giant's Rival: The USSR and Latin America.* Pittsburgh: University of Pittsburgh Press, revised edition, 1987.

BUSZYNSKI, LESZEK. *Soviet Foreign Policy and Southeast Asia.* New York: St. Martin's Press, 1986.

CAMPBELL, KURT M. *Soviet Policy Towards South Africa.* New York: St. Martin's Press, 1986.

CARR, EDWARD HALLETT. *The Bolshevik Revolution, 1917-1923.* Vols. 1, 2, 3. New York: Macmillan, 1951, 1952, 1953.

DINERSTEIN, HERBERT S. *The Making of a Missile Crisis: October 1962.* Baltimore: Johns Hopkins University Press, 1976.

DISMUKES, BRADFORD, and JAMES M. MCCONNELL (EDS.). *Soviet Naval Diplomacy.* Elmsford, N.Y.: Pergamon Press, 1979.

DUNCAN, W. RAYMOND. *The Soviet Union and Cuba.* New York: Praeger, 1985.

HORN, ROBERT C. *Soviet-Indian Relations: Issues and Influence.* New York: Praeger, 1982.

KATZ, MARK N. *The Third World in Soviet Military Thought.* Baltimore: Johns Hopkins University Press, 1982.

KLINGHOFFER, ARTHUR JAY. *The Angolan War: A Study in Soviet Policy in the Third World.* Boulder: Westview Press, 1980.

LEGVOLD, ROBERT. *Soviet Policy in West Africa.* Cambridge: Harvard University Press, 1970.

MCLANE, CHARLES B. *Soviet Strategies in Southeast Asia.* Princeton: Princeton University Press, 1966.

MENON, RAJAN. *Soviet Power and the Third World.* New Haven: Yale University Press, 1986.

RUBINSTEIN, ALVIN Z. *Moscow's Third World Strategy.* Princeton: Princeton University Press, 1989.

STEVENS, CHRISTOPHER. *The Soviet Union and Black Africa.* New York: Holmes and Meier, 1976.

VALKENIER, ELIZABETH KRIDL. *The Soviet Union and the Third World: An Economic Bind.* New York: Praeger, 1983.

VARAS, AUGUSTO (ED.). *Soviet–Latin American Relations in the 1980s.* Boulder: Westview Press, 1987.

WHELAN, JOSEPH G. and MICHAEL J. DIXON. *The Soviet Union in the Third World: Threat to World Peace?* Elmsford, N.Y.: Pergamon Press, 1986.

9
The Soviet Union and the Middle East

In the Third World it is the Middle East that has drawn most of the Soviet attention, and it is there that the Soviet Union and the United States have consistently had their most serious crises. Tension between them in the decades ahead seems inevitable, because of the region's intrinsic strategic and economic significance.

The importance of the Middle East needs no elaboration. Geographically, it is the land bridge linking Europe to Africa and Asia; strategically, it commands key air routes and maritime communications and lies south of the soft underbelly of the USSR; economically, it possesses vast amounts of oil, the critical energy resource of the next generation; and politically, as a region experiencing simultaneous political, social, religious, and economic turmoil and rivalry, it suffers from the systemic instability that attracts superpower involvement.

Soviet strategy in the Middle East is directed toward four areas: (1) the non-Arab Muslim tier of states situated along the USSR's southern border, namely, Turkey, Iran and Afghanistan; (2) the Arab-Israeli sector of the Arab world and the eastern littoral of the Mediterranean; (3) the Persian Gulf–Arabian Peninsula region; and (4) the North African littoral, from Libya westward. Soviet interest in each subregion developed independently in response to a changing combination of security concerns, military capabilities, local opportunities, and U.S. policy. From the mid-1950s, when the post-Stalin leadership first tentatively sought to improve its position in some parts of the Middle East, to the 1980s, when it has become deeply enmeshed in all sectors of the Middle East, Moscow has broadened its military probes and political horizons from regions contiguous to its imperial system to those lying well beyond its essential security belt. The revolution in military technology and the enormous growth of

Soviet military capabilities have made the USSR's strategic outreach global.

Moscow's Southern Tier: Turkey, Iran, and Afghanistan

The most important component of the USSR's Middle East policy has been the relationship with Turkey, Iran, and Afghanistan. In the 1950s, Soviet vulnerability in the south to nuclear strikes by the U.S. Strategic Air Command (SAC) heightened the Kremlin's already well-honed obsession with security. Previously, Russia had not been threatened from the south. Successive czars had expanded in the eighteenth and nineteenth centuries at the expense of the enfeebled Ottoman and Persian Empires; absorbed the feudal Central Asian Turkic-speaking Muslim khanates of Bokhara, Khiva and Samarkand; and reached the border of Afghanistan by the 1880s. Acquiring real estate always loomed large in Russian military thinking. Temporary Russian military weakness after the Bolshevik Revolution and World War I led the new communist regime to emphasize "peaceful coexistence." From 1919 to 1945, Moscow lacked the strength or opportunity to do otherwise than maintain the status quo with its southern neighbors. Victory in World War II, however, revived the imperial impetus. Encouraged by his successes in Europe, Stalin tried in 1945–1946 to wrest territorial concessions from Turkey and Iran and to acquire a UN trusteeship over Tripolitania (Libya), but failed, largely as a consequence of determined U.S. opposition. He did indirectly affect developments in the Arab East, however, by supporting the United Nations' partition of Palestine in November 1947 and by recognizing Israel in 1948 in order to weaken the British position in the area. Indeed, even though 1948–1949 was a period of mounting anti-Semitism in the Soviet Union, Stalin's sanction for the sale of Czech arms to Israel at that critical time was a crucial factor in the survival of the infant Israeli nation. But aside from this, during the Stalin period, Moscow was a sideline observer of the political controversies plaguing the Middle East.

In 1953 the change of leadership in the Kremlin brought with it a readiness to chart new approaches to improve the USSR's security and strategic position in the Middle East. Geographical contiguity mandated special attention to improving relations with Turkey, Iran, and Afghanistan. This courtship started slowly but was pursued consistently. The Note to the Turkish Government from Soviet Foreign Minister V. M. Molotov on May 30, 1953, heralded the start of a campaign to repair the damage done by Stalin and to reestablish the accommodation that had prevailed in the 1920s. The Note was significant for its unequivocal apology and renunciation of territorial ambitions. By the early 1960s, Ankara was slowly responding to the proffered Soviet olive branch as Washington sought détente with Moscow and as alignments changed in the Arab world. Moscow was prudent and generous. It avoided military provocation, extended economic assistance, and exploited Ankara's disillusionment with Washington which was triggered by the U.S. removal of Jupiter missiles from Turkey several months after the Cuban missile crisis (arousing Turkish suspicions of a Soviet-American deal at their expense); and which was reinforced by the Cyprus crises of 1964 and 1974. Extensive Soviet economic commitments have resulted in the construction of important industrial projects, including an iron and steel complex, an oil refinery, and an aluminum plant, and Soviet loans to Turkey for economic projects have been larger than those extended to any less-developed country in recent years. In 1975 Kosygin's suggestion of a nonaggression pact was politely rejected, but during Turkish Premier Bulent Ecevit's visit to Moscow in June 1978, the two governments signed a political document on the principles of good neighborly and friendly cooperation, similar to a 1972 communiqué issued from Ankara during a visit by Soviet President Nikolai Podgorny.

All of this helps explain the ease with which Moscow was able to carry out its military deployments and overflights of Turkish (and Greek) airspace during the 1973 October War and the 1977–1978 Somali-Ethiopian war. Turkey looked the other way. In July 1976, at the height of Turkey's anger at the U.S. arms embargo over Cyprus, the Turks interpreted the 1936 Montreux Convention flexibly and, by designating the USSR's Kiev-class carrier an antisubmarine cruiser, permitted it to be the first carrier ever to transit the Turkish straits.

In the late 1980s, Soviet relations with Turkey must be accounted a success for Soviet policy. The Turks remain wary—500 years of suspicion, hostility, war, a common frontier, and Moscow's perennial ambition to control the Turkish straits are all givens in Turkish thinking—but the bear has been almost benign. The frontier has been quiet, though Moscow occasionally protests the presence of U.S. monitoring stations on Turkish territory. No threatening Soviet military buildups and no serious incidents have taken place. Indeed, the current state of Soviet-Turkish relations epitomizes the progress Moscow has made toward undermining containment, encouraging the de facto nonalignment of the entire rimland region from Greece to Afghanistan, and ensuring an easy access to the eastern Mediterranean and the Arab East.

Soviet-Iranian relations, poor between 1945 and 1961, improved gradually after 1962, when the shah announced that no United States military bases or missile sites would be permitted on Iranian territory. Although Iran was a member of the pro-Western CENTO military pact, she did not keep a large military force along the Soviet-Iranian border, a fact that made her participation in CENTO tolerable to Moscow and played an important role in the Soviet-Iranian rapprochement. Economic ties expanded significantly. The USSR built a major steel plant and various industrial projects; in return, it received natural gas and oil. Increasingly the government-to-government relationship improved to the point that the shah even returned Soviet defectors.

Iran experienced serious social unrest and political protests, the frustrated responses of different groups to rampant inflation; urban blight; agrarian dislocation; extensive corruption; and modernization on the one hand, and dictatorial rule, repressive policies, and rising expectations on the other. For complex reasons, the disparate groups in opposition to the shah found a unifying symbol in the late spring of 1978: Ayatollah Ruhollah Khomeini, the octogenarian religious leader who had been exiled by the shah in 1962. Events moved with tumultous rapidity, so that by mid-January 1979, the shah was forced into exile; within a month, Khomeini had returned and established an Islamic republic.

The Soviet role in these momentous and unexpected developments remains a subject of speculation. In the early stages of the antishah protests—from late spring to early fall 1978—Soviet commentators generally restricted themselves essentially to reporting what was happening in the cities and oil fields. They did not turn against the shah or proclaim his imminent demise. Moscow, like Washington, was surprised by the shah's ineptness. Only gradually did Soviet broadcasts begin to criticize the shah's government, attack United States involvement in Iran, and demand that U.S. imperialism be kicked out of the country.

A turning point in the Kremlin's attitude came on November 19, 1978, when Brezhnev issued a statement noting Moscow's opposition to any outside interference in Iran. In effect, he warned the United States that if it attempted to act directly to keep the shah in power, the Soviet Union might undertake an intervention of its own in accordance with a 1921 Soviet-Iranian treaty concerning threats to the territorial integrity of the country. By January 1979 Moscow had decided that the shah would not hold. Soviet anti-American agitation acquired an incendiary dimension, and Communist agents played an important (but as yet only imperfectly understood) role in aggravating labor unrest in the oil fields (where the Communists were influential among the minority Arab and Kurdish workers), thereby contributing to the general economic paralysis that finally undermined the shah's position.

The fall of the shah was in general a boon to Moscow and, of course, a grievous blow to the United States. Soviet benefits are considerable and primarily strategic. The American-manned intelligence-gathering stations situated along the Soviet border were shut down; Iranian arms purchases from the United States ended and Iran withdrew from the role of policeman for the West in the Persian Gulf. Moscow watched with understandable satisfaction Khomeini's intense anti-Americanism, Iran's withdrawal from CENTO (which collapsed shortly thereafter), and the legalization of the Tudeh (Communist) party. Despite different political systems and antithetical ideologies, Soviet leaders expected basic continuation of extensive economic relations, quiet borders, and a prudent, pragmatic handling of divergent regional interests.

Relations with Khomeini's Iran, however, have proved pricklier than Moscow had reason to expect. The issues that loom large in Soviet-Iranian relations wax and wane in importance, largely as a consequence of the vagaries of the domestic turmoil in Iran, but also because of Iran's absorption with the United States during the period from February 1979 to January 1981 (when the 444-day hostage crisis ended) and with Iraq since its invasion in September 1980. The principal issues are Soviet attempts to normalize relations, the USSR's occupation of Afghanistan, the Iran-Iraq war, the inability to agree on a price for Iranian natural gas, and Soviet interference in Iran's internal affairs. A few comments about each should indicate the strained and self-limiting character of Soviet-Iranian ties and the difficulties the Soviets face in their courtship of Iran under Khomeini.

The Soviet Union's quest for normalization and continuation of the good state-to-state relationship that it had had with the shah has been hampered by the suspicion of communism shared by Khomeini's supporters, by the traditional Iranian fear of the covetous colossus to the north, by the Communist coup in Afghanistan in April 1978, and by Moscow's insistence on reaffirming, despite Tehran's repeated repudiations, the application of Articles 5 and 6 of the 1921 Soviet-Iranian treaty. These articles stipulate that Soviet forces may intervene in Iranian affairs if a third country threatens to attack the USSR from Iranian territory or if Moscow considers its border threatened. The latter has been a particularly sore point, a reminder that for more than 150 years successive generations of Russian leaders have looked on Iran as their natural sphere of influence and that Moscow's support for the principles of equality between nations and noninterference in the internal affairs of other countries bears little resemblance to the way it, in practice, deals with weaker powers.

Soon after coming to power, the Khomeini regime criticized the USSR's intervention in the internal affairs of Afghanistan, and Ayatollah Khomeini exhorted the Afghans to resist their Communist puppet rulers. Moscow's attempts to ingratiate itself with Tehran by adopting a pro-Iranian position in the hostage crisis that erupted on November 4, 1979, when militants seized the U.S. Embassy, failed to silence Iranian criticisms. Since the Soviet military intervention of December 1979, the issue has been a running sore in their relations. Not even the Iraqi attack on

September 22, 1980, and Iran's obvious desire that the Soviet Union be a disinterested observer instead of a partisan patron of Iraq as could be expected from the 1972 Soviet-Iraqi friendship treaty, mitigated Tehran's hostility on the Afghan issue (which in 1989 is disappearing).

The Iran-Iraq War has posed dilemmas for Moscow, which seeks to avoid alienating either side. The essential Soviet position, set forth in *Izvestiia* the day after the war began, is that the conflict was a vestige of the two countries' colonial past; that the United States seeks to exploit the situation in order to establish control over the region's oil; that Washington hopes the conflict will lessen Iran's ability "to resist the imperialist pressures that are being brought on it"; and that the United States sees the conflict as an opportunity to reorient Iraq's foreign policy toward the West.[1] In this entangled situation, the Soviet government has been selling arms to both sides and playing for time in the hope that a termination of hostilities will enable it to continue its courtship of both Tehran and Baghdad.

Soviet-Iranian relations are complex. A major irritation to the Kremlin was Khomeini's crackdown on the Tudeh Party. In February 1983, many members were arrested. At the end of April, Nureddin Kianuri, the Tudeh leader, publicly confessed that the party had been trying to subvert the Islamic Republic and had been spying for the Soviet Union. On May 4, Tehran outlawed the Tudeh and expelled a number of Soviet diplomats. Iran's help to the anti-Soviet resistance movement in Afghanistan and hostility to the Soviet Union's stepped-up arms sales to Iraq were additional factors contributing to the worsening relationship between the two countries.

As often happens in its approach to regional politics, the Soviet leadership reacts to events rather than initiating them. The signal of a desire for better relations came from Tehran. By 1984 the Iranian government realized that increased tension with Moscow redounded to Iraq's benefit, and it set out to improve the atmosphere, first, with the symbolic whitewashing of the anti-Soviet slogans blazoned on the walls of the Soviet embassy, and second, by an exchange of economic delegations. In February 1986, amidst fierce fighting on the Iran-Iraq front, First Deputy Foreign Minister Georgii Korniyenko became the highest ranking Soviet official to visit Tehran since Khomeini's 1979 revolution; in December, the Iranian-Soviet Standing Commission for Economic Cooperation met in Tehran for the first time in six years. In August 1987 the two countries agreed to large scale economic cooperation, including projections for expansion of natural gas deliveries by the early 1990s; construction in the areas of power generation, steel, and oil refining; and the return of Soviet technicians, removed in 1985 because of Iraqi air attacks.

But unforeseen developments have left the future of the Soviet-

Iranian relationship in a state of renewed uncertainty. Iran's concern over growing Soviet involvement in the Gulf increased in 1985 when the USSR normalized its relations with Oman and the United Arab Emirates and made repeated overtures to Saudi Arabia. Gorbachev's activism, underlying which is a quest for greater influence in the region, was evident with the introduction of a Soviet naval presence in the Gulf. Since September 1986, when Iran intercepted a Soviet ship bound for Kuwait with a cargo of weapons and held it for several days before releasing it on the grounds that it had been found to be carrying only "cement," the USSR has used its warships to convoy Soviet merchant ships bound for Kuwait (with cargoes destined in the main for Iraq). This is the same tactic employed by Washington, which started escorting ships earlier in the year. As the "tanker war"—consisting of Iraqi and Iranian attacks on merchant ships suspected of trading with the other side—intensified, the issue of freedom of the seas became a matter of concern to the Soviet Union and the United States. Also prompting greater Soviet involvement were the revelations in November 1986 of the U.S. sale of arms to Iran (which has influence with the Shiite hostage-takers in Lebanon) in its attempt to ransom American hostages and open a political dialogue with Tehran.

Moscow is proceeding prudently in its search for a position that will enhance its leverage in the region. Though critical of the U.S. and West European naval buildup and mine-sweeping operations in the Gulf, it has done much the same thing, including its reflagging of several Kuwaiti ships. It supports the UN Security Council Resolution 598 of July 20, 1987, which called for a ceasefire in the war between Iran and Iraq and a return to prewar boundaries, but has been reluctant to support proposals that call for the imposition of sanctions on Iran, for fear that this would foreclose improved relations with Tehran and benefit the U.S. policy of isolating Iran. Nevertheless, it continues as Iraq's principal arms supplier.

For the moment, Moscow is looking to the long term, encouraging Iran's anti-Americanism, maintaining connections to both belligerents, and awaiting developments. In neighboring Afghanistan, it faces a more immediately pressing problem.

The roots of Soviet interest in Afghanistan can be traced to Russian imperial expansion into Central Asia in the nineteenth century and to the "great game" of power politics between Russia and Britain. Russia's expansion to the Oxus River, the northern border of Afghanistan, heightened Britain's fear for the security of its Indian Empire. In 1907, faced with threats to their security in Europe and the Far East, Russia and Britain agreed to respect a buffer role for Afghanistan and the status quo along the entire Central Asian periphery. This accommodation ended with the Bolshevik Revolution.

In 1919, Afghanistan proclaimed its full independence—and neutrality. It maintained correct relations with Soviet Russia and the British raj. However, with the end of British rule in 1947 and the establishment of India and Pakistan as new nation-states, Afghanistan started to press claims to the Pashto-speaking tribal areas of Pakistan, and this policy intensified its desire for modernization, especially for modern weapons. Ironically, this covetous course was to end in subjugation to the power that did the most to feed Afghan ambitions, namely, the Soviet Union.

The Soviet courtship of Afghanistan began in 1954 as part of Khrushchev's overall policy of improving relations with Turkey, Iran, and Afghanistan and undermining the U.S. policy of containment. Sensitive to the xenophobia of its weak, semifeudal neighbor, the Soviet government proceeded slowly. Agreements were signed calling for Soviet construction of two large grain elevators, a flour mill, and road-building equipment. Other economic and social projects followed in rapid succession.

However, it was the military relationship, pushed by Prime Minister Muhammad Daoud Khan during his first period in office (1953–1963) that was to be momentous. Unlike the older generation, Daoud did not believe that reliance on the Soviet Union would jeopardize the country's independence. Arrogant and obstinate, obsessed with the ambition to unite the approximately five million Pathans living in Pakistan's Northwest Frontier Province (NWFP) with Afghanistan, he was convinced that with the British departure from India, Moscow had little to gain from swallowing Afghanistan—a tough and unripe nut. Accordingly, he discarded the previous policy of hiring as advisers and technicians only nationals from countries that posed no possible threat and engaged Russians by the hundreds to develop the nation's infrastructure and economy —and to equip and train the army.

Soviet policy had several objectives: to prevent the possibility of Afghanistan's joining any United States-sponsored alliance; to create in Afghanistan a showcase of Soviet aid projects as a way of demonstrating to other Third World countries the benefits of closer ties with the USSR; to offset Chinese inroads; and to draw Afghanistan more intimately into the Soviet sphere of influence, into what Soviet leader Leonid Brezhnev was to term in 1969 a "collective security system for Asia."

In March 1963, King Mohammad Zahir Shah removed Daoud, introduced the country's first constitution, and tried, ineffectually, to take the royal family out of ministerial politics. But he proved to be a reluctant reformer. Modernization proceeded fitfully, enough to stimulate elite demands for a greater role in policymaking but inadequate to satisfy the social groups that it spawned. Meanwhile, Afghan dependence on Soviet economic aid grew. One consequence of Soviet assistance was the development of an efficient all-weather system of highways through the previously formidable Hindu Kush mountains, which facilitated the Soviet invasion of 1979. In July 1973, a group of army officers staged a coup, brought Daoud back to power, and established a republic. Daoud tried, but too late, to veer toward an approximation of the policy that had traditionally been used to preserve independence—*bi-tarafi,* the balancing of external influences. His attempt to become less dependent on the Soviet Union prompted the restive Communists to seize power in a bloody coup on April 27, 1978.

The new Communist government was headed by Nur Mohammad Taraki, one of the founders of the People's Democratic Party of Afghanistan (PDPA) in 1965. The party split in 1968, with Taraki leading a majority faction known as the Khalq (the "masses") and Babrak Karmal heading the smaller, more pro-Soviet, group known as the Parcham (the "flag"). For a time the two Communist groups cooperated, but three months after the coup, Taraki purged the Parchamis, and Babrak Karmal took refuge in East Europe.

Taraki zealously pressed radical reforms, thus alienating the tribes, the religious leaders, and the small urban middle class, depriving himself of both popular support and the loyalty of the thin stratum of administrators and technically trained personnel. Intensifying this alienation was his decision to draw even closer to the Soviet Union. On December 5, 1978, a twenty-year treaty of friendship and cooperation was signed. Moscow greatly expanded its assistance and advisory personnel, and Afghanistan was drawn into a position of total dependence.

Taraki's policies triggered open rebellion. By early 1979, attacks on the regime were so widespread that in April Moscow dispatched a high-ranking military mission to Kabul to evaluate the situation. In September, Taraki fell afoul of intraparty factionalism and was killed in a showdown with his Deputy Prime Minister, Hafizullah Amin. For the next three-and-a-half months, Amin pursued an even more aggressive policy, trying to destroy the Mujahideen (or freedom fighters). Like Taraki, he took Soviet support for granted and welcomed the thickening flow of Soviet soldiers and supplies. The Kremlin, however, had other plans. On December 27, 1979, it intervened in force, killing Amin and installing Babrak Karmal as its man in Kabul. Whatever independence of action the Communist regime had retained in the twenty months after the April 1978 coup came to an end. The decisions for securing Communist rule in Afghanistan were henceforth made in Moscow.

For more than eight years, the Soviet Union waged a brutal war, aptly termed selective genocide, to crush the Afghan freedom-fighters (the *Mujahideen,* or "holy warriors"): it bombed and strafed villages suspected of harboring members of the resistance; burned crops in an attempt to starve the population into submission; mounted repeated offensives to depopulate strategic valleys; and conducted a scorched-earth policy. Out of a population of approximately 16 million, more than 4 million Afghans have fled—over 3 million to Pakistan, the rest to Iran. Despite overwhelming superiority in firepower, the 110,000 Soviet troops have been slowly thwarted, and now the costs to Moscow are rising steeply. The *Mujahideen* are better armed—for example, since late 1986, they have been receiving shoulder-held surface-to-air missiles like the U.S. Stinger, which has virtually neutralized Soviet control of the air, and their perfected hit-and-run strikes and ambushes exact a heavy price, estimated at about 2000 Soviet combat deaths a year.

Soon after coming to power, Gorbachev recognized that the war in Afghanistan was his most urgent and difficult problem in the Third World. In his report to the twenty-seventh congress of the CPSU on February 26, 1986, he called it "a bleeding wound." His dissatisfaction prompted changes on a number of fronts. First, in May 1986, he replaced Babrak Karmal as general-secretary of the PDPA by Najib, a tough, dedicated Communist with a record of complete loyalty to Moscow going back to his student days in the mid-1960s. Second, Gorbachev moved to give credence to his stated aim of bringing Soviet troops home by withdrawing 8000 at the end of October, though Pakistani and Western intelligence sources noted that Soviet force levels in the country remained fairly constant, between 110,000 and 125,000. Third, Gorbachev accelerated diplomatic efforts, both bilaterally and through the U.N.-sponsored talks that had started in 1982 between Pakistan and the Communist regime in Kabul. Fourth, military attacks on the *Mujahideen* were intensified, as was propaganda aimed at dividing and coopting them to support the Najib government with offers of status and rewards. Finally, in January 1987, Najib called for "national reconciliation" and announced a ceasefire, provided that the *Mujahideen* agreed to accept the regime's terms, which were soon shown to be completely unacceptable.

By the end of 1987, Gorbachev seemed to have run out of carrots and sticks. His hopes for cooptation (attracting cadres with a stake in the survival of the Communist regime) and national reconciliation had failed to provide a popular base on which to construct a viable Afghan regime that could survive without Soviet military props; his military escalation—intended to show the impossibility of defeating the Red Army on the battlefield—had not destroyed the *Mujahideen's* will to fight, and the air strikes along the border and incitement of tribal unrest had not cowed Pakistan into cutting down its aid to the *Mujahideen*.

The most serious and unequivocal statement of intention to withdraw from Afghanistan was made by Mikhail S. Gorbachev on February 8, 1988:

> By now documents covering all aspects of a settlement have been almost fully worked out at the Geneva negotiations. They include agreements between Afghanistan and Pakistan on non-interference in each other's internal affairs and on the return of Afghan refugees from Pakistan; international guarantees of non-interference in Afghanistan's internal affairs; a document on the interrelationship of all elements of a political settlement. There is also agreement on establishing a verification mechanism.
>
> So what remains to be done? It is to establish a time frame for the withdrawal of Soviet troops from Afghanistan that would be acceptable to all. Precisely that—a time frame, since the fundamental political decision to withdraw Soviet troops from Afghanistan was adopted by us, in agreement with the Afghan leadership, some time ago . . .

He went on to say that "the Afghans themselves will decide the final status of their country," and that he "would be only too happy to have" a nonaligned, independent, and neutral Afghanistan as a neighbor.

On April 14, 1988, a series of agreements, the most important of which calls for the withdrawal of Soviet troops from Afghanistan, was signed in Geneva between the government of Pakistan and the Soviet-puppet regime in Kabul. On May 15, 1988, the Soviet withdrawal began and is expected to be completed by 1989, leaving in doubt Najib's ability to survive without massive support from Moscow. All this suggests that in the interests of pushing *perestroika* and economic development at home and pursuing priority foreign policy objectives in Europe, the Far East, and arms control negotiations, he is determined to relinquish the prospective geo-strategic gains that are within the USSR's grasp in Afghanistan and cut the Gordian knot that binds Moscow to its endless war there.

If Gorbachev does completely withdraw Soviet forces from Afghanistan and permits the Afghans to reestablish their own independent political system, he will have taken a giant step toward reconciliation with the West, the Muslim world, and China, one that may presage "restructuring" and "new political thinking" in other areas of Soviet foreign policy as well. However, anything less will signify that continuity, not change, is to be expected in the years ahead.

The Arab-Israeli Sector

By concluding an arms deal with Egypt's Gamal Abdel Nasser in August 1955, the USSR discovered that arms were the key to access to the Arab world and erased the diplomatic debits of the Stalin era. The initial targets were Egypt and Syria, both of whom opposed Western military pacts in the area and sought alternative sources of weapons with which to counter their Western-armed regional rivals. Moscow seemed fully in tune with the anticolonialist and anti-imperialist sentiment cresting in the Arab world. Soon afterward, the Arab-Israeli conflict provided Moscow with a convenient issue for exploiting Arab ties with the United States and enhancing its status with radical Arab states. In time, Moscow's goals expanded to include the quest for military privileges and manipulation of Arab oil to weaken the Western world.

Moscow sold Egypt arms with several purposes in mind, primarily to establish firm ties with a key Arab country and to encourage its opposition to the Baghdad pact (established in the spring of 1955 and reorganized as CENTO in 1959, following the revolution in Iraq that brought in an anti-Western regime). When Washington's precipitate withdrawal of its offer to assist Egypt in building the Aswan High Dam provoked Nasser to nationalize the Suez Canal Company in July 1956, the Soviet government upheld the Egyptian action. Moscow also championed Nasser's cause during the Israeli-Anglo-French invasion of Egypt in October 1956, and though it was American rather than Soviet pressure on the invaders that forced their withdrawal and saved Nasser, the Soviet Union's prestige nonetheless rose spectacularly in the Arab world as it replaced Egyptian arms lost to the Israelis in Sinai, lent Egypt and Syria several hundred million dollars for economic development, and supported Arab positions in the UN. However, Moscow was careful to avoid any military actions that might occasion a strong response from the United States, still the preeminent military power in the area.

Arab nationalism posed dilemmas for the Soviet Union in the years immediately after the merger of Egypt and Syria created the United Arab Republic (UAR) and the military made an anti-Western coup in Iraq, in March and July 1958, respectively. Though unhappy over the establishment of the UAR because this "nullified some of the gains made in Syria by both the USSR and the indigenous Communist Party" and also served to strengthen Nasser's bargaining position, "making him less amenable to Moscow's wishes and more immune to Soviet pressure," Moscow reconciled itself to the newest manifestation of Arab nationalism and "chose to continue to protect Soviet interests in the Middle East through cooperation with, not opposition to, Cairo."[2] Pleasantly surprised by the overthrow of the pro-Western Iraqi regime on July 14, 1958, the USSR saw in the emergence of the Qasim government a sharp blow to the Western position in the Middle East (Nasser also considered it a move toward Arab unity). An early and unexpected falling-out between Cairo and Baghdad, however, confronted Moscow with difficult choices. How was it to differentiate between two "progressive" Arab regimes without alienating either? How was it to nourish anti-imperialism without arousing Arab suspicions of communism by pressing for better conditions for indigenous Arab Communists? How was it to strengthen the progressive component of Arab nationalism and at the same time minimize its bourgeois component?

For a time, Moscow backed Abd al-Karim Qasim against Nasser because in contrast to Nasser, who repeatedly expressed interest in improving relations with the Western countries, Qasim was militantly critical. Also in contrast to Nasser, who cracked down on local Communists and asserted that communism was incompatible with Arab nationalism and unity, Qasim brought Communists into the government and relied on their support against his Nasserite opponents; and where Nasser had ambitions to unify the Arab world under his leadership, Qasim represented a force for retaining the existing nation-state system in the Arab world, thus affording Moscow more room for diplomatic maneuver and lessening the likelihood that Arab nationalism would take on a bourgeois complexion that might impede the move toward socialism. Furthermore, Moscow could not fail to regard with utmost concern the possibility, however remote, of a unitary Arab nationalist state, which might exert a strong attraction for Soviet Muslims.

Shrewdly, Khrushchev kept this mini-Cold War with Cairo over strategy, outlook, and issues from interfering with the expansion of economic ties, as exemplified by the USSR's commitment in October 1958 and January 1959 to help build the Aswan High Dam. Aware of Nasser's enormously enhanced position as the standard-bearer of Arab nationalism, Moscow tolerated his anti-Communist outbursts and sporadic moves toward improved relations with the West. Moreover, by 1961–1962, disenchantment with Qasim had set in because of his suppression of Iraqi Communists.

Military considerations were even more important motivations for Moscow's careful courtship of Nasser. In May 1961, Albania evicted the Soviet Union from the naval base it had enjoyed at Vlone on the Adriatic Sea since 1945, and U.S. deployment of Polaris submarines in the Mediterranean was impending. These events prompted friendlier relations with Nasser and serious Soviet efforts to obtain naval facilities in Egyptian ports.[3] This quest for tangible military privileges increasingly absorbed Moscow and muted political differences with Egypt. The collapse of the Egyptian-Syrian federation in September 1961 also helped; and, buttressed by the growing interest of Soviet strategic planners in Aden, the USSR subsidized Egyptian intervention in the Yemeni civil war after 1962.

Once again, in the mid-1960s, as in the mid-1950s, Egypt emerged as the key Arab target of Soviet attention, and Moscow grudgingly acquiesced to its espousal of Arab unity, subordinating ideological and political dilemmas to strategic and military objectives. Although Moscow failed to obtain the coveted naval facilities until Nasser's crushing defeat in June

1967, it benefitted enormously in its broader aim of penetrating the Arab world, by heeding a formula devised by Khrushchev.

> This formula had simple elements: first, the delivery of arms to Arab states, to break their dependence on the West and create a new dependence; second, the building of a political and economic relationship with those states based on the calculated self-interest of each party and the willingness of each to pay something in the coin of the interest of the other; and third, a rather vague ideological solidarity grounded in anticolonialism, anti-imperialism, anti-Zionism, national liberation, revolutionary change, and "socialism" in a sense broad enough to evade definition, for precision in that respect could undermine and destroy the cooperation.[4]

Egypt's disastrous showing in the Arab-Israeli war of June 1967 proved a boon for Moscow, paving the way for the extensive privileges that the Soviet military had sought. The political and strategic consequences of the June War concern us here only insofar as they relate to Soviet policy. Briefly, the background was this: In the spring of 1967, Moscow feared for the future of the pro-Soviet government in Syria. To rally support behind its Syrian client, it spread false reports of an impending Israeli attack against Syria. (To prove that there was no military buildup, the Israeli prime minister even offered to tour the Israeli-Syrian border with the Soviet ambassador, who refused.) Nasser, who had been persuaded by the Soviet Union to sign a defense pact with Syria in November 1966, did not check on Soviet intelligence reports; he mobilized his army in Sinai and ousted the UN Emergency Force, which had kept the Egyptians and Israelis apart since 1957. At this point, Nasser went beyond Soviet expectations. Instead of settling for the tactical political triumph of liquidating UNEF—the last vestige of Israel's advantage from the 1956 war—and thus diverting the supposed threat away from Syria, he announced the closing of the Straits of Tiran, blocking Israel's outlet to the Red Sea and Indian Ocean, and moved the mass of his army into position for invasion of Israel. However, the combination of Israeli air superiority and surprise was decisive, and in a lightning campaign from June 5 to 10, the Israelis defeated the Egyptians in Gaza and Sinai, the Jordanians in Jerusalem and on the West Bank, and the Syrians on the Golan Heights.

Soviet leaders, unwilling to abandon their ambitions in the Arab world, poured new weapons and Soviet advisers into Egypt and Syria. Cairo's dependence was total; the army and air force had to be reequipped and retrained to handle advanced weaponry, and the economy required imports of food, industrial materials, and machinery, much of which Moscow bankrolled. Between 1967 and 1969 alone, the Soviet investment into Egypt was in the range of $3 to $4 billion. Nevertheless, against Soviet wishes, Nasser started a "war of attrition" against Israel along the length of the Suez Canal in March 1969; but this effort backfired. In early 1970, Moscow was forced to up its ante to the point of committing 20,000 combat troops to man missile sites and the air defense of Egypt's heartland. In its complete dependence on the Soviet Union, Egypt granted significant concessions: naval facilities at Alexandria and Port Said, the assignment of airfields for the almost exclusive use of Soviet forces, and approval for the transformation of Mersa Matruh into a naval "facility" (the term Third World countries prefer to "base," since it does not imply surrender of sovereignty or smack of colonial rule) to be used by the Soviet Mediterranean fleet. These privileges marked the high point of Soviet presence in any Arab country. In saving Nasser, Moscow demonstrated that it was prepared to go beyond the supply of arms and advisers to support prized clients and pursue imperial objectives in the Third World, even if these jeopardized the USSR's quest for détente with the United States.

When Nasser died in late September 1970, Moscow expected continuity in leadership but instead watched a struggle for power that resulted in the virtual elimination in May 1971 of Nasser's entire entourage, on which it had predicated its aim of consolidating and preserving the privileged Soviet position in Egypt. Seeking to stabilize relations with Anwar Sadat, the victor in the succession struggle, and to institutionalize its political and military presence, Moscow pressed for the Soviet-Egyptian treaty of friendship and cooperation of May 27, 1971. Article 7 of the treaty held that "in the event of development of situations creating, in the opinion of both sides, a danger to peace or violation of peace, they will contact each other without delay in order to concert their positions with a view to removing the threat that has arisen or reestablishing peace." For the first time, the USSR bound itself to a military commitment in the Third World—a measure of Egypt's importance to Moscow and of the USSR's growing military confidence. Moscow hoped that the treaty would assure its position in Egypt and serve as a model for cementing ties with other Third World countries. (And indeed, similar treaties were signed with India in August 1971, Iraq in April 1972, Somalia in 1974, Angola in October 1976, Ethiopia in November 1978, Afghanistan in December 1978, the People's Democratic Republic of Yemen in October 1979, and Syria in October 1980, to mention some of the most important ones for the Soviet Union.)

Despite the treaty, the Soviet leadership found Sadat difficult. Cairo wanted more weaponry than Moscow, influenced by its developing détente with the United States, was prepared to deliver; the Egyptian military was restive over the patronizing attitude of Soviet advisers; and the completion of the Aswan Dam in January 1971 brought new requests for major economic commitments. Also, Sadat helped to suppress a Communist-inspired coup in the Sudan in July 1971, subsequently cracked down on Egyptian Communists, and made independent efforts to deal with the United States and diminish its support of Israel. On July 18, 1972, he publicly announced the expulsion from Egypt of Soviet military personnel (between 15,000 and 20,000), including all Soviet pilots. Of the once extensive Soviet military presence in Egypt, only the naval facilities were permitted to remain more or less as before. This stunning turn of events demonstrated that neither a major presence nor heavy dependency would necessarily bring influence to the patron, and that a superpower unable or unwilling to project its military power directly into the domestic politics of a client state was vulnerable to the vagaries of a client's change of attitude or policy.

By January 1973, Moscow and Cairo had effected a reconciliation, Sadat unilaterally extending Soviet naval facilities beyond the April 1973 expiration date and Brezhnev again turning on the arms tap, in part for strategic reasons and in part for Arab oil money. In the summer of 1973, Soviet leaders—perplexed by the contradictions arising out of their interest in détente, their ambitions in the Arab world, and their rivalry with the United States—sought to accentuate the positive and minimize the negative. It remained for Sadat to influence the pattern not only of Soviet-Egyptian but also of Soviet-American relations.

When Sadat and Syrian President Hafez Assad launched the fifth Arab-Israeli war on October 6, 1973, they started a conflict that Moscow did not want but did nothing to stop. The Soviet leadership risked the budding détente with the United States in order to back its Arab clients, going nearer to the brink of a confrontation with the United States than ever before, even during the 1962 Cuban missile crisis. By 1973, the Soviet Union had achieved strategic equivalence with the United States and both sides had sizable conventional forces deployed in proximity, so that a small incident might easily have triggered a chain reaction. Moscow acted very much the generous and protective patron, saving Egypt and Syria from another military disaster and enabling both to emerge from the war with significant strategic and political gains.

But Sadat far from being grateful, repaid Soviet help with contumely and a political rebuff. For a combination of personal, strategic, political, and economic reasons, Sadat turned sharply to Washington, openly alienating the Soviet Union. Acrimony and increasing friction characterized Soviet-Egyptian relations for the next two-and-a-half years, as Sadat looked to Washington for economic assistance and for political solutions to the Arab-Israeli conflict. On March 15, 1976, Sadat unilaterally abrogated the 1971 treaty; a month later, he announced the cancellation of facilities for the Soviet navy. In less than five years, the formerly impressive Soviet military presence in Egypt had turned to sand.

The end of the Egyptian connection forced Moscow to search anew for a secure foothold in that part of the Arab world directly involved in the Arab-Israeli conflict. Thus, while the United States was fashioning two disengagement agreements on the Egyptian-Israeli front and a first-stage pullback in the Syrian-Israeli sector, the Soviet Union was looking elsewhere for an active role and a constituency for itself. It built up Syria's military capability, reluctantly supporting Assad's intervention in Lebanon in 1976; it sold massive amounts of arms to Iraq and Libya; and it followed the lead of the Arab rejectionist front in espousing the maximalist demands of the Palestine Liberation Organization.

President Jimmy Carter took office in January 1977 determined to press for a comprehensive Middle East settlement. Deteriorating relations with the Soviet Union prompted by the president's abrasive emphasis on the human rights issue and introduction of sudden changes in the SALT negotiations led Secretary of State Cyrus Vance to seek Soviet cooperation on the Arab-Israeli problem, in the hope that progress on a Middle East settlement would have a salutary effect on negotiations in other sectors. On October 1, 1977, the Soviet Union and the United States issued a joint statement that would have moved the Middle East negotiations to a Geneva venue and included all the parties. However, Israeli objections and congressional opposition rendered the statement ineffective within a week. This led Sadat to take matters into his own hands. The result was his historic trip to Jerusalem on November 19, 1977, and the pursuit of a separate Egyptian-Israeli accord. Once again the Soviet Union was left outside the bargaining process.

Moscow denounced Sadat's initiative as "an act of capitulation" and strongly supported the position of the hard-line Arab states—Syria, Iraq, Libya, and Algeria—who sought to prevent any Egyptian-Israeli agreement. It also bitterly criticized the United States for reneging on the joint statement and encouraging a separate accord, allegedly at the expense of Arab unity and the Palestinians. During the months that followed, Moscow watched the ups and downs of the Egyptian-Israeli talks and Washington's inability to bring matters to a conclusion. By the end of July 1978, the Soviet Union had reason to expect an American failure—then came the August 8 announcement in Washington of a meeting to be convened on September 5, 1978, at Camp David, Maryland. President Carter's personal commitment and involvement made the difference. The Egyptian-Israeli-American negotiations bore fruit in the signing of a formal treaty between Egypt and Israel on March 26, 1979.

Soviet officials insist that a conflict as extensive and explosive as that between the Arab states and Israel cannot be settled without the cooperation of the Soviet Union. They claim that what happens in the Middle East is a matter of vital national interest to the USSR and that Soviet strategic concerns encompass the entire region and not merely the areas bordering on the USSR. However, though the Soviet Union wants to be treated as an equal of the United States, it is hamstrung by its tactical blunder in having broken diplomatic relations with Israel in June 1967, by the residual suspicion with which it is viewed by most Arab parties, and by the Arabs' inability to forge a common policy, thus leading the militants to prefer Moscow as a patron than as a broker of a settlement.

In the aftermath of the Egyptian-Israeli reconciliation and peace treaty of March 26, 1979, Moscow strengthened ties with members of the radical, anti-American, anti-Camp David component of the Arab world, notably Syria, the PDRY, and the Palestine Liberation Organization (PLO). Syria has long been important in the USSR's political-ideological effort to establish sound relations with a key Arab country. The first to receive Soviet arms (in the fall of 1954, admittedly on a small scale), it was attractive because of its radical secular anti-Western political outlook, its toleration of Communist party activity, and its bitter opposition to any compromise with Israel. In the early 1970s arms flowed to President Hafez Assad, to whose defense Moscow rallied during the October War and whose obduracy toward U.S. efforts to promote a Syrian-Israeli agreement was rewarded with massive quantities of arms. Moscow was unhappy with Syria's military intervention in Lebanon in June 1976, but did nothing to pressure Assad to withdraw—on the contrary, continually upgrading its commitments and transfers of weapons.

The situation in Lebanon and growing Syrian domestic opposition stemming from ethnic and religious sectarianism forced Assad into a closer political relationship with Moscow. Assad's tightly knit, tough, secretive leadership is primarily Alawite, members of a Shiite Muslim sect representing only about 10 percent of the Syrian population, which is predominately Sunni, the orthodox mainstream of the Islamic religion. On October 8, 1980, in Moscow, Assad gave the Kremlin the treaty it had sought for almost a decade and signed a twenty-year treaty of friendship and cooperation. Moscow's advantages are the following: access to Syrian port facilities, prestige in the Arab world as a consequence of having finally persuaded Syria to conclude a friendship treaty, support by a key Arab country on the issue of Afghanistan, and a decreased likelihood that Syria will improve relations with the United States.

The treaty's utility to Syria became evident in June 1982, soon after Israeli forces invaded Lebanon. A series of Israeli-Syrian confrontations in the sky over the Bekaa Valley resulted in the downing of more than 80 Syrian Soviet-built MiG aircraft. In addition, the Israelis, using pinpoint bombing, knocked out all of Syria's Soviet-provided mobile surface-to-air missile sites (SAMs) in Lebanon. Furious over foreign reports depreciating the value of Soviet weaponry and intent both on reassuring Syria of its commitment to the 1980 treaty and on signaling Israel not to carry the war to Syria, Moscow quickly replenished Syria's losses of aircraft, tanks, armored personnel carriers, and SAMs. In political terms, its military resupply and buildup of Syria was a response to Camp David and President Reagan's Middle East initiative of September 1, 1982, and a warning to Washington not to underestimate the USSR's determination to play an active role in the Arab-Israeli sector of the Middle East.

Soviet diplomacy under Gorbachev has sought to improve relations with moderate Arab states such as Egypt, Jordan, and Saudi Arabia and to drum up interest in an international conference that would seek a comprehensive settlement of the Arab-Israeli conflict. Intrinsic to this process have been changes in the approach to Israel.

The first sign that the Soviet government was rethinking its policy towards Israel was *Izvestiia*'s publishing on May 12, 1985 of a telegram from Israeli President Chaim Herzog on the occasion of the 40th anniversary of the Allied victory in Europe. In printing the Israeli message in the commemorative celebration, Moscow gave rare diplomatic affirmation of Israel's right to exist. By the time that (then) Prime Minister Shimon Peres met Soviet Foreign Minister Shevardnadze at the U.N. in New York in late October, the Soviet-Israeli dialogue had become front-page news.

Indeed, in the period prior to the first Gorbachev-Reagan summit meeting in Geneva on November 19–20, 1985 and the CPSU Congress in late February 1986, hints of an imminent Soviet restoration of diplomatic relations with Israel and an easing of restrictions on the emigration of Soviet Jews were heard with increasing frequency from Soviet sources and foreign dignitaries who visited Moscow or dealt with Soviet officials abroad. But both the summit and the party congress came and went with no change. For several months, there was virtual silence. Then, in early August 1986, the Soviets proposed a meeting in Helsinki to discuss "consular affairs." Though nothing came of the one day session, periodic discussions during the year that followed produced a low-level breakthrough: in July 1987, a Soviet consular delegation arrived in Israel on a 90-day visa, the first visit by Soviet diplomats in more than twenty years. Its ostensible purposes were to survey the property of the Russian Orthodox Church and check on the situation of the few dozen Soviet citizens living in Israel; the real ones are more political and potentially far-reaching. In late July 1988, rather than risk the nonrenewal of its delegation's visas, Moscow admitted an unofficial Israeli consular delegation. Since then, each side has granted limited extensions.

However, Gorbachev seems to be no more willing than were his predecessors to risk jeopardizing good relations with prime Arab clients in order to advance the prospect of an Arab-Israeli settlement, witness his kid-gloves treatment of Syrian President Assad. Notwithstanding persisting policy differences over Syria's instigation of Palestinian opposition to Yasir Arafat's leadership of the PLO and Syria's policy in Lebanon, Gorbachev has kept the arms tap open. The continued closeness of the two countries is evident in Gorbachev's promise of additional weapons and acceptance of Assad's invitation to visit Syria; in their mutual condemnation of Israel and call for an independent Palestinian state; in their stated non-acceptance of the Egyptian-Israeli peace treaty; and in their failure in joint communiques to mention UN Security Council Resolutions 242 and 338 as the basis for future negotiations to achieve a comprehensive settlement.

Still, there are signs of a gradual thaw in Soviet policy toward Israel. First, contacts between Soviet and Israeli officials are continuing as the game of diplomatic cat-and-mouse goes on. Second, there has been an increase in Jewish emigration. Whereas in 1986 only 914 Soviet Jews were permitted to emigrate, in 1987 about 8100 were. Third, virulent, anti-Zionist, anti-Semitic and anti-Israeli propaganda has abated. Gorbachev has on a number of highly visible occasions taken a determined stand against "any manifestation of nationalist narrow-mindness and boastfulness" as in Zionism and anti-Semitism. Finally, the gradual improvement in Polish and Hungarian relations with Israel, whose purpose is eventual diplomatic normalization, could be taking place only with Moscow's approval. All this suggests that Gorbachev wants an international conference, if only to establish the USSR's equality with the United States in the Arab-Israeli arena.

A few words may be appropriate at this juncture about the PLO. There was an unwarranted rush to assert that Moscow suffered a severe blow to its credibility as a patron-protector because of its failure to intervene in Lebanon and defend the PLO from a crushing military defeat at the hands of Israel in the summer of 1982. True, Moscow helped arm, train, and encourage the PLO for years, but in this it was more a camp follower of the hard-line, radical anti-American Arab regimes it courted. Its attitude toward the PLO has evolved as a function of its perceived need to align itself with the mainstream of the anti-American coalition in the Arab world. Thus, as the PLO was accorded a more central position by Arab leaderships, Moscow increased its support. But to use the extent of the Soviet Union's readiness to fight on behalf of the PLO as a litmus test of its credibility with those Arab regimes with whom it has a treaty relationship or close ties is to misread Soviet policy egregiously. Moscow never agreed to act as the PLO's protector. It was under no obligation whatsoever—moral, legal, or military—to lift a hand in Lebanon on behalf of the PLO, to whom no single Arab government had provided help. In all likelihood, Gorbachev, like his predecessors, will take his position on the

PLO from that of Syria, currently Moscow's prime client in the Arab world.

The Gulf and the Arabian Peninsula

The differentiated policy Moscow has pursued in the Third World—the adaptability, persistence, and pragmatism as well as the opportunistic and low-risk character of that policy—is very apparent in the USSR's drive to penetrate the Arabian Peninsula. In recent years, particularly since the oil and energy crises roared onto the international scene in the wake of the October War, the area has assumed greatly increased importance in Soviet calculations. A geographically strategic land mass lying to the south of the USSR's Muslim, non-Slavic union-republics and flanked by busy sea routes whose choke points at the Strait of Hormuz and the Strait of Bab al-Mandab expose Western economic vulnerability to any cutoff of oil, the peninsula is an obvious target for U.S.-Soviet rivalry in the Middle East.

The Soviet Union's interest in the Arabian Peninsula started in the late 1920s and early 1930s, when Moscow established relations with Yemen and Saudi Arabia. However, the essentially marginal commercial ties of that time never took hold. Moscow's attempts to establish firm footholds on the peninsula lagged far behind its efforts in other regions, in part for want of opportunity but also because the less explosive political tensions offered few quick rewards. Post-Stalin Soviet diplomacy made its first inroad on the peninsula with the treaty of friendship signed with Yemen in Cairo on October 31, 1955, though not until 1968 did the USSR become directly and intimately involved in the Yemeni sector.

Moscow's readiness to assume extensive economic and military commitments in pursuit of strategic interests in the Arabian Peninsula was first demonstrated in Iraq. The military coup that overthrew the pro-Western Hashemite monarchy in Baghdad on July 14, 1958, brought the Soviet Union into an important tributary of Middle East developments quite independent of its growing involvement with Egypt and the Arab-Israeli conflict. After an initial halcyon period, Soviet-Iraqi relations went through a trying ten-year phase, primarily as a result of the changing fortunes of the Iraqi Communist party. But this did not prevent the steady expansion of government-to-government ties, because regardless of the group in power, Baghdad pursued an anti-Western policy, which Moscow found congenial.

By the late 1960s, with the Baath party in power in Iraq, Soviet-Iraqi relations improved. Moscow looked favorably on the Baath's anti-Western and radical orientation, its determination to settle the Kurdish issue, its greater tolerance of local Communists, and its growing reliance on Soviet assistance and arms. Not only did Moscow's concern over its southern tier ease as a consequence of Iraq's nonalignment and the shah's decision in 1962 to bar U.S. military bases and missiles from Iranian territory, but its intrusive activities in the gulf and Arabian Peninsula region were aided by changes in the strategic environment: the end of the British imperial presence in the gulf; the creation of independent ministates along the eastern littoral of the Arabian Peninsula, which fueled residual Iraqi-Iranian-Saudi rivalry; and the growth of Soviet military capability.

Symptomatic of the improving Soviet-Iraqi relationship was the fifteen-year treaty of friendship and cooperation signed on April 9, 1972 (and subsequently renewed in 1987 for a five-year period, in accordance with the provisions contained in Article 12). The treaty helped convince Baghdad of Moscow's readiness to back the Baath's decision to settle the Kurdish problem, nationalize Western oil holdings, and oppose the threat from the shah of Iran. When the Kurds rejected the Baath's offer of limited autonomy in March 1974 and the civil war was gradually resumed, Moscow sided with Baghdad. The Soviet leadership's desertion of the Kurds and its support for the Baath furthermore dissuaded the shah from interference.

Moscow's aim was to consolidate relations with Iraq, but also to prevent an Iraqi-Iranian conflict that could have scuttled the Soviet-Iranian rapprochement. The effort succeeded well, and the Soviets used a limited display of military force (overt shipments of sophisticated weapons and occasional strafing runs by Soviet-piloted MiG-25s along the Iraqi-Iranian border) without alienating either party. The Iraqi-Iranian agreement of March 1975 sealed the fate of the Kurds and exempted the USSR from having to take sides in a regional conflict whose outbreak would have jeopardized its quest for better relations with both countries. In this instance, the USSR proved to be a force for stability and the territorial status quo. Yet Soviet influence did not increase appreciably.

Soviet-Iraqi relations have been adversely affected by the Iran-Iraq War. Since the fighting broke out in September 1980, Moscow's calls for a peaceful settlement have gone unheeded, and it saw again, as it did in Egypt in the 1970s, that in the Middle East, nothing fails like success. It had hoped to maintain good relations with both sides, but was prevented from pursuing its courtship of Iran because of Khomeini's hostility to communism, his opposition to the USSR's war in Afghanistan, and the USSR's ties to Iraq. Moscow also found relations with Iraq strained, because of strongman Saddam Hussein's conviction that it preferred Iran to Iraq, his dissatisfaction with the level and reliability of Soviet arms deliveries, and his repression of local Communists and expulsion of Soviet diplomats on charges of spying. Although the Soviet Union has been

Iraq's principal arms supplier since late 1983, its diplomacy has not been too successful. It was unable to prevent Baghdad's restoration of diplomatic relations with Washington in November 1984, and its failure to persuade Syria (which, although an Arab state, sides with Iran) to restore the functioning of the Iraqi pipeline that traverses Syrian territory resulted in Iraq's contracting to build an oil pipeline to the Mediterranean through Turkey, further linking Iraq to Western markets.

Despite the Soviet sales (for cash) of advanced fighter aircraft, T-72 tanks, and air-to-surface missiles that serve to upgrade Iraq's capacity for precision strikes against merchant ships and Iranian targets, despite the more sympathetic Soviet commentaries on Iraq's desire for a peaceful and just end to the war, and despite the presence of several thousand Soviet technicians, Moscow knows that the future of its relationship with Iraq is highly unpredictable, with prospects for gains bleak indeed.

The Yemeni sector of the Arabian Peninsula, stretching in a northerly direction along the Red Sea and eastward along the Gulf of Aden, has received attention second only to Iraq in Moscow's quest for footholds on the peninsula. Soon after the 1955 treaty of friendship, Moscow gave Yemen small amounts of economic and military assistance to encourage its opposition to British rule in the Aden–South Yemen region. For a short time after Yemen's accession to the union formed by Egypt and Syria in February 1958, Nasser was uneasy over the influx of Soviet technicians and advisers into Yemen, fearing that the country might come under Soviet domination and that Imam Ahmad might provoke a war with the British in Aden. A military coup in September 1962 and the proclamation of the Yemen Arab Republic (YAR) led Nasser to commit Egyptian forces in order to prop up the pro-Egyptian putschist Brigadier Abdullah al-Sallal, whose forces were no match for the Zaidi tribes supporting Imam al-Badr (who had succeeded to office on the death of his father a week before Sallal's coup). Thus began Nasser's Soviet subsidized Vietnam: the 60,000 to 80,000 troops were Egyptian; the weapons and supplies were Soviet. Moscow funneled most of its aid through Cairo, avoiding direct involvement in the civil war that pitted the Egyptian-backed republicans and Shafeite tribes against the Saudi-backed royalists and long-dominant Zaidis.

In contrast to its behavior in Iraq, Moscow tried in Yemen to upset the status quo and exploit regional instability. Soviet objectives included deepening Nasser's dependence, with the hope of obtaining naval facilities that would replace the loss of the Soviet base in Albania; intensifying pressure on the British in Aden and on Saudi Arabia; and establishing close ties with a new progressive force and preventing its overthrow by reactionary, Western-supported forces. Without the Soviet wherewithal, Nasser could not have sustained his overseas adventure. Indeed, it is difficult to imagine that he would have gotten so enmeshed in the first instance but for Soviet assurances and encouragement. Certainly he would not have been able to sustain five years of demanding, inconclusive conflict.

Nasser's defeat in the June War forced him to withdraw and leave the field to the Saudis. Consequently, Soviet prospects in Yemen declined. At the same time, the British crown colony of Aden and the associated surrounding miniprotectorates were emerging to independence under the name of the South Arabian Federation. Instead of fostering the nationalist coalition of the pro-Egyptian Front for the Liberation of Occupied Southern Yemen (FLOSY), the British shortsightedly allowed power to gravitate toward the National Liberation Front (NLF), an umbrella organization for a motley mixture of Marxist-Leninists and Maoists, out of hostility towards Nasser after their humiliation in 1956. When the British left in November 1967, the NLF seized power in Aden and soon extended its control over the entire country, whose population is about one-third that of the neighboring YAR. In June 1969, the more radical faction of the NLF gained control; it changed the country's name in November 1970 to the People's Democratic Republic of Yemen (PDRY) and rammed through drastic institutional arrangements designed to secure its base of power.[5] A marked radicalization and militancy, including a proclaimed policy of spreading revolution to the entire Arabian Peninsula, triggered Saudi enmity and attracted additional Soviet-bloc aid.

From the start, the PDRY cultivated close relations with the Soviet Union. Military assistance, economic aid, and Soviet, Cuban, and East German advisers and technicians poured in, the first shipment of Soviet arms arriving in August 1968. Moscow's assistance has been essential not only for the internal retention of power, but also for waging an ongoing fight with the YAR and sustaining the Dhofari rebellion that started in western Oman in 1965 (the Dhofaris used PDRY territory as training and staging areas and sought with PDRY assistance to overthrow the pro-Western regime in Oman). By the mid-1970s, the Dhofaris were defeated militarily by a combination of Iranian troops and British advisers, and they were stripped politically of leverage when the financially sorely pressed PDRY leadership decided to accept Saudi financial assistance in return for normalization of relations in March 1976. This meant an end to support for the Dhofari insurgency.

The PDRY-Saudi rapprochement was short-lived, and very possibly the coup de grace was administered by Soviet agents. A series of bizarre and complex events in June 1978 resulted in the assassinations of the top leaders in Sana and Aden in the course of a factional struggle in which personal animosities underlay differing ideological and political outlooks. The previous murders in October 1977 of President Ibrahim al-Hamdi, of the Yemen Arab Republic, and his brother had strengthened the faction of Ahmad al-Ghashmi, who then became president. Al-Gashmi, who favored better relations with Saudi Arabia and the PDRY, was murdered in June 1978. Within a matter of days it appeared that the deed had been planned in Aden to frame the PDRY's president, Salim Rubayyi Ali, a pragmatist who reciprocated al-Ghashmi's desire for accommodation. Behind the plot was his rival, the more ideological and militantly pro-Soviet Adb al-Fatah Ismail al-Jawfi. One week later, in the struggle for power at the top that broke out between Ismail's Soviet and East German-trained People's Militia and Rubayyi Ali's army units, Ismail triumphed and his opponent was killed. The Soviet role in these events is impossible to document but Moscow's preference for the outcome is not.

First, Moscow stood to lose from Rubayyi Ali's opening to the YAR and Saudi Arabia, so its support for Fatah Ismail was understandable. The sharp increase in Soviet arms shipments after July 1978 suggests a desire to buttress Ismail's position and demonstrate the USSR's reliability in the face of Arab criticism of the PDRY. Second, the Soviet Union has further consolidated its presence in the PDRY since the assassination of Rubayyi Ali. A friendship treaty was signed in October 1979. Not even the deposal of Fatah Ismail in April 1980 and his replacement by Ali Nasir Muhammad changed the essentials of the USSR-PDRY relationship. It remained intact even after the civil war of January 1986 between rival party and tribal factions of the ruling Marxist and pro-Soviet Yemeni Socialist Party (YSP) that resulted in the flight of President Ali Nasser Muhammad. Moscow appears to have been caught by surprise; but some Western analysts believe that, sensing his vulnerability, it tipped the scales against him. In any event, within a few weeks a new party secretary, Ali Salem al-Bidh, was installed, and at the end of Feburary he attended the CPSU's congress. Soviet advisers, withdrawn in the early days of the fighting, quickly resumed their central role in running the economy and training the military.

Faced with a serious threat to the USSR's position in a strategically important client state and embarrassed by the shoot-out between factions of the Soviet-subsidized YSP leadership, Gorbachev maneuvered adeptly to throw his support behind the technically "rebel" group. To repair the damage, he has poured generous amounts of economic and military assistance into the country, and the USSR has consolidated its formidable military presence, flying intelligence missions from PDRY airfields, using Aden and the island of Socotra for its naval ships, and intriguing (with Cuban and East German proxies) to train anti-Western radical groups and keep the pressure on the Saudis. To safeguard the chips it holds in a complicated political game on the Arabian Peninsula, Moscow is taking nothing for granted and is not stinting on resources.

On the other side of the peninsula, the Soviet Union's inroads are far less tangible, but nonetheless not devoid of incremental gains. In the fall of 1985, Oman and the United Arab Emirates (Abu Dhabi, Dubai, Ajman, Sharjah, Fujayrah, Umm al-Qaywayn, and Ra's al-Khaymah) joined Iraq and Kuwait as Gulf countries having diplomatic ties with the USSR. Bahrain, Qatar, and, of course, Saudi Arabia continue to keep the Soviets at a distance. The constraints on Soviet penetration of the lower gulf stem from fundamentalist Islamic propensities, an intrinsic traditionalism, stable oligarchies, and strong prevailing ties to British and American expertise and technology, as well as suspicion of the USSR's military buildup of Iraq and military intervention in Afghanistan, Saudi influence, and the absence of politically destabilizing regional rivalries.

Tiny Kuwait established diplomatic ties with the Soviet Union in March 1963, after Qasim was overthrown and Moscow showed itself unwilling to uphold Baghdad's territorial claims against Kuwait. Its motives have been to signal to the Saudis not to take it for granted, to buy some Soviet goodwill as a form of protection against Iran or a renewal of Iraqi pressure, and to put Washington on notice that the oil-rich Arabs might turn to Moscow for weapons if the United States stops pressuring Israel to relinquish Arab lands.

All Moscow can do is bide its time and await disruptive developments. Lack of opportunity limits Soviet options; without clients eager to exploit the Soviet connection for their own ends, Moscow lacks the entanglement essential for political maneuver and influence. Its repeated feelers for normalization of relations with Saudi Arabia have thus far been rebuffed. Moscow has trouble finding suitable levers for an initial penetration. Whereas elsewhere in the Arab world it has found militancy against Israel to go hand-in-hand with a general policy of anti-imperialism and an invariable readiness to improve relations with the Soviet Union, in the Gulf the Saudi leadership's hostility to communism, its perception of threat from the Soviet presence in Afghanistan, and its need to maintain a principled position in the face of the challenge from Khomeini's brand of puritanical Shi'ism militate against any early change in Saudi policy.

The Soviet approach to the Arabian Peninsula has been pragmatic and low-key. Moscow has adapted to regional upheavals with flexibility and shrewdness, in the main tempering its activism to political circumstances. Opportunism, not ideology, impels Soviet policy. The USSR has been quick to establish diplomatic ties and a presence, assist prospective client states, and prove its reliability as a provisioner and superpower protector. The inhibitions on greater activism come primarily from the preferences and domestic pressure of the clients themselves and not from considerations relating to prospects for the Soviet-American relationship or to the power of the United States, whose capacity for affecting developments on the peninsula has diminished considerably. The USSR has been a generally accommodating patron; its ups and downs with Yemen, the PDRY, and Iraq have turned more often on their political variability than on its own mistakes. With the exception of possible complicity in the Yemeni assassinations, the Soviets have not been well placed to meddle effectively in leadership quarrels and have wisely concentrated on maintaining good government-to-government relations, reinforcing convergent policy goals, and providing such assistance as is necessary to keep a client in power.

The level and character of Soviet involvement have been determined (except in Afghanistan) by each Middle East country. Though reluctant to accede to all requests for arms, Moscow has nonetheless given what support has been necessary to assure a client's security, without (it must be noted) always being able to obtain comparably significant returns—witness the limited nature of Soviet naval privileges in Umm Qasr in the 1970s during the halcyon years of relations with Iraq. In rendering military assistance, the USSR has avoided mindless polarization of regional conflicts. Initially it benefited from the feuds between Iraq and Iran, Iraq and Kuwait, the YAR and the PDRY, the PDRY and Oman, and Iraq and Saudi Arabia by developing a close working relationship with one party to the dispute; but having once forced a connection, it prefers generally to dampen regional conflicts and, as in the Iraqi-Iranian and Iraqi-Kuwaiti cases, to improve its relations with both parties and help mediate disputes. Moreover, Moscow's commitment of military power has been prudent, designed to achieve limited and specific military and political ends and to satisfy the prime client without unnecessarily alarming the United States.

Moscow accepts the dilemmas that result from courting opposing sides in regional disputes and the periodic frustration with unmanageable clients as the lot of a superpower pursuing a multiplicity of goals in an age of complexity and change. Thus, it knows that the 1972 treaty with Iraq aroused suspicions among the Arabs of the lower gulf and temporarily scuttled Soviet efforts to effect a diplomatic breakthrough, and that the Dhofari revolt fed the shah's fears and stimulated his military buildup, which was a bulwark against the emergence of pro-Soviet regimes in the gulf as long as Iran was stable. Even the replacement of the pro-Western shah by a revolutionary, anti-Western regime has not been an unmixed blessing for the Soviet Union. The more Moscow builds up the PDRY, the more resistance it may encounter from North Yemen, Saudi Arabia, Sudan, and Egypt. In case after case, its efforts to exercise influence arouse nationalist resentment and resistance; and to the extent that Moscow tries to mediate local disputes, it confronts divergent tugs that set limits to the influence it can wield over either party.

Recent developments on both sides of the Bab al-Mandab Strait, in Afghanistan, and in Iran raise inevitable questions about Soviet involvement and specifically about the extent to which Moscow has benefited from its patient courtship of key countries of the Persian Gulf–Arabian Peninsula area. The regional opportunities to which Moscow has responded have been internally generated. What Moscow has done—and done with alacrity—is to cater to clients, some of whom have sought protection against external threats (as in the case of Iraq in 1974–1975), or to reinforce regimes with strong anti-Western biases (the PDRY, for instance). All of this has been intended to demonstrate the Soviet Union's credibility as a patron-protector. Above all, when presented with a combination of opportunity and invitation, Moscow has repeatedly not been constrained by considerations of its relations with the United States, a phenomenon that often puzzles Washington.

Moscow's tangible benefits in the Arabian Peninsula have on the average been modest. Its position in the PDRY is better now than at any time since the British withdrawal in late 1967 opened the way for the Soviet Union to engage the new Arab state. Privileged access to Aden, the best port in that part of the world, facilitates the Soviet navy's forward deployment; unlike Berbera (in Somalia), Aden has ample supplies of fresh water (which may be more important than fuel oil). It is also cooler by ten degrees and has better docking, storage, and repair facilities; it lacks only Berbera's isolation from heavy traffic. The Soviet navy has also made use of the island of Socotra, but more as an anchorage to escape the monsoon swells and heat than as a significant facility.

Aden is certainly satisfactory for Soviet naval needs, though Moscow has yet to test the extent to which it can exploit the port in time of tension. Far more valuable to the Soviet military have been the air privileges accorded it. Since late 1978, Ilyushin-38 reconnaissance patrol aircraft have been flying on antisubmarine warfare (ASW) and intelligence missions. Moreover, the ability to give Aden as a destination made it easier for the Soviets to obtain overflight permission from Turkey, Iraq, and Iran for airlifting supplies and personnel to Ethiopia during the intensive resupply effort in late 1977–early 1978. In other words, access to PDRY airfields expedited Soviet intervention in the Horn—certainly a handsome short-time return on Moscow's investment.

Moscow has sensed that the Yemenis are a key to the future of the peninsula. Forming the most numerous single Arabic-speaking group and dispersed throughout Arabia, they are a multiplying, energetic, economically backward, and socially depressed people, whom the Saudis view with great suspicion. Yemeni unity is as much an anathema to Saudi Arabia as Yemeni radicalism.

Of the two superpowers, the USSR has been the one sedulously courting both Yemens. Not only did Moscow arm the PDRY and support its guerrilla war against Oman—the first time that the Soviet Union openly encouraged a client to upset the existing territorial status quo—but it also intrigued to bring regimes more congenial to its political aims to power in Aden and Sana. Though it could not prevent a limited PDRY-Saudi reconciliation in 1976, the USSR may have been instrumental in arresting that development. It has shipped enormous quantities of arms to the PDRY, and at the same time has held out tantalizing offers of quick arms deliveries to Sana, with assurances that Soviet leaders will use their good offices to restrain the PDRY. Nowhere has the Soviet attempt to use arms transfers as an instrument of diplomacy, or Moscow's unwillingness to aggravate regional arms races for the promotion of political ends, been more blatant. If its present close relationship with the PDRY could be extended to the YAR as well, the Soviet Union's psychological impact would be felt far beyond the Yemens.

In addition to polarizing the peninsula as a result of direct superpower interventions, a militant Yemeni nationalism could, by politicizing the Yemeni work force—now the most important in Saudi Arabia—undermine Saudi rule. If the Saudis become afflicted by an Iranian-type modernization virus, their Yemeni workers could be an aggravating catalyst; the way would be open for the Balkanization of the Arabian Peninsula and with it, a surge in Soviet prospects. So far the Saudis have kept the USSR at a distance, but fear of Yemeni nationalism, compounded by an untoward dangerous twist to the Iranian revolution and perceptions of the United States as indecisive, unreliable, and excessively military-minded in groping for ways to meet the Soviet challenge in the Arab world, could lead them to normalize relations with the Soviet Union.

Prior to the Soviet military invasion of Afghanistan in December 1979, there were signs of an incipient Soviet courtship of Saudi Arabia. In late January 1979, O. A. Grinevskii, the head of the Near Eastern department of the USSR Ministry of Foreign Affairs, made a special visit to Kuwait to reassure Arab leaders in the gulf about the USSR's interest in maintaining friendly relations and about its lack of responsibility for the turbulence in Iran. At the same time, Igor Beliaev, a leading Soviet specialist on the Middle East, published an article suggesting that the time might be ripe for a Soviet-Saudi rapprochement.[6] Noting that "the Soviet Union and Saudi Arabia have never been at war with each other and they have never had any implacable conflicts," he opined that different social systems were no reason for mutual enmity, especially since both countries shared many important foreign-policy objectives, namely, opposition to Israel's occupation of Arab lands and recognition of "the right of the Arab people of Palestine to self-determination and the creation of their own independent state and also the return of East Jerusalem to the Arabs." He suggested that Saudi Arabia's anti-Sovietism was deliberately fostered by Western circles seeking to keep the countries apart and alienated. Beliaev also implied that the special relationship that Washington was trying to nurture with Riyadh—witness the sale of F-15 fight bombers and other advanced weaponry—was vitiated by the "anti-Arab essence" of the Camp David agreements, which the United States was desirous of imposing on the Arabs. Overall, Beliaev struck a tune he hoped would arouse Saudi interest.

A little more than a month later, in an interview with the Beirut magazine *Al Hawadith*, Prince Saud al-Faisal, the Saudi foreign minister, acknowledged the importance of the Soviet Union in world affairs and said that his country often appreciated "the positive policy adopted by the Soviet Union towards Arab issues." A resumption of Soviet-Saudi diplomatic relations would be an enormous achievement for Soviet leaders.[7] But the Afghan crisis has chilled Saudi interest.

Western uneasiness over its vital interests in the area is understandable, but there is no cause for excessive pessimism. A few observations may be appropriate.

First, Soviet influence is thus far very limited. With the possible exception of its relations with the PDRY, Moscow is not in a position to shape the domestic or foreign policies of the countries of the Arabian Peninsula. What it seeks is a presence that could act as a springboard for the future.

Second, again with the possible exception of the PDRY, none of the countries of the area wants to see a consolidated Soviet presence. Each of them would like to use the Soviet Union for its own purposes, just as Moscow seeks to exploit, and not be exploited by, its Arab clients. A convergence of some goals often gives the impression that the Russians are achieving more than they are—for instance, note the limited dividends that Moscow has realized from its Iraqi connection. The confining of Soviet influence is a theme running through the policies of all the countries in the region.

Third, though developments on the Arabian Peninsula can no longer be isolated from changing power-political relationships in the Arab East, the Horn of Africa, or the peninsula's northern tier (Turkey, Iran, Afghanistan, and Pakistan), they are likely to continue to be determined primarily by factors indigenous to the peninsula itself.

Finally, the Soviet threat in the Arabian Peninsula is not a military one, though large-scale Soviet arms transfers and assignments of Cuban and East German personnel do provide the Soviet-subsidized PDRY with mischievous clout. Basically, Moscow seeks influence, not instability, though it will not be above exploiting and aggravating the latter in the quest for the former.

The North African Littoral

Until recently, the North African littoral was fairly remote from Soviet intrusive activities. But in this fourth subsystem of the Middle East, regional rivalries have also paved the way for Soviet involvement. In Libya, Qaddafi's conflict with Egypt since the October War, as well as his attempts to subvert Chad, Tunisia, and the Sudan, has made Soviet arms dealers welcome and helped to forge a strange relationship between a megalomaniac and a cunning Kremlin bent on earning hard currency from Libya's enormous oil wealth, positioning itself to have ready access to the stockpiles of arms it is selling, and destabilizing Central Africa through Qaddafi's restless intrigues. Both the USSR and Libya have a common interest in undermining the position of the United States in the region. Farther to the west, the undeclared war between Algeria and Morocco over former Spanish Sahara leads Algeria to look to Moscow for modern weapons (for which it pays in hard currency) and aggravates regional instability.

Throughout the Arab East, the Soviet Union maintains an active diplomacy and seeks to expand economic ties. Its primary aim is to weaken the strategic position of the United States. Strategic advantage, not oil or the spread of communism, impels Soviet policy—hence Moscow's readiness to absorb setbacks and bide its time. Proceeding on the assumptions derived from Lenin's theory of imperialism, the Soviet leadership sees a weakening of the West in the Middle East as a key to improving its own bargaining position in Europe, which remains strategically the pivot of Soviet aspirations.

Notes

1. *Izvestiia,* September 23, 1980.
2. Oles M. Smolansky, *The Soviet Union and the Arab East Under Khrushchev* (Lewisburg, Pa.: Bucknell University Press, 1974), 80.
3. George S. Dragnich, "The Soviet Union's Quest for Access to Naval Facilities in Egypt Prior to the June War of 1967," in Michael MccGwire, Ken Booth, and John McDonnell (eds.), *Soviet Naval Policy: Objectives and Constraints* (New York: Praeger, 1975), 252–69.
4. John C. Campbell, "Communist Strategies in the Mediterranean," *Problems of Communism,* Vol. 28, No. 3 (May–June 1979), 5.
5. Haim Shaked and Tamar Yegness, "Continuity and Change in Saudi Arabia, Yemen and South Yemen, 1967–1973," in Itamar Rabinovich and Haim Shaked (eds.), *From June to October: The Middle East Between 1967 and 1973* (New Brunswick, N.J.: Transaction Books, 1978), 299–301.

6. Igor Beliaev, "Saudi Arabia: What Next?," *Literaturnaya gazeta,* No. 5 (January 31, 1979), 14.

7. The advantages of a Soviet link may, however, have palled on the Saudi leadership since late November 1979, when approximately 500 heavily armed and well-trained guerrillas attempted to undermine the Saudi regime by seizing the Grand Mosque in Mecca. Preliminary reports indicate that they were trained in Aden, very likely under Soviet sponsorship. See *New York Times,* December 17, 1979.

Selected Bibliography

BRADSHER, HENRY S. *Afghanistan and the Soviet Union. New and expanded edition.* Durham: Duke Press Policy Studies, 1985.

COLLINS, JOSEPH J. *The Soviet Invasion of Afghanistan.* Lexington: Lexington Books, 1986.

FREEDMAN, ROBERT O. *Soviet Policy Towards the Middle East Since 1970,* 3rd ed. New York: Praeger, 1982.

GOLAN, GALIA. *Yom Kippur and After: The Soviet Union and the Middle East Crisis.* Cambridge: Cambridge University Press, 1977.

———. *The Soviet Union and the Palestine Liberation Organization.* New York: Praeger, 1980.

HEIKAL, MOHAMED. *The Road to Ramadan.* London: Collins, 1975.

EL-HUSSINI, MOHREZ MAHMOUD. *Soviet-Egyptian Relations, 1945–85.* New York: St. Martin's Press, 1988.

KATZ, MARK N. *Russia and Arabia: Soviet Foreign Policy Toward the Arabian Peninsula.* Baltimore: The Johns Hopkins University Press, 1986.

KRAMNER, ARNOLD. *The Forgotten Friendship: Israel and the Soviet Bloc 1947–1953.* Urbana: University of Illinois Press, 1974.

PAGE, STEPHEN. *The Soviet Union and the Yemens.* New York: Praeger, 1985.

RO'I, YAACOV (ED.). *From Encroachment to Involvement: A Documentary Study of Soviet Policy in the Middle East, 1945–1973.* New York: John Wiley, 1974.

RO'I, YAACOV. *Soviet Decision Making in Practice: The USSR and Israel, 1947–1954.* New Brunswick, N.J.: Transaction Books, 1980.

RUBINSTEIN, ALVIN Z. *Red Star on the Nile: The Soviet-Egyptian Influence Relationship Since the June War.* Princeton: Princeton University Press, 1977.

———. *Soviet Policy Toward Turkey, Iran, and Afghanistan.* New York: Praeger, 1982.

SELLA, AMNON. *Soviet Political and Military Conduct in the Middle East.* New York: St. Martin's Press, 1981.

SMOLANSKY, OLES M. *The Soviet Union and the Arab East Under Khrushchev.* Bucknell, Pa.: Bucknell University Press, 1974.

YODFAT, ARYEH. *The Soviet Union and the Arab Peninsula.* New York: St. Martin's Press, 1983.

III

Instruments of Soviet Diplomacy

10
The Military Dimensions of Soviet Foreign Policy

Military power has brought a new dimension to Soviet foreign policy: for the first time in its history, the USSR is truly a global power. Not only can it intervene effectively to preserve its imperial system in Eastern Europe and the Far East, but its nuclear weapons can shower enormous destruction on the United States, and it can project conventional military power beyond its continental confines into the Third World. This overall military capability has reinforced the basic world outlook and ambitions of Soviet rulers, strengthened their confidence, and provided them with a wider range of options for dealing with adversaries. Militarily, the Soviet Union can hold up its end of the global balance of power with the United States.

The aims of Soviet military policy have evolved since 1917 from preservation of the Soviet state and defense against external threat to expansion of the Soviet empire and promotion of global objectives. The basic aim is still to defend the Soviet homeland, a theme that dominated Soviet thinking during the 1917-to-1945 period, but following the annexations and expansion after World War II, the military was assigned the additional task of defending the entire Communist camp. As a result of the direct assistance rendered by the Red Army, the People's Republic of China and North Korea consolidated their power in the Far East.

Through the deployment of its units in occupied Germany and Austria, and then on the basis of bilateral agreements in Poland, Hungary, and Romania,

> the Soviet Army on the one hand improved the security of the Soviet Union, and on the other hand helped the weak communist parties in East Germany, Poland, Czechoslovakia, Hungary, Romania, and Bulgaria to take power and initiate a gradual social transformation. . . . In this way, and with full use of the Soviet armed forces, the basic goals of Soviet foreign policy in World War II were realized: the capitalist encirclement of the USSR and its isolation were broken, a belt of socialist states along Soviet borders was created, and the Soviet Union acquired the position of a world power.[1]

Discouraging intrasystemic efforts to break away from Moscow's hegemony or a Marxist-Leninist political system, the Soviet armed forces suppressed rebellions in Eastern Europe in 1953, 1956, and 1968, and, by demonstrating overwhelming military force and determination, dissuaded the Western powers from any intervention. In addition to their deterrent function, they have enabled Soviet diplomats to negotiate with NATO countries from a position of strength.

Finally, the Soviet military has been an indispensable adjunct of Moscow's "forward policy" in the Third World. In country after country in the Middle East, Southern Asia, Africa, and Latin America (thus far, primarily only in Cuba), Soviet arms, advisers, and sheltering shields have aided client states and undermined Western positions. In a number of instances, Soviet combat forces have actually participated in engagements to defend and promote the interests of beleaguered Third World clients. This international outreach signifies the metamorphosis of Soviet foreign policy from a continental-based strategy to a global strategy.

From Strategic Inferiority to SALT I

After 1945, Soviet foreign policy was geared to the consolidation of the empire in Eastern Europe. In view of the American nuclear monopoly, Moscow placed a premium on maintaining a commanding conventional capability in the area. Implicit in Stalin's strategy of neutralizing the U.S. nuclear advantage, by which the United States could strike targets in the Soviet Union without fear of retaliation, was the belief that the United States could be deterred by the USSR's deployment of substantial conventional forces in the European theater and by the impression that those forces would be used "for a rapid advance to the Atlantic" if America tried nuclear blackmail; moreover, these same forces "also provided insurance against defections in East Europe."[2]

The Soviet strategy of deploying strong forces in Central Europe heightened Western fears, prompting the establishment of NATO and the West's rearmament, responses that Stalin had hoped to forestall. Essentially, however, this has remained the centerpiece of Moscow's approach, though by the late 1960s the USSR had developed a credible nuclear capability of its own, thanks to the investment and impetus given to nuclear programs during the Stalin years.

The Soviet Union was the first to test an intercontinental ballistic missile (ICBM) successfully, in late August 1957, and it placed the first space satellite, Sputnik I, in orbit on October 4, 1957. These scientific achievements emboldened Khrushchev to seek political advantages—prematurely, as it turned out. Convinced that the balance of world forces was shifting to the Soviet camp, he precipitated a new crisis over Berlin in November 1958, hoping to wrest concessions from the West—at a minimum, its recognition of East Germany. The year 1959 proved to be an inconclusive one, notwithstanding Khrushchev's visit to the United States. Then on May 1, 1960, a U.S. spy plane was shot down while on a routine mission over the Soviet Union, an event that aborted the summit meeting that had been scheduled for mid-May in Paris. The incident revealed the hollowness of Khrushchev's strategic claims, which the Soviet military had known all along because this was the first U-2 they had been able to shoot down ever since the U.S. intelligence missions had started in 1955, and because they knew how few ICBMs were available (for technical and economic reasons) in the Soviet arsenal. In fact, the undeniable Soviet strategic (that is, nuclear) inferiority to the United States was one of the considerations that had led Khrushchev to shy away from supporting Mao Zedong during the 1958 Quemoy crisis and to resist his pressure for a tougher stance toward the United States. At that time, writes Andrei Gromyko in his memoirs, Mao sought Soviet cooperation "for a plan to lure United States troops into the heartland of China, then attack them with Soviet nuclear weapons."[3]

In January 1960 Khrushchev proposed a far-reaching reform of the Soviet military establishment that called for reliance on nuclear-armed missiles to deter any would-be attacker and for a sharp reduction in military manpower to ease the severe labor shortage in Soviet industry. Elements in the military pressed for acceleration of the buildup of strategic forces beyond what Khrushchev thought necessary, as part of the revolution in Soviet military doctrine being formulated by the high command. With other domestic priorities attracting his support, Khrushchev sought an alternative that would minimize defense expenditures on strategic weapons systems and still satisfy the military. Accordingly, to strengthen the credibility of the USSR's nuclear deterrent, Khrushchev agreed in the spring of 1962 to implant short- and intermediate-range ballistic missiles

(IRBMs) in Cuba. Not only would the success of this stratagem have enhanced Soviet prestige, punctured Chinese criticisms that Khrushchev was behaving timidly vis-à-vis U.S. imperialism, and demonstrated Moscow's credibility as a patron, but "the force of some forty MRBM [medium-range ballistic missiles] and IRBM launchers dispatched to Cuba would have narrowed in one quick stroke the actual margin of the U.S. advantage in strategic forces, for it would have had the effect, as Raymond Garthoff has pointed out, of transforming readily available missiles of 1100 to 2200-mile range into 'ersatz' intercontinental missiles. In terms of the Soviet Union's then-existing first-strike salvo capability against targets in the United States," this would have meant an increase of 80 percent.[4]

Khrushchev's failure in Cuba strengthened his opponents in Moscow. An ever-larger percentage of Soviet defense expenditures was committed to an accelerated buildup of strategic forces, while Soviet diplomacy worked to slow down the U.S. program through a combination of disarmament proposals and extensive antiwar propaganda. When the Kremlin backed down during the Cuban missile crisis, the Soviet military was determined—as the Soviet UN delegate, Vasily Kuznetzov, warned his American counterpart—that this would be the last time the Soviet Union would bow to America's nuclear superiority.

Between late 1953 and 1960, as the leadership sought to adapt to the nuclear age, Soviet military doctrine and the composition of the military forces that were to serve as the instruments of Soviet foreign policy underwent a searching review. The debate was started in November 1953 in the journal of the general staff, *Voennaia mysl'* (Military Thought), by its editor, Major-General Nikolai A. Talenskii. His arguments, which were bitterly fought but eventually accepted by the traditionalists, implicitly challenged Stalin's dogma that the Soviet Union was destined to win any future war by virtue of the advantage of "permanently operating factors," such as a stable, loyal home front; high morale of the army; quality of leadership; and so forth. He tried to convince the leadership that the principles of military science needed revision and that they operated with equal validity for both sides; he also pointed out that the introduction of nuclear weapons required a far-reaching modification of the laws governing the strategy and conduct of war.[5]

By January 1960, when Khrushchev unveiled the essentials of a new military doctrine, the Soviet high command had embraced Talenskii's basic argument and moved far beyond it, in what came to be called "the revolution in military affairs," the term used to describe the enormous changes wrought in warfare by nuclear weapons and missiles. Henceforth Soviet military writings made it clear that since nuclear war was possible, it had to be analyzed and prepared for like any other war. The USSR's military doctrine and strategic concepts have been constantly modified and refined, in keeping with the development of a burgeoning arsenal of sophisticated and varied delivery systems and nuclear weapons.

Starting in 1960 (before the 1962 Cuban missile crisis), the Soviet leadership embarked on a buildup of its Strategic Rocket Forces, which were established as a separate arm of the Soviet armed forces; on the development of theater nuclear weapons, in accordance with a general program of modernizing and upgrading all weapons systems; and on the strengthening of anti-air defense and civil defense. The aims were to improve the country's ability to absorb a possible nuclear attack and to enhance deterrence. In the late 1950s, the Kremlin had decided to give priority to IRBMs and MRBMs (just as earlier it had concentrated on medium rather than long-range bombers) because most NATO military bases were located in Western Europe, and the early ICBM (SS-6) "was too ungainly a beast, and much too expensive, to deploy widely"; the SS-6 was a good rocket for Khrushchev to rattle when the West did not know how few he had, but after the Cuban crisis, Moscow realized that it had a significant missile gap to overcome and acted accordingly.[6]

There were other shifts of emphasis as well. Whereas Khrushchev wanted to rely primarily on the Strategic Rocket Forces, essentially emulating U.S. reliance on massive retaliation to ensure deterrence, his successors opted for across-the-board investment, building up not only nuclear but conventional force capabilities so as to obtain maximum flexibility in foreign policy. This policy was to pay off handsomely in the 1970s, when the Soviet capability to project military power greatly enhanced its prestige and attractiveness among Third World clients and contributed to the globalization of its rivalry with the United States.

Moscow's determination to redress its inferiority to the United States in strategic weapons brought impressive results. During the 1965-to-1969 period, the USSR tripled the number of ICBMs (in 1967 alone it more than doubled its force, from 340 to 720) and greatly expanded the number of submarine-launched ballistic missiles (SLBMs). By the end of the 1960s, it exceeded the U.S. ICBM force (which has not been increased at all) of 1054 land-based ICBMs, 656 Polaris SLBMs, and approximately 400 to 600 long-range bombers that were deemed sufficient by Washington for an assured destruction capability. Having developed what President Richard Nixon and Secretary of Defense James Schlesinger were later to term "essential equivalence," Moscow agreed to enter into the Strategic Arms Limitation Talks (SALT) with Washington.

As far back as 1964, President Lyndon Johnson had proposed a freeze on strategic weapons, but he had been rebuffed by Soviet leaders, who wanted a stronger hand for the next nuclear facedown. His next invitation to discuss limitations on offensive and defensive delivery systems, on January 27, 1967, was accepted in principle by the Soviet government in March 1967, but not until June 27, 1968 did Moscow formally agree to open talks. The reasons for the prolonged delay are obscure; we can only surmise that they were due to the combination of sharp differences within the Politburo over how to deal with the United States, the calculation that a delayed response would aggravate political cleavages in the United States and postpone deployment of a thin anti-ballistic missile system (ABM), and the determination to overcome the U.S. advantage in strategic weapons before commencing the talks. The Soviet invasion of Czechoslovakia then intervened, leading Washington to postpone the start of SALT. Another year passed before the new Nixon administration was ready to start negotiations in Helsinki on November 17, 1969.

The talks dragged on into 1970 and 1971, in an international environment of high U.S.–Soviet tension in the Arab–Israeli sector (until late 1970), Soviet border troubles with China, the USSR's military assistance to North Vietnam in support of its war against the United States, and the Indo–Pakistani war and resulting emergence of East Pakistan as the new, independent nation of Bangladesh. In the spring of 1972, even though the United States was bombing and mining North Vietnamese ports, the Kremlin decided to conclude the SALT I agreement, for reasons of its own—whether from satisfaction at having completed its planned expansion of strategic forces, a desire to give impetus to its policy of détente with the United States and garner the long-term economic credits that were a likely part of the package, concern that further delay might jeopardize the entire process, or uneasiness over the Sino-American reconciliation, epitomized by Nixon's visit to China in February.

The Payoff in SALT

SALT I was signed by President Nixon and CPSU Secretary Brezhnev on May 26, 1972. It consisted of three agreements. The first is a treaty of unlimited duration on the limitation of anti-ballistic missile systems, entered into force on October 3, 1972. The treaty prohibits the development of an ABM system, but originally permitted each side to protect its national capital and one ICBM silo launcher area; a protocol was signed in 1974 restricting each side to only one ABM deployment. The second agreement was a five-year interim agreement that entered into force on October 3, 1972. It fixed Soviet ICBM and SLBM launchers at 2350 and American launchers at 1710, thus marking the first time in the nuclear era that the USSR and the United States had agreed to set up quantitative limits on their strategic delivery systems (that is, missiles capable of striking the other's homeland). Bombers were not covered by the agreement.

Though it formally expired on October 3, 1977, both sides respected its provisions until a follow-up agreement was reached (but never ratified) in Vienna in June 1979. The third set of documents dealt with interpretations of technical issues such as radars, testing, and so on. The two parties agreed to rely on national technical means (NTM) to monitor the treaty. NTM refers to verification by sophisticated methods of data collection, which include photographic, radar, and electronic surveillance capabilities, seismic instrumentation to provide information on the location and magnitude of underground nuclear explosions, and sea- and ground-based systems to detect and identify military activities; it implies a prohibition on interfering with the other side's space satellites or on concealing flight test data essential for verification.

There were several immediate advantages to SALT I for the USSR; each presumably interested constituency in the Soviet political-military establishment realized some preferred objective, however imperfectly. Politically, the Soviet Union was recognized by the United States as a full-fledged and equal nuclear superpower. In the decade since the Cuban crisis, it had moved from inferiority to strategic equivalence. Militarily, through the ban on ABM development, the USSR nipped in the bud the American deployment of a more technologically advanced ABM system, and it negotiated a quantitative edge in offensive delivery systems. This included provision for 313 heavy missiles, compared to none for the United States—a quantitative advantage that became qualitative with the deployment of MIRVed missiles, that is, those capable of carrying more than one nuclear warhead. Economically, the USSR avoided the strains that an ABM race would have brought and was able to concentrate on upgrading its offensive capability. SALT also enabled Moscow to invest heavily in research and development, looking ahead to the upgrading of existing weapons systems and the development of new ones. Finally, Moscow's policy of promoting détente, one aim of which was to slacken U.S. defense efforts, was greatly enhanced.

The 1972 Moscow summit also helped Soviet diplomacy in Europe, by facilitating the convening of CSCE and the accompanying Western recognition of the territorial status quo in Europe and Moscow's sphere of influence in Eastern Europe—prime postwar Soviet objectives. However, the budding Soviet-American détente went awry in October 1973 over the Arab–Israeli war, in 1974–1975 over competition in Angola, and in 1977–1978 over the Horn of Africa. These regional quarrels, coupled with mounting congressonal criticisms of SALT I and the Watergate affair, which forced Nixon to resign in August 1974, made a new agreement limiting offensive weapons more difficult to negotiate.

At Vladivostok in November 1974, President Gerald Ford and Brezhnev agreed to guidelines that established quantitative equality in strategic delivery vehicles; each side was to be permitted a limit of 2400 ICBMs, SLBMs, and heavy bombers as well as a ceiling of 1320 MIRVed missiles. Secretary of State Henry Kissinger exultantly reported that the Vladivostock accord (which was never ratified) put "a cap on the arms race," but closer examination revealed that it had considerably raised the threshold of the number of deliverable nuclear weapons. There were other criticisms, too. Critics alleged that Soviet technological advances and larger throw-weight capacity on newly developed MIRVed missiles could give the USSR a capacity by the 1980s to destroy the U.S. land-based ICBM force in a first-strike attack. Further complicating the negotiation of a follow-up SALT agreement was the intrusion of technology in the form of cruise missiles (a guided missile remaining within the Earth's atmosphere, capable of being launched from the ground, aircraft, or ships and delivering nuclear warheads with great accuracy in large numbers, but thus far with much smaller ranges than an ICBM or IRBM); mobile missiles of increasing range and accuracy; and MIRVed missiles that could not be distinguished from non-MIRVed missiles (as someone observed, we can detect the make of a car from space satellites, but there is no way of knowing what its engine power is). The verification problem and the political aspects of arms control versus force reduction, to mention but a few of the complicating variables, placed formidable obstacles in the path of a new SALT agreement.

The Soviet government was prepared to sign an accord on offensive missiles based on the Vladivostok formula, but in March 1977 the new Carter administration offered its own proposals for a sharp reduction in the quantitative limits, which would have affected Soviet production schedules and imposed qualitative constraints on the Vladivostock ceilings. For substantive as well as procedural reasons (Soviet leaders do not like surprises sprung on them in negotiations, least of all with public fanfare), Moscow demurred, and the 1972 interim agreement on offensive missiles lapsed in October 1977. However, a month before, the two governments had stated their willingness not to take any action inconsistent with the provisions of the interim agreement, pending negotiation of SALT II.

After two years of protracted negotiations in an environment of deteriorating Soviet-American relations, the USSR and the United States reached an agreement that was closer to the Vladivostok proposals than the Carter administration's original counterproposals. SALT II produced none of the euphoria of SALT I. On June 18, 1979, at a summit meeting in Vienna, Brezhnev and Carter signed an agreement stipulating that it would "remain in force through December 31, 1985, unless replaced earlier by an agreement further limiting strategic offensive arms." In its essentials, SALT II set a ceiling of 2250 strategic delivery systems, effective January 1, 1981 (prior to this, each party had been permitted 2400). It placed a limit of 1320 on the number of such delivery systems that can be MIRVed. The Soviet Union was permitted to retain a 308-to-0 advantage in heavy silo-based ICBMs (SS-18)—it successfully resisted U.S. pressure to reduce the number of heavy missiles to 150—in return for agreeing to equal aggregate force levels. The Backfire bomber, which it insisted is a medium bomber, was not included in the formal agreement, but Brezhnev gave assurances that the USSR "does not intend to give this airplane the capability of operating at intercontinental distances," nor does it plan "to increase the Backfire's capability in any other manner, including in-flight refueling" or increase the aircraft's present production rate. SALT II also placed limitations on the development of cruise missiles with a range in excess of 600 kilometers. Compliance with the treaty would have been by national technical means of verification.

Though the Soviet government was ready to ratify the agreement promptly, the U.S. government was not able to do so. Carter wanted quick ratification but encountered increasing opposition from the Senate. First, critics of SALT argued that the treaty gave the Soviets too many advantages, including the already-mentioned capability possibly to destroy the entire U.S. land-based ICBM force in a first-strike attack by the mid-1980s. Second, in the summer and early fall of 1979, Carter himself fed the anti-SALT forces by initially magnifying the significance of the Soviet military presence in Cuba and then accepting the status quo when Moscow refused to make even token concessions to help him sell SALT domestically. Third, the anti-Soviet mood in the United States spread in the wake of Moscow's unhelpful position on the seizure of American embassy personnel in Tehran in early November 1979 by Iranian radicals demanding extradition of the shah. The final blow to early ratification was the Soviet invasion of Afghanistan in December, as Moscow decided to extirpate Afghan nationalist opposition to the Communist regime that it had helped to bring to power in April 1978. On January 2, 1980, President Carter formally requested the Senate to postpone considerations of the SALT II treaty indefinitely. The chill in Soviet–American relations put the SALT process into deep freeze.

When the Reagan administration took office in January 1981, Moscow encountered a far more skeptical attitude in Washington toward arms control, as well as a determination to upgrade U.S. strategic and conventional forces and to press forward, in accordance with NATO's 1979 decision, with the deployment of modernized Pershing-IIs and GLCMs (ground-launched cruise missiles) in Western Europe, starting in December 1983. The principal Soviet aim in Europe was to forestall this deployment.

In November 1981, Moscow and Washington began two sets of negotiations: START (strategic arms reduction talks, the new name given to SALT by the Reagan administration) and INF (intermediate-range nuclear forces, also known as theater nuclear forces or Euromissiles), which deals with weapons systems having a range of between 300 and 3500 miles.

Almost from the very beginning, START showed little movement. A fundamental asymmetry in force structuring, reflecting very different strategic outlooks and military situations, lay at the heart of the impasse at Geneva. As against the U.S. force of 1045 land-based ICBMs with 2145 warheads and 568 SLBMs (submarine-launched ballistic missiles) with 5152 warheads, the USSR had operational 1398 ICBMs with 5654 warheads and 980 SLBMs with 2688 warheads.[7] Moscow rejected the basic U.S. proposal, which called for a reduction of warheads to 5000, of which no more than half could be in land-based ICBMs, because this would require the USSR to dismantle a sizable proportion of its existing strategic deterrent.

Moscow directed far greater attention to the INF talks. It rejected Reagan's "zero option" proposal, which called for the dismantling of all the triple-warhead Soviet SS-20s (whose deployment had started in 1977 and prompted NATO's 1979 decision/response) in return for U.S. renunciation of its scheduled Pershing-II deployment. Moreover, while mounting an all-out propaganda campaign against the scheduled deployment, the Soviet leadership put an increasing number of SS-20s into operation, indifferent to the uneasiness this occasioned.

In an atmosphere of escalating recrimination, Moscow broke off the INF talks on November 23, 1983, as the first Pershing-IIs were deployed in West Germany and Britain; and on December 8, it recessed START, refusing to fix a date for the resumption of either. One week later, the negotiations in Vienna on conventional force reductions were also adjourned, with no time set for the next meeting. For the next eighteen months the matter remained deadlocked. There were no arms-control talks and, amid worsening relations, both superpowers deployed modernized versions of their INF arsenals.

On March 10, 1985, Chernenko died, and, on March 12, the day following the election of Mikhail S. Gorbachev as the CPSU's new general secretary, U.S.–Soviet talks on nuclear arms control and weapons in space resumed in Geneva. The timing was purely fortuitous, because the resumption had been approved in a meeting in Geneva between Secretary of State Schultz and Soviet Foreign Minister Gromyko in January, while Chernenko was still alive. Behind the Kremlin's decision to return to the bargaining table may have been, first, its realization that having failed to stop the U.S. deployment of Pershing-IIs through an aggressive campaign of propaganda and political intimidation, it had to find a way of neutralizing the military threat that they posed to the Soviet Command and Control Headquarters near Minsk; and, second, its concern over President Reagan's Strategic Defense Initiative (SDI) proposal (commonly called "Star Wars") of March 23, 1983, in which he embarked the United States on a quest for a space-based missile defense system.

Gorbachev's interest in stabilizing the nuclear relationship is serious. Though there was no breakthrough at the first Gorbachev-Reagan summit in Geneva in November 1985, his suggestion of a freeze on all INF deployments in Europe to be followed by reductions on both sides was suggestive of the flexibility to come. In January 1986 he issued a major statement on arms control, which, among other things, called for deep cuts in offensive forces, an end to nuclear testing, the development of appropriate verification procedures, and the elimination of Soviet and U.S. medium-range missiles in Europe, "as a first stage on the path to freeing the European continent of nuclear weapons." At the party congress the following month, he discussed the general problem of arms control and disarmament at great length and with considerable candor:

> The character of present-day weapons leaves a country no hope of safeguarding itself solely with military and technical means, for example, by building up a defense system, even the most powerful one. The task of ensuring security is increasingly seen as a political problem, and it can only be resolved by political means. . . . Security cannot be built endlessly on fear of retaliation, in other words, on the doctrines of "containment" or "deterrence." Apart from the absurdity and amorality of a situation in which the whole world becomes a nuclear hostage, these doctrines encourage an arms race that may sooner or later go out of control.
>
> In the context of the relations between the USSR and the USA, security can only be mutual. . . . The highest wisdom is not in caring exclusively for oneself, especially to the detriment of the other side. It is vital that all should feel equally secure, for the fears and anxieties of the nuclear age generate unpredictability in politics and concrete action.

Though dismissing the policies that are pillars of Western security—containment and deterrence—Gorbachev's implicit call for strategic stability and "mututal security" and his renewed interest in the SALT/START process elicited receptive reactions in many Western quarters. Still, the hurdles were formidable: disagreement over what constituted adequate verification and Moscow's insistence that an agreement on intermediate-range missiles be tied to U.S. readiness to forego development of a space-based missile defense.

In late May 1986, the Reagan administration, which was sharply divided over the issue of whether the Soviets were violating the 1972 ABM treaty by heavily encrypting, or encoding, information from their missile tests and by constructing a new network of defensive radars in Central Asia, announced that it would no longer be bound by the provisions of the (unratified) SALT II treaty, unless Soviet policy changed. When the Rejkjavik summit five months later ended acrimoniously, arms control prospects were very dim.

On February 28, 1987, Gorbachev unexpectedly offered to sign an INF agreement, without any preconditions. We can only speculate on his reasons for decoupling INF from SDI: perhaps his advisers argued that any advances in missile defense could easily and economically be encountered by merely expanding the number of offensive missiles; perhaps it was the prohibitive costs of persisting in an unchecked nuclear arms build-up; perhaps the realization that the original Soviet deployment of SS-20s had been a mistake, the consequence of which had been a startlingly threatening Western response; perhaps a desire to "create an atmosphere of greater trust" that would improve Soviet-American relations and restore the USSR's prestige in Western Europe.

The third Gorbachev-Reagan summit, held in Washington, D.C. in December 1987, was crowned by the signing of an INF treaty calling for the total elimination of all intermediate and shorter-range missiles and GLCMs with a range of between 300 and 3500 miles. All the missiles of this type were to be destroyed no later than three years after the treaty went into effect. The treaty includes provisions for on-site inspection, under which "each party shall have the right, for 13 years . . . to inspect by means of continuous monitoring."

With this precedent-setting treaty in hand, the two superpowers have intensified their quest for a formula that will result in deep cuts in strategic nuclear forces, that is, long range ICBMs; also a problem are SLCMs (sea-launched cruise missiles) and ALCMs (air-launched cruise missiles). The difficulties are significantly greater than the ones encountered in negotiating the INF treaty. Briefly, the superpowers must agree on the number of warheads to be carried by missiles and bombers, the number of allowable heavy ICBMs (the most destabilizing weapons system), and very elaborate inspection procedures, since START limits but does not ban a dual category of weapons system, namely, ICBMs and bombers. Also, because testing would be permitted and a logistical infrastructure retained, the capacity for cheating under any SALT/START agreement is greater than under the INF treaty.

The Buildup of Conventional Forces

Another dimension of Soviet military policy with far-reaching foreign policy implications has been the sustained buildup of Soviet conventional force levels. Ever since 1945 the USSR has maintained large military forces in Central and Eastern Europe. Originally designed to deter

Western interference with the imposition of the Soviet imperium in Eastern Europe and to ensure internal security in the bloc, by the 1980s Soviet forces could, if required, assume an offensive role capable of overrunning key sectors of NATO. The aim of making the USSR the dominant military power in Europe has been achieved; the preservation of this preeminence is what drives Soviet policy and has given it impressive momentum in acquiring new weapons systems and deploying combat-ready divisions in Europe. Most reliable estimates of the military balance assign the Soviet-dominated Warsaw Pact a margin of at least two to one over NATO forces. This military might is both a type of insurance and a threat to the West. Given the present nuclear stalemate between the superpowers, in the event of a crisis or an opportunity in Europe, Moscow will not lack the wherewithal for influencing a preferred political outcome with its army, widely accepted in the West as the most powerful in the world. What is particularly notable about the Soviet army is its high state of battle readiness, its offensive capability for a massive breakthrough on several fronts, and its ability to carry on sustained operations for several weeks without reinforcements from the Soviet Union proper. Moreover, there is evidence to suggest that the USSR intends to maintain high defense expenditures in the 1990s, notwithstanding difficult domestic economic and social problems.

Apart from the influence that the forward deployment of powerful Soviet conventional forces has on diplomacy in Europe—for example, in discouraging challenges to Moscow's rule in Eastern Europe and in prompting the MFR talks that began in Vienna in 1973 as an outgrowth of SALT I—and in relations with China, the consequences for Soviet policy in the Third World have been incalculable. Military power is the arm of Soviet diplomacy that has made the USSR a real rival of the United States in the Middle East, Africa, and South Asia. In the mid-1950s Moscow could frustrate the Western powers and their diplomacy by sending arms to anti-Western Third World leaders; in the 1960s it could enable prized clients to engage in overseas adventures (for example, Nasser's intervention in Yemen from 1962 to 1967) and avoid lasting defeats (for example, by rearming the Egyptian and Syrian armies after their trouncing by Israel in June 1967). But in the 1970s it could intervene directly to protect clients from defeat and provide decisive assistance to produce political and military outcomes regarded as congenial to the spread of Soviet influence—for example, in Angola in 1975, in Ethiopia in 1977–1978, in the People's Democratic Republic of Yemen in 1978, and in Afghanistan in 1979–1980.

Until the early 1970s the Soviet Union lacked the military capability to project military power in a decisive fashion outside of the Eurasian land mass, a shortcoming that hampered the conduct of a forward policy in the

Third World. This has changed. The development of a long-range air transport capability; the construction of a blue-water fleet and a large, versatile merchant marine; and the availability of huge stockpiles of surplus weapons have provided the Kremlin with the military clout it needed for interventions in friendly environments in Africa, the Middle East, and Vietnam. In late 1977–early 1978, the USSR poured more than $2 billion in weapons, ammunition, and supplies, (with essential personnel) into Ethiopia, changing the entire complexion of regional affairs in the Horn without in any way diminishing its military capability in Europe. Its war in Afghanistan was waged without draining men or material from the European or Far Eastern military theaters. With the growing saliency of security issues in Soviet foreign policy, the Soviet military has become an indispensable and prominent adjunct of Soviet overseas policy, and many features of its most modern force additions bespeak an intention to play an active role in the Third World (see Chapters 8 and 9).

Arms Control Measures

Disarmament has been a subordinate but nonetheless useful component of Soviet military and diplomatic strategy. Linked to the traditional imperial and Soviet Russian policy of maintaining a large standing army, it has been a political tool for trying to redress adverse military balances. It was Czar Nicholas II who was instrumental in convening the first world disarmament conference in 1899. Throughout the 1920s and 1930s, when threats loomed from Japan and Germany and when Britain and France were seriously regarded as advocates of another capitalist coalition to destroy the Soviet state, the Soviet government was in the forefront of campaigns for universal disarmament—for example, Litvinov's proposal in 1927 to the League of Nations Preparatory Commission on Disarmament. At the same time it did everything possible to build up the Red Army. By the mid-1930s, Soviet policy in Europe changed for a few years, and diplomacy shifted from disarmament to collective security.

What is important to keep in mind is that Russian leaders have never regarded disarmament as a panacea for ensuring peace; they have always used the appeal of disarmament for political ends. Thus, any detailed examination of Soviet disarmament policy reveals that Moscow has exploited the theme as a means of compensating for military and technological inferiority, trying to induce a rival to offer unilateral concessions and limit its military programs, and gaining support internationally and among pacifist-minded groups whose domestic lobbying might affect their government's policies.

The disarmament issue became prominent in the United Nations at a very early stage. At the first meeting of the UN Atomic Energy Commission in June 1946, the United States made a comprehensive proposal for controlling the atom. The Baruch Plan called for the establishment of an international agency to control, own, and operate all nuclear facilities "from the mine to the finished product" and provided for the *eventual* destruction of existing nuclear weapons, but only after an adequate international inspection system had been set up. Molotov attacked the proposal as intended to guarantee the United States monopolistic possession of the atomic bomb, warning that "no single country can count on retaining a complete monopoly. Science and its exponents cannot be shut up in a box and kept under lock and key. . . . It must not be forgotten that atomic bombs on one side may draw a reply in atomic bombs, and perhaps something else to boot, from the other side." (The USSR was then intensely engaged in its own effort to build a bomb.)

By 1947 the Cold War took over and disarmament had become a dead issue. To block Western rearmament programs, the Soviet government regularly condemned NATO and launched a global propaganda campaign calling "for the unconditional abolition of atomic weapons and the branding of any government which first used such weapons against another as guilty of war crimes against humanity." In March 1950, the World Peace Congress, a Soviet-front organization, met in Stockholm and initiated the Stockholm Peace Campaign, which gathered millions of signatures throughout the world in an attempt to mobilize international public opinion against the United States and its deterrent policy based on nuclear weapons. (Moscow's detonation of an atomic bomb in September 1949 was conveniently ignored.) The campaign ran afoul at the outbreak of the Korean War, but it demonstrated the enormous potential of antinuclear campaigns and resistance to rearmament that could be exploited by Soviet propaganda.

After Stalin's death, the Soviet leadership decided on a more conciliatory approach toward the West. This thaw in the Cold War raised expectations in the West for disarmament, though the inadequacy of provisions for internal inspection was in insuperable hurdle to agreement. At the fall 1954 session of the UN General Assembly, the Soviet delegate called for the reduction of conventional arms by 50 percent, the establishment of a temporary commission under the Security Council to study methods of controlling nuclear weapons, and an end to their manufacture. These proposals provided a basis for negotiation because they avoided previous Soviet insistence that talks be preceded by the immediate prohibition of nuclear weapons.

On May 10, 1955, the Soviet government presented concrete and detailed proposals calling for a gradual reduction of conventional forces to fixed levels, the destruction of nuclear stockpiles after these levels had been reached, and the establishment of measures to prevent surprise attack. Though recommending the creation of "control posts at the big ports, railway junctions, motor roads, and in airfields. . . . to see that no dangerous concentrations of land, air, or naval forces are effected," the Soviet proposals failed to provide for an actual inspection system. Nevertheless, they were important for two reasons. First, they recognized the need to limit nuclear stockpiles and safeguard against surprise attack. Second, they encouraged further discussions. At the Big Four summit conference in Geneva two months later, President Eisenhower responded with his "open skies" proposal, under which each country would carry out aerial photography of the other to detect and thereby to discourage any concentration of military forces that might be used to launch a surprise attack. Moscow was not about to expose the Soviet Union to such detailed intelligence reconnaissance (though within a decade or so the development of space satellites was to provide each superpower with exactly this type of information-gathering capability).

Speaking to the UN General Assembly in 1959, Premier Khrushchev unveiled his proposal for general and complete disarmament (GCD)—a policy the Soviet government has propounded ever since. While GCD was a chimerical notion that no nation, least of all the Soviet Union, really took seriously, it ushered in a period during which Moscow devoted more attention to partial measures in order to improve its military position and relationship with the United States. In the decades since then, Soviet diplomacy in the general field of disarmament has sought to narrow the areas of Soviet-American competition in strategic weapons, reduce the danger of accidental war, and ensure the best possible bargaining environment for the USSR by giving particular attention to four broad issues: (1) limiting nuclear testing, (2) protecting against surprise attack, (3) restricting outer space to peaceful purposes, and (4) confining the proliferation of nuclear weapons. Progress has been piecemeal and painstakingly slow, but without further agreements on these issues no sound structure of arms control is possible.

Limiting nuclear testing. The Soviet government has been an advocate of a nuclear test ban since it was first proposed by Indian Prime Minister Nehru in 1954. In March 1958, having completed a series of A-bomb explosions, Moscow announced its unilateral renunciation of further tests. (It was aware at the time of the West's intention to do testing during the summer.) However, by October, the Soviet government resumed testing, as military and strategic considerations outweighed the propaganda advantage accruing from advocacy of the ban.

Before March 1958, the United States had rejected proposals calling for a cessation of nuclear tests unless they included a ban on the production of nuclear weapons. Moscow countered with the demand that the *use* of nuclear weapons be outlawed. It also argued that linking a test ban with an end to bomb production was not practical, for while a cessation of tests could be verified, a production cutoff could not. The United States modified its position and agreed to a moratorium on nuclear testing for one year, effective October 31, 1958; this agreement lasted almost three years.

On August 31, 1961, amid mounting tensions over Berlin, Laos, and the Congo, the Soviet government abrogated the informal moratorium without warning and resumed testing in the atmosphere the next day. This was done despite Khrushchev's statement to the Supreme Soviet on January 14, 1960, that the "Soviet Government, prompted by the desire to provide the most favorable conditions for the earliest possible drafting of a treaty on the discontinuance of tests, will abide by its commitment not to resume experimental nuclear blasts in the Soviet Union unless the Western Powers begin testing atomic and hydrogen weapons" (at the time, Khrushchev had found it convenient to ignore France's continued testing). It was also done despite the gathering in Belgrade of the first summit meeting of nonaligned Afro–Asian countries, a group opposed to all testing and the target of intensive Soviet diplomatic attention since the mid-1950s. Khrushchev justified breaking the moratorium on several grounds: the requirements of Soviet security, the inability to agree on a treaty, and the testing by France during the time of the moratorium, allegedly with NATO's blessing. What Khrushchev did not mention was the intense pressure of the Soviet military to test new weapons and catch up to the United States.

After the Cuban missile crisis, the Soviets redoubled their efforts to improve relations with the United States, at the same time that they gave top priority to overcoming their glaring inferiority in strategic weapons. The Treaty Banning Nuclear Weapons Tests in the Atmosphere, in Outer Space, and Under Water was signed in Moscow on August 5, 1963. This was the first concrete result to emerge from post-1945 disarmament negotiations. The treaty does not cover underground testing, ostensibly because of the inability to agree on an acceptable system of on-site inspections but more likely because of the possibility that seismic instruments would not detect all possible violations and because of the resistance from each country's military establishment, which wants to continue testing of low-yield weapons. The treaty is self-executory: it continues to be operative for as long as each signatory observes it. In the event of a putative violation, "each Party shall in exercising its national sovereignty have the right to withdraw from the treaty."

Why did the Soviet Union sign the limited test ban treaty? Khrushchev said that these considerations were controlling: to end the radioactive contamination of the atmosphere (since 1964 the French and the Chinese have been the gross pollutors), to decrease international tension and pave the way for a settlement of the German problem, to slow down the arms race to allow greater attention to domestic problems, and to ease the negotiation of an agreement on measures to prevent surprise attack. Four other factors may have been equally important. First was the urgency of improving relations with the United States, dramatized by the Cuban crisis, in order to enable Moscow to concentrate on narrowing the gap in strategic delivery systems. Second, the Soviets realized that further atmospheric testing was not necessary for national security, which could be assured with existing weapons and with expanded underground testing of smaller-yield weapons. Third, the growing rift with Beijing was absorbing Soviet energies. Fourth, the Kremlin hoped that the treaty might help forestall the proliferation of nuclear weapons to other countries, especially to West Germany.

Increasingly reliable ways of distinguishing between natural seismic phenomena and weapons testing enhance the feasibility of further limitations on nuclear testing—the ultimate aim being a comprehensive test ban treaty (CTB). Still, how little progress has been achieved since the 1963 treaty is illustrated by both sides having signed but not ratified two subsequent treaties: in June 1974, the Treaty Between the USA and the USSR on the Limitation of Underground Nuclear Weapons Tests (also known as the Threshold Test Ban Treaty), which prohibits explosions above 150 kilotons (about eight times the explosive power of the bomb dropped on Hiroshima); and in May 1976, the Treaty Between the USA and the USSR on Underground Nuclear Explosions for Peaceful Purposes (commonly referred to as the Peaceful Nuclear Explosions Treaty), which limits peaceful nuclear explosions to 150 kilotons and provides for extensive verification procedures, including on-site inspections.

Gorbachev has pushed a CTB. In July 1985 he announced a unilateral moratorium on all nuclear testing from August 6 until January 1, 1986, and invited the United States to follow the Soviet lead. Throughout 1986 he extended the moratorium, arguing that ending of nuclear testing "would accelerate the process of entirely eliminating nuclear arms. The logic in this is simple: without nuclear testing the nuclear weapons, which both sides have stockpiled in abundance, cannot be upgraded." To demonstrate its readiness to accept reasonable on-site inspection, Moscow allowed a group of private U.S. citizens (Natural Resources Defense Council) to set up seismic monitoring equipment at three sites that are 200 miles from a major testing center at Semipalatinsk, in Soviet Central Asia. However, in the absence of any reciprocal restraint from the United

States, the USSR resumed underground nuclear testing shortly after ending its moratorium on February 28, 1987. By the end of the year, it had staged about 20 tests.

The U.S. opposed a CTB on two grounds: without on-site inspection, it was impossible to distinguish between low-yield nuclear-weapons tests and natural seismic phenomena; and some testing was necessary in order to develop better nuclear weapons, and this was especially true for the development of nuclear-powered X-ray lasers as part of the "Star Wars" anti-missile defense. Now, with the extensive inspection procedures mandated by the INF treaty and the greater sophistication of seismic detection, the "cheating" argument has lost much of its former cogency. Therefore, the case against a CTB rests mainly on the need for continued weapons testing.

Protection against surprise attack. As the military capability of the superpowers increases, there is ever greater need to avoid any kind of war between them and to create safeguards against surprise attack. Such safeguards are difficult to build into a treaty. Advances in military technology inevitably give rise to conflicting national assessments of areas of possible compromise; in some instances they make agreement less imperative, in others, even more so. Thus, on the one hand, fear of surprise attack has been allayed by the development of space satellites and high-altitude photography, which enable each superpower to gather reliable information about troop movements, missile placements, and the military testing of the other. These national technical means of verification reduce the need for international inspection. On the other hand, each side fears that the other may make a major technological breakthrough that could abruptly shift the strategic balance of power.

At the heart of concern over surprise attack is the attention given to preventing misunderstandings in moments of crisis. A pioneering agreement establishing a direct communications link between Moscow and Washington was signed in Geneva on June 20, 1963, and became operational on August 30, 1963. This hot-line teletypewriter link is intended for use only in extreme situations requiring immediate and direct communication between the top political leaders of the two countries. It was used for the first time on June 5, 1967, when the Soviet government wanted to ascertain American intentions in the Arab–Israeli war that had started earlier that day.

Two other agreements designed to lessen the fear of surprise attack and the danger of nuclear war through inadvertence were signed on September 30, 1971. One is intended to prevent overreaction in the case of an accidental launch of a nuclear weapon; it calls on each party to notify the other immediately "in the event of an accidental, unauthorized or any other unexplained incident involving a possible detonation of a nuclear weapon" and for advance notification of planned missile launches "if such launches will extend beyond its national territory in the direction of the other party." The second agreement improves the hot-line service by providing for a direct communications connection via satellite.

As noted earlier (Chapter 6), confidence-building measures (CBMs) at the conventional force level are being explored within the context of the MFR talks in Vienna, CSCE, and UN disarmament forums. The resumption of MFR talks in mid-March 1984 was the first small step toward reactivating Soviet–American arms control negotiations which Moscow broke off late in 1983. The Stockholm Conference on Confidence- and Security-Building Measures and Disarmament in Europe, which met from January 1984 to September 1986, produced "the first *militarily significant* confidence- and security-building measures to grow out of the Helsinki Final Act of 1975." These include: (1) prior notification of land exercises involving over 13,000 troops or 300 battle tanks, amphibious landings of more than 3000 troops, or transfers of forces numbering more than 13,000 troops to areas where they might constitute a threat to signatory members; (2) invitations to observers from all participating states "to monitor exercises and transfers when they meet or exceed 17,000 troops, and amphibious and parachute activities at 5,000 troops"; (3) one year's prior notice of military activities in the field involving more than 40,000 troops; and (4) verification that allows each state to conduct an inspection of a suspect activity on 48 hours' notice, although no more than three a year need be granted by the same state.[8] These provisions are important because they provide for on-site inspections and because the Soviets seem willing to consider CBMs, irrespective of the general climate of East–West relations. War through inadvertence is deemed as dangerous as war through advertence.[9]

There has been little movement in the MFR talks, but change may be coming. Gorbachev's acceptance of on-site inspection for nuclear arms control and elimination of a whole category of weapons and his emphasis on the idea of "reasonable sufficiency," all hint at "a Soviet readiness to reconsider the conventional arms balance in Central Europe."[10] However, the threat to NATO remains, in the offensive character of Soviet conventional forces in Central Europe. Thus far, this has not diminished.

Still, the open Soviet discussions of a possible shift to a defensive strategy that would rely on a military balance at low levels and on less threatening deployments, including a withdrawal of tanks and other offensive weapons from forward military positions in East Germany, suggest reevaluation of Soviet military doctrine. Even the Soviet military are beginning, for reasons of their own, as Robert Legvold has noted, "to question many aspects of prevailing doctrine. The changing character of the modern battlefield, the emergence of new technologies calling into question the primacy of the tank, and NATO's own evolution toward more offensive strategies are forcing the General Staff's shrewdest strategists to think long and hard about the war of tomorrow. How they eventually choose to respond to the *military* challenge may not be utterly at loggerheads with the kind of posture Gorbachev and his supporters may begin insisting on for *political* reasons."[11]

Restricting outer space to peaceful purposes. In an age when man has walked on the moon, lived in space for months at a time, and launched unmanned probes to Venus, Mars, and Saturn, the military implications of peaceful exploration of outer space are ever-present. In 1967, the Soviet Union and the United States joined through the UN in signing a treaty prohibiting nuclear weapons in outer space or on any celestial bodies. However, by the late 1970s, the Outer Space Treaty had not prevented an ominous race to develop an antisatellite capability: a hunter-killer satellite that would paralyze an adversary's "strategic nervous system" by destroying its communication and early-warning satellites.[12]

The Soviet Union has been testing anti-satellite (ASAT) weapons since 1968. Such a weapon, designed to destroy communications, navigation, and intelligence satellites, "consists of a simple bomb maneuvered into orbit alongside its intended victim. When the bomb explodes, shrapnel riddles its target like a shotgun blast. . . . No treaty prohibits placing such weapons of *pinpoint* destruction in orbit."[13] Efforts to negotiate a ban on ASATs were started and broken off during the Carter administration. In August 1983, five months after President Reagan's "Star Wars" speech, Andropov called for a moratorium on the testing of such weapons, but the deterioration in Soviet–American relations that followed the USSR's downing of a Korean airliner a month later and the impasse over the Pershing-II deployment at the end of 1983 temporarily eclipsed concerns over the arms race in space.

Unlike an ASAT weapon, an antiballistic missile (ABM) system is designed to destroy incoming missiles carrying nuclear warheads. In answer to the view that SDI contravenes the provisions of the 1972 ABM treaty, which is of indefinite duration and which prohibits the development, testing, or deployment of "sea-based, air-based, space-based, or mobile land-based" ABM systems or components (Article V), Reagan argued in late 1985 that the testing of systems that were not in existence at the time the treaty was signed is not banned.

The Soviet Union, which has been spending almost as much on strategic defense as on strategic offensive forces, has pressed for a treaty banning weapons and the use of force in space. The United States counters with the difficulty of verification, the advanced research the Soviets have undertaken in laser, particle beam, kinetic energy, and microwave technologies, and the USSR's network of ballistic missile early warning radars (both in operation and under construction) that could provide an ABM system far in excess of that which is permitted by treaty. An example of this capability was cited in late 1987 by General John L. Piotrowski, who is responsible for U.S. military activities in space, when he announced that the Soviet Union has developed lasers capable of knocking out reconnaissance satellites at an altitude of 400 miles and damaging those at 750 miles.[14]

In calling for negotiations on all aspects of the U.S.–Soviet rivalry in space, Gorbachev stresses particularly the need to contain SDI. On numerous occasions he has warned that SDI will accelerate the race in strategic offensive weapons and compel retaliatory measures in the field of both offensive and defensive weapons. He sees SDI as "an instrument for ensuring U.S. military domination" and says that it "destroys strategic stability" (that is, the current reliance on mutual assured destruction, MAD). One Western analyst notes that both superpowers possess "an assured capability to deliver an annihilating retaliatory strike on an aggressor even after subjection to a first strike. Hence Moscow views SDI as inherently destabilizing precisely because it threatens to undermine the more equalizing reality of M.A.D. in present-day conditions."[15] According to Marshal Sergei F. Akhromeyev, the chief of the Soviet General Staff, the U.S. SDI effort seeks to solve two problems: "to create a space-based nuclear shield for itself, and at the same time to cut down the number of strategic forces to a certain level, 6,000 warheads on each side. Given this number of warheads on each side, it is possible, at least in theory, to create a space-based nuclear shield."[16] The implication is that this makes an attack on the Soviet Union feasible, since it provides the United States with sufficient protection from "an annihilating retaliatory strike."

In trying to restrict SDI, Gorbachev has several objectives: to prevent the United States from effecting a technological breakthrough that could diminish the USSR's security and degrade its offensive capability; to avoid having to divert scarce resources to a new and extremely costly phase of the arms race; to exploit the differences within NATO; and to use arms control to limit a possible U.S. military–technological advantage, as Moscow did in the early 1970s when it used the SALT I treaty to curtail the U.S. lead in ABM development. Whatever his primary goals, Gorbachev's opposition to SDI, coupled with his call for the elimination of all nuclear weapons by the year 2000, underscores an apparent shift in Soviet doctrine in the late 1980s to a strategy of greater reliance on general-purpose conventional forces. At a time when U.S. strategic forces are being modernized and expanded, the USSR's diplomatic quest for the "denuclearization" of space—and Europe—poses an array of new political and military challenges to the NATO alliance.

SDI did bring Gorbachev to the summit in November 1985, and it did lead to the INF treaty, with extensive provisions for on-site inspection. The effort to reconcile SDI with the ABM treaty may produce a major breakthrough in the START negotiations and usher in a new era of political-diplomatic maneuvering to reshape and sustain the nuclear deterrent at levels commensurate with the concept of "equal security."

Confining the proliferation of nuclear weapons. Moscow's interest in limiting the proliferation of nuclear weapons goes back to 1957 and rearmament of the Federal Republic of Germany. In the early 1960s the USSR assailed the U.S. proposal to provide NATO with a multilateral nuclear force, which was intended to satisfy Bonn without actually permitting it to acquire an independent nuclear capability. The entry of China into the nuclear club in October 1964 and the growing number of countries on the threshold of acquiring a nuclear capability (India, Israel, Pakistan, Sweden, and Japan) raised the importance of nonproliferation in Moscow's overall disarmament policy.

In general, Soviet opposition to the diffusion of nuclear weapons stemmed from a number of pragmatic considerations involving its perception of national security and strategic interests, such as "a) concern that further nuclear spread might eventually add Nth-power threats to the physical security of the Soviet Union; b) concern that proliferation would undermine the stability of the prevailing U.S.–Soviet nuclear dominance over the international arena by introducing less nuclear principalities led by men of questionable responsibility and rationality; c) fears that local use of nuclear weapons in regional crises might generate enormous escalatory pressures threatening to embroil the superpowers in an unwanted nuclear confrontation."[17]

In 1968 the Soviet Union and the United States cosponsored a UN resolution that resulted in the 1970 Non-Proliferation Treaty (NPT). The USSR has looked favorably on the establishment of nuclear-free zones in regions now lacking nuclear weapons and where regional members agree not to manufacture, stockpile, or use nuclear weapons (Latin America has such a treaty). Its ultimate aim, of course, is to see such nuclear abnegation extend to Western Europe, and especially to West Germany. Its strong condemnation of certain nonsigners of NPT (notably Israel and Japan) but not of others (India, for one) indicates that Soviet leaders view the issue as much in its political as in its military context. Though Moscow has "solemnly" promised to assist "any nonnuclear signatory of the treaty who becomes the victim of aggression or threatened aggression with the use of nuclear weapons," the treaty remains vague on who decides when and how to implement the "guarantee" of assistance. In light of Bonn's commitment to nonproliferation, the issue has for the time being lost some of its former salience for the USSR.

Another step to curtail nuclear proliferation centered on barring the "emplanting or emplacing" of nuclear weapons on the ocean floor more than twelve miles offshore. The issue was originally raised in 1967 by Ambassador Arvid Pardo of Malta, who urged the United Nations to demilitarize the seabed "beyond the limits of present national jurisdiction and to internationalize its resources in the interest of mankind." The superpowers pushed the military aspect but showed little interest in the economic one. On February 11, 1971, the USSR, the United States, and Great Britain signed a treaty prohibiting "any nuclear weapons and launching installations or any other facilities specifically designed for storing, testing, or using such weapons" from the ocean seabed beyond a twelve-mile coastal zone. The treaty does not ban nuclear-armed submarines or the emplacement of submarine detection devices, items that the Soviet Union tried to include but that the United States forestalled because of the difficulties of verification and the military's interest in perfecting anti-submarine defenses.

During the 1970s, while negotiating SALT and the aforementioned various arms control-related measures, the Soviet Union is estimated to have spent upwards of $100 billion more than the United States on strategic nuclear weapons and delivery systems alone. It now has strategic equivalence with the United States. The CIA estimates that Soviet military expenditures take approximately 13 to 14 percent of the Soviet GNP, roughly twice the American figure. From 1966 to 1976, the USSR's military expenditures increased by 4 to 5 percent a year; from 1977 to 1985, by about 2 percent a year. The recent lower rate of growth is due to the general slowdown in Soviet economic growth, to inefficiency in Soviet industry, and to the higher cost of modern weaponry. Nonetheless, Soviet policy continues to maintain a huge military capability, conventional as well as nuclear. One CIA estimate holds that the USSR maintains an army of over 210 divisions, of which 40 percent are considered combat-ready. "Rather than modernizing all units, the Soviets generally concentrate on upgrading equipment holdings of their frontline divisions in Eastern Europe and the western USSR. As of 1986, their Ground Forces inventory included approximately: 53,000 tanks; 55,000 armored troop carriers; 34,000 pieces of tube artillery; 6,300 tactical surface-to-surface multiple rocket launchers; 1,600 tactical surface-to-surface missile launchers; and 4,300 major surface-to-air missile launchers." The air force had some 10,000 fixed-wing aircraft and 4000 helicopters. The Soviet navy has about 300 major surface combatants and over 380 submarines, many of which are increasingly nuclear-powered.[18]

Does this Soviet buildup signify a quest for strategic superiority or a distinctive view of deterrence that considers the development of a "war-fighting" and a "war-winning" military capability as the best type of credible deterrence? John Erickson has analyzed the Soviet concept of deterrence as rooted in "denial":

> . . . designed to prevent the United States from the actual initiation of hostilities, to reduce the prospect of making military gains at the expense of the Socialist camp (an objective which has steadily committed the Soviet Union to a global role), to assure the survival of the Soviet system (hence the priority accorded to strategic defence) and, through the development of actual military (war-fighting) capability, to minimize the incentives for attacking the USSR by guaranteeing counterstrike—hence the "mix" of pre-emptive and secondary retaliatory forces. What has certainly become increasingly prominent in Soviet military–political thinking is the idea of a "more protracted" war—should it come to war—with consequent emphasis on survivability and sustainability, including wartime force reconstitution.[19]

However, despite statements by Soviet leaders that the USSR is not building a first-strike capability, that it is not aiming for strategic superiority, and that Soviet forces are not a "military menace" to the West, Western uneasiness over Soviet intentions remains.

Trends

Soviet military (and by transference, foreign) policy has been consistently misperceived and misunderstood because it has not conformed to what the West expects it to be. Soviet leaders have acted on a set of assumptions very different from those of the West, concerning the meaning of nuclear weapons for foreign policy, the centrality of political aims in military policy, and the kinds of uses to which military power can be harnessed in the pursuit of foreign policy. At least part of the continuing U.S. perplexity over Soviet policy is due to a stubborn unwillingness to draw the necessary implications from the direction that military doctrine and strategic thinking has taken in the Soviet Union and to accept the asymmetries in Soviet and American thinking and policy as intrinsic to the continuing superpower rivalry.

First, the Soviet Union surprised the United States by its unrelenting drive to overcome strategic inferiority, irrespective of cost, and by the speed with which this was accomplished. In the early 1960s, the U.S. civilian leadership thought that Moscow wanted its own assured destruction capability and would settle for a credible force of 400 to 500 ICBMs and symbolic parity, if only to free resources for the civilian sector of the economy. Consequently, Washington failed to appreciate the Kremlin's profound determination never again to be in the position it held during the Cuban missile crisis and its complete rejection of the political implications that would follow its acceptance of institutionalized inferiority. Undaunted by this misassessment, Washington thought that if it exercised restraint, the USSR would automatically follow suit once it caught up to the United States. Instead, the USSR has kept the momentum of its military buildup, bargaining hard and making concessions only if it has something to gain, that is, if it can effect a trade-off between an incipient U.S. technological advantage and an obsolescing Soviet system.

Second, whereas U.S. strategic and military policy has been formulated by civilian strategists and arms control specialists who have believed that limiting the arms race is essentially a technical, not a political, problem and who have sought strategic stability, not superiority—in 1974, Kissinger expostulated: "What in God's name is the meaning of strategic superiority? What do you do with it?"—the Soviet counterpart developed with the full participation of and significant contributions from professional military officers and with a more conscious effort to tailor military policy to political goals. Inevitably, this resulted in the greater influence of historical factors on Soviet decision-makers—the traditional Russian stress on mass, bigness, and numbers to compensate for weakness and insecurity. Nowhere is this more apparent than in the differing Soviet and American attitudes toward nuclear war.

Soviet military doctrine regards nuclear war as a war that has to be won, like any other. The U.S. position that nuclear war would be a catastrophe for both sides, with no winners and no losers, helps explain its lack of interest in civil defense programs and its willingness to bargain away the ABM chip. The Soviet approach does not mean that Moscow wants a nuclear showdown or expects a nuclear war. But it is frighteningly pragmatic. It assumes that nuclear war is possible and that such a war, if it should come, however horrible to contemplate, "must be survivable and some kind of meaningful victory attainable. . . . Not so to believe would mean that the most basic processes of history, on which Soviet ideology and political legitimacy are founded, could be derailed by the technological works of man and the caprice of an historically doomed opponent."[20] Accordingly, Soviet leaders have invested heavily in civil defense organization and structurally reinforced factories designed to withstand any but direct or near-direct hits, and they have trained the Red Army to cope with nuclear attack. They have also consciously tried to anticipate the problems of preserving the existing social system after a nuclear holocaust.

Third, when SALT began, the United States assumed that the guiding principle would be the preservation of stability through mutual assured destruction (the ability to destroy an "unacceptable" percentage of the adversary's population and industry) and that the aim of the negotiations was strategic stability. That was never the Soviet goal. Soviet leaders have been indifferent to the static, illusory, apolitical concept of stability. They have regarded destabilizing technologies with greater equanimity than the West and sought to exploit them for political ends. In January 1977, in a major speech at Tula, Brezhnev rejected "the allegations that the Soviet Union is going beyond what is sufficient for defense, that it is striving for superiority in arms, with the aim of delivering a 'first strike.'" He said that he accepted the "essential equivalence" that existed between the Soviet Union and the United States in the realm of nuclear weapons and rejected the possibility of strategic nuclear superiority. But at the same time the Soviet military started deploying MIRVed intermediate range nuclear missiles (SS-20s) and continued modernizing its ICBM forces.

Concomitantly, Soviet military doctrine has stressed the importance of advanced technologies in revolutionizing conventional means of waging nonnuclear war. This doctrinal shift is associated with the thinking of Marshal Nikolai V. Ogarkov, who was chief of the Soviet General Staff from 1977 to 1984. Though removed from this post in September 1984, presumably because of his insistence on increased defense expenditures to match the U.S. military buildup during the first Reagan administration, his influence among Soviet military thinkers is evident in the attention being devoted to adapting emerging technologies to conventional theatre operations.[21]

Fourth, the USSR's overall military buildup has been consistently underestimated. Soviet technological and industrial expertise in the military sphere—whether in developing an atomic or hydrogen bomb, an ICBM force, land-based silos with a reload capability, MIRVs, enormous quantities of diverse and high-quality weapons from tanks to SAMs, long-range air transport, or the navy's helicopter carriers, missile-firing ships, and roll-off–roll-on merchant vessels—has always surprised Western analysts. Even the navy, the stepchild of the Soviet armed forces, has surged impressively forward. In 1982, the USSR launched the largest submarine in existence, assigned the NATO codename Typhoon, which has twenty missile tubes, and each missle is MIRVed. (The U.S. equivalent, the Ohio class, carries MIRVed Trident missiles.)

Fifth, American leaders have all too often approached negotiations with the Soviets in an intellectually patronizing way, as if they have been assigned the mission of educating Soviet leaders to the dangers of nuclear war and strategic instability. With a far richer experience in safeguarding vital national interests than the civilian strategists who dominated the U.S. establishment in the 1960s and 1970s, the Soviet leadership and general staff was quite able to determine its national interests without an assist from Washington. Throughout the postwar period, Soviet propaganda has denounced the U.S. policy of negotiating from "positions of strength," probably because Moscow fully appreciated just how important it was to be in such a position when negotiating. Soviet leaders know how essential military power has been in preserving their East European empire, discouraging outside interference, obtaining Western acceptance of the division of Europe, and enabling them to compete with the United States in the Third World.

Sixth, the military's role in Soviet foreign policymaking is significant. Though the precise weight of military considerations is impossible to determine in any specific instance, their importance was evident in the decisions to invade Afghanistan, resupply the Syrians in 1982, and send a naval force to the Caribbean in March 1984, at a time of U.S.–Soviet tension over Nicaragua and El Salvador. The visibility of leading Soviet marshals suggests the considerable political prominence of the military establishment, not only in Soviet society as a whole where it has great prestige and commands vast economic resources, but also institutionally, in the making of foreign policy. The voice of the military is heeded in matters relating to security in Eastern Europe, China, military doctrine, and procurement and industrial policies.

Seventh, the Soviet Union has a long history of seeking advantage through arms control and disarmament. In the past, its proposals have aimed at imposing limitations on adversaries in those areas in which it was weak, while leaving untouched those in which it was strong (for example, Moscow's insistence on the ABM treaty in return for SALT I and its current attention to halting SDI). Nor does the USSR negotiate away advantages, as the negotiations in START and MFR show. Adherence to the INF treaty stands to bring it more, militarily and politically, than it surrenders.

According to Peter Vigor, the Kremlin's approach to arms control negotiations is likely to be traditional:

> It will seek to conserve its present formidable ability to wage large-scale war successfully, should such a conflict break out; and to wage it whether by conventional means or nuclear means or both. This demands the retention by the Soviet Union of very large armed forces and numbers of weapons. In addition, the Kremlin, by means of suitable disarmament agreements, will seek to prevent the USA from profiting by its genius for applied technology and introducing into its arsenal ever newer, ever more sophisticated and ever more costly weapons systems. In addition, the USSR will be willing to ban those particular sorts of weapons systems which it regards as being not very profitable militarily from the Soviet point of view, or else, although being profitable, as being potentially far *more* profitable to those whom it regards as its enemies.[22]

Finally, lacking a grand strategy, the United States has projected onto the Kremlin its own ambivalence and confusion over the relationship between military policy and foreign policy. But there has never been any mirror image in this realm. Moscow has fashioned a functional nexus between the political and military components of its foreign policy, and it is a firm believer in the ability of military power to provide additional foreign-policy options and political advantages. Understanding this central theme of Soviet policy is crucial for future assessments and actions pertaining to the Soviet–U.S. strategic interaction.

Notes

1. Anton Bebler, "The Armed Forces' Role in Soviet Foreign Policy," *Delo,* March 20, 1976; translated by Zdenko Antic in *Radio Free Europe Research Paper,* RAD Background Report, No. 70 (Yugoslavia), March 25, 1976.
2. Thomas W. Wolfe, *Soviet Power and Europe 1945–1970* (Baltimore: Johns Hopkins University Press, 1970), 33–34.
3. See Philip Taubman, *New York Times,* February 22, 1988.
4. Wolfe, *op. cit.,* 98, see also Raymond L. Garthoff, "The Meaning of the Missiles," *Washington Quarterly,* Vol. 5, No. 4 (Autumn 1982), 77–80, excerpts.
5. Herbert S. Dinerstein, "The Revolution in Soviet Strategic Thinking," *Foreign Affairs,* Vol. 36, No. 2 (January 1958), 244–45. See also Harriet Fast Scott and William F. Scott, *The Armed Forces of the USSR* (Boulder: Westview Press, 1979), 39–47.
6. William T. Lee, "Soviet Military Policy: Objectives and Capabilities," *Air Force Magazine* (March 1979), 55.
7. *The Military Balance 1983–1984* (London: International Institute for Strategic Studies, Autumn 1983), 3, 11.
8. John Borawski, "Confidence and Security-Building Measures in Europe," *Parameters,* Vol. XVI, No. 4 (1986), 69–70.
9. Bruce Allyn, "Soviet Views of CBMs," in John Borawski (ed.), *Avoiding War in the Nuclear Age: Confidence-Building Measures for Crisis Stability* (Boulder: Westview Press, 1986), 126.
10. Robert Legvold, "Gorbachev's New Approach to Conventional Arms Control," *The Harriman Institute Forum,* Vol. 1, No. 1 (January 1988), 2. See also Bernard E. Trainor, *New York Times,* March 7, 1988.
11. *Ibid.,* 6.
12. Herbert Scoville, Jr., and Kosta Tsipis. *Can Space Remain a Peaceful Environment?* (Muscatine, Ia.: Stanley Foundation, 1978).
13. Ben Bova, "Soviet Space Offensive," *OMNI* (July 1982), 63.
14. *New York Times,* October 24, 1987.

15. Mary C. Fitzgerald, *Soviet Views on SDI* (Pittsburgh: University of Pittsburgh Center for Russian and East European Studies: The Carl Beck Papers, No. 601, May 1987), 48.
16. *New York Times,* October 30, 1987.
17. Benjamin S. Lambeth, "Nuclear Proliferation and Soviet Arms Control Policy," *Orbis,* Vol. 14, No. 2 (Summer 1970), 308.
18. Directorate of Intelligence, CIA, "The Soviet Weapons Industry: An Overview" (Washington, D.C.: September 1986), 4.
19. John Erickson, "The Soviet View of Deterrence: A General Survey," *Survival,* Vol. XXIV, No. 6 (November–December 1982), 246.
20. Fritz Ermarth, "Contrasts in American and Soviet Strategic Thought," *International Security,* Vol. 3, No. 2 (Fall 1978), 144.
21. Mary C. Fitzgerald, "Marshal Ogarkov on the Modern Theater Operation," *Naval War College Review,* Vol. XXXIX, No. 4 (Autumn 1986), 6–25.
22. P. H. Vigor, *The Soviet View of Disarmament* (London: The Macmillan Press Ltd, 1986), 170.

Selected Bibliography

BURROWS, WILLIAM E. *Deep Black: Space Espionage and National Security.* New York: Random House, 1987.

COLLINS, JOHN M. *U.S.-Soviet Military Balance: Concepts and Capabilities 1960–1980.* New York: McGraw-Hill, 1980.

DANIEL, DONALD G. *Anti-Submarine Warfare and Superpower Strategic Stability.* Urbana: University of Illinois Press, 1986.

DEAN, JONATHAN. *Watershed in Europe: Dismantling the East–West Military Confrontation.* Lexington: Lexington Books, 1987.

DOUGLASS, JOSEPH D., JR. *Soviet Military Strategy in Europe.* New York: Pergamon Press, 1980.

HOLLOWAY, DAVID. *The Soviet Union and the Arms Race.* 2nd ed. New Haven: Yale University Press, 1984.

HORELICK, ARNOLD L., and MYRON RUSH. *Strategic Power and Soviet Foreign Policy.* Chicago: University of Chicago Press, 1966.

JOHNSON, NICHOLAS L. *Soviet Military Strategy in Space.* Boston: Jane's Publishing Co., 1987.

KELIHER, JOHN G. *The Negotiations on Mutual and Balanced Force Reductions.* New York: Pergamon Press, 1982.

LOCKWOOD, JONATHAN SAMUEL. *The Soviet View of U.S. Strategic Doctrine.* New Brunswick, N.J.: Transaction Books, 1983.

MACKINTOSH, MALCOLM. *Juggernaut: The Russian Forces, 1918–1966.* New York: Macmillan, 1967.

MCCGWIRE, MICHAEL. *Military Objectives in Soviet Foreign Policy.* Washington, D.C.: The Brookings Institution, 1987.

OBERG, JAMES E. *Red Star in Orbit.* New York: Random House, 1981.

RANFT, BRYAN, and GEOFFERY TILL. *The Sea in Soviet Strategy.* Annapolis, Md.: The Naval Institute Press, 1983.

SUVOROV, VIKTOR. *Inside the Soviet Army.* New York: Macmillan, 1983.

VIGOR, P. H. *The Soviet View of Disarmament.* New York: St. Martin's Press, 1986.

WATSON, BRUCE W. *Red Navy at Sea: Soviet Naval Operations on the High Seas, 1956–1980.* Boulder: Westview Press, 1982.

11
Soviet Policy and the World Communist Movement

Ever since March 1919, when the Comintern was established, the Soviet Union has been considered the godfather of the world Communist movement, the term favored by Soviet writers for the collectivity of almost a hundred Communist and workers' parties. It has committed enormous resources to this instrumentality in order to advance Soviet foreign-policy interests.

Paradoxically, Moscow's manipulation of foreign Communist parties to defend Soviet state interests was never managed with more telling effect than in the period of the USSR's maximum weakness. At the time of Soviet diplomatic isolation and military vulnerability in the 1920s and 1930s, the world Communist movement was truly the handmaiden of Soviet policy. There was no questioning of Stalin's injunction that internationalism required proletarians of all countries to support the Soviet Union, since an internationalist is one who "unhesitatingly, unconditionally, without vacillation, is ready to defend the USSR because the USSR is the basis of the world revolutionary movement, and it is impossible to defend and to advance [this movement] unless the USSR is defended."[1]

In the late 1980s, when Soviet military power and international influence are greater than ever before in the USSR's history, the movement is split, unruly, and dominated by nationalism. The CPSU leadership finds itself challenged not only by ruling parties within the Communist world (the "world socialist system," in the Soviet lexicon) but also by nonruling Communist parties that often lack much political influence in their own countries. Moscow must learn to adapt to the increasingly fragmented character of the world Communist movement, because it sees no way to stop the centrifugal tendencies that make the movement as much a source of embarrassment and disunity as of strength and prestige.

Before exploring the factors that produced the present erosion of the once unchallenged Soviet leadership over the world Communist movement and its transformation from monolithism to polycentrism, along with the effect that this has had on Soviet foreign policy, we must look briefly at the nature of Soviet authority, past and present, and the parameters within which it operates.

In general, authority may rest on one or more elements: it may be based on the charismatic personality of an outstanding figure; it may devolve upon an individual or group who is in the vanguard of a quest for a shared objective and who for the moment embodies the transcendent idea; it may be forcibly imposed by those who control the instruments of coercion; or it may come from the voluntary accession of affiliated members whose own weakness leads them to rely on the external source of authority represented by one of the preceding.[2] As we look at Soviet history since 1917, we can distinguish the periods in which one or another of these bases of authority was ascendent.

From 1919 to 1945, the world Communist movement was characterized by two fundamental considerations: the existence of the Soviet Union as the *only* Communist state, and the complete subservience, especially under Stalin, of foreign Communist parties to the will of Moscow. Those who disagreed either quit or were expelled from the movement. During this period, authority devolved upon Moscow because of the esteem in which it was held by the membership despite periodic disagreements, and not because Moscow was in a position physically to compel obedience. The early adherents to Soviet authority willingly followed Lenin, who uniquely combined "the individual prestige of a charismatic personality with the authority of the idea of world revolution."[3] Stalin's authority came from manipulation of symbols, personalities, bureaucracy, and the use of force.

Foreign Communists accepted Moscow's policies, often at the sacrifice of their own interests and prospects for power. They did so because the Soviet Union, as the only Communist state, embodied the ideal of world revolution; because the realization of world revolution was feasible only as long as the Soviet state survived and thrived; because of the exalted feeling that comes from membership in a universalistic movement; because Moscow's approbation meant that an otherwise political nonentity would be "taken seriously not merely by his party but also by his fellow countrymen, for whom he personifies Moscow's power locally";[4] and because of the power over an organization, however small, that flowed to a leadership willing to do Moscow's bidding. Their blind obedience brought disaster to many parties in the 1920s and 1930s, including the German, Chinese (before Mao), Indonesian, and Spanish. During the honeymoon period of the Nazi–Soviet pact, West European Communists did nothing to help their countries resist German aggression; not until Hitler's attack on the Soviet Union in June 1941 did they take up arms against nazism. In all of this, Soviet state interests transcended those of world revolution, though Moscow rationalized the former in terms of the latter, and the party faithful voluntarily did as Moscow asked.

The big change in the world Communist movement came in 1945, when the Soviet Union extended its authority over Eastern Europe through the Red Army. With this coercive instrument, it created new Communist states, although at the time they were merely compliant, exploited Soviet imperial possessions. Intent on subordinating Yugoslavia to Soviet wishes, Stalin tested his authority, trying by dint of his prestige to have Tito removed, but he failed and, unwilling to use the Red Army to compel obedience, resorted to excommunication. But the heretic survived and in the process retained his credentials as a Communist and a revolutionary.

However, Tito's rejection of Soviet authority was a minor matter compared with the situation that was inherent in Mao's conquest of mainland China. At first Mao acknowledged Moscow's ideological preeminence and leadership in foreign affairs. The charisma of Stalin and the convergence of national interests ensured unity, and the nature of Soviet authority did not become an issue as long as Stalin lived. Stalin died in 1953, and the turning point in the relationship of authority between Moscow and Beijing came in February 1956. Khrushchev's denunciation of Stalin at the CPSU's twentieth congress compromised his own standing in Beijing and led Mao to stake his claim to leadership of the world Communist movement. The November 1957 attempt to paper over the policy differences between Moscow and Beijing failed, and the rift widened. It became public knowledge after 1960, and forced foreign Communist parties to take sides. The quarrel ended Moscow's pretension to speak for all parties on matters of doctrine and policy. Its authority was being challenged by a major center of power fully qualified to carry on the mission of the proletariat to bring about world revolution and communism.

At the heart of this struggle for authority is what Benjamin Schwartz has called "the myth of the Communist party," that is, the ascription to "the Communist party—conceived of as the total Communist movement"—of the "transcendental and messianic qualities attributed by conventional Marxism to the world proletariat."[5] But there is a contradiction inherent in the myth: "The infallibility and monolithic unity presupposed in the myth can be maintained only so long as there is an unquestioned ultimate instance of authority."[6] Lenin's unquestioned authority derived from his charismatic influence and unshakable conviction that he was uniquely endowed to apply the "changeless and universal truths" of Marxism to the specific situations faced by the proletariat in other countries. Stalin, lacking Lenin's powerful personality, derived his authority from a combination of bureaucratic and coercive methods. He also benefited from an international context in which defense of the socialist homeland took on a crusading zeal that subordinated all other considerations.

De-Stalinization and Polycentrism

By Khrushchev's time the rival claimants of authority in Beijing and Belgrade were forcing Moscow to confront the challenge of reconciling unity with diversity. But Moscow lacked the instruments necessary for restoring bloc unity: it had neither the charismatic leader nor the monopoly of force. A series of irreversible developments inevitably weakened its attempts to reassert Soviet authority in the Socialist camp and in the world Communist movement: the USSR's de-Stalinization that spread to Eastern Europe and nurtured nationalistic demands for greater independence; the Sino-Soviet dispute that enabled the mice in the socialist camp to play, while the two cats fought; the Soviet leadership's surrender, implicit in its acceptance of the notion of "many roads to socialism," of the prerogative of proclaiming the universality of the Soviet model, in return for support of the Soviet position in the dispute with China and on major foreign-policy issues; Moscow's readiness to discard the former exploitative economic relationship with Eastern Europe and seek bloc cooperation; and its realization that greater independence from the center was essential to preserve the communist character of the countries in Eastern Europe.

The monolithism that existed until 1948 is part of the "ancient" history of international communism. The Kremlin has since had to cope with three different kinds of Communist parties in order to exercise what remains of its once preeminent authority. First, there are the ruling Communist parties that are part of the Soviet bloc and that can, in extreme circumstances, be brought into line by the Red Army. Second, there are the ruling parties that lie outside of Moscow's ability to impose its authority if need be and with whom Moscow's relationships are as complex as the one with Beijing; these are to be found in Yugoslavia, Albania, North Korea, Cuba, Vietnam, Kampuchea, and Laos. Third, there are the nonruling Communist parties, which for convenience may be roughly divided into two groups: those permitted to operate openly, which possess a solid core of electoral support, have prospects for attaining a measure of parliamentary power, and are found primarily in Western Europe but also in Japan and India; and those proscribed in ways that severely limit their political possibilities, at least through legitimate channels, and which exist in the Third World. The first two categories of parties and their relationships with Moscow have already been discussed, primarily in Chapters 5 and 7; here we shall predominantly treat the third category.

Authority Versus Autonomy

Moscow has used two types of forums in its efforts to reimpose a measure of authority: the international meeting, epitomized by the conferences of world Communist and workers' parties held in Moscow in 1957, 1960, and 1969 (and supplemented by frequent annual gatherings of the dozen or so leading Communist-front organizations in the fields of labor, education, science, and culture); and the regional forum, intended primarily for European Communist parties, exemplified by the meetings in 1967 in Karlovy Vary, Czechoslovakia, in 1976 in East Berlin, and in 1980 in Paris.

In the wake of de-Stalinization, the revolutions in Eastern Europe, the shock and disillusionment that reverberated through Western nonruling Communist parties, and the call by Italian Communist party (PCI) chief Palmiro Togliatti for the independence of all Communist parties and their right to determine their own strategy for achieving socialism (he coined the term *polycentrism*), the 1957 Moscow conference sought to restore unity to the movement. In addition, a Soviet-edited journal, *Problems of Peace and Socialism,* was set up the following year to replace the Cominform's organ, *For a Lasting Peace, For a People's Democracy.* A unity of sorts was fashioned, acknowledging the leading position of the Soviet Union in the struggle against imperialism and condemning revisionism, which meant the Yugoslavs. Moscow and Beijing closed ranks, leaving Yugoslavia out and the Italian and Polish Communists uneasy. However, Sino-Soviet relations soon worsened, and at an accelerating pace.

By the 1960 Moscow conference of eighty-one Communist parties, the cracks in the Sino-Soviet relationship could no longer be puttied over. The exchanges were "frank" (a Soviet euphemism for bitter disagreement). The final document was more "a collation" of views than a compromise; its very "ambiguities and qualifications were so numerous that it could hardly serve as a guide for any of the Communist parties."[7] There was no agreement on the fundamental issue of authority within the world Communist movement, and the seeming accord hardly outlived the conference. So ended Moscow's former unquestioned sway.

Ironically, the Chinese were the ones pressing for a formulation that would recognize "the camp of Socialism headed by the Soviet Union," in order to alienate Yugoslavia and other revisionists, while Khrushchev disclaimed any interest in reestablishing Moscow's hegemonial role. In general, the Moscow declaration reflected the Soviet views in a way that "was sufficiently ambiguous so that the Chinese could (and did) interpret it in their favor: on the 'nature of the present epoch,' on the relative danger of dogmatism and revisionism, on local war (where Khrushchev after the conference recognized the justness and inevitability of 'wars of national liberation' but condemned 'interstate' wars), on the destructiveness of world war (where in general the statement took the Soviet position), on disarmament, on underdeveloped areas (where the compromise ideological concept of a 'national democracy' was outlined), on peaceful transition to Socialism, and on Communist strategy in capitalist countries (which reflected primarily the Soviet view), and on Yugoslavia."[8]

An indication of how far the Soviet Union's authority had slipped can be seen in the difficulty Moscow experienced in trying to convene an international Communist conference to condemn or excommunicate Beijing. Khrushchev determined in late 1963 to hold such an ecumenical kangaroo court but encountered stiff opposition from the Yugoslav, Romanian, Polish, and the Italian party leaders. The PCI's secretary-general, Palmiro Togliatti, told his Central Committee in April 1964: "When talk arose of a new international meeting of all Communist parties to examine and assess the attitude of the Chinese comrades . . . this . . . was likely to end in another excommunication . . . ; and it appeared to us unnecessary and dangerous." Togliatti, a highly respected veteran Communist—a survivor of the Stalin period—carried his criticism of Khrushchev's course and his insistence on the independence and equality of all parties to the Kremlin itself and to the movement as a whole.

Togliatti died of a stroke while on vacation with Khrushchev in the Crimea in August 1964, but not before publishing an extraordinary memorandum on the problems of the world Communist movement. In it he opposed an international conference as untimely, and urged a continual round robin of working groups to defeat and alter the Chinese views. He called for "the unity of all socialist forces in a common action, going also beyond ideological differences, against the most reactionary imperialist groups." Deploring "the old atheist propaganda" as counterproductive to reaching the Catholic masses and coming to grips with the challenge posed by a changing Vatican, he denounced the "cult of Stalin" and stressed the need to study "the political errors" that gave rise to it. He cited the worrying centrifugal tendency of nationalism among the socialist countries and noted that "in this lies an evident and serious danger with which the Soviet comrades should concern themselves." For all of these reasons, he said, "we would be against any proposal to create once again a centralized international organization. We are firm supporters of the unity of our movement and of the international workers movement, but this unity must be achieved in the diversity of our concrete political positions, conforming to the situation and degree of development in each country."[9]

Khrushchev and his successors have not heeded all of Togliatti's advice, but neither have they ignored his admonitions or the impact that the memorandum had on the evolution of the world Communist movement.

At the time of Khrushchev's deposal in October 1964, Moscow could count on attendance by only forty-six parties, not the seventy Khrushchev had originally claimed. Brezhnev postponed the December conference, convening instead a "preparatory meeting" in Moscow in March 1965, which was attended by only eighteen of the twenty-six parties invited. Faced with widespread resistance to the excommunication of the Chinese and to any return to the monolithism of the Stalinist period, Soviet leaders groped through subsequent meetings in 1967 and 1968 for a way to accommodate both the diversity demanded by foreign parties and the minimal unity the Kremlin could accept and still retain the authority necessary for promotion of foreign-policy priorities.

Far from forging the movement's unity, the world conference finally held in Moscow from June 5 to 17, 1969, demonstrated conclusively that the Balkanization of world communism had taken place. The very holding of the conference was a minor feat of sorts for Moscow. Seventy-five parties attended (five did not sign the final document)—the remaining twenty-five followed China and stayed away (absentees who had been present in 1960 included the Communist parties of Vietnam, North Korea, Japan, Burma, and Indonesia). The final document, which did not mention China or the Soviet invasion of Czechoslovakia, was a bland mélange of generalities. The conference left the movement pretty much where it had been before and where it has remained ever since: polycentric, beset with divergences, wedded on paper to a common ideology that frays badly when used, and firm in rejecting any attempt to restore the CPSU's former leading position in the movement; its professions of unity reduced mainly to denunciations of U.S. imperialism (though, as opponents noted, the USSR seeks continually to reach agreements with the United States on a variety of issues.).

Moscow fared no better in the regional conferences of European Communist parties the most important of which was held in East Berlin in June 1976.[10] Moscow failed even with the timing: it had wanted the conference a year earlier, to link it to the Conference on Security and Cooperation in Europe, hoping thereby to "lessen the effect of the concessions that the East Europeans would have to make in Helsinki with regard to 'Basket 3' (the freer movement of information, ideas, and persons); at the same time, it would at least implicitly reaffirm the status of the CPSU as *primus inter pares* (or *imparies*) in the European Communist movement."[11]

The conference document signed by the twenty-nine participants was not what Moscow wanted. It stressed the voluntary cooperation of the participating parties, "strictly adhering to the principles of *equality and sovereign independence* of each party, noninterference in internal affairs and respect for their *free choice* of different roads in the struggle for social change of a progressive nature and for Socialism" (italics added). In the seven years since the 1969 international conference, Moscow had made no headway in regaining any of its former authority. Indeed, the statements of individual leaders had become even more forceful in the assertion of their independence. For example, the PCI's Enrico Berlinguer said that the solidarity of the world Communist movement "is based on recognition that each party elaborates autonomously and decides in full independence its own political line, both internal and international. . . . The truth is that . . . there is not and cannot be any leading party or leading state. . . . "

What Moscow wanted was stated on several occasions by Konstantin Zarodov (then Russian editor-in-chief of *Problems of Peace and Socialism,* the theoretical journal of pro-Moscow and independent Communist parties) and others: acceptance of the "unchanged necessity for 'a revolutionary democratic dictatorship of the Proletariat', led 'from above' by the [Soviet] Communist party," which, by virtue of its historical experience, should in essence have the "right to impart ideological and political lessons to other CP's."[12] Moscow wanted the conference to adopt a "general line," but it did not. To ensure the participation of the Yugoslav, Romanian, Italian, Spanish, and even French party leaders, Moscow had to swallow such bitter pills as equality of parties; independence in interparty relations; no special status for the CPSU, though it could claim support for its foreign policy vis-a-vis the capitalist world; no criticism of any party; no binding requirements; and no acceptance of the venerable concept of "proletarian internationalism"—since the days of Lenin and Stalin the symbol of Soviet authority in world Communist affairs—but replacement instead "by the ostensibly less restrictive concept of 'international proletarian solidarity,' [and] the subsequent insistence by Moscow on treating the two concepts as functional equivalents suggests that the Eurocommunist victory was more apparent than real."[13]

By the time of the pan-European Communist conference on peace and disarmament convened in Paris at the end of April 1980, the Eurocommunist swell had crested. The conference attracted twenty-two delegations, but was boycotted by the Italian, Spanish, British, Swedish, Yugoslav, and Romanian parties, whose reasons were as various as their opposition to the USSR's invasion of Afghanistan, dissatisfaction with the lack of preconference consultations, and interest in exploring closer cooperation with the non-Communist socialist Left. To overcome the disarray in the movement, Moscow used the forum to launch a major propaganda campaign against NATO's decision to deploy new intermediate-range nuclear missiles, and to muster support for its Afghan policy.

After 1969, Moscow stopped convening world conferences of Communist parties, because of Chinese opposition and its own inability to control the views of key leaderships among the ruling and nonruling Communist parties alike. It has also come to realize that even the regional conferences have serious shortcomings, but continued to support them in those areas in which its influence over the parties concerned remains high (especially in the Middle East and Latin America).

Eurocommunism

The new independence shown by West European Communist parties has been termed "Eurocommunism." Many consider that Eurocommunism came of age in the statement issued by Enrico Berlinguer and Georges Marchais in mid-November 1975, all the principles of which were included in the June 1976 document issued at the East Berlin meeting. Continued agreement by the Italian and French Communist parties (PCI and PCF, respectively), the most important in Western Europe, was a development the Kremlin could not ignore.

Eurocommunism heralds the entry of West European Communist parties into the political mainstreams of their respective countries, and their professed commitment to an evolutionary quest for power and a readiness to share office in coalition with non-Communist parties. It also implies greater independence from Soviet ideological and political authority; rejection of the concept of the dictatorship of the proletariat; and formal acceptance of the principles underlying Western pluralist democratic societies, including free elections, toleration of competing parties, and respect for fundamental civil liberties and majority rule. A variegated, multifaceted adaptation of nonruling West European Communist parties to their national political environments, Eurocommunism signifies the right of party leaderships to develop their own tactics in the quest for power. Even the "Stalinist" leaders—Cunhal in Portugal and Marchais in France—toe only that part of the Soviet line that suits their own situation: thus, both dropped the phrase "dictatorship of the proletariat" from their respective party programs as a convenience, to avoid alienating groups to whom the term means "fascist" or "Stalinist." Psephological tactics mandate doctrinal flexibility. This adaptation to reality is pure Leninism, and Moscow can live with it, especially since neither Cunhal or Marchais disputes Soviet leadership of the world Communist movement or the USSR's policy in the Third World including Afghanistan or the suppression of Solidarity in Poland.

The differences between the Cunhal-Marchais breed of Eurocommunist and the self-styled democratic/libertarian Berlinguer-Carrillo breed reflect different political contexts, challenges, and constituencies. A Marchais, for example, is against the Common Market and attacks the flight of the boat people from Vietnam as part of a campaign to denigrate the Vietnamese regime and communism, because to do so is popular among large segments of his country's populace; a Berlinguer defends the EEC and calls for aid to the refugees for the same reason. Neither checked with Moscow before deciding which position to adopt, and Moscow is not overly sensitive to this kind of polycentrism, which does no harm to Soviet foreign-policy aims in Europe. Carrillo and Berlinguer in particular tried to organize closer cooperation and political initiatives to draw the Latin parties into a joint approach to "the problem of how to face up to the crisis in European society." They predicted increasing economic and social tensions, a prognosis shared by many in Moscow.

There are times, however, when Eurocommunism seriously troubles Moscow, as when it seems to be eroding the basis for the USSR's extant authority and claim to special status in the world Communist movement. The Carrillo affair is a good example. In early 1977, after decades of clandestine existence, the Communist party of Spain (PCE) emerged as a legal party in the post-Franco period and contested seats in the parliamentary elections in April. The brouhaha between Moscow and the PCE's secretary-general, Santiago Carrillo, broke out shortly after publication of his book, *Eurocommunism and the State.* Carrillo angered Moscow on a number of counts: he criticized and rejected the Soviet model of socialism; equated the military hegemony of the USSR with that of the U.S., cautioned Eurocommunist parties to avoid the embrace of either, and suggested that Spain might join militarily with its neighbors (NATO members) to protect itself against invasion; criticized the deformation of Soviet society, the persistence of Stalinism and the "cult of personality" in the USSR, and the PCE's past blind obedience to the CPSU; called for an objective evaluation of Trotsky's role in history; referred to Khrushchev's fall as "a sort of palace coup"; and accused the Soviet leadership of trying to perpetuate dogmas and relationships that "may have some propagandistic value for the type of system that has been achieved in the USSR" but that have no relevance for the Communists in Western Europe.

The initial Soviet answer was a heavy barrage that appeared in late June 1977 in *Novoe vremya* and had the effect of raising the specters of Soviet censorship of foreign Communists and another excommunication campaign similar to that launched against Yugoslav leaders in 1948.[14]

Moscow attacked Carrillo for transgressing the correct norms of proper interparty relations by denigrating Soviet achievements, society, and foreign policy and shamelessly echoing Western charges concerning Soviet human-rights violations. It may have reacted this sharply out of fear that the Eurocommunist summit that Carrillo, Berlinguer, and Marchais held in Madrid in March 1977 was the precursor of some form of anti-Soviet coalition within the Communist movement.

It is probable that Soviet leaders used Carrillo's book, which was hastily written and not always very analytical, as a pretext to criticize the Italian and French party leaders, who are far more important on the European scene and whose behavior could have serious repercussions in Eastern Europe. The very weakness of the PCE made it a good surrogate target for the bigger fry. The criticisms were delayed until after the Spanish elections (in which the PCE fared poorly), perhaps to avoid the accusation that Moscow was trying to sow factionalism or undermine a Eurocommunist party with which it was at odds. One lesson Moscow hoped other parties would learn from the Spanish case was that anti-Sovietism does not pay. The snipping, like the phenomenon, which is apt to remain a feature of the European scene, occasionally turns up some choice morsels, such as Carrillo's comparison of the Kremlin to the Spanish Inquisition: Soviet leaders have forgotten that "the world Communist movement is no longer a church and Moscow is no longer Rome. We cannot accept the existence of a 'Holy Office' within the Central Committee of the Soviet Communist Party with the power of dispensing excommunications or blessings."[15]

By the end of the 1970s, however, Carrillo's ideological assertiveness reverted to political acceptance of the Soviet line, for example, criticism of NATO's decision to deploy new missiles, attacks on the United States as the main enemy of peace, and opposition to Spain's entry into NATO. In November 1982, a month after a stinging electoral defeat of the PCE at the hands of the Socialist Party, he was deposed by "Spanish comrades who considered him still too Stalinist and authoritarian in internal party affairs."[16] His successor, Gerardo Iglesias, advocates the kind of independence of Moscow that, ironically, first placed Carrillo in the forefront of Eurocommunism. In January 1984, a splinter group led by the sixty-nine-year old Ignacio Gallego broke away and established a rival, avowedly pro-Soviet PCE, which is committed to the Leninist principles of centralized party leadership and is "resolutely" opposed to Eurocommunist manifestations of "revisionism."[17] It is his party that Moscow recognizes.

The French Communist Party (PCF), rightly considered one of the closest to Moscow among the major nonruling parties, has found it difficult to deal with Eurocommunism. In an effort to arrest the erosion of electoral strength and restore the PCF's political fortunes, party leader

Georges Marchais shifted from his 1977 policy of cooperation with the socialists and support for the concept of Eurocommunism and in 1978 stood for opposition to the socialists and the "Euroleft" strategy, only to shift back again in 1981 to cooperation with them and participation until 1984 in the government of Socialist President François Mitterand. As a minority member of the Socialist Party–led government, the PCF had to accept, at least tacitly, official French criticism of the USSR's policy toward Afghanistan and Poland and its shooting down of the Korean airliner in September 1983. For Marchais, who controls the party's professional apparatus, participation in the Mitterand government was a calculated risk, one that Moscow apparently supported. His decision to break with Mitterand in July 1984 only accelerated the PCF's decline. In the March 1986 parliamentary elections, the party's vote dropped to less than 10 percent, the lowest since its creation in 1921. It is doubtful that the glow of Gorbachev and *glasnost* will help the old-guard Stalinist party of Marchais at the polls.

Among the nonruling West European Communist parties, only the Italian Communist party (PCI) has taken a consistently independent line. Ever since the 1960s, when it embarked on the path to power by parliamentary means and opposed all Soviet attempts to reestablish authority over the world Communist movement, the PCI has been the leading proponent of Eurocommunism. Under the leadership of Enrico Berlinguer and Alessandro Natta (who became head of the party in June 1984, when Berlinguer died), it has pushed the concept of "new internationalism," which calls for open dialogue and cooperation with Catholic, socialist, and bourgeois groups and which criticizes the Soviet doctrine of "proletarian internationalism." In 1978, Berlinguer engineered the withdrawal of the PCI-backed CGIL trade union movement from the Soviet-dominated World Federation of Trade Unions. He denounced the USSR's intervention in Afghanistan and repression in Poland, restored relations with the Chinese Communist Party, and upheld Italy's membership in NATO. Soviet hostility manifests itself in various ways, such as refusal to allow PCI delegates to speak at CPSU congresses and scathing denunciations in *Pravda,* which has accused the PCI of "direct aid to imperialism" and support to "anti-communism and to all forces hostile to the cause of socialist progress in general."[18] Some improvement has taken place under Gorbachev. However, judging by the coolness manifested toward the Soviet Union by the PCI leadership at its seventeeth congress in April 1986, relations between the two parties are not likely to change significantly until Moscow permits a far greater degree of autonomy in Eastern Europe.

The very different kinds of policies followed by nonruling European Communist parties, the mixed success that they have had at the ballot box, and the sterility of the political dialogue between Communist and non-Communist Left suggest that the heydey of the Eurocommunist challenge to Moscow has passed. As West European Communist leaders experiment with programs and tactics capable of eliciting greater support, they increasingly direct their attention inward and not toward far-ranging criticisms of the Soviet Union or Soviet socialism.

The Japanese Variant

The growing assertiveness of the nonruling Communist parties in Western Europe has absorbed but not monopolized Moscow's attention. There is in Asia a less well-known counterpart to the phenomenon of Eurocommunism. It is clearly manifested in the behavior of the Japan Communist Party (JCP). Founded in 1922, the JCP is the best-organized and strongest Communist party in non-Communist Asia, with a membership of about 300,000. It has undergone tortuous reversals; finally, in the 1970s, it succeeded in establishing an image of nonviolence, accepted the parliamentary system, and emerged as the third most important party in the Diet.

After World War II, the JCP slavishly followed the Soviet line. In 1950, the Cominform "suggested" a revolutionary tack that led the Japanese leadership to admit its mistakes and adopt a violent approach, with the result that for the next five years, the party had to go underground.[19] From the mid-1950s to the mid-1960s—from the USSR's de-Stalinization to the CPR's Cultural Revolution—the JCP drew closer to Beijing; it opposed Moscow because of the U.S.–Soviet limited nuclear test ban treaty (1963), the Soviet détente with the United States, and the lingering resentment over the humiliation that party leaders had suffered at Stalin's hands for advocating the very kind of policy that Brezhnev had come to espouse. Soviet leaders were accused of meddling in intra-JCP activities, encouraging factionalism, and seeking improved relations with the JCP's arch-foes, the socialists.[20] However, by late 1966, the JCP's pro-Beijing position on the Sino-Soviet dispute came a cropper in the revulsion against Mao's Cultural Revolution and his rejection of a common front with Moscow in support of North Vietnam's struggle against U.S. imperialism. This led the chairman of the JCP, the octogenarian Kenji Miyamoto (the party's secretary-general is Tetsuzo Fuwa), to pioneer a policy of independence from both Beijing and Moscow, and it gave rise to statements such as the one in support of Dubcěk during the 1968 Czech crisis. The JCP edged toward a reconciliation with Moscow, sending a delegation to the CPSU's twenty-fourth congress in March 1971 (it had not been present at the previous congress in 1966), but matters proceeded slowly, and it did not attend the twenty-fifth congress in February 1976.

The effort to normalize relations led the CPSU and the JCP to sign a joint statement of reconciliation in Moscow on December 25, 1979, but a new stumbling block appeared when, two days later, the Soviets moved into Afghanistan. At the twenty-sixth congress of the CPSU in February 1981, the JCP denounced the Brezhnev Doctrine, explicitly citing Afghanistan, and a series of polemical exchanges ensued.

Moscow's troubles with the JCP stem from a variety of causes. Ideologically, the JCP has over a period of years been discarding traditional formulations such as the "dictatorship of the proletariat" in favor of "the power of the laboring class," which lacks the threatening overtones associated with "dictatorship," and it rejects Moscow's attempts to reassert domination over the world communist movement, contending that "there is no such thing as a 'leading party.'" On foreign policy the JCP has become a tenacious advocate of the Soviet return of all the Kuril Islands, not just the "northern territories." Although eliciting denunciations from Moscow for "chauvinistic, nationalistic attitudes," the JCP's ultranationalist stand is designed to help the party "erase its prewar image as an alien group organized and manipulated by the Communist International in Moscow" and to overcome its relative isolation at home.[21]

Relations between the CPSU and the JCP started to improve in 1984. After suffering a sharp electoral setback the previous year, the Japanese Communists responded to Soviet overtures for the two to cooperate in using the nuclear issue "to organize a kind of anti-nuclear international united front": as the only country in the world that has been atom-bombed, Japan was the place to give particular attention to the anti-nuclear issue in 1985, "the 40th anniversary of Hiroshima and Nagasaki," thereby associating the JCP with an issue that could not help but prove popular and generate anti-American feelings.[22] Under Gorbachev the gradual improvement in relations between the two parties has continued. A JCP delegation attended the Soviet party congress in 1986, and high-level meetings have taken place on a regular basis. Moscow has a strong interest in nurturing the relationship with this well-organized, well-positioned party because, beyond "the visible legal party, there is the potential for secret infiltration of labor unions (particularly those composed of government employees, who are more radical than their counterparts in the private sector), industry, the educational network, and even Japanese security forces."[23] It also seeks to encourage the JCP's opposition to the U.S.-Japanese security pact, U.S. "imperialism" in Asia, Beijing's growing ties to the United States, and the possibility of a Washington-Beijing-Tokyo axis. Japan's emergence as a leading world power lends new significance to Moscow's multilayered connections with a prominent Communist party, many of whose activities, overt and covert, bring tangible benefit to the Soviet Union.

The Kremlin's Dilemmas

How is Soviet foreign policy affected or apt to be affected by Eurocommunism? An obviously complex question, this needs to be differentiated from the more general considerations of the relationship between the Soviet Union and the weblike phenomenon known as the world Communist movement. If Soviet foreign-policy priorities are seen as avoidance of nuclear war, maintenance of the cohesion of the USSR and its imperial system in Eastern Europe and promotion of peaceful coexistence and détente with the West—with all that this entails for Soviet leaders in trade, technological borrowing, and forestalling a stronger NATO—then it can be stated with reasonable certainty that Eurocommunism does not now affect the overall strategic balance between the Soviet Union and its prime adversary, the United States, or the USSR's military hegemony in Eastern Europe. The Soviet capability to pursue these specific objectives is not fundamentally weakened by the phenomenon of *nonruling* Communist parties playing a more assertive role in their respective polities and speaking out more frequently and forcefully in ways critical of the USSR's past and present authority within the world Communist movement. The erosion of Soviet authority in this sphere does not directly affect its capacity for conducting a multifaceted diplomacy in other spheres that touch more concretely on vital Soviet security interests.

Yet, the Kremlin realizes that Eurocommunism does pose long-term challenges for Soviet foreign policy (1) globally, within the world Communist movement; (2) regionally, within the bloc, especially in Eastern Europe; (3) diplomatically, in relations with the countries of Western Europe; and (4) internally, in intraparty debates on the proper strategy and tactics to adopt in dealing with the capitalist world.

First, at the global level, Eurocommunism further weakens Soviet authority within the world Communist movement. What Titoism began and the Sino–Soviet split aggravated, Eurocommunism chips away at still more—namely, Moscow's loss of its leading role in guiding the policies of foreign Communist parties in ways that effectively supplement Soviet diplomatic activities. The additional leverage Moscow once had through the calibrated manipulation of unconventional diplomacy has significantly waned. Diversity has superseded monolithism, complexity supplanted simplicity, and criticism replaced blind acceptance of abrupt political turnabouts. Moscow can no longer summarily issue commands to foreign Communist parties. When it acts as it did in Hungary in 1956 or Czechoslovakia in 1968, it must expect dissonance and disillusionment among foreign Communists. Thus far, the price has not been too high.

Second, in Eastern Europe, Eurocommunist formulations may encourage indigenous reformers to demand greater autonomy, thereby intensifying the danger that another "Czech spring" will break out elsewhere in the bloc. If Moscow did not trust the Czechoslovak leadership to superintend the internal liberalization in 1968, fearing that the Czech virus might spread, it must be even more anxious over the continual flow of heretical and fermenting ideas from West European Communists to their comrades in Eastern Europe, not to mention the difficulty of squelching ideas such as equality of parties, nonintervention in party affairs, and respect for the right of each party to find its own road to socialism—principles that the Soviet leadership seemingly accepted at Moscow in 1969 and East Berlin in 1976. Soviet leaders have shown little tolerance for deviations from the political and institutional forms that were grafted onto Eastern Europe after 1945. For them to tolerate the validity of the pluralist and democratic procedures formally espoused by the PCI and PCE would be to give inadvertent support and legitimacy to dissidents in Eastern Europe, and ultimately even in the Soviet Union.

In theory, at least, there is no reason for East European parties not to covet for themselves what their counterparts profess in Western Europe, but the spillover effect could prove politically dangerous. Soviet leaders know, and fear, that "Eurocommunism is a promising source of ideological justification and political leverage" for the East Europeans in their quest for greater independence from Moscow:

> It tends to reinforce the image East Europeans have always had of their historic role in Europe as a bridge between East and West and, more recently, as a kind of ideological potting shed for the introduction of Western ideas into the Soviet Union.[24]

Moscow knows enough about the unanticipated consequences of social and political forces to sense the threat to its East European imperium that lies untapped in some unforeseen mixture of Eurocommunist ideas, "the potential effects of Basket III of the Helsinki Final Act, and the economic difficulties in some countries of the Eastern bloc."[25]

Third, Soviet government-to-government relations with key countries in Western Europe could be adversely affected if the local Communist parties were in a position to influence their countries' foreign policy, either through participating in a coalition government or through coming to power on their own, because the closer a Communist party comes to power, the more difficult becomes the Soviet task of exploiting divisions within the capitalist world. Indeed, Moscow's chances to establish and maintain close diplomatic relations with a non-Communist government are better when the nonruling Communist party is weak to the degree that its non-Communist rivals perceive it as no domestic threat. Moscow has traditionally tried to maintain good interparty and interstate relations and has been careful to keep the two components of its foreign relations separate. Occasionally, as in Indonesia in the early 1960s and the Sudan in 1971, internal conflicts between the party and the state have created government-to-government tensions. But in the main, Soviet diplomacy has successfully promoted good relations with a government while at the same time managing good relations with the Communist party challenging the policies of that government.

If a Communist party did come to power, Moscow would make the appropriate accommodation. However, judging by past experiences with China, North Korea, Yugoslavia, and Albania, it has no reason for assuming that a Communist accession to power in Western Europe would automatically be a net gain for Soviet foreign policy. Indeed, since such a development would undoubtedly exacerbate pressures in Eastern Europe for greater independence, Moscow may well prefer that Eurocommunists remain perennially in the opposition. It knows that the more nationalistic Communist parties become, the less compliant they are apt to be to its wishes. Bolshevization is a thing of the past and Stalinism is passé. Autonomist propensities spell trouble.

Finally, Soviet leaders are divided on how to deal with Eurocommunism. We may therefore expect to see all kinds of zigs and zags in Moscow's responses, ranging from polemical campaigns in the vein of the Carrillo–*Novoe vremya* affair to frequent party get-togethers to keep the lid on the more serious disputes to cooperation with contentious parties, such as the JCP, on specific issues that can bridge the political-ideological divide. As far back as the early 1970s, "the ever-present duality between Soviet *raison d'état* and revolutionary commitment" was taking on particular intensity in the intra-Kremlin debate on how to respond to revolutionary situations, first in Chile and then in Portugal, with Soviet hard-liners such as Mikhail Suslov and Konstantin Zarodov favoring preservation of the party's separate identity, direct action, and the use of revolutionary means to gain power, and moderates such as Leonid Brezhnev and Vadim V. Zagladin leaning toward coalition-building, electoral alliances, and a gradual transition toward socialism.[26] Soviet writings acknowledge that Soviet leaders differ on the implications of Eurocommunism for Soviet foreign policy.

Moscow distrusts Eurocommunism. Its criticisms, forcefully stated in the campaign against Carrillo, have been expressed even more astringently by East European surrogates. Thus, the Bulgarian party leader, Todor Zhivkov, labeled the "so-called Eurocommunism" an anti-Soviet creation of the class enemy, and Vasil Bilak, the secretary of the Czechoslovak CP Central Committee, said, "Its content is traitorous. It is a deliberate effort to split the international Communist movement according to geographical zones and various regions, to incite all that breaks the unity of our movement."[27] These sentiments mirror Moscow's real feelings toward West European Communist parties, which it sees "much as Lenin had viewed the Bolsheviks': namely, 'Better fewer but better.' What the CPSU—both the statesmen and the ideologues—wanted from the PCI (as from the French and Spanish Communists) was that it grow in orthodoxy, not in numbers. Given a choice, the Kremlin leaders—if their past conduct was any clue to the future—would prefer to see the Italian Communists [for example] remain in the opposition rather than become a coalition partner in the national government of Italy."[28]

To begin with, in the absence of the Red Army, Moscow knows that there is nothing it can do to prevent foreign Communists from speaking out, short of excommunicating them or breaking up the entire movement, which is probably what would happen if it tried the tactics of 1948 in the 1980s. Its authority is no longer sufficient to intimidate a maverick into silent submission to Moscow's views on the promotion of world revolution. Lacking Lenin's moral stature or Stalin's coercive apparatus, Gorbachev must rely on persuasion and consensus—time-consuming, untidy, and often frustrating procedures.

Furthermore, Moscow finds the support given by the West European Communist parties to Soviet foreign policy positions more than ample recompense for the ideological and political difficulties these parties cause. Soviet proposals usually (though not always, as we have already seen) meet with their unqualified approval on a wide and significant range of issues including disarmament, the Middle East, opposition to the modernization of nuclear and conventional forces, the establishment of nuclear-free zones, and criticism of U.S. policy. The net effect is reinforcement for Moscow's general foreign-policy line. If not exactly a Trojan horse, the Communists and their affiliated, manipulated Communist-front organizations help mold public opinion in ways congenial to the promotion of Soviet foreign-policy aims in Europe, and this is what matters most to Moscow. If the Communists were to come to power, they would most probably not become Soviet puppets, but their success would undoubtedly weaken U.S. influence, which would suit Moscow just fine.

Next, for all the attention given in the West to the Eurocommunist challenge to the Soviet Union, Moscow senses that it is an even more immediate problem for the United States and its NATO allies. NATO's southern flank is beset with rivalries and serious internal difficulties, and leftist revolutions or parliamentary triumphs are not impossible. A sizable Communist component in the government of Greece, Portugal, Italy, Spain, or France could destabilize NATO (the entry of Communists into the coalition government of Iceland in 1978 did not produce any changes in foreign policy, but Iceland's homogeneous, democratic society is quite different from those of NATO's Mediterranean members).

In addition, Moscow temporizes with the would-be Eurocommunists because it realizes that they need Moscow as much as Moscow needs them. However much they may criticize Moscow on this doctrinal point or that foreign-policy issue, they will not—they dare not—split with Moscow, because without affiliation with the Soviet Union they are just another political party, which the faithful would quit in disillusionment and for which they would find a substitute elsewhere.

The West European Communists may criticize Moscow to display their independence to their countrymen and enhance their internal prestige for electoral contests, but they will not reject the mythology of the Bolshevik Revolution and the Soviet role in building socialism. Nor have they so far been willing to democratize their party organizations. Every Communist party remains totalitarian, a state within a state. Each is hierarchically structured to prevent grass-roots revolts and is led by a small elite of tough, shrewd, pragmatic leaders, whose first commandment is "Thou shalt stay in power." Their followers follow for a number of reasons, an essential one being the umbilical tie to the Soviet Union. Party leaderships have tiffs with Moscow and temporarily remain aloof from intraparty gatherings, but they usually return to the fold.

Soviet leaders know it is important for West European Communist leaders to present an independent and democratic image, but they are not always certain how to react to a Carrillo or a Berlinguer. Aware that human rights are one of the most sensitive issues for Western parties, they continue to harass and imprison dissidents and to refuse visas to those wishing to emigrate. They persevere because of their confidence that in any showdown their foreign constituencies would be reluctant to leave the fold.

Despite this, Moscow distrusts Eurocommunists; it has always been opposed to foreign Communist leaders acting together outside of its orbit. Much of this distrust is explainable in terms of Soviet paranoia, whose traditional Russian antecedents are compounded by a heavy overlay of Leninist secretiveness and suspicion of the outside world; some stems from a reluctance to lose any of the leverage that comes with control of the world Communist movement. The Kremlin deals with oppositionists in the non-ruling parties in a number of ways: (1) quiet diplomacy, in which the International Department of the CPSU's Central Committee plays a key role in disseminating the official line and trying to bring recalcitrant Communists into the fold; (2) limited political warfare that utilizes the non-Communist bourgeois press to put forward, through interviews given by leading Soviet officials, rebuttals of criticisms leveled at Moscow by foreign Communists and that seeks to drive a wedge between the local

Communist factions in an effort to find and foster individuals who are pro-Moscow and in this way build up pressures inside the local party to fashion a policy congenial to the USSR; (3) publication of the journal *Problems of Peace and Socialism,* officially sponsored by sixty-nine Communist parties and located and printed in Prague in thirty-two languages; and (4) the convening of multilateral gatherings, regional party conferences, and meetings of Communist-front organizations, such as the World Peace Council and the World Federation of Democratic Youth.

Finally, Eurocommunism is a pill that Moscow swallows to keep alive its pretensions to ecumenism. Moscow needs the international movement not only to justify the legitimacy of its ideology and of one-party rule in the USSR, but also because "a total break with major Communist parties could possibly prove even more harmful to the internal legitimacy of the Soviet-bloc regimes than proclamation of even serious heresies by those nonruling parties while still in communion with the ruling ones."[29] Its belief in the utility of the world Communist movement for the promotion of Soviet foreign-policy interests helps explain the Kremlin's readiness "not only to grant the nonruling parties an almost complete autonomy with regard to strategy and tactics [which cannot in any event be proscribed], but also to react to deviations from the Soviet interpretations of Communist doctrine and to public critiques of Soviet and Soviet-bloc actions with comparative moderation, and to confine attempts to exert pressure in cases they consider extreme chiefly to nonpublic channels."[30] After all, if Moscow has been shaken by Eurocommunism, imagine how the Eurocommunists had been shaken by de-Stalinization and détente.

On a number of occasions, Gorbachev acknowledged the diversity within the world Communist movement and the independence of individual parties. At the twenty-seventh CPSU congress in February 1986, he noted that there cannot be "an identity of views on all issues":

> We consider that the variety of our movement is not a synonym for disjointedness, just as unity has nothing in common with uniformity, with a hierarchy, with interference by some parties in the affairs of others, with an aspiration by any party for a monopoly on truth. The Communist movement can and must be strong through its class solidarity and the equal cooperation of all fraternal parties in the struggle for common goals. That is how the CPSU understands unity and it intends to foster it in every way.[31]

At a meeting commemorating the seventieth anniversary of the Bolshevik Revolution, he said that "the days of the Comintern . . . and even of binding international conferences have passed; but the international Communist movement exists":

> All parties are fully and irreversibly independent. We said that as long ago as the 20th congress. True, it took time to free ourselves from the old

> habits. Now, however, this is an immutable reality. . . . The movement is open to dialogue, to cooperation, to interaction and alliance with all other revolutionary, democratic, and progressive forces.[32]

The policy-relevant significance of this expressed desire for reconciliation and cooperation with all foreign Communist parties has yet to be determined.

From the foregoing analysis, we may hazard a number of propositions concerning the *present* relationship between Soviet foreign policy and the world Communist movement, to help fix the areas and limits of its importance to Moscow.

First, the significance of international communism as a tool of Soviet foreign policy is greatly exaggerated. The core of the Soviet threat, whether to the West, China, Japan, or the Third World, is military and political, not ideological or subversive, though the latter aspects of foreign policy are occasionally effective, as with the coup in Afghanistan in April 1978. Nonruling Communist parties are rarely in a position to deliver—when and where Soviet policymakers want it—the kind of assistance that would make a difference in the promotion of concrete policy objectives.

Second, Western observers tend to overrate the extent of Soviet influence over nonruling Communist parties because of a persisting propensity to view all of them as compliant and effective proxies of Moscow and to attribute to these parties a capacity for influencing policy that few of them possess.

Third, the authority that Soviet leaders wield within the world Communist movement is constrained by Moscow's need to accommodate to divergent interests and outlooks, by ingrained opposition of nonruling Communist parties to Moscow's ever again acquiring the kind of authority it held prior to 1953, and by the evolutionary assertiveness of the independent Communist parties (for instance, Yugoslavia and Vietnam), as well as by the very range and increasing complexity of the foreign-policy issues that Moscow must deal with.

Fourth, the diversity and disunity of the movement is no charade intended to lull the West into inactivity. It is a real and permanent development, as momentous in its own way as the schism in the Christian church in the sixteenth century.

Finally, Soviet leaders continue to use the movement as best they can in their ongoing global rivalry with the United States.

Notes

1. Jane Degras, *Soviet Documents on Foreign Policy,* Vol. II (New York: Oxford University Press, 1952), 243.

2. For a particularly thoughtful discussion and application of these generalizations to the relationship between the Comintern and Soviet foreign policy, see Bernard S. Morris, *Communism, Revolution, and American Policy* (Durham: Duke University Press, 1987), 7–22.
3. *Ibid.,* 10.
4. *Ibid.,* 13.
5. Benjamin Schwartz, "Sino-Soviet Relations—The Question of Authority," *The Annals of the American Academy of Political and Social Science,* Vol. 349 (September 1963), 42.
6. *Ibid.,* 44.
7. Donald S. Zagoria, *The Sino-Soviet Conflict 1956-1961* (Princeton: Princeton University Press, 1962), 367–68.
8. William E. Griffith, "The November 1960 Moscow Meeting: A Preliminary Reconstruction," *The China Quarterly,* No. 11 (July–September 1962), 55.
9. *New York Times,* September 5, 1964.
10. For the best account of the background and significance of the East Berlin Conference of European Communist and Workers' Parties, see Kevin Devlin, "The Challenge of Eurocommunism," *Problems of Communism,* Vol. 26, No. 1 (January–February 1977), 1–18.
11. *Ibid.,* 3.
12. *Ibid.,* 5.
13. Robert F. Miller, "Eurocommunism and the Quest for Legitimacy," in T. H. Rigby and Ferenc Fehér (eds.), *Political Legitimation in Communist States* (New York: St. Martin's Press, 1982), 136.
14. U.S. Information Agency, Office of Research, *The European Communist Media Debate on the Santiago Carrillo-NOVOE VREMYA Controversy: Search for or Avoidance of a Definition of Eurocommunism* (R-25-77) (Washington, D.C.), November 15, 1977.
15. *The Guardian,* June 30, 1977.
16. *New York Times,* December 19, 1982.
17. Foreign Broadcast Information Service/ USSR, January 17, 1984, G11.
18. *Pravda,* January 24, 1982.
19. Rodger Swearingen, "Japanese Communism and the Moscow-Peking Axis," *The Annals of the American Academy of Social and Political Science,* Vol. 308 (November 1956), 63–75.
20. Sheldon W. Simon, "New Soviet Approaches to the Japanese Left," *Asian Survey,* Vol. 6, No. 6 (June 1966), 319–26.
21. Peter A. Berton, "Japanese Eurocommunists: Running in Place," *Problems of Communism,* Vol. XXXV, No. 4 (July–August 1986), 21.
22. *Ibid.,* 26.

23. *Ibid.*, 27.
24. Charles Gati, "The 'Europeanization' of Communism?" *Foreign Affairs,* Vol. 55, No. 3 (April 1977), 546.
25. Heinz Timmermann, "Eurocommunism: Moscow's Reaction and the Implications for Eastern Europe," *The World Today,* Vol. 33, No. 10 (October 1977), 379.
26. Joan Barth Urban, "Contemporary Soviet Perspectives on Revolution in the West," *Orbis,* Vol. 19, No. 4 (Winter 1976), 1360, 1391–96.
27. Kevin Devlin, "Comrade Bilak and the Eurocommunists," RFE Research, RAD Background Report/119 (June 22, 1977), 3.
28. Joan Barth Urban, *Moscow and the Italian Communist Party: From Togliatti to Berlinguer* (Ithaca: Cornell University Press, 1986), 350.
29. Richard Lowenthal, "Moscow and the 'Eurocommunists,'" *Problems of Communism,* Vol. 27, No. 4 (July–August 1978), 47.
30. *Ibid.*, 48.
31. FBIS/SOV/Party Congresses, February 26, 1986, O 33.
32. FBIS/SOV/GOSR 70th Anniversary, November 3, 1987, 59.

Selected Bibliography

ASPATURIAN, VERNON V., JIRI VALENTA, and DAVID P. BURKE (EDS.). *Eurocommunism Between the East and West.* Bloomington: Indiana University Press, 1980.

BORKENAU, FRANZ. *World Communism.* Ann Arbor: University of Michigan Press, 1962.

BRAUNTHAL, JULIUS. *History of the International: World Socialism 1943–1968.* Boulder: Westview Press, 1980.

BROWN, ANTHONY CAVE, and CHARLES B. MACDONALD. *On a Field of Red: The Communist International and the Coming of World War II.* New York: Putnam, 1982.

CLAUDIN, FERNANDO. *The Communist Movement: From Comintern to Cominform.* 2 vols. New York: Monthly Review Press, 1976.

GODSON, ROY, and STEPHEN HASLER. *"Eurocommunism": Implications for East and West.* London: Macmillan, 1978.

KINDERSLEY, RICHARD (ED.). *In Search of Eurocommunism.* New York: St. Martin's Press, 1981.

MCKENZIE, KERMIT E. *Comintern and World Revolution, 1928–1943.* New York: Columbia University Press, 1964.

MORRIS, BERNARD S. *Communism, Revolution, and American Policy.* Durham: Duke University Press, 1987.

SCALAPINO, ROBERT A. *The Japanese Communist Movement, 1920–1966.* Berkeley: University of California Press, 1967.

STAROBIN, JOSEPH R. *American Communism in Crisis, 1943–1957.* Cambridge: Harvard University Press, 1972.

STIEFBOLD, ANNETTE EISENBERG. *The French Communist Party in Transition: PCF-CPSU Relations and the Challenge to Soviet Authority.* New York: Praeger, 1977.

SWEARINGEN, RODGER, and PAUL LANGER. *Red Flag in Japan: International Communism in Action, 1919–1951.* Cambridge: Harvard University Press, 1952.

TIMMERMANN, HEINZ. *The Decline of the World Communist Movement: Moscow, Beijing, and the Communist Parties in the West.* Boulder: Westview Press, 1987.

TOKES, RUDOLF L. (ED). *Eurocommunism and Détente.* New York: New York University Press, 1979.

URBAN, JOAN BARTH. *Moscow and the Italian Communist Party: From Togliatti to Berlinguer.* (Ithaca: Cornell University Press, 1986).

12
Soviet Diplomacy in the United Nations

The antecedents of the Soviet attitude toward the United Nations are to be found in the Kremlin's ideological perceptions and diplomatic experience with the League of Nations. The League was created after World War I to preserve an international system based on capitalism and colonialism and epitomized the antithesis of the world revolution and anticolonialism propagated by Soviet and Comintern leaders. Dominated by Britain and France and their visceral fear of communism, it barred the USSR from membership. During the 1920-to-1934 period, Moscow saw it as an instrument of "imperialism" designed to promote the encirclement and eventual destruction of the Soviet state. Lenin called it "a League of bandits." Maxim Litvinov, then deputy foreign minister, termed it "a masked league" engaged in anti-Soviet intrigues. He said the Soviet Union had no desire to be a member, knowing that "it would then be confronted, in the form of partners, or even judges, with states, many of which have not even recognized it, and [which] consequently do not conceal their enmity toward it, and with others, even among those which have recognized it, which even now behaved toward it with ill-concealed hostility."[1]

Expediency, however, dictated accommodation. Global realignments of power prompted the Soviet Union and the Western powers to draw closer together in the face of the common threat from Hitler. When Hitler discarded Rapallo, Stalin could no longer rely on the special relationship with Germany. He turned to France, which was interested in reviving a variation of the pre-1914 Franco-Russian alliance against the threat of a strong and expansionist Germany. To ease the way for the Franco-Soviet rapprochement, which the French believed would be facilitated by Soviet membership, Stalin—who was increasingly concerned also over Japan's military threat in Manchuria and Korea—joined the League of Nations.

On September 18, 1934, in his maiden speech, Foreign Minister Litvinov sought to allay the League's anxieties over the presence of a Marxist-Leninist member in a bourgeois political organization:

> I should like further to state that the idea in itself of an association of nations contains nothing theoretically inacceptable for the Soviet state and its ideology. . . . The Soviet state has . . . never excluded the possibility of some form or other of association with states having a different political and social system, so long as there is no mutual hostility and if it is for the attainment of common aims.[2]

For the next few years, Litvinov championed the concept of collective security and tried to fashion an effective security arrangement with Britain and France. However, the Western sellout at Munich and Hitler's subsequent readiness (in contrast to Britain and France) to meet Stalin's stiff terms for friendship set in motion the chain of events that resulted in the Nazi–Soviet pact and the outbreak of World War II. The denouement of the Soviet Union's experience in the League came after its invasion of Finland; the League, already an anachronism in a dying era, denounced the USSR's aggression and expelled it from the organization on December 14, 1939.

As World War II drew to a close, the enthusiasm of the Western powers for a new international organization was not shared in Moscow, but Stalin obliged Roosevelt and Churchill once he had secure guarantees for safeguarding Soviet interests. The Soviet Union joined the United Nations as an act of accommodation, not out of conviction. Its aim was to ensure that the League's successor would not become an anti-Soviet alliance; and its participation was predicated on the assumption that the United Nations would function primarily to handle political and security problems, and that the ultimate responsibility for the maintenance of international peace and security would devolve upon the permanent members of the Security Council, the five great powers: the USSR, the United States, Britain, France, and China. In essence, Stalin envisaged an extension in peacetime of the wartime condominium of the United States, Britain, and the Soviet Union, which would preserve the peace, determine and respect spheres of influence, and settle disputes among themselves at clubby summit meetings. The USSR approved the UN Charter, but only after the inclusion of the veto power in the Security Council and the provision that amendments to the charter would be subject to the approval of the five permanent members.

Unlike influential private circles in the United States, Soviet leaders never had any illusions about what the UN was and what it was not. They considered the UN *"an inter-state organization, an organization of sovereign independent states":*

> As an inter-state organization, the United Nations does not, and cannot, stand above states; it is not and cannot be a self-sufficient body, independent of states. . . . It is for this reason that no United Nations body, except the Security Council, can take any decisions, binding on all member states of the Organization, on any question except administrative matters and procedural questions.[3]

There was no visionary interest in integration or supranational institutions. Soviet writers denounced all proposals to transform the UN into a world parliament, emphasizing that this would undermine the concept of national sovereignty.

The Early Years

The Cold War and the polarization of political alignments dominated the period from 1945 to 1953. From the very first session of the Security Council in January 1946, when the USSR was severely criticized for its failure to withdraw Soviet troops from Iran in accordance with the 1942 treaty among Iran, Britain, and the USSR, Moscow felt its isolated minority position in the UN. Its attention was riveted on issues directly affecting Soviet interests. To offset Western "mechanistic voting" majorities, the Soviet government used the veto, which Molotov strongly justified in a speech at the UN on September 14, 1946. He noted that the veto prevents one group of powers from organizing themselves to act against one or another of the five permanent members and that its very existence encourages frank discussions on disputed issues and provides an incentive for concessions and eventual agreement; and he pointed out that unlike the League, which in theory was built on the principle of equality of large and small states, the United Nations institutionalizes a process of ensuring that the interests of the great powers in matters of international peace and security are not ignored.

During the first postwar decade, the USSR exercised the veto eighty times, usually to keep out new members pending a deal with the United States on quid pro quos. The USSR has also used the veto to prevent attempts to interfere in any way with its hegemonial position in Eastern Europe and to assist client states. For example, in December 1971, during the Indo-Pakistani war, it vetoed a resolution calling for a cease-fire and troop withdrawals, because the Indian government, which was favored by Moscow, was not yet interested in halting military operations; and in July 1979, the mere threat of a veto was sufficient to terminate the UN Emergency Force (UNEF) operation in Sinai, a move favored by the anti-Sadat Arab states that Moscow was courting. In 1960 Khrushchev himself warned the General Assembly (which at the time was discussing possible revisions of the charter) that "if there is no veto, there will be no international organization; it will fall to pieces."

Stalin's only interest in the United Nations was to ensure that it would not serve an anti-Soviet function or interfere with the realization of Soviet objectives in Eastern Europe. Moscow thwarted all UN efforts to function in that region; it denounced UN reports implicating the Communist governments of Albania, Bulgaria, and Yugoslavia for their role in fueling the Greek civil war, and it refused entry to economic survey missions and investigators of human rights violations. The USSR also tried to keep the UN's authority as circumscribed as possible. It interpreted the concept of national sovereignty to mean the exclusion of any outside interference in the domestic affairs of Soviet-bloc countries.

But consistency is not a strong card in the ongoing international game of weakening the enemy. When the target of interference was non-Communist countries, especially Western-dominated colonial areas, adherence to a narrow interpretation of the charter's provisions on sovereignty and nonintervention in the domestic affairs of member states was supplanted by espousal of the principles of national self-determination and the need to act against "threats to international peace." These principles were given a very broad interpretation by Soviet officials, who wished to align themselves with Third World countries and undermine the overseas empires of the Western powers.

During the Stalin period, the USSR was slow to perceive the advantages of active participation in the UN. Wedded to the two-camp conception of international alignments, Moscow made tactical errors on colonial questions, alienating Indonesia, India, and the Philippines, among others; and its support for the creation of Israel in 1948 alienated the Arabs. A miscalculation with far-reaching consequences occurred in January 1950, when the USSR abruptly walked out of the Security Council, the General Assembly, and the other UN bodies over the question of Chinese representation; Moscow argued that the People's Republic of China, proclaimed on October 1, 1949, and not the Kuomintang regime of Chiang Kai-shek, was the legitimate government of China and should be seated in the Security Council. The USSR announced a boycott of all UN organizations and activities until the PRC's admission was procured. The resultant absence of the Soviet Union at the time of the North Korean aggression on June 25, 1950, enabled the Security Council to pass resolutions calling for the cessation of hostilities, the withdrawal of North Korean forces from South Korea, and the rendering of all possible assistance to South Korea by UN members. No doubt Moscow assumed that the UN, like the

League, would take no effective action to repel the aggression; hence its absence from the council. It returned on August 1, 1950, but too late to block the UN's authorization of a police action to "restore international security in the area."

The Western powers, realizing that the Security Council's decisiveness had been possible only because of the absence of the Soviet delegate, used their commanding voting majority in the General Assembly to pass the Uniting for Peace Resolution on November 3, 1950. This stipulates that if, because of the lack of unanimity of its five permanent members, the Security Council fails to act in a situation threatening international peace and security, the General Assembly itself may discuss the problem and recommend appropriate measures, including the use of armed forces. The effect of the American-engineered resolution was a de facto amendment of the charter and an enhanced role for the General Assembly in the sphere of security affairs. The Soviet Union condemned the resolution on the grounds that the Security Council is the sole body responsible under the charter for initiating and implementing measures to preserve the peace, and that the assumption of such authority by the General Assembly was illegal; and that the procedures for amending the charter had been violated. (Ironically, by the 1970s, it was the United States that bitterly criticized the General Assembly's arrogation of powers as unwarranted and contrary to the charter and that objected to interpretations of the charter as too flexible.)

It was during the Korean War that the Soviet leadership came to the realization that participation in the United Nations was important, not just to prevent the UN's being used by the United States as an anti-Soviet instrument, but to establish closer relations with the emerging Afro-Asian group of nonaligned countries, which were neither Western puppets nor necessarily opposed to policies advantageous to Moscow. Moscow perceived that it could actively exploit, not merely thwart, the UN to keep the West on the defensive and strengthen the international position of the Soviet Union. Stalin's death brought a new flexibility and activism to Soviet policy in the UN.

Decolonization

The process of decolonization has now been virtually completed, but in the early postwar years the issue of independence for colonial areas occupied a central place in UN deliberations. From the beginning Moscow staked out a position in the UN debates that placed it in the vanguard of anticolonialism. The USSR did not face any agonizing dilemmas; its imperial system did not include Asian or African territories agitating for independence. Moscow generally applauded the mushrooming national liberation movements, including peoples' wars waged against colonial regimes. But though aware that such struggles weakened its Western rivals, Moscow offered only moral support and rhetorical encouragement during the first postwar decade. That it did not offer tangible assistance can perhaps be explained in part by its absorption with internal reconstruction, consolidation of Soviet rule in Eastern Europe, and an unwillingness to confront American power in areas lying outside the Soviet imperium, and in part by a lack of capability for projecting military power.

Such ambitions as the USSR had in 1945 to become the administering authority for one of the trusteeships that were to be established for former Italian colonies, that is, Libya and Somaliland, were blocked by the United States. But the Soviet Union did join the call in the United Nations for the dismantling of the British, French, Dutch, and Portuguese overseas empires. As India, Burma, Ceylon, Indonesia, and the Philippines became independent, Moscow was ideologically supportive but otherwise passive, precluded from any active role by geographical distance, ignorance of local conditions, isolation in the UN, the absence of meaningful contacts with Asian national liberation leaders, and military inferiority.

By the mid-1950s, when the anticolonial movement assumed an increasingly radical bent, Moscow moved into the Third World, with a view toward hastening the end of Western domination and establishing a permanent Soviet presence. In rapid succession it extended aid to Afghanistan, India, Burma, Egypt, Indonesia, Iraq, and Guinea. In 1960, seventeen new nations—sixteen of them African—became independent and members of the UN. Premier Khrushchev shrewdly seized the moment to propose a declaration, subsequently adopted in modified form as General Assembly Resolution 1514 (XV), embodying the most radical denunciation of colonialism in all of its aspects and calling for the independence of all colonial countries and peoples. The abstention by the Western powers enhanced the political impact of the Soviet proposal among the African and Asian leaders.

The following year the Soviet Union again laid claim to a bold initiative, proposing the establishment of the Special Committee on the Situation with Regard to the Implementation of the Declaration on the Granting of Independence to Colonial Countries and Peoples (known informally as the Special Committee of Twenty-four) to ensure that Resolution 1514 (XV) was implemented and decolonization brought to a successful completion. Under the weight of its African membership, the committee militantly pressed for independence of the Portuguese colonies (Angola, Mozambique, Guinea-Bissau) and of Zimbabwe (Rhodesia); and since the late 1970s, it has zeroed in on South Africa and urged independence for Namibia, the former German colony of Southwest Africa that was taken over by South Africa after World War I and administered as a possession until the late 1970s, when Pretoria grudgingly acquiesced to Namibia's independence, on the condition that Cuban and Soviet troops first leave Angola.

The Soviet Union has supported radical Afro-Asian resolutions in the General Assembly (regarding them as recommendations only, albeit ones requiring careful attention, and not as legally binding obligations under international law); but in the Security Council, it shies away from the demands of the militants for military action under the Uniting for Peace Resolution. Thus, in the General Assembly, it cultivates its image as a concerned anticolonialist power, while in the Security Council, it opposes any broadening of UN operational responsibilities or financial levies on member states. Because it had no direct links with Afro-Asian colonial areas and could not bring influence to bear on Britain, France, or Portugal outside the framework of the UN, the USSR used the UN as the forum in which it could directly address itself to the decolonization issue and hope to exert some leverage, if only by exhortation and escalatory, declaratory initiatives. For Moscow, the colonial issue has gone a long way politically.

Peacekeeping

United Nations peacekeeping operations have become useful adjuncts of the USSR's efforts on behalf of Third World clients and exploitation of tensions between the Western powers and developing countries. Moscow's policy has been quintessentially Leninist, judging each operation in terms of Soviet interests and of its effect on U.S.–Soviet rivalry in the region involved. Soviet leaders have not tried to establish precedents or principles to guide future UN efforts, but rather have acted only to take whatever advantage a particular crisis offered them.

The first UN peacekeeping operation was organized after the combined British, French, and Israeli attack on Egypt at the end of October 1956 and the paralysis of the Security Council because of the British and French veto. Though in principle deploring the General Assembly's allegedly unconstitutional assumption of authority for international security under the Uniting for Peace Resolution, the Soviet Union in practice was not averse to the resolution's application to the 1956 Middle East crisis, and merely abstained when the assembly created the United Nations Emergency Force (though it formally objected to financing the operation by levies assessed on all member states, insisting that the aggressors should bear the costs). UNEF suited Soviet aims: to bring about a withdrawal of British, French, and Israeli forces; to preserve

Nasser in power; to weaken the position of Britain and France in the Middle East; and to sow discord in NATO.

At the same time, however, Moscow bitterly opposed the General Assembly's attempted intercession in the Hungarian crisis of November 1956, arguing that the "unrest" was purely an internal matter and came under the domestic jurisdiction of the Hungarian government—despite the presence of 5000 Soviet tanks and 250,000 Soviet troops. In this instance, it invoked Article 2, paragraph 7 of the UN Charter, which says that the United Nations shall not "intervene in matters which are essentially within the domestic jurisdiction of any state" nor shall it "require members to submit such matters to settlement." Eastern Europe was off limits to the United Nations.

In the Congo crisis of mid-1960, the USSR approved the United Nations Peacekeeping Operation in the Congo (ONUC) in order "to ensure the immediate and unconditional withdrawal of the Belgian troops," but soon reversed itself when the possibility of acquiring a foothold in the Congo disappeared. It has not opposed the United Nations Force in Cyprus (UNFICYP), created in March 1964 to keep Greek and Turkish Cypriots separated, in part because the operation has been financed by voluntary contributions, in part because the nonaligned government of Cyprus has favored the peacekeeping operation, and in part because Moscow considers that festering tensions are useful in its attempt to improve relations with Greece and Turkey and weaken NATO's southern flank. Even though the Turks intervened in July 1974 and established military control over 40 percent of the island—where according to Ankara, they will remain until a settlement that safeguards the rights of the Turkish Cypriot community is concluded—Moscow continues to give its approval, but no funding, to the semiannual renewals of UNFICYP's mandate, an indication of the importance that it places on maintaining good relations with Turkey.

In 1964–1965, the Soviet Union's unwillingness to help finance the peacekeeping operations that it supported politically precipitated a major crisis in the UN. At issue was the Soviet conception of what should be the outer limits to political and economic commitments by UN organizations. The USSR (as well as France) refused to pay its assessed share of the UNEF and ONUC operations on the ground that they were not legal, having been authorized by the General Assembly and not the Security Council. As mentioned, it maintained that the charter invests the Security Council with the sole responsibility for defining the terms, including the financial terms, under which armed forces may be employed by the UN to maintain international peace and security. To substitute the General Assembly or the UN Secretariat for the Security Council (and its Military Staff Committee) is to undermine the principle of great-power unanimity that is embodied in the charter and that must be controlling in situations involving the use of armed forces under UN auspices. Moscow dismissed the July 1962 advisory opinion of the International Court of Justice, which ruled that the UNEF and ONUC operations were legitimate expenses of the United Nations and thus subject to the budgetary authority of the General Assembly, as devoid of legal value, since advisory opinions are not binding on the parties. Also, in company with such other countries as France and the Arab nations, the USSR insisted that full responsibility for these operations must be borne by the countries most directly responsible for their having been undertaken by the United Nations.

The financial crisis erupted in late 1964, at the nineteenth session of the General Assembly, when the United States delegation contended that Article 19 of the charter should be invoked against delinquent countries. Under this article, a nation that falls two years behind in paying its assessments "shall have no vote in the General Assembly." With Moscow threatening to withdraw from the UN—having refused to pay its assessment in the regular UN budget for activities it considered illegal—the General Assembly adjourned in February 1965 without debating the issue. The crisis passed soon thereafter, only because the United States, sensing the reluctance of the membership to implement Article 19, decided not to press the issue. From time to time, Moscow indicated that it would make a "voluntary contribution" to help ease the UN deficit caused by peacekeeping expenditures, but not until September 1987 did it do so (see below).

Political considerations have determined the USSR's policy on peacekeeping, as developments in the Middle East have shown. In the aftermath of the Suez War of October 1956, UNEF contingents were stationed in Gaza and Sinai and for one decade helped create a situation that allowed the uneasy truce between the Egyptians and the Israelis; but Nasser's summary termination of the UNEF presence on May 18, 1967, set in motion the chain of events that triggered the Arab-Israeli war of June 5 to 10, 1967. In the wake of the Egyptian defeat and with the approval of the Security Council, the secretary-general assigned UN observers to the Suez Canal zone, but they played a minor role.

After the 1973 October War, the Security Council, with Soviet approval, established two peacekeeping forces to preserve the peace and uphold the interim agreements reached between Israel and Egypt, and Israel and Syria: a second UNEF in Sinai, and the United Nations Disengagement Observer Force (UNDOF) on the Golan Heights. During the 1974-to-1978 period, the USSR went along with a series of six-month extensions because the Arab states wanted them. However, Egyptian President Anwar Sadat's decision to sign a separate peace treaty with Israel on March 26, 1979, polarized the Arab world and precipitated Soviet opposition to a renewal of UNEF, that is, the UN units supervising the gradual

Israeli withdrawal from Sinai and safeguarding the peace in that sector. Rather than incur a Soviet veto, Washington accepted the withdrawal of the 4000-man armed force on July 24, 1979, and the substitution of the unarmed United Nations Truce Supervisory Organization (UNTSO), which has operated in different parts of the world since 1949 and which is directly responsible to the Security Council, unlike UNEF; and it is a part of a non-UN policing force.

Just as the USSR's opposition to UNEF's continuation was in deference to the wishes of the Arab states opposed to Sadat's treaty with Israel, so its support for UNDOF's renewals has been conditioned by the desires of Syria, Moscow's prime client in the Arab world. Since May 1974, UNDOF's 1300-man force has supervised the ceasefire and disengagement between Syria and Israel on the Golan Heights, which has remained quiet even during the worst period of Israeli-Syrian fighting in Lebanon's Bekaa Valley in the summer of 1982.

In late February 1984, the Soviet government vetoed a French proposal to create a UN peacekeeping force for Beirut that was intended to replace the dismantled eighteen-month effort of the four-nation (USA, France, Britain, and Italy) non-UN multinational force to protect the beleaguered Lebanese government of Amin Gemayel. As with the cases of UNEF, UNDOF, and UNIFIL (the United Nations Force in Lebanon established in March 1978 as a way of forestalling Israeli intervention in strife-torn southern Lebanon), Moscow took its cue from Damascus.

The first sign of a change in Soviet policy came on April 18, 1986, when the USSR voted with the fourteen other members of the UN Security Council to renew UNIFIL's mandate for another three months, whereas on previous votes it had abstained. Even more unexpected was the Soviet delegate's statement that Moscow intended to pay its assessed share of the UN operation.

On September 17, 1987, in a major article in *Pravda,* Gorbachev proposed the wider use of "UN military observers and UN peacekeeping forces in disengaging the troops of warring sides, and observing ceasefire and armistice agreements." The plan would also entail greater use of the permanent members of the UN Security Council, who could act as guarantors of regional security; cooperation in "uprooting international terrorism"; and more frequent use of the International Court of Justice "for consultative conclusions on international law disputes." Initial reaction to Gorbachev's proposals was one of skepticism, in part because six days later Foreign Minister Shevardnadze suggested that the United Nations should take over from the United States and the West European countries the responsibility for ensuring the safety of navigation in the Persian Gulf.

On October 15, Gorbachev's sweeping proposals for revitalization of

UN functions—not just in the area of peacekeeping—gained credibility when the Soviet government announced that it was paying its $225 million debt to the UN, of which $197 million was for peacekeeping operations and $28 million for the regular budget. With this sharp policy reversal, Gorbachev enhanced Soviet prestige and highlighted U.S. indebtedness, which is larger than any other country's. There is speculation that "Moscow may want a stronger United Nations to help extricate it from numerous Third World conflicts with a minimum loss of face"; and also that it is seeking "a propaganda victory at America's expense, posing as the champion of internationalism at a time when the United States is growing increasingly disenchanted with this role."[4] It will be some time before the policy implications of this new Soviet attitude toward UN peacekeeping can be assessed. In the short term, Moscow gained plaudits, but not votes, as the UN General Assembly passed resolutions criticizing the Soviet Union's intervention in Afghanistan and support for Vietnam's occupation of Kampuchea and did not adopt Gorbachev's call for a committee to implement his plan for a comprehensive system of international security (CSIS).

Global Issues

The growing politicization of the less-developed countries (LDCs) and the escalation of their demands for a New International Economic Order (NIEO) have been applauded by the Soviet Union, which sees these pressures weakening the international system long dominated by the Western powers. Yet Moscow's actions on behalf of the LDCs bear little resemblance to its principled declarations. On issue after issue, when push comes to shove, its approach is to safeguard Soviet state interests and refuse to contribute in any significant fashion, arguing that the problems are a legacy of colonialism and imperialism, and hence the responsibility of the Western countries. The USSR's approach is best exemplified in its record on the issues of economic development, the law of the sea, environmental protection, and food to the needy.

Economic development. During the Stalinist period, the Soviet Union did not contribute "one Red ruble" to UN programs designed to promote the development of the new nations. Soviet delegates criticized the West's emphasis on agriculture and light industry and, oblivious of the resource base and immediate needs of developing countries, insisted that only heavy industry could make the countries truly independent. They opposed any kind of direct investment, saying that it led inevitably to political interference, but refused to assist in the creation of a fund that would instead disburse loans and credits, allegedly because the amounts contemplated were inadequate to the task. Nonparticipation in any of the UN economic and technical assistance programs was the policy.

When Stalin died this damaging legacy was ended, and the USSR began to contribute to UN technical assistance programs. It sought thereby to make its bilateral assistance, which it was then dangling before developing countries, respectable and desirable. The Soviet courtship of the LDCs in turn induced Soviet participation in UN activities, though Moscow was more interested in image-building than nation-building. It opposed the view that aid should be given primarily in the form of grants and insisted that the problem "could not be solved by the creation of a charitable society." Neither the establishment of the Special Fund in 1959 nor the UN Capital Development Fund in 1966 brought forth any generous Soviet response. Moscow's niggardliness reinforced the impression that its small contributions to UN programs was the price it paid to play power politics in the United Nations.

In the 1950s and 1960s, Soviet delegates argued to often-sympathetic delegates that "the principal sources of means for the economic development of underdeveloped countries should be their own exploitation of their natural resources and natural wealth." The elites of these countries found the Soviet diagnosis of their economic backwardness plausible, sufficiently familiar inessentials to be readily accepted, and comforting to believe, as it relieved them of any responsibility for their present malaise and instead blamed foreign rule, exploitation of national wealth by foreign monopolies, forced dependence upon a single crop, and lack of industry.

In the 1970s, especially after the dazzling success of the OPEC nations in revolutionizing their economic situation and the adoption by the nonaligned movement at its 1973 summit meeting in Algiers of a charter for a New International Economic Order, the LDCs deluged the General Assembly with resolutions for redistributing the world's wealth. In particular, at the United Nations Conference on Trade and Development (UNCTAD), first convened in 1964 and then in 1968, 1972, 1976, 1979, and 1983, they pressed for higher commodity prices, lower tariffs, concessionary loans, more favorable terms of trade, and debt rescheduling.

Moscow's reaction to all of this has been to play up the anti-Western, anti-imperialist, and anti-colonial animus underlying LDC demands and to repudiate Western efforts to link the industrialized capitalist and Soviet-bloc socialist states together or to equate "the socialist community countries with the imperialist countries." Despite its oft-proclaimed sympathy for the plight of needy Third World countries, the Soviet Union offered little and played an insignificant part in UN deliberations. It consistently opposes recommendations for new international funds to be provided by "rich" developed countries, of which it is one, arguing that new investment could be obtained from savings realized through Soviet proposals for disarmament and reduction of military budgets; and rejects attempts to explain Third World difficulties in terms of differences between a "rich North" and a "poor South." In October 1981, for example, at the time of the Cancun Conference, which was attended by twenty-two countries (eight Western states, twelve LDCs, plus China and Yugoslavia, but not the USSR), Moscow dismissed as "downright hypocrisy . . . the fashionable appeals in some nonsocialist countries' capitals to the socialist community to 'share with the West the burden of aid' to the developing states. . . . What is this imperialist 'aid' if not an occasional crumb to the liberated countries out of what Western monopolies have plundered from them."[5]

Nor has Moscow altered its commercial practices. Soviet foreign-trade organizations exact high prices for their products (unless political considerations are controlling, as in dealing with Cuba); they buy primary products at the lowest possible prices and will not increase their purchases—for example, of cocoa beans, coffee, or fresh produce—to assist the producing countries in disposing of surpluses (and, incidentally, to give Soviet consumers a better choice of food); and Soviet terms of trade are rarely more favorable than those offered by the Western countries. Indeed, as a practitioner of the double standard, the USSR is notorious. For example, in the mid-1970s, it began requiring Western firms to purchase some of the finished goods produced in the factories built by them in the Soviet Union; however, when Moscow helps LDCs (India is a case in point), it resists such "industry-branch" or cooperative arrangements and does not wish to link its production needs to the supplies from Soviet-built factories in Third World countries. In the international economic arena, the Soviet Union is very much the tight-fisted state power vis-à-vis the LDCs, looking out for its own interests; in UN meetings, it throws out the same old line of discussing the problems of LDCs without attaching any new bait.

The law of the sea. Examination of another global issue shows that the emergence of the Soviet Union as a major naval and maritime power has had the curious effect of aligning it with the United States against the LDCs on many issues affecting the regulation of the high seas. The necessity of clarifying and modifying traditional practices on such issues as the establishment of the limits of the territorial seas, innocent right of passage, fishing rights, and exploitation of the mineral resources to be found on the seabed prompted the 1958 convening of the United Nations Conference on the Law of the Sea (UNCLOS I); a second conference was held in 1960, and a third was started in 1973 and ended in April 1982. By early 1988, the UNCLOS-III treaty had been ratified by only thirty-five of the sixty governments needed to bring it into force. Neither the USSR nor any other leading maritime power, such as the United States, Great Britain, or Japan, has yet ratified it. The net effect of the widespread objections to key sections of the treaty has been to set off a wave of restrictive domestic legislation that has driven another nail into the coffin of the long-dominant sixteenth- and seventeenth-century notion of freedom of the seas.

The Soviet Union has long been a vigorous advocate of retaining the traditional freedom of the seas. Though claiming twelve miles for its territorial sea since 1927, in opposition to the Western-preferred norm of three miles, it favored the traditional limiting of national jurisdiction over fishing zones. However, as many countries unilaterally extended their territorial waters and claims to exclusive fishing rights in these waters, the USSR followed suit. Thus, on December 10, 1976, the Supreme Soviet extended to 200 miles the coastal waters limit over which the USSR was prepared to exercise control on all fishing, most likely in response to similar actions by other states, including the United States, which were unwilling to await the final results of UNCLOS III. The move was taken reluctantly, because the Soviet fishing fleet is enormous and ranges from the English Channel to the waters off the Arabian Peninsula to Antarctica, and Moscow would have preferred to avoid the complications of impinging on national jurisdictions. Like the United States, the Soviet Union is adapting to the restraints imposed by increasingly nationalistic governments on previously unfettered fishing rights. On March 1, 1984, it officially established sovereignty over all mineral and maritime resources within the 200-mile zone.

An issue of particular strategic significance on which the superpowers find themselves aligned against radical Third World countries is the right of innocent passage through international straits where the extension of sovereignty to twelve miles offshore (from the present generally practiced three-mile limit) would restrict the free movement of naval ships. However, whereas the USSR advocates a twelve-mile limit for territorial waters, it disputes the extension of the present right of innocent passage through international straits to straits that are situated wholly within the territorial waters of one country—for example in Soviet territorial waters. (The United States favors this extension.) Thus, when "in 1967, the United States sent two coastguard ice-breakers, the *Edisto* and the *Eastwind*, along the Northern Sea Route, outside a line 12 nautical miles from the Soviet Arctic coast, intending them to pass through the Vilkitskogo Straits,"[6] they were turned back at the straits by the Soviets, who contended that these waters are "Historic Bays and Straits" for which no right of innocent passage is held to exist under Soviet law. Though "Soviet law in fact refrains from defining Soviet historic or internal waters—either theoretically or geographically"—Soviet jurists include all the Arctic Seas "in the category of what are called 'historic internal waters.'"[7] The effect is to deny other countries access to the vast Arctic areas north of the Soviet Union and innocent passage through straits located in Soviet waters. On a related issue, the Soviet Union allows merchant ships the right of innocent passage through its territorial waters (that is, twelve miles off shore), but insists that naval vessels must obtain prior permission, a position the United States rejects. In February 1988, while passing through Soviet territorial waters off the Crimea in the Black Sea, two U.S. warships were scraped from behind by Soviet warships, after refusing an order to leave. The incident showed the danger inherent in leaving unresolved differing interpretations of freedom of the seas.

One global issue on which the USSR is sharply at odds with LDCs relates to their proposals for exploitation of the minerals of the seabed lying in international waters. Moscow opposes LDC proposals for creating a supranational authority, under the aegis of the General Assembly, that would be responsible for mining the polymetallic nodules found on the ocean floor and distributing the earnings to needy countries; it has repeatedly cautioned against turning the United Nations into "some kind of philanthropic society."

Environmental protection. The Soviet government does, however, recognize the need for international cooperation to control pollution of the environment. The oil and industrial wastes in the Caspian and Baltic seas; the depletion of marine life in foreign and international waters that could affect the Soviet diet, which relies heavily on fish it catches there; and the growing toxicity of the atmosphere are but three of the spheres that it acknowledges need attention. Although the USSR had been active in the preparatory meeting of the UN Conference on the Human Environment, it saw fit not to attend the 1972 conference for the political reason that East Germany, not then a member of the UN, had been excluded as a voting member. However, Moscow did go along with the creation of the UN Environment Program in 1973 and contributes to its activities. One area in which it has become very active is nuclear-reactor safety. Since the accident on April 26, 1986 at the Chernobyl nuclear power plant, the radioactive fallout of which affected all Europe, the Soviet government has encouraged the UN International Atomic Energy Agency to expand its program (which began in 1982) of inspecting nuclear reactors around the world and exchanging information on reactor safety.

Soviet analysts increasingly write about the emergence of new and complex global problems ranging from energy and raw-materials scarcity to eradication of diseases, including AIDS, and from developing the resources of the oceans to regulating communications. They attribute this vast network of problems to the profound political changes in international alignments and attitudes and the multifaceted phenomenon they call the scientific and technological revolution (STR). As they see it, the STR arose out of military needs but now compels qualitative changes in international economic relations and socioeconomic patterns.

Food to the needy. Over the years the Soviet Union has refused to participate in multilateral efforts to provide food assistance to needy countries, for example, it declined to work with the International Wheat Council in negotiations for a new international Food Aid Convention and to cooperate with the UN Food and Agricultural Organization. It maintains that a solution to the food problems depends first on the steps taken by the LDCs themselves to improve agricultural production and second on the additional resources that should be given by the "imperialist" powers and monopolies, which continue to exploit the natural and manpower resources of the developing countries.[8] This results in a policy of minimal contributions to countries afflicted by drought, as many African countries were at various times during the 1980s. Soviet clients, such as Ethiopia and Mozambique, were encouraged to look to the West for food relief.

A change in Soviet attitude toward global issues may, however, be in the making. At the twenty-seventh party congress, Gorbachev acknowledged the interdependent character of states in the international system and the need to solve "the global problems on which the fate of civilization depends." The leadership thus, uncharacteristically, recognized a view that had been gaining adherents among influential Soviet analysts of Third World and international economic developments during the previous decade. They had tentatively but increasingly argued that the problems of Third World countries were not useful levers "for tilting the balance of power in favor of the Soviet Union," but were threats to international stability and peace; and conceding that the Soviet bloc countries did not have all the answers, they urged "the broad, constructive cooperation of all the advanced countries in solving the problems that create unrest in the LDCs—overpopulation, food shortages, and backwardness."[9] In the Soviet context, the term "global problems" is potentially ideologically divisive because it "suggests that such problems transcend class and economic rivalries and that their solution requires a nonclass approach. . . . What is more, once it is admitted that global problems do exist, the logic is that ideological rivals like the United States and the Soviet Union must work together to solve them."[10] However, proof again that one thaw does not a spring make, the professed concern for developmental, environmental, and ecological issues has not, thus far, been followed up by any fundamental shifts in policy in the various UN specialized agencies and regional economic commissions. Continuity has been the characteristic of Soviet behavior in these forums.

Organizational Issues

With the exception of its expressed hostility to Secretary-General Trygve Lie during the early stages of the Korean War, the USSR paid little attention to the UN Secretariat during the Stalinist period. Until 1960, Moscow assigned few Soviet nationals to the secretariats of international organizations, a reflection of its general depreciation and lack of understanding of the value of such groups in shaping the implementation of policy and gathering intelligence. Not until Khrushchev's troika proposal at the 1960 session of the General Assembly did Moscow begin to assign more of its nationals to a wide range of posts in international organizations.

The failure of the Soviet Union to gain a foothold in the Congo turned Khrushchev against Secretary-General Dag Hammarskjöld, because of his allegedly partisan handling of the ONUC peacekeeping mission. Speaking before the General Assembly on September 23, 1960, the Soviet premier attacked the office of the secretary-general and the entire concept of an impartial international civil service. He proposed replacement of the secretary-general by a three-man directorate representing the three political blocs—Western, Communist, nonaligned—and justified it on the ground that the UN should reflect the changed alignment of political forces in the world. On another occasion, Khrushchev declared that "while there are neutral countries, there are no neutral men. You would not accept a Communist administrator and I cannot accept a non-Communist administrator. I will never entrust the security of the Soviet Union to any foreigner. We cannot have another Hammarskjöld, no matter where he comes from among the neutral countries."[11] The troika proposal was rejected because the African and Asian countries saw that it would give the USSR a veto over Secretariat activities with which it disagreed.

Moscow's use of its nationals as intelligence agents in international organizations was confirmed by Arkady N. Shevchenko, the Soviet citizen who was undersecretary-general for political and security affairs, when he defected to the West in April 1978. He said that because of the UN, New York had become "the most important base of all Soviet intelligence operations in the world. . . . Soviet intelligence officers have become a Trojan horse behind the wall of the United Nations."[12]

The Soviet Union has usually tailored its position on organizational issues such as membership and accreditation of nongovernmental groups, including national liberation movements such as the Palestine Liberation Organization (PLO), to the sentiments prevailing among its Third World constituents. But exceptions have clearly occurred, as in differences between the USSR and Third World nations over restructuring the composition of international secretariats; Soviet reluctance to expand the membership of the Security Council (from eleven to fifteen) and the Economic and Social Council (from eighteen to twenty-seven) during the decade from 1955 to 1965; and Soviet opposition to increasing the UN budget or expanding the UN's authority in the economic, social, and humanitarian realms.

Sino–Soviet Interaction

For a little more than a decade after the PRC took its place in the United Nations in 1971—a development Moscow had advocated since 1950, albeit with less conviction after 1961—the most caustic criticisms of USSR policies came from its former ally and Communist neighbor. These attacks were particularly troublesome since China, unlike the Western powers, could not be dismissed as representative of a socioideological outlook whose demise was foreshadowed by the "correlation of forces" that Moscow saw shifting toward the Communist world. Being both non-Western and underdeveloped, China in addition enjoys a natural link to the Afro-Asian bloc that Moscow courts and seeks to influence, and can in this relationship place a mirror to distinctly unflattering Soviet warts.

Though public recriminations have been rare since Gorbachev came to power, Sino–Soviet wrangling in the UN provides a glimpse into the depth of the two countries' differing perceptions, policies, and objectives. How much is tactical and how much is substantive is difficult to say. Whereas the USSR opposes revision of the charter, China insists on the need for fundamental changes that would give the Third World more authority and eliminate superpower domination, especially of the Security Council—though one wonders whether Beijing would really agree to dispense with the veto.

China mocks Soviet professions of interest in international cooperation, calling what Moscow actually practices "not internationalism, but great-power chauvinism, national egoism and territorial expansionism." It states that the USSR's aims are imperial and selfish. In its courtship of Third World countries, China seeks to set itself apart from the Soviet Union and the United States, arguing that the two superpowers are not practicing peaceful coexistence, "only a travesty of peaceful coexistence; the substance is coexisting in rivalry." Though castigating both superpowers as obstinate obstacles to the prohibition and destruction of the nuclear weapons that they are "feverishly developing," Beijing increasingly singled out the Soviet Union for the harsher attacks at the end of the 1970s, when Beijing sought better relations with the United States. For example, at the General Assembly's special session on disarmament in May 1978, Foreign Minister Huang Hua averred that "facts show that this superpower flaunting the label of socialism is more aggressive and adventurous than the other superpower; it is the most dangerous source of a new world war and is sure to be its chief instigator."[13] He labeled Soviet proposals for disarmament "illusory bubbles."

China also belittles the USSR's aid to less-developed countries and lumps the USSR with the United States as developed, industrialized, rich, and selfish. It regards the superpowers as constituting the First World, the Second World being a motley combination of Western Europe and Japan, and the Third World made up of everyone else. This Chinese "three-camp" variation on the Soviet thesis is designed to weaken the Soviet position with the Afro-Asian countries and to broaden the base of its own constituency in the Third World.

Finally, in the initial maneuvering in 1979 over which Kampuchean regime the UN ought to recognize—the ousted, genocidal Pol Pot regime, supported by Beijing, or the Heng Samrin government, brought to office by invading Vietnamese troops and upheld by Moscow—the Chinese demonstrated considerable skill in lobbying support for the unpopular Pol Pot. They mobilized the rebuff to the Soviet-Vietnamese puppet by hammering at a principle widely accepted in the Third World, namely that there can be no justification for a military invasion to change the political character of a government, no matter how gross the violations of human rights.

The nations of Southeast Asia fear Vietnam more than China. As a result, Moscow's special relationship with Vietnam is held at the expense of improved ties with the other countries of the region. For the moment, China is the defender of noninterference in the domestic affairs of member states—the position Moscow had heretofore championed in the Third World. The discussion in the UN rivets world attention on a complex and political dilemma, in a manner not apt to enhance Soviet prestige abroad. On the Afghanistan issue, too, China has effectively hammered at the difference between Soviet professions of principle on nonintervention and actual Soviet policy.

Persisting Motifs

Soviet interest in the UN is an outgrowth of the changed environment within the UN in the 1960s, when the membership more than doubled, America's reliable voting majority came to an end, the LDCs developed a heightened radicalism and anti-Western attitudes on a growing number of political and economic issues, and the Soviet bloc's isolation within the organization drew to a close. One Soviet commentator summed up the UN's usefulness for advancing Soviet aims in this way:

> It facilitates to a certain extent the establishment and development of ties and intercourse between states and in this way provides some prerequisites for an extension of international cooperation in various fields—political, economic, social, and others. The consideration of numerous international problems by UN bodies contributes to the clarification of the views of various states on this or that issue, brings the most important international questions to the notice of a broad public and helps to mobilize the progressive forces of various social groups for the preservation and consolidation of peace and for the peaceful settlement of international issues. In certain instances, UN consideration of international disputes has facilitated their settlement in the interests of world peace and security.[14]

The UN is a forum that enables the USSR to present its views and support nonaligned countries in ways that weaken their links to the West and strengthen their ties to the Soviet bloc. In it, anti-Western sentiments are crystallized, and the United States is kept almost continually on the defensive by the barrage of ever-escalating demands for NIEO, disarmament, and so on.

The USSR participates minimally in the developmental and nation-building programs of the UN. It sees the UN primarily as an arena for political struggle, a place where Soviet leaders can proclaim their commitment to peaceful coexistence of different social and political systems, encourage the demands of the LDCs on the capitalist world, and offer their support on issues that polarize alignments or promote Soviet objectives. Courtship of the nonaligned countries, to detach them from the Western camp and offset Chinese inroads, has high priority. Though Moscow makes and upholds proposals that find favor with the LDCs and seeks to place itself in the forefront of movements for change, it seldom provides substantive support for any of these proposals. It assuredly is unwilling to relinquish the veto or permit any revision of the charter that might give the UN the status of an incipient world parliament. Khrushchev made the Kremlin's views on this sentiment abundantly clear:

> Suppose the delegates of UN member countries suddenly hit on the "grand" idea of resolving to abolish the socialist system in the Soviet Union. What would happen if everybody voted for it except ourselves, the representatives of the socialist countries? What would we say to this? We would say what we Russians usually say in such cases: "Get out!" You took the decision, so live with it; as for us, we will live under our socialist system as we have lived so far. And whoever pokes in his nose—excuse me for the coarse but rather lucid expression—will get a punch in the face!"[15]

Conflict, not cooperation, is the dynamic that impels Soviet behavior in international organizations. No issue is too insignificant, no problem too trivial to be exploited if it holds out the promise of a shred of political advantage. The Soviet government is attentive, active, and insistent in safeguarding its national interests and urging on its clients, whether the issue is advocacy of the non-use of force in international relations and the permanent prohibition of the use of nuclear weapons, exclusion of Israel from UNESCO's activities, or support for restrictions on the dissemination of news by Western press services. And it was the Soviet Union that spawned the crisis in UNESCO over the proposed New World Information Order: at UNESCO's Seventeenth General Conference in the fall of 1972, a Soviet call for the preparation of a "Draft Declaration Concerning the Fundamental Principles Governing the Use of the Media with a View to Strengthening Peace and International Understanding and Combating War Propaganda, Racialism and Apartheid" quickly attracted support as the nonaligned movement, UNESCO's bureaucracy, and the Soviet bloc mounted an attack on the prevailing system of disseminating news. It also encouraged militant proposals on anticolonialism, but refused to facilitate their implementation with increased authority, money, or arms for relevant UN bodies (as was evident, for example, in its unwillingness to contribute to the cost of a proposed UN peacekeeping operation that would supervise the peaceful transition of Namibia from South African control to independence). In 1966, when it sought to mobilize world public opinion against United States involvement in Vietnam, it urged the General Assembly's adoption of a Declaration of the Inadmissibility of Intervention in the Domestic Affairs of States; but in August 1968 and December 1979, indifferent to foreign criticism, it militarily intervened in Czechoslovakia and Afghanistan, respectively. Long an advocate for a definition of aggression, in 1953 and 1956 it proposed that the establishment of a blockade (among other things) should be deemed an act of aggression on the part of the initiator of the blockade; but when Nasser announced Egypt's imposition of a blockade of the Straits of Tiran on May 21, 1967, and thereby helped to precipitate the Israeli response of June 5, 1967, the USSR ignored its own criterion and condemned Israel as the aggressor. Moreover, in February 1969 at the UN Special Committee on the Question of Defining Aggression, with cynical disdain for the legal norms it professes to wish established, it tabled a new draft definition of aggression that omitted provisions contained in previous Soviet drafts. (For example, one 1956 draft position that was dropped defined as an act of aggression the sending of military forces "inside the boundaries of another State without the permission of the government of the latter, or the violation of the conditions of such permission, particularly as regards the length of their stay or the extent of the area in which they stay."[16]

In working tirelessly to undermine the Western conception of what the UN should be, the Soviet Union finds a large and receptive constituency among the authoritarian, antidemocratic governments that increasingly dominate the plenary sessions of international organizations. Moscow's constrictive interpretations of Western proposals are not unwelcome among

Third World countries where the U.S. and West European penchant for human rights does not strike a responsive chord, except on a very selective and politically partisan basis. The USSR proclaims the need for safeguarding human rights but pressures the secretary-general to order UN information centers abroad (specifically, the one in Moscow) to stop accepting individual petitions to the United Nations for redress of discriminatory treatment. While a party to international conventions against terrorism, Moscow wants hijacking left to the present discretionary authority of individual governments; furthermore, it shied away from a U.S. proposal for a new convention requiring signatory nations to suspend air services with any country that did not extradite or punish hijackers or terrorists, ostensibly because the imposition of sanctions is the responsibility of the Security Council, but in fact because the LDCs it courts favor making distinctions between terrorism and acts committed by national liberation movements such as the PLO. On the charged issue of regulating direct broadcasting from space satellites, Moscow has sided with many Third World countries in pressing for regulations that prohibit radio and television transmissions via satellite to foreign audiences unless permission is specifically granted by the respective foreign government.

All of these are segments of an overarching Soviet effort to restructure international law and the norms regulating behavior among states. In conjunction with the LDCs, the USSR seems eager to use international organizations to adopt—through consensus of the Soviet-LDC majority and under the banner of "peaceful coexistence"—a body of "progressive" law that would strengthen "socialism" in the world.[17]

Eschewing the negativism of the Stalin period, the USSR has taken to bloc politics in the UN with a vengeance, exploiting voting majorities (as the United States did in the 1945-to-1960 period) to undermine the West and advance Soviet (and anti-Western) proposals and preferred resolutions. It regards international forums as battlefields for competing ideas and approaches to concrete issues, and has decided that the game is worth the effort. In these multilateral settings, Moscow can demonstrate the unity and sense of purpose of the Soviet bloc "in contrast to the disunity and lack of resolve or common purpose of the West"; and with the assistance of pro-Soviet clients in the Third World, it can, by highlighting the disarray in the West, often frustrate or nip in the bud Western or anti-Soviet moves among the nonaligned countries.[18]

Notes

1. A statement made to the press, as quoted in Jane Degras, *Soviet Documents on Foreign Policy,* Vol. II (New York: Oxford University Press, 1952), 66.

2. League of Nations, *Official Journal,* Special Supplement No. 125 (September 1934), 67.
3. M. Lvov, "United Nations: Results and Prospects," *International Affairs,* No. 9 (September 1965), 4.
4. Paul Lewis, *New York Times,* October 18, 1987.
5. Foreign Broadcast Information Service (FBIS)/USSR International Affairs, October 28, 1981, CC6.
6. Elizabeth Young and Viktor Sebek, "Red Seas and Blue Seas: Soviet Uses of Ocean Law," *Survival,* Vol. 20, No. 6 (November/December 1978), 256.
7. *Ibid.*
8. For example, FBIS/USSR International Affairs, April 3, 1979, CC3.
9. Elizabeth Kridl Valkenier, *The Soviet Union and the Third World: An Economic Bind* (New York: Praeger, 1983), 149.
10. Charles Glickham, "New Directions for Soviet Foreign Policy", Radio Liberty Research, Supplement 2/86 (September 6, 1986), 9.
11. Nikita Khrushchev's interview with Walter Lippmann, *New York Herald Tribune,* April 17, 1961.
12. *New York Times,* September 25, 1979.
13. *New York Times,* May 30, 1978.
14. A. Vorobyov, "The Tenth Anniversary of the United Nations Organization," *International Affairs,* No. 6 (June 1955), 44.
15. N. S. Khrushchev, *On Peaceful Coexistence* (Moscow: Foreign Languages Publishing House, 1961), 286.
16. Radio Liberty Dispatch, "The New Soviet Definition of Aggression," April 9, 1969.
17. John N. Hazard, review of *Soviet Yearbook of International Law 1975,* in *American Journal of International Law,* Vol. 73, No. 2 (April 1979), 319–20.
18. Arieh Eilan, "Conference Diplomacy," *Washington Quarterly,* Vol. 4 (Autumn 1981), 27.

Selected Bibliography

BUTLER, WILLIAM E. *The Soviet Union and the Law of the Sea.* Baltimore: Johns Hopkins University Press, 1971.

DALLIN, ALEXANDER. *The Soviet Union and the United Nations.* New York: Praeger, 1962.

GODSON, ROY. *Labor in Soviet Global Strategy.* New York: Crane, Russak, 1984.

HIGGINS, ROSLYN (ED.). *United Nations Peacekeeping, 1946–1967: Documents and Commentary.* Vol. I: *The Middle East.* London: Oxford University Press, 1969.

JACOBSON, HAROLD K. *The USSR and the UN's Economic and Social Activities.* Notre Dame, Ind.: University of Notre Dame Press, 1963.

JAMES, ALAN. *The Politics of Peacekeeping.* New York: Praeger, 1969.

LALL, ARTHUR. *The UN and the Middle East Crisis, 1967.* New York: Columbia University Press, 1968.

NOGEE, JOSEPH L. *Soviet Policy Towards International Control of Atomic Energy.* Notre Dame, Ind.: University of Notre Dame Press, 1961.

RAMUNDO, BERNARD A. *Peaceful Coexistence: International Law in the Building of Communism.* Baltimore: Johns Hopkins University Press, 1967.

RUBINSTEIN, ALVIN Z. *The Soviets in International Organizations: Changing Policy Toward Developing Countries, 1953–1963.* Princeton, N.J.: Princeton University Press, 1964.

SHEVCHENKO, ARKADY N. *Breaking With Moscow.* New York: Knopf, 1985.

TARACOUZIO, T. A. *The Soviet Union and International Law.* New York: Macmillan, 1935.

VALKENIER, ELIZABETH KRIDL. *The Soviet Union and the Third World: An Economic Bind.* New York: Praeger, 1983.

IV

The Future of Soviet-American Relations and Soviet Strategy to the Year 2000

13

Soviet-American Relations: The Elusive Accommodation

The Soviet Union has been locked in struggle with the United States ever since the end of World War II, when its expansion in Europe and the Far East placed it astride areas that were vital to the United States. An imperial-minded Stalin pursued policies that exacerbated Western insecurity and residual ideological antipathies and that polarized East-West relations. His obsession with security—an understandable reaction to a war that had brought the USSR to the brink of disaster—became more acute as the United States gained obvious superiority in strategic weapons and developed its policy of containment. Tension was endemic.

By the mid-1950s, however, relations between the two blocs had stabilized, and the fear of war in Europe had receded. Soviet possession of nuclear weapons ensured the effectiveness of deterrence. The new leadership inched toward a limited accommodation with the West, based on the preservation of the territorial status quo. But the essentially competitive character of Soviet–American relations did not significantly diminish; indeed, it grew as Moscow's might expanded and assertiveness in the Third World took form. In the consequent globalization of the rivalry, the Soviet–American relationship assumed an adversarial nature in which competition overshadowed cooperation; the latter is served by a mutual desire to avoid nuclear war and direct confrontation of Soviet and American forces, but the former seems destined to persist for the foreseeable future in a wide number of areas.

Our interest here is in the dynamics of the current situation and the troublesome issues that lie ahead; yet in assessing the Soviet–American relationship, we should not ignore certain shared characteristics that hold out a promise—in the long run—of limited détente and attenuation of the impetus to war.

First, the Soviet Union and the United States have never fought a war against one another. This is a remarkable fact of more than 200 years of modern history. Notwithstanding tense crises and local wars, the two superpowers did not go to war with each other over Berlin in 1948–1949, Korea in 1950–1953, Hungary in 1956, Cuba in 1962, Czechoslovakia in 1968, Vietnam in the late 1960s–early 1970s, or the Middle East in 1970 or 1973. Both refrained from taking steps that might have precipitated a direct confrontation between them.

Second, neither covets the territory of the other. There are no outstanding irredentist claims. Real estate is not at the heart of their difficulties. A rivalry that is imperial rather than nationalist in character does not generate volatile emotional passions and thus is far easier for the elites in power to manage domestically and is less likely to get out of hand. Each side can more easily accept limited gains by the other.

Third, as peoples, the Russians and Americans have many positive images of one another. (While the Russians constitute only 52 percent of the total population of the Soviet Union, they are the politically dominant group and their culture pervades the society.) Russians and Americans appreciate each others' literature, music, theater, and sports, as is evident in the general popularity of the visiting artists and cultural troupes of both countries.

Fourth, Soviet and American societies share the admirable but quixotic belief of the eighteenth-century Enlightenment that through science, education, and man's reason, society can be transformed. This fundamental outlook predominates despite mushrooming ecological, social, and economic problems. For both, gleaming technology still stands at the center of the societies that their elites seek to build; for both, technological "fixes" are seen as the cure for man's ills.

Fifth, both the United States and the Soviet Union are disliked and mistrusted by their immediate neighbors. Both have alliance problems. Concerns over maintaining intra-alliance cohesion help to limit each superpower's temptation to interfere directly in the other's primary sphere of influence.

Sixth, as urban, industrialized societies, the two countries face common problems such as alienation, resource depletion, environmental deterioration, and so on. Their racial and nationality problems cause political unrest and absorb an increasing amount of the attention of the leaderships.

Finally, both face the supreme paradox of the nuclear age: Despite ever-increasing military power, their influence over allies and clients is progressively more difficult to manage and maintain. Small nations have found a new lease on autonomy and independence in this nuclear age, and their initiatives often confound the best-laid plans of their patrons and putative masters.

Moscow's Quest for Peaceful Coexistence and Détente

Since the death of Stalin in March 1953, the Soviet leadership has sought to improve relations with the United States and the Western countries for combinations of reasons that have varied over time. The origin of this policy can be pinpointed to the 1954 to 1955 period and Khrushchev's withdrawal of Soviet military power from Austria and Finland. Whatever the other considerations, Moscow's pullback from forward positions in Europe signified its readiness to pare its territorial ambitions somewhat and to seek an accommodation with the West, even at the expense of Soviet relations with China. The Geneva summit conference in July 1955 marked Khrushchev's entry onto the international stage and the beginning of a more open and active Soviet diplomacy.

The process of negotiating with the West however, was erratic and periodically disrupted by intra-Soviet-bloc crises, such as the 1956 upheavals in Eastern Europe, and by tensions with the West, such as the Berlin crisis between 1958 and 1961 (when the wall surrounding West Berlin was erected), the U-2 affair of May 1960 (when the shooting down of a U.S. spy plane over the USSR reminded the Soviet military of their vulnerability to a U.S. nuclear attack), and the Cuban missile crisis of October 1962. The Cuban missile crisis was the most dangerous Soviet challenge to the United States during the Khrushchev period. It had a profound effect on Soviet-U.S. relations and on the acceleration of the USSR's buildup of strategic forces in the 1960s and 1970s.

After Fidel Castro came to power in January 1959, his commitment to revolution elsewhere in Latin America prevented a normalization of Cuba's relations with the United States. Moscow was slow to court Castro, but it denounced the Monroe Doctrine, the better to uphold Cuba's increasingly anti-American policy and revolutionary outlook. In July 1960, Khrushchev said the Monroe Doctrine was dead: it "has outlived its time, has outlived itself, has died, so to say, a natural death. Now the remains of this doctrine should best be buried as every dead body is so that it should not poison the air by its decay."[1] After the abortive CIA-engineered effort to overthrow Castro at the Bay of Pigs in April 1961, Moscow undertook a program of economic and military assistance to Cuba. In the spring of 1962, the Kremlin decided to install intermediate-range missiles in Cuba, ostensibly to protect Castro (who proclaimed himself a Marxist-Leninist) from another U.S.-organized invasion, but primarily to attempt a sweeping shift in the balance of power.

According to Khrushchev, it was during his visit to Bulgaria in mid-May 1962 that he conceived the idea of installing nuclear-tipped missiles in Cuba without allowing Washington to find out about them until it was too late for anything to be done.[2] In late July, after obtaining Castro's permission, Moscow began pouring in men and matériel. On September 2, it announced an expanded program of arms deliveries and the sending of unspecified "technical specialists" to help Cuba meet the "threats" from "aggressive imperialist quarters." On September 11, in a major policy statement, the Soviet government gave assurances of peaceful intent, asserting that "the armaments and military equipment sent to Cuba are designed exclusively for defensive purposes" but warning that "if war is unleashed," the Soviet Union will render assistance to Cuba "just as it was ready in 1956 to render military assistance to Egypt at the time of the Anglo-French-Israeli aggression in the Suez Canal region." During the next few weeks, the Kremlin carried on an intensive program of disinformation and deception, issuing placatory statements and sending diplomats to assure officials in the Kennedy administration, including the president, of the defensive nature of the weapons being introduced into Cuba.

The dramatic account of the "eyeball-to-eyeball" Soviet-American confrontation in the Caribbean is well known. On October 22, President John F. Kennedy told the American people that the United States had "unmistakable evidence" that the USSR was constructing a series of offensive missile sites in Cuba and that the United States aimed "to prevent the use of these missiles against this or any other country and to secure their withdrawal or elimination from the western hemisphere." By the end of October the crisis was over. The denouement was determined by the preponderant U.S. superiority in conventional forces in the Caribbean and not by its advantage in nuclear weapons—6000 to about 300. In this situation, Moscow calculated that Washington would not, despite its edge in nuclear weapons, resort to a nuclear strike because it could not be certain of destroying all the USSR's missiles and thereby avoid the destruction of some American cities.

Though forced to remove the missiles and disappointed at his failure to redress the strategic imbalance between the Soviet Union and the United States, Khrushchev did ensure the security of his Cuban protégé, having extracted a U.S. pledge not to invade Cuba in return for the removal of the missiles. Domestically, his failure to implant the missiles in Cuba and obtain U.S. acceptance of the USSR as an equal in the strategic equation meant that the Soviet military would have its way; a massive and accelerated buildup of strategic forces was undertaken, reflecting the determination of the Soviet leadership never again to have to back down to the United States because of military inferiority.

In the realm of foreign policy, the crisis led to renewed efforts to reach an accommodation through negotiation, "but within a mutually acceptable balance of strategic power." It gave new impetus to the quest for an improvement in Soviet-American relations, leading to the conclusion of the limited nuclear test ban treaty in the summer of 1963 and the establishment "of the so-called hot-line of instant communications between Washington and Moscow. In general, these ameliorating measures were intended to lower the level of tension, facilitate the management of future crises, and clear the way for greater accommodation."[3]

After Khrushchev's deposal in October 1964, the Brezhnev-Kosygin team continued the policy of trying to improve relations with the United States, but headway was slow. Complicating the process were the Soviets' decisions to help North Vietnam, to rearm the Arabs after the June War, to invade Czechoslovakia, and to strengthen Soviet forces in Europe. But West German Chancellor Willy Brandt's *Ostpolitik* and readiness to accept the division of Germany, and the momentum of Moscow's buildup of strategic weapons made the United States receptive to an improvement of Soviet-American relations.

By the early 1970s, the Soviet Union's interest in détente derived from a series of compelling policy objectives that are still operative. First is the desire for Western, especially American, technology and credits to increase industrial and managerial efficiency and modernization in the nonmilitary sectors of the economy. In March 1971, at the twenty-fourth congress of the CPSU, the Politburo made the decision—which had been deferred in late 1969 and frequently discussed in 1970—to seek better relations with the United States in order to assure the importation from that country of large amounts of advanced technology and equipment. It did so after five years of futile efforts to overcome lagging productivity and technological weakness in the nonmilitary sectors of the Soviet economy. In September 1965, the Brezhnev-Kosygin leadership had introduced a series of major economic reforms to overcome the shortcomings that had allegedly resulted from Khrushchev's "hare-brained" policies; but like the fabled monkey who tried to organize the barnyard animals into a symphony orchestra by continually reassigning instruments, they realized that domestic realignments were not sufficient to stimulate innovation and efficiency. For this they would have to run to the West and Japan.

The importation of technology and machinery is a fundamental reason for the USSR's interest in détente. Some argue that it is the *only* reason. By importing on an enormous scale, the leadership seeks to offset the deleterious combination of party and bureaucratic interference in the operation of industry and the imbalances between the military and nonmilitary branches of the economy that account for shortages and shoddy goods and that plague planners and decimate production targets. Western technology has been in vogue before, both under Stalin and Lenin and under the czars. But the scale of the present need is enormous, and meeting it is crucial for overcoming the critical bottlenecks in important economic sectors. With the new impetus toward détente in the late 1980s, Gorbachev has reaffirmed the USSR's desire not only for technology and trade, but also for greater involvement in the global economy and for the establishment of joint ventures with Western businessmen.

A second factor in the Soviet interest in détente is Moscow's China problem. Despite their preponderance of military power, the Soviets are uneasy over the Chinese almost to the point of paranoia. Long-dormant cultural stereotypes of the "inscrutable" Chinese have been revived in the wake of the Sino-Soviet quarrel. The fear of a Chinese threat is aggravated by periodic outbreaks along the thousands of miles of exposed border; by Beijing's vestigial territorial grievances, its growing nuclear capability, and its formal termination of the 1950 treaty of alliance; and by the evolving Sino-U.S. rapprochement. In recent years, Moscow has tried to normalize relations with Beijing, but with little success. Meanwhile, unhappy over the need to maintain large conventional forces along the Chinese border and disturbed as much by China's active challenge to Soviet interests and clients in the Far East as by its potential as a superpower, Moscow seeks détente in the West in order to acquire maximum latitude for dealing with China in the East.

A third important consideration—certainly one that has been a constant in Soviet thinking after 1945—was the desire to obtain formal Western recognition of the territorial status quo in Europe. What gained momentum with Chancellor Willy Brandt's policy of accommodation with the Soviet Union in 1969 was completed at the Conference on Security and Cooperation in Europe in Helsinki in July 1975: the final legitimation of the division of Germany and the Soviet imperial system in Eastern Europe.

Fourth, the Soviets have an interest in stabilizing the strategic arms race and limiting the escalation of defense expenditures. Moscow's keen interest was evident in the SALT I agreement in 1972 and the Ford-Brezhnev accord at Vladivostok in November 1974, when "essential equivalence" or parity was determined (though at a much higher threshold than had been expected by Western proponents of arms control). Nevertheless, the Carter administration's attempt in March 1977 to lower the quantitative ceilings that had been agreed to at Vladivostok occasioned bitter Soviet opposition, which led to the formal lapsing of SALT I. Moscow's agreement to the on-site inspection mandated by the INF treaty, its campaign for deep cuts in strategic delivery systems in the

SALT/START talks, and its efforts to contain the competition in the exotic-expensive, hi-tech realm of SDI-type research and deployment all suggest that the Soviets do want to stabilize the arms race, if only to keep their own swollen arms budget within tolerable economic limits and also to avoid an open, all-out weapons competition with the United States.

Finally, Moscow views détente as a form of political struggle that is compatible with avoidance of nuclear war. It sees no essential contradiction between seeking much-needed economic and technological supplements to its industrial network and simultaneously maneuvering for strategic and political advantages to improve its overall global position vis-à-vis the United States. For Moscow, this is the competitive aspect of peaceful coexistence.

Ideological Struggle: Systemic or Sideshow?

Prior to 1945, a weak, isolated Soviet Union resorted to the idea of peaceful coexistence to buttress its essentially defensive strategy. Peaceful coexistence was a policy dictated by weakness; but by the end of the Stalin period and particularly under Khrushchev and Brezhnev, it was refashioned for a strong, internationally vigorous, imperial Soviet Union.

Attempts to understand Soviet foreign policy frequently founder on differences of interpretation concerning the Soviet meaning of "peaceful coexistence." To many in the West, the term signifies the maintenance of status quo in the international arena, with any changes to take place gradually and in accordance with some generally accepted code of conduct that preserves stability and a balance of power between the two rival security systems. To the Soviets, on the other hand, it implies a strategy of conflict, short of nuclear war, in which the Soviet camp is strengthened and extended to encompass new members. As an authoritative Soviet publication explains:

> Peaceful coexistence is a specific form of class struggle between socialism and capitalism. In peaceful competition with capitalism, the socialist system will win, that is, the socialist method of production has decisive advantages over the capitalist system. . . . Peaceful coexistence concerns relations between states. It does not touch upon relations within states; it does not touch upon the revolutionary struggle for the transformation of society.
>
> Peaceful coexistence among the states of the two [different] systems does not mean compromise in ideological questions. The bourgeois and communist world outlooks cannot be reconciled; moreover, this is not necessary for peaceful coexistence among states. Each can maintain its own position on ideological questions without having this serve as a road-

block preventing cooperation in economic questions and in questions concerning international peace and security.

Naturally, the concept of peaceful coexistence as a condition of relations among states is inapplicable to the internal relations of a state. Therefore, the attempts of the revisionists to extend the concept of peaceful coexistence to class relations within a state are absurd. The recognition of the necessity and possibility of peaceful coexistence does not signify rejection of the class struggle, of the idea of the inevitability of the victory of communism over capitalism.[4]

What often confuses Westerners is the way the term can be variously used, at some times to convey a spirit of conciliation and at others, conflict. Thus, speaking before the United Nations General Assembly on September 28, 1960, Khrushchev stated:

> . . . we do not want to impose our order by force upon other countries. Let those who determine the policy of states with a social order differing from ours also renounce futile and dangerous efforts at dictating their will. It is time for them also to recognize that the choice of one way of life or another is a domestic matter for each people. Let us build up our relations, taking into consideration the hard facts of reality. And this will be peaceful coexistence.

A few months later, speaking in Moscow to Communist officials, he declared: "The policy of peaceful coexistence, as regards it social content, is a form of intense economic, political, and ideological struggle of the proletariat against the aggressive forces of imperialism in the international arena."

Perhaps nothing illustrates the ambiguity of the term better than Khrushchev's attempt to explain away the implied threat in the ominous words "We will bury you." For example, on one occasion, at a reception at the Polish Embassy in Moscow on September 4, 1959, he went out of his way to reaffirm the USSR's belief in the peaceful competition implied in peaceful coexistence and to calm Western uneasiness:

> Some representatives of the capitalist countries reproach me for having allegedly said that we shall bury capitalism. I have already said that I want only one thing—that they should understand me correctly. The imperialists are digging their own grave. Such is their nature. Karl Marx long ago explained how this is being done, but they still do not understand it.
>
> I want to say only one thing: You must know that physically we shall not dig a grave for you. If you like the capitalist system so much, live under capitalism to your heart's content as long as you can, but how long you will be able to do so I cannot tell.[5]

In general, to the Soviets, peaceful coexistence means competition and incessant struggle in all spheres short of total war. "Imperialist" wars will be resisted, just as all national liberation movements will be aided, irrespective of the effect on Soviet–U.S. relations. Khrushchev's successors share his firm belief that the balance of world power is shifting inexorably toward the Soviet camp and that capitalism is no more capable of preventing the triumph of communism than feudalism was of forestalling the advent of capitalism. Implicit in peaceful coexistence are continued rivalry, endemic suspicion, and unrelenting effort to weaken the adversary in order to alter the correlation of world forces through a combination of political, economic, cultural, and ideological means. As Brezhnev told the 1976 CPSU congress:

> Some bourgeois leaders affect surprise and raise a howl over the solidarity of Soviet Communists . . . with the struggle of other peoples for freedom and progress. This is either outright naiveté or more likely a deliberate befuddling of minds. It could not be clearer, after all, that détente and peaceful coexistence have to do with interstate relations. This means above all that disputes and conflicts between countries are not to be settled by war, by the use or threat of force. Détente does not in the slightest abolish, nor can it abolish or alter, the laws of class struggle. . . .
>
> We make no secret of the fact that we see détente as the way to create more favorable conditions for peaceful socialist and communist construction.[6]

When relations between the Soviet Union and the West began to improve in the early 1970s, the world *détente*—the French word for a relaxation of international tension—was widely used in the West. In the English language, it connotes not only easing tensions but also developing extensive, friendly relations in all areas of national interaction. During the heady days after the signing of SALT I in May 1972, the Soviets too began to use the word *détente* in conjunction with calls for peaceful coexistence. But the crucial term for the Soviets is peaceful coexistence, not détente. It is important that we understand their usage of *détente* and not extrapolate Soviet interpretations from our own. There is nothing to suggest that the Soviet interpretation foresees a time or a situation in which the USSR and the United States will end up as friends, settling their differences congenially around the bargaining table.

In the United States, as in Western Europe, there were many who behaved as if the mere use of the term had suddenly transmuted the essence of the conflictual Soviet-American relationship. Events since 1974 have battered at sanguine views of interdependency and the cooperation it is supposed to foster. In the past, détente was oversold, and there is good reason to be skeptical of a flowering of Soviet-American relations in the 1990s.

In the past, Soviet ideology has been highly malleable. Policy shifts occasioned by changes in the correlation of forces were incorporated in refurbished ideological formulations. Thus Khrushchev, recognizing in 1956 that nuclear weapons had made war between great powers unthinkable as a means of acquiring tactical political and strategic advantages, announced in a sweeping doctrinal change that war between capitalism (that is, the United States) and communism (the Soviet Union) was no longer "fatalistically inevitable." But though Khrushchev dropped the inevitability-of-war thesis from Moscow's doctrinal baggage, he did not say that war was impossible, nor did he cease in his efforts to undermine his adversaries and extend Soviet influence, and neither did he suggest that peaceful coexistence means cooperation with other powers to alleviate global ills. Moreover, as one keen British analyst has observed, for the Soviets even the word "peace" has a very different usage: whereas in English, "peace" is a positive term, connoting goodwill, friendship, and harmony, in official Soviet use it is a state of being or relationship that can only occur when capitalism disappears and communism triumphs, when all "exploiting classes" have been eliminated. In the Russian, "peace," with its English implications is used for ridiculing opponents, for describing "illusory and Utopian" positions."

> If, for instance, the Russians are talking about a "peace policy," they may be meaning "a policy of avoiding armed conflict", or they may be meaning "a policy designed to further a communist takeover"; or they may be using the expression (and frequently are) in both these senses at once. The one thing, however, of which one can be quite certain is that they are *not* using it in the sense of "peace and goodwill towards the bourgeois world"; since this is, by definition, a concept which it is impossible for a communist to hold.[7]

Under Gorbachev's "new political thinking," we are witnessing less contentious formulations. In the 1985 edition of the authoritative Soviet *Diplomatic Dictionary,* the term peaceful coexistence is defined more benignly than during the Khrushchev and Brezhnev periods. There is no elaboration of its historical and ideological significance in the struggle between the capitalist and the communist systems nor any effort to single out the national-liberation movement in the Third World for particular attention. Maintaining that peaceful coexistence means "neither preservation of the social and political status quo in the world, nor weakening of ideological struggle," the 1985 usage of the term, which is linked to international détente, implies a live-and-let-live approach to the West that contrasts with the more combative attitude of the Brezhnev period.

In its fourth programmatic document (the previous one had been adopted in 1961, the second in 1919, the first—Karl Marx's *The Communist Manifesto*—in 1848), the CPSU declared that "the peaceful coexistence of states with different social systems . . . is not simply the absence of war. It is an international order under which good-neighborliness and cooperation, not military power, would dominate, and broad exchanges of scientific and technical achievements and cultural values to benefit all peoples would take place." This roseate formulation is, however, tempered by the assertion that the present era is one "of the transition from capitalism to socialism and communism and of the historic competition of the two world social and political systems . . . an era . . . of the struggle against imperialism [that is, the United States] and its policy of aggression and oppression."

At the twenty-seventh congress in February 1986, Gorbachev emphasized the need for cooperation in an increasingly interdependent world:

> We are realists and are perfectly well aware that the two worlds are divided by very many things, and deeply divided, too. But we also see clearly that the need to resolve most vital problems affecting all humanity must prompt them to interaction. . . .
>
> Such interaction is essential in order to prevent nuclear catastrophe, in order that civilization could survive. . . . The realistic dialectics of present-day development consists in a combination of competition and confrontation between the two systems and in a growing tendency towards interdependence of the countries of the world community. This is precisely the way, through the struggle of opposites, through arduous effort, groping in the dark to some extent, as it were, that the contradictory but interdependent and in many ways integral world is taking shape. . . .
>
> . . . that means recognizing that in the present situation there is no alternative to cooperation and interaction between all states. Thus, objective conditions—and I stress objective—have arisen in which the confrontation between capitalism and socialism can take place only, and exclusively, in the form of peaceful competition and peaceful rivalry. For us, peaceful coexistence is a political course which the Soviet Union intends to rigorously keep to in the future.[8]

The array of new formulations, proposals, and policies introduced by Gorbachev needs to be explained and debated as we try to ascertain their significance.

The New Cold War

An examination of Soviet-American relations reveals the persistence of basic asymmetries that complicate the process and prospects of moving toward a less dangerous world. These asymmetries arise from the different values, perceptions, interests, and ambitions of their respective leaderships. They need not lead to war, for reasons mentioned earlier, but they assuredly hold out little prospect for cooperation and friendship.

The first asymmetry relates to the general posture of the United States and the Soviet Union in world affairs today. Whereas the United States seeks stability and melioration of regional conflicts, the Soviet Union generally sees them (the Iran-Iraq War is an exception) as an opportunity to weaken the West. Soviet ambitions in black Africa, a low-priority area until the mid-1970s, have been whetted by the ascendancy in Angola, Mozambique, and Ethiopia of leaderships professing a belief in Marxism-Leninism, and Soviet military involvement is widespread, notwithstanding the additional strains this has imposed on relations with the United States. Readiness to commit economic and military resources to Third World clients shows no signs of flagging, as is evident in Central America with support for Cuba and the Sandinista regime in Nicaragua. Underlying Soviet readiness to accept the higher costs of an imperial policy is a belief in what might be called incrementalism: the view that modest gains, systematically garnered, can undermine the geopolitical foundations of an adversary and bring benefits, which over time can produce qualitative changes in the diplomatic environment within which the USSR operates and in the balance of power itself. To Soviet leaders, the nuclear age has not rendered obsolete the time-honored principle of strengthening one's position by undermining the alliances and alignments of an adversary.

A second asymmetry inheres in the disparity between the conventional force levels and capabilities of the Soviet Union and those of the United States, and between the Warsaw Pact and NATO. The ratio of two to one has been bandied about for many important categories of weapons. However, the Soviets enjoy greater advantages in such crucial categories of conventional weapons as tanks, artillery, motorized armored personnel carriers, and attack helicopters.

Third, a fundamental asymmetry lies in the way in which each superpower relates to the members of its respective alliance system. There is no need to detail here how little control the United States exercises over the behavior of its NATO allies. Furthermore, NATO's southern flank is going through a period of grave internal troubles that calls into question the very viability of the alliance in the Mediterranean. In the short run, at least, there is little that the United States can do to set the alliance in order. Certainly it cannot impose the kind of outward discipline on its allies that the Soviet Union can within the Warsaw Pact. The Romanians may behave like mavericks, but Bucharest remembers Prague in August 1968. It is careful to stay within the narrow limits of asssertive autonomy allowed by Moscow. The Brezhnev Doctrine is a writ no national Communist regime in Eastern Europe can afford to forget or ignore. Moscow's mailed fist keeps its reluctant allies in line.

A fourth asymmetry adversely affecting the ability of the two superpowers to reach meaningful political-military accords is the differing approach and attitude toward China. Moscow is uneasy over the kind of relationship that Washington seeks to establish with Beijing. Ever since Nixon's 1972 visit to China, the USSR has warily watched U.S. overtures, fearing that they presage a military buildup of China. In a remarkably candid interview, Dr. Georgii Arbatov, a member of the CPSU Central Committee and director of the Institute for the USA and Canada (an important Soviet think tank), noted that any effort to reequip the Chinese army "cannot be considered a step that can be reconciled with good intentions" toward the Soviet Union. The United States has to make a crucial decision, he continued: Does it want to build the bridge across the river or along the river? What kind of international situation does it want to create "in this dangerous nuclear age? . . . If you do want détente in Europe, let us say, if you want arms reduction, you would be very unwise and inconsistent and even self-defeating if at the same time you tried to fan up dangerous situations in another part of the world."[9]

The Soviets tell the fable of two hunters who are stalking tigers. They separate, and then one shouts, "I found a tiger!" The other cries, "Why don't you bring him back?" "He won't let go of me" is the answer. The moral is for the United States to be careful not to let the Chinese drag it too far away from better relations with the USSR. The Kremlin blamed Carter for encouraging the anti-Soviet statements (the attacks on "hegemonism") of Deng Xiaoping, the deputy premier and vice-chairman of the CCP, during his visit to the United States in February 1979. It also believed that China's invasion of Vietnam a month later was made possible only because of tacit support from Washington. The United States's backing of China in its quarrel with Vietnam, its preferential treatment of China economically, and the fear that it may seek to modernize China's military machine all heighten Soviet uneasiness about American policy.

A fifth asymmetry is the difference between the open society of the United States and the closed society of the Soviet Union. In the United States, public opinion, private lobbying, and Congressional attitudes can influence official policy (as they did on the issues of Vietnam, Cyprus, Lebanon, and El Salvador, for example); in the Soviet Union, they cannot. There are no tugs in the USSR between the executive and legislative branches of government to complicate the conduct of foreign policy or exasperate allies. If there are détentists or antidétentists in the Kremlin, we have no sure way of identifying them and little likelihood of directly influencing the outcome of whatever Soviet internal debate on foreign policy may be going on at any given time. Gorbachev seeks to encourage initiative in the management of the economy; but he shows no sign of easing the Kremlin's highly centralized control of foreign policy.

The differences in the two political systems reinforce the suspicions harbored by top leaders and complicate the tasks not only of negotiation but also of the communication of strongly held attitudes. Thus, Moscow's insensitivity to the political difficulties that its military presence in Cuba creates for a U.S. administration that would like to stabilize the arms race, expand trade, and improve relations derives partially from its erroneously attributing to the United States the mode of decision-making that operates in the Soviet Union. For example, Soviet leaders appear not to appreciate fully the independent and powerful role that the Congress plays in shaping U.S. foreign policy.

Sixth, there is a profound asymmetry in the way in which each country tends to view the other. U.S. leaders often think that they and Soviet leaders see the world similarly; the Soviets know better! The Soviet perception of the Soviet-American strategic relationship differs markedly from the American. The Soviet military and political establishment has held that the way to security is through a preponderance of military power. Thus, the USSR countered the U.S. offer of "essential equivalence" in the strategic nuclear field with a concept of "equal security" that was tantamount to assured superiority. In this respect, Gorbachev's proposal for "reasonable sufficiency" may represent a narrowing of past differences over actual force levels and deployments.

In 1835, Alexis de Tocqueville, a French nobleman who had been sent on a mission to study penal institutions in America, wrote, prophetically, of democratic America and despotic Russia, and of the characteristics that differentiate them, their societies, and their *Weltanschauung:*

> There are at the present time two great nations in the world, which started from different points, but seem to tend towards the same end. I allude to the Russians and the Americans. Both of them have grown up unnoticed; and while the attention of mankind was directed elsewhere, they have suddenly placed themselves in the front rank among the nations, and the world learned their existence and their greatness at almost the same time . . . .
>
> The American struggles against the obstacles that nature opposes to him; the adversaries of the Russian are men. The former combats the wilderness and savage life; the latter, civilization with all its arms. The conquests of the American are therefore gained by the plowshare; those of the Russian by the sword. The Anglo-American relies upon personal interest to accomplish his ends and gives free scope to the unguided strength and common sense of the people; the Russian centers all the authority of society in a single arm. The principal instrument of the former is freedom; of the latter, servitude. Their starting-point is different and their courses are not

> the same; yet each of them seems marked by the will of heaven to sway the destinies of half the globe.[10]

Finally, there is the difference in each leadership's view of the idea of linkage in foreign policy. Moscow rejects Washington's contention that accommodation and progress in one area depend on improvements and melioration of tensions in other areas as well. The Kremlin never shared the assumption, which was crucial in the Nixon-Kissinger approach to the Soviet Union, that the signing of the SALT I agreement implied Soviet restraint, for example, in Africa or the Middle East; it rejected any overt linkage between improved Soviet-American relations and Soviet support for national-liberation movements and regimes pursuing an anti-Western foreign policy. Moscow argued that the building of détente has to proceed agreement by agreement, that it applies to those issues on which accord has been reached. Détente is not, in its view, a reward for good behavior, but a necessity of the current era. In this respect, the Soviets have, ironically enough, been the issue-specific problem-solvers, and the Americans, the global generalizers and conceptual philosophers. In the past, the absence of a common frame of reference has resulted in disaster for détente.

Dilemmas of an Imperial Policy

By the second half of the 1970s, Moscow's ambitions in the Third World had seriously compromised its efforts to improve relations with the United States. The optimistic expectations for détente raised by the signing of SALT I and the subsequent round robin of summit visits had begun to wane by the convening of the Conference on Security and Cooperation in Europe in July 1975. A number of developments adversely affected the Soviet-American relationship: the near-confrontation during the Arab-Israeli war in October 1973; the resignation of Richard Nixon in August 1974; the uncertainty that followed the military coup in Portugal in April 1974 and led to the Portuguese Communist party's coming close to gaining effective control of the country; and the passage of the Jackson-Vanik amendment restricting U.S. credits to the USSR and denying most-favored-nation treatment in tariffs until Moscow eased restrictions on the emigration of dissidents, and the USSR's consequent abrogation of the economic agreement reached with Nixon for the repayment of World War II lend-lease debts. The Soviet-Cuban intervention in Angola in late 1975, which successfully brought to power a pro-Soviet regime, and the USSR's intervention in Ethiopia in 1976–1977 also contributed to the growing difficulties.[11]

In the late 1970s and early 1980s, the USSR and the United States stood essentially in an adversarial relationship. From the start of the Carter administration in January 1977, Soviet leaders went from uncertainty to disappointment, and then to uneasiness over their relations with the United States. In their view, the principal responsibility for the steady deterioration in Soviet-American relations rested with Washington. They were annoyed by Carter's stress on human rights, which was viewed as a move toward intensification of ideological struggle. His letter, written soon after taking office, to the dissident nuclear physicist Andrei Sakharov, and his support for Anatoly Shcharansky, the Jewish refusnik (that is, one who seeks to emigrate from the USSR), when the latter was arrested by Soviet authorities in 1977 and accused of working for U.S. intelligence, were especially irritating to the Soviets. More important, after a visit to Moscow by Secretary of State Cyrus Vance, Kremlin officials sharply criticized the Carter administration in March 1977, for seeking to undermine the essentials of the SALT II agreement that Moscow had regarded as all but sealed by negotiations with the Ford administration.

In Geneva in May 1977, Vance suggested cooperation on the Arab-Israeli problem as an indication of Washington's desire to put relations back on track. After some very secret discussions (only Carter, Vance, and National Security Council Adviser Zbigniew Brzezinski were involved on the American side), a U.S.-Soviet statement on the Middle East was issued on October 1, 1977, calling for a return to the Geneva venue and agreement on bringing the PLO into the negotiating process. However, within a week the Carter administration was forced by Israeli and congressional objections to renege on the agreement, to the ire of Moscow. Sadat's dramatic initiative and trip to Jerusalem and Carter's subsequent efforts on behalf of a separate Egyptian-Israeli agreement reinforced Moscow's view that divergence rather than convergence characterized Soviet-U.S. aims in the Middle East. Moscow questioned Washington's seriousness about détente.

During the following year the relationship continued to be troubled. Moscow resented the Camp David process that brought an Egyptian-Israeli treaty on March 26, 1979, without Soviet participation; the encumbrances that Washington placed in the way of greater trade and technological imports from the United States; U.S. attention to the normalization of Sino-American relations, at the expense, Moscow thought, of Soviet-American relations; and the fracas in August–September 1979 over the Soviet "combat brigade" in Cuba. Developments in Afghanistan and Iran further aggravated the Soviet-American relationship: a Soviet-backed Communist coup in Kabul in April 1978 triggered an anti-Communist nationalist guerrilla war that brought increasingly blatant Soviet involvement, culminating in December 1979 in a formal Soviet military invasion to prop up its Afghan puppets; and the toppling of the pro-Western regime of the shah in February 1979 ushered in a time of turmoil in Iran, highlighted by the seizure of U.S. embassy personnel in Tehran in early November 1979 and Moscow's unhelpful attitude throughout.

Symptomatic of the soured state of Soviet relations with the United States was the imbroglio over Cuba—it was hardly a crisis—that erupted in July 1979. Soon after President Carter returned from his Vienna meeting with Brezhnev, reports surfaced in Washington of a Soviet military buildup in Cuba. The administration's mishandling of the issue led to an escalation of tensions with Moscow out of all proportion to any substantive threat. Terming the Soviet combat brigade of 2600 men, 40 tanks, 60 armored personnel carriers, and other equipment an "unacceptable" military presence, Carter apparently expected the Kremlin to make some token concessions or conciliatory statements assuring the United States of the nonthreatening character of these troops, if only in the interest of strengthening his hand against the opponents of SALT II in the U.S. Senate. But Moscow obdurately denied that any buildup had taken place, insisting that the Soviet military presence in Cuba had not significantly changed since the 1962 Khrushchev-Kennedy understanding that settled the Cuban missile crisis. An editorial in *Pravda* set the Soviet tone:

> In this connection the need arises to recall the true state of affairs concerning Soviet military personnel in Cuba. For seventeen years now, a training center has existed in Cuba at which Soviet military personnel have helped Cuban servicemen to master Soviet military equipment used by the Cuban armed forces. Neither the number nor the functions of the said Soviet personnel have changed throughout all these years. All contentions about the arrival in Cuba of "organized Soviet combat units" are totally groundless. . . .
>
> It is also perfectly clear that the Soviet military personnel in Cuba do not and cannot pose any threat, either as regards their size or their functions, to the United States or any other country.[12]

Moscow refused to budge and successfully faced down Washington's efforts to pressure a change in the size and character of the Soviet military presence in Cuba. The advent of the Iranian hostage crisis in November 1979 and the Soviet invasion of Afghanistan the following month finished off efforts to improve Soviet-American relations during the Carter administration.

During the 1970s, however, all was not tension and disagreement. After Nixon's 1972 visit to Moscow and the signing of the SALT I agreement, the two countries concluded a series of agreements covering such diverse fields as science, public health, culture, space, housing, agriculture, oceanography, and nuclear energy, whose underlying rationale—at least for Washington—was the creation of a network of interdependence that would help stabilize and strengthen détente in the political-military fields.

Whither Détente

In the early 1980s, Soviet-American relations were at an all-time low. When Ronald Reagan entered the White House in January 1981, he brought with him a profoundly hostile attitude toward the Soviet Union, which he characterized as an "evil empire." Within days of taking office, he said that the only morality Soviet leaders recognize "is what will further their cause, meaning they reserve unto themselves the right to commit any crime, to lie, to cheat in order to obtain that."[13]

The Soviet press quickly responded in kind, but the Kremlin, though blaming the United States for poisoning the atmosphere of relations between the two countries, sounded a few conciliatory notes. After all, it had negotiated agreements with the conservative, anti-Communist Nixon administration, so it approached Ronald Reagan in much the same way. At the Twenty-sixth CPSU congress in late February 1981, Brezhnev said there was a need for "an active dialogue at all levels" and "We are prepared to have this dialogue," and he suggested the possibility of a summit conference.[14] But none of his proposals—for example, the suggestions that a special session of the UN Security Council be convened to discuss ways of "improving the international situation and preventing war," or that the two sides agree to "a moratorium on the development in Europe of new medium-range nuclear missile weapons of the NATO countries and the Soviet Union, that is, to freeze the existing quantitative and qualitative level of these weapons, naturally including the U.S. forward-based nuclear weapons in this region"—was attractive to the Reagan administration, whose agenda gave top priority to a massive and rapid defense buildup and force modernization to counter the growing threat that it perceived from the Soviet Union. Whether on missiles, Afghanistan, Poland, Persian Gulf security, CBMs, Central America, the Far East, southern Africa, or conventional force levels in Central Europe, Soviet and American leadership perceptions were virtually diametrically different.

In early May, the Soviet media accused Secretary of State Alexander M. Haig, Jr. of "rabid anti-Sovietism and anti-Communism." Condemnations of the Reagan administration's military buildup intensified, as Moscow mounted a major "peace offensive" hoping to forestall the Pershing-II/cruise missile deployment and to split the Western allies by playing on West European fears of Reagan's inexperience, strident anti-Soviet rhetoric, and opposition to the Soviet-European natural-gas pipeline project.

Throughout 1982 and 1983 Soviet-American relations went from bad to worse, leaving little of detente intact. In Europe, Moscow alleged U.S. interference in Poland's internal affairs, when the Reagan administration imposed sanctions against the Jaruzelski regime in the wake of the crack-down on Solidarity; decried U.S. opposition to East-West trade and the natural gas pipeline accord (Reagan grudgingly lifted sanctions against participating American and West European firms in November 1982); and bitterly opposed the deployment of Pershing-IIs, using propaganda, pressure, and infiltration of antiwar groups in an attempt to forestall the deployment that began in November 1983. In the Third World, Moscow expanded its military commitments to Syria, opposed U.S. involvement in Lebanon, and continued to wage its war in Afghanistan; in Central America, it used Cuba to funnel arms to rebels in El Salvador and build up the Sandinista government in Nicaragua; in Africa, it denounced U.S. backing of South Africa, involvement in the nonaggression treaty that South Africa and Mozambique signed in March 1984, and hostility toward "progressive" regimes; and in Southeast Asia, it upheld Vietnam's policy in Kampuchea and Laos. Moscow's mistrust was heightened by fears that Washington intended to provide China with advanced weaponry and technology. The USSR's downing of a civilian Korean airliner on the night of August 31/September 1, 1983, which Reagan called a "crime against humanity," occasioned a Soviet charge that the United States was "mounting a worldwide rabid anti-Soviet campaign."

Beyond the specifics of Soviet-American disagreements and differing perceptions of security and international problems, and even beyond the stridency and anger that characterized so many of their public exchanges, there was a dangerous impasse over how and what to negotiate. Perhaps more than ever before in the postwar period, Soviet leaders discerned in the attitudes and actions of the U.S. "ruling circles" confirmation of their worst fears of a sorely wounded but still powerful capitalist America trying to stem its decline by recourse to military power and ideological warfare. They saw in Reagan's policies a "crusade against communism," a basic unwillingness to negotiate, and a propensity toward high-risk, unpredictable behavior. On the eve of the Pershing-II deployment, a Soviet diplomat averred that "Détente has been deliberately murdered by the United States."[15] Aleksandr N. Yakovlev, director of a leading Soviet think tank, told a Japanese audience that "our relations with the United States are indeed at a very low level, whatever yardstick we use. A lot of bitterness, unpleasantness, and danger—I would say much danger—have accumulated in these relations."[16]

Perhaps realizing the parlous situation into which they were rapidly drifting, the superpowers agreed in January 1985 to resume formal talks on the whole range of nuclear issues. With the advent of the Gorbachev era two months later, their relationship underwent a rapid turnabout, so that by the end of the second Reagan administration the Soviet general secretary and the American president had held four summit meetings.

In any evaluation of future prospects for Soviet-American relations, it is essential that Western analysts give serious attention to several contentions that the Soviet elite believe go a long way toward explaining the erratic course of détente in previous decades.

First: The United States is not prepared to deal with the Soviet Union on the basis of equality. Soviet leaders think the United States has been unwilling to recognize the Soviet Union as an equal superpower, with global and legitimate interests whose views must be considered in the management of the international system. Moscow believes that Washington has yet to accept the parity that was implicit in the signing of SALT I—that it is unwilling to face up to the new power situation in the world. A minor incident illustrated this point. In April 1978 a U.S. congressional delegation visited Moscow and met with Kremlin leaders. During one session at the Ministry of Defense, Marshal Ogarkov responded to a question by referring to Brezhnev's Tula speech of January 18, 1977, in which he had rejected as "absurd and utterly unfounded" allegations of the Soviet Union's striving for a first-strike capability; Ogarkov reiterated that the USSR was not seeking nuclear superiority and noted that the United States did not seem reconciled to the Soviet Union's attainment of nuclear parity, but instead yearned for the old days of its former nuclear superiority, which, he added, was a thing of the past, as the United States would have to learn to accept.[17]

Second: The United States seeks advantage instead of accommodation from its military buildup. While invariably explaining their own deployments, force modernization, and military decisions in benign, defensive, or reactive terms, Soviet officials see Washington's unwillingness to take SALT I any further and its huge military expenditures as confirmation of their worst fears. *Pravda* put the matter thus:

> If someone in Washington cherishes the hope that it will thus be possible to insure unilateral military advantage for the USA, it is a futile hope. The Soviet Union will not permit such a turn of events to occur.[18]

Finally: The United States, especially under the Reagan administration, embarked on a campaign of primitive anti-Sovietism and venomous anticommunism that aimed at nothing less than isolating the Soviet Union in the world and spreading calumny about its social-political system. For example, on September 28, 1983, Yuri Andropov denounced Ronald Reagan for striving to "pile heaps of slander on the Soviet Union, on socialism as a social system. . . . One must say bluntly—it is an unattractive sight when, with a view to smearing the Soviet people, leaders of such a country as the United States resort to what almost amounts to obscenities alternating with hypocritical preaching about morals and humanism:"

> Starting with a scare about the "Soviet military threat," they have now proclaimed a "crusade" against socialism as a social system. Attempts are being made to convince people that there is no room for socialism in the world; . . . malicious attacks on the Soviet Union produce a natural feeling of indignation. But our nerves are strong, and we do not base our policy on emotions.[19]

Perestroika or Peredyshka?

Is Gorbachev interested in the kind of extensive restructuring (*perestroika*) of foreign policy that he is pushing internally or is he seeking a respite (*peredyshka*) to gain time to modernize the Soviet economy and better prepare it for military-political competition with the United States in the twenty-first century? He has already gone much further in the arms control field and in bilateral relations with the United States than anyone would have thought possible when he came to power in March 1985. The dynamism he introduced in Soviet foreign policy poses new challenges to the United States.

Mikhail S. Gorbachev was born in 1931, in Stavropol, an agricultural area between the Black and Caspian Seas, located in the RSFSR. Before graduating from Moscow University in 1955 with a degree in law, he worked on a machine-tractor station and gained recognition as a leader in the Komsomol (the Young Communist League). After joining the party in 1952 he rose rapidly, attracting the attention of Brezhnev and Andropov for his work in the Stavropol region. There he remained throughout his professional career, until called to Moscow in November 1978 to become a member of the CPSU Secretariat, responsible for agriculture. Two years later, he was appointed a voting member of the Politburo as well. He has impressed foreign leaders, who describe him as intelligent, extremely self-assured, energetic, well-informed, having a solid grasp of difficult issues, unshakable in his views, argumentative, a skilled debater, and a shrewd negotiator. In brief, Gorbachev is a formidable national leader.

During the process of consolidating his power and reordering the country's foreign policy agenda, Gorbachev carried out sweeping personnel changes. Perhaps most important was the elevation of Andrei Gromyko to the ceremonial position of chairman of the Presidium of the Council of Ministers (the titular post of president of the USSR) and his replacement as foreign minister by Eduard Shevardnadze, the head of the Georgian SSR, who had shown himself to be efficient and reform-oriented. Among the many other appointments Gorbachev has made in the foreign affairs field, two warrant attention because they illustrate the importance that he attaches to relations with the United States and with the West in general: Anatoly Dobrynin, the USSR's ambassador to the United States from 1962 to 1986, elected to the CPSU Secretariat in March 1986 and made responsible for foreign policy; and Aleksandr Yakovlev, who first came to the United States in the late 1950s as part of the Soviet-American cultural exchange and who served many years as ambassador in Canada, elected at the same time as Dobrynin and put in charge of ideology and culture. Both are members of Gorbachev's inner circle of advisers.

By mid-1985 Gorbachev assumed the diplomatic offensive, presenting the United States with a range of arms control proposals aimed at drastically reducing offensive weapons, and accepting Reagan's proposal for an early summit. The first of the four summits that the two leaders held was convened in Geneva in November 1985 and succeeded in taking the frost out of Soviet-American relations. The second, in Reykjavik, Iceland, in October 1986, foundered on Gorbachev's heavy-handed attempt to kill SDI. At the third, held in Washington, D.C. in December 1987, there was a precedent-setting agreement abolishing an entire category of weapons—intermediate range missiles—and instituting an elaborate procedure for on-site inspection to verify the consequent INF treaty. The fourth, was held in Moscow from May 29 to June 2, 1988; while it did not break important new ground, it may serve to strengthen the case for regular summits, even in the absence of concrete achievements.

Summits can play a variety of roles: they test the intentions of one's opponent; reach understandings on "gray areas," issues and regions that are of interest but are not vital to national survival; and they normalize high-level meetings as part of a longer term process of stabilizing diplomatic relationships. However, given the regular changes of presidents in the United States, institutionalizing summits could mislead Moscow into assuming continuities in policy that would not be forthcoming. And, unless they are accompanied by a steady record of achievements, which may be expecting far too much given the erratic record of the 1970s and 1980s, they can degenerate into trivializing media opportunities devoid of substance.

The shift in Soviet policy from acrimony to accord was unveiled in Moscow's readiness to accept Reagan's conditions for an INF treaty: no linkage of U.S. and Soviet missile and nuclear systems to those possessed by Great Britain and France; elimination of an entire category of weapons; and agreement to on-site inspection to ensure adequate verification. Improved relations with the United States seem to be the centerpiece of

Gorbachev's "new political thinking" in foreign affairs. How far he is prepared to go, not only in efforts to reduce nuclear and conventional force levels, but in altering the character of military deployments in Central Europe, will have to be determined in the coming years through relevant bilateral and multilateral negotiations. Arms control has dominated Gorbachev's American agenda, but for any long term improvement in U.S.-Soviet relations to take hold, there will have to be progress toward solutions of regional conflicts, ending of human rights abuses, and expansion of economic ties.

The release from prison in early 1987 of prominent dissidents such as Yuri Orlov (one of the founders in 1976 of the Moscow Helsinki Group to monitor human rights violations in the USSR), Anatoly Koryagin (a psychiatrist who spoke out against the KGB's misuse of psychiatry to change political behavior), and Sergei Grigoryants (a literary critic and activist on human rights issues); the increase in Soviet Jewish emigration from less than 900 in 1986 to more than 8000 in 1987; and the passing in January 1988 of national legislation making illegal the incarceration of individuals in psychiatric hospitals controlled by the secret police on the basis of hearsay and without judicial approval are signs of change under Gorbachev. In the economic realm, *perestroika* encourages the establishment of joint ventures with foreign investors and the grant of more autonomy to some ministries engaged in foreign trade, evidence of the desire to engage the Soviet Union more heavily in the international economic system. For the moment, however, notwithstanding expressions of keen interest on both sides in expanding trade, the Soviet Union and the United States do little business with each other, less than one percent of either country's GNP.

A number of factors impel Gorbachev to undertake far-reaching changes at home and abroad. First, he seeks to reverse the Soviet Union's stagnation. Realizing, and acknowledging, that economic and social problems have proliferated at a rate far greater than had originally been thought possible, he has geared his policies toward revitalizing the economy, tackling corrosive social alienation that is manifested in widespread alcoholism and corruption, and restoring a sense of élan and purposefulness to a population that has grown cynical, selfishly acquisitive, and unwilling to work hard in the absence of rewards for merit or productivity. To raise the standard of living and the quality of life, Gorbachev must stimulate production and efficiency in the economy's civilian sectors—industrial, agricultural, and service. He knows that defense expenditures consume too large a proportion of the country's GNP; that the quality of consumer goods and services is poor; and that necessary technological changes, including the intensive use of computers and photocopiers, may entail social and political headaches. However, allowing a policy of drift for another decade or two could well reduce the Soviet Union to the status of a second rate economic and military power.

Second, Gorbachev's move toward a Soviet military doctrine that emphasizes "reasonable sufficiency" rather than "superiority" suggests that influential sectors of the political-military elite recognize the need for a new allocation of scarce resources: their aims are still the defense of the Soviet Union, preservation of the Soviet imperial order, and a major role in world affairs, but to be realized these goals require a lengthy period of addressing debilitating domestic problems.

Third, looking at the international environment, Gorbachev does not see any immediate threats that necessitate military expenditures of the magnitude allocated by his predecessors. The USSR is not threatened with invasion or attack, and it possesses more than enough power for deterrence, defense, and power projection in the Third World. Indeed, its military power may have reached the limit of what can be usefully applied to the process of expanding Soviet influence and interests; in Soviet terms, the military component of the "correlation of forces" (the multifaceted concept used by the Soviets to evaluate the international situation and the USSR's overall relationship to key adversaries) is sound in the present global context and needs to be augmented by economic and political means. By downgrading the military instrument, or at least using it only in selective Third World situations, and upgrading diplomatic, political-cultural, and economic instruments, the USSR may be able to improve its strategic position and undermine U.S. attempts to forge an anti-Soviet alignment in the decades ahead. The present epoch offers opportunities for advance through nonmilitary means, an assessment that accords with Gorbachev's outlook.

Finally, there is the "X" factor: the personality and outlook of Gorbachev. A leader has come on to the Soviet political scene with a vision of what must be done to prepare the Soviet Union to enter the next century in a position of strength. This vision is harnessed to a drive, determination, and intelligence that have been absent from the Soviet leadership since the eras of Lenin and Stalin. According to Richard Nixon, Gorbachev is abler than Khrushchev or Brezhnev, the two Soviet leaders with whom he dealt while in office. Of his two hour meeting with him in July 1986, Nixon reports that "it was the most impressive performance I have witnessed in nearly 40 years of meetings with world leaders."[20] Leadership is important. Nothing is inevitable in the rise and fall of great powers. That the Soviet leadership has chosen as its head someone whose policies and outlook differ so radically from those who were his mentors and superiors is testament to the resiliency and strength of the Soviet system of oligarchic authoritarianism.

Notes

1. *Pravda,* July 13, 1960.
2. *Khrushchev Remembers* (Boston: Little, Brown, 1970), 546–47.
3. Joseph G. Whelan, *Soviet Diplomacy and Negotiating Behavior: Emerging New Context for U.S. Diplomacy* (Washington, D.C.: Committee on Foreign Affairs, 1979), 360–61.
4. "Mirnoe sosushchestvovanie" [Peaceful coexistence], *Diplomaticheskii slovar'* [*diplomatic dictionary*], Vol. II (Moscow: Politizdat, 1961), 299.
5. *Soviet News,* No. 4107 (September 8, 1959), 142.
6. L. I. Brezhnev, "Report of the CPSU Central Committee and the Immediate Tasks of the Party in Home and Foreign Policy," *Socialism: Theory and Practice,* No. 3 (March 1976), 39.
7. P. H. Vigor, *The Soviet View of War, Peace, and Neutrality* (London: Routledge & Kegan Paul, 1975), 165, 169.
8. FBIS/SOV/Party Congresses, 26 February 1986, 0 9, 0 30.
9. *London Observer,* November 12, 1978.
10. Alexis de Tocqueville, *Democracy in America,* Vol. 1. Edited by Phillips Bradley. (New York: Vintage, 1959), 452.
11. For example, Henry Kissinger, *Years of Upheaval* (Boston: Little, Brown, 1982), passim.
12. *Pravda,* September 11, 1979.
13. *New York Times,* January 30, 1981.
14. *Pravda,* February 24, 1981.
15. *New York Times,* November 26, 1983.
16. Foreign Broadcast Information Service/USSR International Affairs, March 9, 1984, AA5.
17. Author's discussion with one of the U.S. attendees, March 1984.
18. As quoted in the *New York Times,* January 2, 1983.
19. *New York Times,* September 29, 1983.
20. Richard Nixon, "Dealing with Gorbachev," *New York Times Magazine* (March 13, 1988), 30.

Selected Bibliography

BELL, CORAL. *The Diplomacy of Détente: The Kissinger Era.* New York: St. Martin's Press, 1977.

BRZEZINSKI, ZBIGNIEW. *Game Plan: A Geostrategic Framework for the Conduct of the U.S.-Soviet Contest.* Boston: Atlantic Monthly Press, 1986.

CALDWELL, DAN. *American-Soviet Relations: From 1947 to the Nixon-Kissinger Grand Design.* Westport, Calif.: Greenwood Press, 1981.

FINDER, JOSEPH. *Red Carpet.* New York: Holt, Rinehart and Winston, 1983.

GELMAN, HARRY. *The Brezhnev Politburo and the Decline of Détente.* Ithaca: Cornell University Press, 1984.

HYLAND, WILLIAM G. *Mortal Rivals: Superpower Relations From Nixon to Reagan.* New York: Random House, 1987.

JAMGOTCH, NISH, JR. *Sectors of Mutual Benefit in U.S.-Soviet Relations.* Durham: Duke University Press, 1985.

KENNAN, GEORGE F. *The Nuclear Delusion: Soviet-American Relations in the Atomic Age.* Rev. ed. New York: Pantheon, 1983.

LENCZOWSKI, JOHN. *Soviet Perceptions of U.S. Foreign Policy.* Ithaca: Cornell University Press, 1982.

MCDOUGALL, WALLACE. *The Heavens and the Earth: U.S.-Soviet Competition in Space.* New York: Basic Books, 1984.

NOGEE, JOSEPH L. and JOHN SPANIER. *Peace Impossible—War Unlikely: The Cold War Between the United States and the Soviet Union.* Glenview, Ill.: Scott, Foresman/Little, Brown, 1988.

NYE, JOSEPH S. (ED.). *The Making of America's Soviet Policy.* New Haven: Yale University Press, 1984.

RICHMOND, YALE. *U.S.-Soviet Cultural Exchanges, 1958–1986: Who Wins?* Boulder: Westview Press, 1987.

ROSITZKE, HARRY. *Managing Moscow: Guns or Goods?* New York: Morrow, 1984.

SCHWARTZ, MORTON. *Soviet Perceptions of the United States.* Berkeley: University of California Press, 1978.

TAUBMAN, WILLIAM. *Stalin's American Policy.* New York: W. W. Norton, 1982.

ULAM, ADAM B. *The Rivals: America and Russia Since World War II.* New York: Viking, 1971.

WHITE, RALPH K. *Fearful Warriors: A Psychological Profile of U.S.-Soviet Relations.* New York: Free Press, 1984.

14
Soviet Strategy to the Year 2000*

What probable trends will shape Soviet foreign policy in the year 2000 and beyond? The Chinese say it is very difficult to make predictions, especially about the future. Sociologist Daniel Bell once observed that any attempt to forecast trends is extremely hazardous because of "the variabilities of accident, folly, and simply human cantankerousness." Still, there is benefit to be derived from speculating, from stimulating the imagination to visualize what might be and what needs to be done to bring about a possibly more secure tomorrow. But first, it might be useful to recall the recent, unanticipated developments that greatly affected Soviet foreign policy, to distinguish the continuities and the discontinuities, and from this perspective enhance our insight into the present and find a basis for projections into the future.

The advent of the Gorbachev era invites comparison with the Khrushchev era. Both leaders were confronted by major domestic and foreign policy dilemmas. Khrushchev's decisions—what he did and what happened, though causality is not always certain—are a matter of record. Gorbachev has manifested some indications of what he would like to do and has shown himself skillful in consolidating power and initiating a diverse range of policies at home and abroad.

Many of the essentials of Khrushchev's foreign policy were embraced by his successors; in the main, they also guide Gorbachev's policy, allowing

---

* An expanded version of this chapter appears in Alvin Z. Rubinstein, *Moscow's Third World Strategy* (Princeton: Princeton University Press, 1989).

for the tactical differences that reflect the new circumstances. These essentials are a disposition toward loosening controls on the individual members of the Soviet bloc, consonant with continued Soviet military-political hegemony; parity with the United States in the nuclear field; peaceful coexistence with the West, by which is meant cooperation in certain sectors but, in all else, competition short of war as part of an unrelenting effort to derive advantage from Western weaknesses; and the projection of Soviet power into the Third World. There is no reason to expect the Kremlin to downgrade any of these policies.

Continuities

Though no two situations or sets of circumstances are exactly alike, the task of locating Gorbachev somewhere along the spectrum of probable behavior may be facilitated by the identification of essential similarities in the past and in the present. The following generalizations are offered tentatively, in the spirit of encouraging thought.

The similarities are striking:

- the struggle for power at a time of mounting economic and political dilemmas;
- the quest for rationalization of Soviet-East European economic relationships, subject to Moscow's strategic control;
- the need to improve relations with the United States; and
- the readiness to pursue Soviet objectives in the Third World though aware of possible adverse consequences for Soviet-American relations.

First, in the struggle for political ascendancy, each had to revamp the structure of power that he inherited. The key to Khrushchev's success was de-Stalinization; for Gorbachev it is de-Brezhnevization. Whereas de-Stalinization entailed the end of one-man rule that rested on the tyrannization of the party by the secret police and the restoration of the party as the preeminent political institution of Soviet society, de-Brezhnevization requires renewal of the middle level bureaucracies that administer the country's economic, social, and political institutions. Gorbachev appears to have consolidated his position as the leading figure in the Communist Party. Having staffed the Politburo, the Secretariat, and the Central Committee with like-minded contemporaries, he must now ensure that they impose his priorities and values on the various levels (national, republic, obkom, raikom) of the political system and implement his "new political thinking." De-Brezhnevization is essential for the success of Gorbachev's campaign to modernize the economy, weed out corruption, and foster the acceleration of economic development. He may be forced to a more modest setting of his sights by the obdurate resistance of the bureaucracies that flourished during the Brezhnev-Andropov-Chernenko periods. As Khrushchev learned, wielding political power does not guarantee one the ability to transform the way in which the economy is operated.

Second, Eastern Europe is no less a problem for Gorbachev than it was for Khrushchev. In the past, when confronted with a choice between viability and cohesion, Moscow opted for the latter. Its absorption with security has overshadowed its willingness to permit more rational, less exploitative economic relationships with its East European satellites. Khrushchev sought to decentralize the empire that Stalin had created from 1945 to 1953, to enhance its economic utility to the Soviet Union, but he was not prepared for the disruptive tidal consequences of de-Stalinization. As matters turned out, the effort at imperial decompression threatened the very foundations of Soviet rule. His successors groped unsuccessfully for a formula that would foster sustained economic growth and permit a considerable measure of autonomy within politically tolerable parameters. Brezhnev tried to loosen things up in Comecon, encouraging a degree of specialization and greater integration among the members, but Moscow's insistence on ultimate administrative and political control reinforced propensities toward bureaucratic inertia and innate conservatism in dealing with economic issues.

Gorbachev is wary of the dangers of economic and political reform in Eastern Europe. He remembers the upheavals of 1956 and recognizes the persistence with which the nationalism and national interests of individual East European countries complicate Soviet objectives in the socialist camp. Moscow's call for bloc cohesion to counter "imperialism's anticommunist crusade" has not, however, been followed up by any specific or long-term initiatives. Being undecided about what to do, Gorbachev has permitted each bloc member to cope with problems in its own way—at least for the time being. Vladimir V. Kusin of Radio Free Europe notes that Gorbachev has not relaxed Moscow's "grip on the area to the point where disintegration might, or almost certainly would, ensue":

> He has eschewed endorsing market-based reform for individual countries or as an underpinning of CMEA. He has prodded all of the client states into domestic action designed to increase efficiency, discipline, and thrift, and he asked them to cut corruption and abuse of power. He affirmed the Soviet primacy in coordinating the way the East-West relationship was to be shaped and conducted.
>
> Nevertheless, Gorbachev has fine-tuned rather than bulldozed. . . . The Hungarians continue their reforms, and so far the Czechoslovaks go ahead with their non-reforms. He has conceded that national peculiarities and interests do not have to be trampled underfoot but could be amicably

> dovetailed in order to produce internationalist ideological satisfaction. He has given his client states the right to deal with the West as long as they eschew countering Soviet strategic objectives, comply with CMEA's integration plans, and avoid becoming dependent on Western mercies. . . .
>
> In at least one respect Gorbachev has so far failed to provide an adequate answer to the East European challenge. He has not charted a credible path toward making the region economically healthy.*

Third, Soviet-American relations in the 1980s, as in the 1960s, are in a state of flux. Normalization for any sustained period is elusive: for Khrushchev there were crises over Berlin and Cuba; for Gorbachev, SDI, Afghanistan, and force levels in Central Europe are among the contentious issues preventing a meaningful improvement in relations. Nonetheless, Gorbachev, like Khrushchev, was able to set in motion initiatives that conveyed a sense of the centrality that Moscow placed on the U.S.-Soviet relationship. And he, too, seeks better relations with the United States for much the same reasons: the USSR's need for Western technology and credits; its quest for stability in Europe; concern over China; and interest in limiting or at least stabilizing the nuclear relationship.

Finally, the USSR persists with policies in the Third World irrespective of their adverse consequences for U.S.-Soviet relations. The essential continuity in the policy pioneered by Khrushchev, driven forward by Brezhnev, and thus far sustained by Gorbachev, suggests that the policy is considered strategically sound by the key oligarchs in the party, military, and government, notwithstanding occasional setbacks and possible differences over particular aspects of it. Afghanistan may be a litmus test of Gorbachev's future intentions toward the Third World. If he does, in fact, withdraw all Soviet troops from Afghanistan and permits the Afghan people to decide their own future, including a return to an independent, non-Communist, nonaligned status—as he has indicated an intention to do—his policy will have to be reevaluated.

Changes

Let us lead into our examination of the equally important differences between the two eras by noting one change, minor in itself, that may, however, have long-term significance. Under Khrushchev, the slogan "peaceful competition" was emblazoned everywhere. He took it seriously and believed that the Soviet experience could serve as a model for the world, especially in the newly independent countries of Africa, Asia, and

---

* Vladimir V. Kusin, "Gorbachev and Eastern Europe," *Problems of Communism,* Vol. XXXV, No. 1 (January–February 1986), 53.

the Middle East. By the 1970s, Brezhnev dropped the slogan, realizing that the Soviet Union was not going to catch up and surpass the U.S. economy and move into the communist stage of bountiful production and consumption by the next decade. Gorbachev is realist enough to know that there is no possibility of the Soviet Union's competing economically with the United States in the foreseeable future. This modified expectation could presage a fundamental change of outlook and policy. Gorbachev's determination to ensure that the Soviet Union remains a world power will, presumably then, be based on military, not economic strength, and on skill in exploiting political divisions and rivalries in different regions of the world. The strategic context within which the Soviet diplomacy seeks to advance Soviet goals can be enhanced by political as well as military means.

There have been a number of changes in the international situation and in the Soviet-American relationship which must make Gorbachev's foreign policy outlook different from Khrushchev's and which must influence Soviet policy in the future:

- Gorbachev's U.S.S.R. is far stronger and is a credible nuclear power;
- Gorbachev has many more options in the Third World;
- the Far East is a major foreign policy problem; and
- U.S. influence in the international system is less in the 1980s than it was in the 1950s.

Whereas in the 1950s the Soviet Union was a significantly weaker military power with no credible nuclear force and no long-range bomber or SLBM capability, in the 1980s it enjoys essential equivalence or parity with the United States in the nuclear field. Khrushchev operated from military inferiority, but Gorbachev commands an imposing array of powerful forces. Whereas Khrushchev's reach was continental, Gorbachev's is global; and whereas Khrushchev was driven by a need to catch up to the United States in strategic weapons or dramatically offset the gap with lesser systems, Gorbachev's problem is how to preserve the reliance on MAD, confine SDI, and use political means to keep the arms race from draining away resources needed for domestic modernization.

Gorbachev is better positioned militarily, but he faces tougher obstacles in arms control: the issues are more complex, more interrelated, more momentous in their potential consequences than in Khrushchev's day, thus his active efforts to exploit public diplomacy for wresting concessions from the United States at the negotiating table. In public, Gorbachev sounds flexible; in private, the Soviet position is tough and purposeful, insisting that any deep cuts in offensive weapons must be preceded by agreed limits on the development of a space-based defense system.

Gorbachev is more adept than Khrushchev in projecting an image of reasonableness and pragmatism abroad, but he is also far more respectful of the military and far less likely to be high-handed with them in his efforts to trim defense expenditures. Today, the military may be even more influential in commanding scarce resources, partly because of the U.S. arms buildup under the Reagan administration, partly because of the mushrooming costs of defense modernization, and partly because the party leadership is sensitive to the military's need to absorb the defeat in Afghanistan. The world is a more dangerous place for the Soviet Union than it was in the 1950s. Then, the only military threat was the American nuclear capability, which, while real enough, was sheathed for deterrent purposes. In present circumstances, however, besides the ever-present nuclear problem, NATO forces are stronger, relative to Soviet bloc forces, than they were thirty years ago; China is an antagonist not an ally; the war in Afghanistan has been an unanticipated drain; and commitments in different parts of the Third World complicate the military's preparedness posture.

Next, Gorbachev's foreign policy attitude toward the Third World is significantly different from Khrushchev's in taking the offensive and probing forcefully for advantage. It is not merely strategic denial that Moscow seeks, but strategic debasement—the weakening of U.S. policy regionally and globally, and the dissipation of its resources in areas of marginal utility to the Soviet Union. Judging by preliminary evidence, Gorbachev's inclination is to exploit further the cost-effective indirect strategy of frustrating U.S. policy and aggravating discord in the Western alliance that his predecessors stumbled upon and gave their consensual support to over a period of three decades.

Over the past 20 years, the Soviet Union has developed a power projection capability to safeguard clients and influence events in ways that were previously beyond its ken; and the Third World environment within which it operates has undergone a polarization and militarization that enhance the value of what Moscow is best equipped to provide, namely, protection and a method of institutionalizing power. The change in outlook in much of the Third World dovetails nicely with the strong military hand that Gorbachev has to play. Though prime clients such as Cuba and Vietnam receive economic assistance, Moscow's main contributions are military.

Gorbachev's activism in the Third World is generated by commitment to the underlying strategic rationale that was so persuasive for his predecessors, but that, more than ever before, relies on military power. Gone is the belief in the suitability of the Soviet model of development; gone is the perceived need to develop close economic ties as a condition for long-term, politically meaningful relationships; and gone, too, is the ideological optimism for socialism in our time.

His approach is dominated by strategic-military considerations. Equally important, he believes that these are what motivate Third World clients to look to the Soviet Union. The result is a reciprocal courtship that is mutually cynical in its outlook and expectations. Thus, unlike Khrushchev, with his hopes of a de facto alignment between the Soviet camp and the new nations based on shared ideological affinities, Gorbachev looks at the Third World without illusions and with a cold eye for strategic advantage.

Third, the Far East is a more serious foreign policy problem for Gorbachev than it was for Khrushchev. Sino-Soviet relations turned sour under Khrushchev, though not until the late 1950s. The twin shocks of de-Stalinization and détente with the West rocked Mao Tse-tung's belief in a bipolar world that would keep the Soviet Union and the United States ideological-political antagonists. When Khrushchev's espousal of "peaceful coexistence" and doctrinal revision asserting that war was no longer "fatalistically inevitable"—the ideological rationale for Moscow's unwillingness to use its nuclear power on China's behalf to regain Taiwan—came into conflict with Mao's revolutionary line, then personal antipathies further worsened the deteriorating political relationship.

Khrushchev had no reason to fear China militarily; Gorbachev does. Indeed, for the first time since the 1920s and 1930s, a Soviet leadership has cause for concern over the threat to its security from an Asian power. Khrushchev squandered Stalin's bequest of a military-political alliance with a dependent, ideologically-congenial China. Gorbachev must find a way of restoring normalcy to a relationship that has profound implications for Moscow's future in the Far East and for the U.S.-Soviet relations as well.

Finally, the overall strategic environment within which the Soviet-American rivalry operates has become far less congenial to the United States than formerly and perhaps better-suited to the advancement of Soviet rather than American purposes. Relatively speaking, the Soviet Union's geostrategic, military, political, and even economic situation may be better off than that of the United States. Gorbachev's Soviet Union has major problems, but so does the United States. The USSR is not a backward country. Indeed, in terms of resource potential, it may be far better positioned to expand its economic strength in the 21st century than any other country in the world. It alone is capable of pursuing a policy of autarchy. True, the Soviet economy lags perennially behind countries of the West and Japan, but to lag behind is not to falter. The Soviet Union can absorb increased military spending by squeezing a nationalistic and politically compliant population. Lagging behind the United States by five or even ten years in high-tech military fields does not mean that the USSR is becoming increasingly weaker militarily or unable to pursue the kinds of diverse policies that it has over the past thirty years. Gorbachev is realist enough to appreciate that Soviet militarism drains men and resources and keeps the USSR from modernizing as extensively as he would like. Also, he is probably ideological enough to sense that the U.S. economy has profound problems (for example, the chronic U.S. balance of payments deficit, the Third World indebtedness, and the rising pressures for protectionism), any one of which could catapult the Western world into a depression having severe domestic social, economic, political, and military consequences.

Observations

Moscow will not risk war with the United States in order to acquire territory, but neither will it become a status quo power, averse to risk or to exploiting opportunities to improve its strategic position and weaken that of its main adversaries—the United States, Western Europe, and China. The Kremlin seeks influence, not territory. In this sense, the Soviet Union has become basically an intrusive, rather than expansionist, power. By this I mean that there is no reason to believe its security needs and political ambitions will impel it toward additional territorial acquisitions. Whatever were the special circumstances that led the Soviet Union to invade Afghanistan, my argument is that Soviet policy there does not typify Kremlin aims elsewhere in the Third World; if anything, the USSR's experience may bring home to the Kremlin the exorbitant costs of new conquests and occasion, in the future, greater caution in comparable circumstances of geostrategic temptation.

Of course, what Gorbachev does will depend not only on his ambitions and the Soviet Union's capabilities for exploiting opportunities abroad, but also on the West's responses to its own internal challenges and the problems of managing the international system that it dominates. What the West and Japan do inevitably affects what the Soviet Union can or cannot do: cohesion in NATO and cooperation among the Western nations, whether on defense, trade, or finance, strengthen stability in Europe and enhance deterrence; a resolution of the growing range of U.S.-Japanese tensions is essential for the future of economic growth and political stability in the Pacific Basin; and so on.

Extrapolation from the recent past is inevitable. The thrust of the analysis presented here is toward essential continuity in the decade or so ahead. After all, successive leaders from Khrushchev to Gorbachev have pursued objectives that, in their fundamentals, seem to have enjoyed widespread support among the oligarchs in the party and the military; preservation of the imperial system in Eastern Europe; improved relations with the United States, including arms control agreements if possible; normalization of ties with China and Japan; and competitive rivalry with the United States in the Third World. Within each of these broad issue areas there is latitude for toughness or accommodation, forceful power projection or studied equivocation, expanded commitments or political diffidence. We can generally agree on what Soviet policy actually is, if not always on what motivates the leadership.

Gorbachev's style is new. It features skillful public relations, cultivation of an image of reasonableness, bold initiatives designed to exploit NATO divisions, and activism on a scale that suggests a man in charge. What is at issue is his intent. In this connection, it might be well to remember Andrei Gromyko's observation that Gorbachev is a man who smiles, yet whose smile has "iron teeth."

Gorbachev may want Western trade and technology and a respite from the escalating arms race, but the USSR's experience must make it wary of reliance on détente to obtain the assistance needed for modernization. Stabilizing the strategic arms race is high on Gorbachev's agenda, but developing the kind of confidence in the efficacy of agreements and their follow-on verification that would lead to deep cuts in defense spending will take a minimum of five years, probably longer. In the absence of a profound transformation of the Soviet-American political relationship, Moscow's ability to borrow heavily in international financial markets and attract American capital will be limited. Accordingly, the Soviet leadership may decide to focus on developing its own enormous but underutilized resource base.

It will be years before the fate of Gorbachev's economic restructuring is known. That policy has three main components: institutional change relating to the issue of centralization versus decentralization; managerial authority with its tie-in to the entire incentive system; and correlation of the pricing mechanism and the flow of information. How this three-fold process of incipient and extensive change might affect foreign policy issues is simply impossible to hazard at this early date. For the foreseeable future, therefore, the dictates of geography and established approaches to security and transactions with the outside world should be the principal criteria used to speculate about Soviet policy.

This would suggest that the Gorbachev generation will do whatever is required to preserve the Soviet empire, maintain strategic nuclear equivalence with the United States, and ensure the "equal security" it considers vital for its national security. The old Russian maxim, "Better one army too many, than one division too few," is as operative today as in the past.

The area of the world that seems least likely to experience a withdrawal or diminution of Soviet power is Eastern Europe. Soviet domination of Eastern and Central Europe will remain nonnegotiable. Moscow will not relinquish strategic-military control over its forward positions in Europe; nor will it, under any circumstances that can be imagined in the years ahead, permit the reunification of Germany. Whatever the costs of empire, they will be borne in the center of Europe because the Soviets have come to perceive this area as vital for the stability and preservation of their imperial system.

Nationalism in the empire is an old Russian bogey. It is an ever-present challenge to the stability of Russian rule. In Eastern Europe it bedevils Moscow's quest for economic integration and haunts the contingency planning of the Soviet General Staff which must continually worry about the reliability of the East European forces in the Warsaw Pact under varying conditions of danger. Barring an upheaval inside the Soviet Union—an unlikely development—the region will remain Soviet-controlled and communist, but divided, dispirited and, for the most part, profoundly antipathetical to the Soviet Union.

Toward Western Europe, Soviet aims will remain the same. They are the derangement of NATO; perpetuation of a favorable military balance through an adroit and adapting mixture of force modernization, a strong forward deployment in Central Europe (long a cardinal tenet of Russian military doctrine), and diplomatic blandishments; improved relations with the main European actors, with special attention to economic ties; and maintenance of a friendly and nonnuclear Federal Republic of Germany. Overall, Soviet strategy seems wedded to the same general approach in the 1990s that brought it such handsome benefits in the 1970s.

Soviet policy in the Third World is not apt to change significantly under Gorbachev. It has proven itself time and again to be a cost-effective way of weakening U.S. power at the center by engaging it in regions that are of marginal interest to the Soviet Union. Unlike Europe or the Far East, where relatively stable political-military constellations or entities coincide generally with territorially-delineated centers of established authority, the Middle East, Southern Asia, Africa, and Central America are characterized by unanticipated dealignment and systemic instability, and are therefore natural arenas for superpower rivalry, with minimal risk of direct confrontation.

Gorbachev has yet to shed any clients; though in Afghanistan he seems to be writing off Najib. Elsewhere in the Third World the Soviet outreach has not been reined in, not even slightly. Economic difficulties at home are no apparent bar to continuation of present policy, which is predominately military in character. If few new ventures have been undertaken, it is only because the promising opportunities have not presented themselves to Soviet leaders for possible underwriting.

If continuity is to be the pattern of Gorbachev's policy in the Third World, then there is little likelihood of any significant improvement in Soviet-American relations. Détente collapsed in the 1970s because of Soviet imperial greed. Starting with the 1973 October War, the Soviet leadership saw the defense of existing relationships in the Arab world as more important than the prospective advantages of cooperating with the United States to stop a dangerous regional conflict and nurture the relaxation ushered in by the SALT I accords. Since then, the Kremlin has availed itself of every opportunity to interfere in regional conflicts, despite the adverse effects this has had on its relationship with the United States. The list is long and need not be elaborated.

If, however, Gorbachev is serious about wanting better relations, the Third World will be the likely place to begin. It is there that the stakes are expendable, the effects on Soviet security negligible, and the moderation of policy likely to bring benefits in the form of Western credits and trade. Nowhere could a signal of intent be so clearly sent. Afghanistan would be an obvious point of departure, as would Nicaragua, and at far less strategic cost.

Gorbachev has set himself the formidable task of modernizing Soviet society, of bringing it into the 21st century. Given this concentration on renewal at home, it would make a great deal of sense to maintain course abroad, and especially to focus efforts on improving the Soviet position in Northern and Central Europe, the Far East, and along the southern tier of the USSR. Rivalry with the United States will go on, but barring unplanned and uncontrollable cataclysmic developments threatening Soviet stability or the security of the Soviet empire, the prognosis for the foreign policy of Gorbachev, or his successor, to the year 2000, is for the continuity of core interests.

Selected Bibliography

BIALER, SEWERYN. *The Soviet Paradox: External Expansion, Internal Decline.* New York: Knopf, 1986.

COHEN, STEPHEN F. *Rethinking the Soviet Experience.* New York: Oxford University Press, 1985.

COLTON, TIMOTHY J. *The Dilemma of Reform in the Soviet Union.* Revised and expanded edition. New York: Council on Foreign Relations, 1986.

GORBACHEV, MIKHAIL S. *Perestroika: New Thinking For Our Country and the World.* New York: Harper & Row, 1988.

HANSON, PHILIP. *Trade and Technology in Soviet-Western Relations.* New York: Columbia University Press, 1981.

KOSTECKI, M. M. (ED.). *The Soviet Impact on Commodity Markets.* New York: St. Martin's Press, 1984.

PIPES, RICHARD. *Survival is Not Enough: Soviet Realities and America's Future.* New York: Simon and Schuster, 1984.

VALENTA, JIRI, and WILLIAM POTTER (EDS.). *Soviet Decisionmaking for National Security.* Boston: Allen & Unwin, 1984.

VIGOR, P. H. *The Soviet View of War, Peace, and Neutrality.* London: Routledge & Kegan Paul, 1975.

WHITING, ALLEN S. *Siberian Development and East Asia: Threat or Promise?* Stanford: Stanford University Press, 1981.

YANOV, ALEXANDER. *Détente After Brezhnev: The Domestic Roots of Soviet Foreign Policy.* Berkeley: Institute of International Studies, 1977.

———. *The Russian New Right: Right-Wing Ideologies in the Contemporary USSR.* Berkeley: Institute of International Studies, 1978.

Index

Other Books by Alvin Z. Rubinstein

Moscow's Third World Strategy

Anti-Americanism in the Third World (co-editor)

The Great Game: Rivalry in the Persian Gulf and South Asia (editor)

The Arab-Israeli Conflict: Perspectives (editor)

Soviet Foreign Policy Toward Western Europe (co-editor)

Red Star on the Nile: The Soviet-Egyptian Influence Relationship Since the June War

Soviet and Chinese Influence in the Third World (editor)

The Foreign Policy of the Soviet Union

Soviet and American Policies in the United Nations: A Twenty-five Year Perspective (co-editor)

Yugoslavia and the Nonaligned World

the Challenge of Politics (co-editor)

Soviet Writings on Southeast Asia (co-editor)

Communist Political Systems

The Soviets in International Organizations: Changing Policy Toward Developing Countries, 1953–1963